Early French Feminisms, 1830–1940

To those thousands of French women, many unknown, who from 1789 to 1945 dedicated their lives to becoming citizens of the Republic in a movement also known as feminism

Early French Feminisms, 1830–1940

A Passion for Liberty

by

Felicia Gordon

Principal Lecturer in European Philosophy and Literature, Anglia Polytechnic University, UK

and

Máire Cross

Senior Lecturer in French Studies, University of Sheffield, UK

Edward Elgar
Cheltenham, UK • Brookfield, US

Published by
Edward Elgar Publishing Limited
8 Lansdown Place
Cheltenham
Glos
GL50 2HU
UK

Edward Elgar Publishing Company
Old Post Road
Brookfield
Vermont 05036
US

British Library Cataloguing in Publication Data
Gordon, Felicia
    Early French Feminisms, 1830–1940:
    Passion for Liberty
    I. Title   II. Cross, Máire
    305.420944

Library of Congress Cataloguing in Publication Data
Gordon, Felicia
    Early French feminisms, 1830–1940 : a passion for liberty / by
Felicia Gordon and Máire Cross.
        p.   cm.
    Includes bibliographical references and index.
    1. Feminists—France—Biography.   2. Feminism—France—History.
3. Women socialists—France—Biography.   4. Socialism—France—
History.   I. Cross, Máire.   II. Title.
HQ1615.A3G67   1996
305.42'092'244—dc20
[B]   95–42408
                                                                                                      CIP

ISBN 1 85278 969 7

Typeset by Manton Typesetters, 5–7 Eastfield Road, Louth, Lincolnshire LN11 7AJ, UK.
Printed and bound in Great Britain by Hartnolls Limited, Bodmin, Cornwall

Contents

Illustrations

Preface and acknowledgements

This 'Reader' arose out of a desire to present the writings of five women – Flora Tristan, Jeanne Deroin, Pauline Roland, Madeleine Pelletier and Hélène Brion – and some lesser known aspects of French socialist feminism to the non-French reader.

By linking socialist feminist experiences from Flora Tristan to Madeleine Pelletier we hope to share our excitement at finding a common thread of polemical issues in the lives of the women chosen. The work is a combination of two distinct chronological parts. We have translated all texts included in this book.

We are indebted to Anglia Polytechnic University, Cambridge and The University of Northumbria at Newcastle for financially supporting our research, and to our colleagues for their encouragement.

Our grateful thanks go to the staff of the following libraries in Paris: Archives Nationales, Bibliothèque de l'Arsenal, Bibliothèque de Documentation Internationale Contemporaine, Bibliothèque Historique de la Ville de Paris, Bibliothèque Marguerite Durand, Bibliothèque Nationale and Institut Français de l'Histoire Sociale; likewise to the Bibliothèque Municipale in Castres and the Institute of International Social History in Amsterdam.

We greatly appreciate the attention that Conrad J.H. Smith has given to the manuscript and his thoroughly useful corrections.

1. Introduction

'Whoever is really worthy of freedom does not wait for it to be given to them; they take it.' (Madeleine Pelletier; motto on masthead of Hélène Brion's journal, *La Lutte féministe*)

The five women writers and political activists whose works are collected in this volume – Flora Tristan, Jeanne Deroin, Pauline Roland, Madeleine Pelletier and Hélène Brion – were representative of that small minority of French women in the mid-19th and early 20th centuries who contested the post-revolutionary Napoleonic settlement on gender roles, which accorded the 'Rights of Man' to men alone.[1] Though France had invented the concept of human rights and enshrined them in the 'Rights of Man', it accorded few rights to women, of property, personal autonomy or civic participation. French women had, however, actively participated in the revolutionary struggles and labour movements which shook France in 1789, 1830, 1848 and 1871. Unlike the United States, where solidarity with the anti-slavery cause helped the campaign for women's suffrage, and unlike Britain, where links with the labour movement strengthened the women's suffrage movement, in France, the undoubted contribution of women at all levels of revolutionary, socialist and trade union activity did not result in enfranchisement or other forms of public recognition. French women did not gain the vote until 1944 under General De Gaulle's provisional government and exercised this right for the first time in 1945.

The writings of the five feminist socialists collected here, many of which are available for the first time in English, establish the depth of their political commitment and help to explain how within the French historical situation their struggles remained largely unavailing, though not unremembered. This 'Reader' seeks to recuperate their words as well as their deeds and to allow their distinctive voices to speak within a contextual setting. Flora Tristan, Jeanne Deroin and Pauline Roland belonged to the 1830 to 1848 phase of socialist feminist activism. The period of political repression which followed the Second Republic of 1849 effectively curtailed radical political activity until the advent of the Third Republic. Madeleine Pelletier and Hélène Brion, coming of age at the turn of the century, represent a second wave of socialist feminist involvement which in its turn experienced the political repression of the First World War and the subsequent draconian laws relating to the birth control or neo-Malthusian movement as well as the German occupation during the Second World War.

The authors included in this anthology demonstrate a commonalty of women's experience over a period of 100 years and bear witness to a persistent thread both of political protest and of repression of those women who challenged established values. Their personal strategies of protest were as important as their declared public ones. For this reason we have included a range of genres: polemical articles, autobiographical memoirs and selections from unpublished correspondence. Like many women legally excluded from public life, Tristan, Deroin, Roland, Pelletier and Brion saw their writing as a vital mode of action, bridging the then rigidly separated public and private spheres.

Our approach towards writing history and in treating historical texts in this anthology has been primarily empirical. Recent work which has emphasized the importance of language as discourse and which de-structures the subject, though usefully undermining the notion of the transparency of language or the idea of the unitary self, may risk distancing the very subjectivities or persons which working-class men and women attempted to construe as valid subjects or citizens.[2] While we recognize the subjective side of our authors' experiences – which was indissolubly linked to their public roles, as the letters and autobiographical sections demonstrate – we are anxious to emphasize their political commitment, the public aspect of their work.

In contextualizing the personal and political trajectories of these early socialist feminists, one is struck by the centrality of the French Revolution of 1789 as the source of their inspiration, in particular the beliefs deriving from that event of the possibility of a new civilization founded on messianic religious impulses (visible in the Saint-Simonian and other utopian movements), faith in progress, in the transforming power of education, the importance of civic rights as a force for political education, and, finally, a sense that the Revolution remained to be completed. Turning first to the generation of 1830 to 1850, that of Flora Tristan, Jeanne Deroin and Pauline Roland, this period. which included two failed revolutions (1830 and 1848) illuminates what was to become a continuously troubled history of relations between feminists and their fellow socialist militants.

PERIODICITY OF PROTEST

The 19th and early 20th centuries in France were marked by dramatic political events manifested by relatively frequent changes of regime from the restored Bourbon monarchy of 1815, which was replaced by the Orleans version in 1830 followed by the Second Republic in 1848. Louis Napoléon, after assuming the Presidency of the Second Republic took on his predecessor's title of Emperor. The Second Empire lasted until the Franco-Prussian War of 1870 and the founding of the Third Republic.[3] Alongside these changes in formal political organization and in response to rapid industrial and social change, a number of new social and political theories emerged, among them, feminism, democratic republicanism and varieties of utopian socialism.

Feminist socialists of the 1830 to 1850 generation, as well as those of the '*Belle Epoque*', perceived themselves as, and were, in fact, excluded from the public sphere in politics, in education and from trade unions, then called 'associations'. Such women imagined a new social organization in which the 'new woman', emancipated from the social and sexual constraints of the past, would be both an agent of change and would benefit from social transformation. Social and personal emancipation for women, they believed, were inseparable. Yet though the gender dimension of their protest was vital, as we see in the writings included in this anthology, it was by no means an exclusive preoccupation. Tristan, Roland and Deroin, as well as Brion and Pelletier after them, claimed their right to citizenship through other struggles on the political Left, notably through socialism, pacifism and neo-Malthusianism.

FLORA TRISTAN, PAULINE ROLAND AND JEANNE DEROIN: THE FIRST WAVE OF PROTEST

Flora Tristan (1803–1844), Pauline Roland (1805–1852) and Jeanne Deroin (1805–1894) remain significant by reason of their political participation and their intellectual trajectories in the 1830 to 1850 period. Their activism initially was partly made possible by the state's relative tolerance of political activity during the initial euphoria of the revolutions which ushered in the July Monarchy and the short-lived Second Republic, and partly by the upsurge of feminist, socialist and republican activity. However, the Second Empire brought with it a prolonged period of political repression and, while Tristan died before the events of 1848, Roland and Deroin both underwent imprisonment and exile. Roland's untimely death in 1852 was a direct consequence of her period of deportation in Algerian prison camps.

The early feminists discovered a forum for political debate and activity within the utopian socialist Saint-Simonian movement. Founded by Henri de Saint-Simon (1760–1825), the movement envisaged a new social order based on technological achievement and economic co-operation between all classes. Social antagonisms would give way to rational order. Saint-Simon's disciple, Prosper Enfantin, referred to as 'The Father' in Saint-Simonian parlance, revitalized the movement after 1825 by conceptualizing a new social structure built on love rather than competition. In this order, women were to be

central, though not equal, participants. Emphasizing a theory of sexual difference, Enfantin thought that women represented the realm of feeling and of
the body which would be fully valued within his new society. He elaborated
the idea of a 'Woman Messiah', who was still to be awaited, but at the same
time he excluded actual women from the organization. At the centre of the
Saint-Simonian messianic ideal could be found not only the idea of hierarchy,
but the notion that sexual relations lay at the heart of all social relations and
that reform in this area was as vital as economic or technological advance.

The Saint-Simonians tended to a middle-class leadership, but appealed
strongly to male artisans and women from diverse social backgrounds, among
them Pauline Roland and Jeanne Deroin. To articulate but disadvantaged
working-class women the Saint-Simonians promised economic, social and
sexual liberation. In concrete terms, the context of Saint-Simonian debate
encouraged women to participate in utopian communities, to establish their
own women's groups and to found their own newspapers, to one of which, a
journal called *La Tribune des Femmes*, Jeanne Deroin was a major contribu-
tor. The existence of a forum for working-class women to express their ideas
in print is of inestimable importance in the development of this strand of
socialist feminism.

After 1835, however, the government imposed heavy press censorship. In
addition, thanks to police surveillance and new laws banning workers' organizations, it became extremely difficult to hold meetings or to disseminate
Saint-Simonian ideas. Nevertheless, because literacy had become widespread
among male workers and even among working-class women, the regime
found it increasingly difficult to contain dissent and to prevent debate, which
continued to flourish by private correspondence, in newspapers, books and
pamphlets. These often clandestine modes of communication became vital to
the dynamics of opposition politics. Within this culture of political opposition, Tristan, Roland and Deroin gained a voice both for their class and their
gender. Largely self-educated, they made a precarious living by writing and
entered the public sphere through their publications. For such women the act
of writing itself became, as for succeeding generations, a primary means both
of self-definition and of emancipation.

Socialist feminists did not only encounter opposition from official authority, whether of the Church or the state. Within the workers' movement too,
powerful voices such as Proudhon's actively opposed women's demands for
full social and economic participation.[4] The resistance of Proudhonian socialists to equal pay, trade union participation or the suffrage for women has a
long history on the French Left. Thus Tristan's call for women's right to
work, Jeanne Deroin's demand for the vote, Pauline Roland's appeal for
equal membership of women and men in 'associations' were met with derision by elements of the socialist press.[5] Opposed by a repressive state appara-

tus, these feminists simultaneously found few expressions of solidarity within the political opposition which was their ideological home.

As has been suggested, this generation of feminists took their inspiration from the Revolution of 1789. The writings of Deroin, Roland, Tristan, as later those of Pelletier and Brion, demonstrated that the French Revolution had forged a vocabulary and a sense of historical momentum, namely the belief in progress, which feminists could draw upon, as had Mary Wollstonecraft during the Revolution itself. The discourse of individual rights, the 'Rights of Man', illuminated the flagrant violations of those rights in French society, particularly the exclusion of women from full citizenship. Women demanded their rights in the name of equality, that virtue enshrined in the revolutionary republican triumvirate, 'liberty, equality, fraternity'. Thus Flora Tristan argued that all men and women should have the right to work and that the working class must complete the revolutionary process begun in 1789 by emancipating women, as the bourgeoisie had formerly freed the serfs. Similarly when Pauline Roland was tried for subversive activities in 1851, she insisted on addressing her judges as 'Citizen', a term redolent of the 1789 upheavals.

A Challenge to the Saint-Simonian Movement and to Republicanism

While Flora Tristan was active between 1835 and 1844, Pauline Roland and Jeanne Deroin first pursued their political campaigns in the early period of the July Monarchy (1830 to 1848), and were even more prominent in the closing days of the Second Republic which lasted from 1848 to 1852. Their relation to the Saint-Simonian movement was complex and differed in each case. As a young woman, Pauline Roland had embraced Saint-Simonian doctrine uncritically and enthusiastically and attempted to live by its precepts, particularly with regard to freedom in sexual relations. Inspired by the teachings of her tutor in the movement, Desprez, she left Normandy and moved to Paris where she succeeded in launching herself as a teacher and as a writer of articles for an encyclopaedia. Her commitment to political and sexual freedom led her to take sole responsibility for her three children whom she bore to two different fathers. She refused to accept financial assistance for their maintenance until she was imprisoned and destitute. Her devotion to Saint-Simonian principles caused her to experience terrible hardship and insecurity.

Like Pauline Roland, Jeanne Deroin was engaged in the early days of Saint-Simonianism. As a working-class woman she was one of the many who found inspiration in the new religion which valued women for their alleged morally uplifting influence. Deroin, however, directly challenged the Saint-Simonian doctrine of sexual difference by arguing for complete equality between the sexes and for female emancipation through education. Like Roland, she sought independence and when she married she retained her own surname as a sign of autonomy. An active militant in 1848, she was briefly imprisoned along with Pauline Roland, and in 1852, rather than agreeing to be silenced by the authorities, she chose exile in London. Though cut off from her fellow militants, she continued to write, publishing a moving lament on Pauline Roland's tragic death.

It is instructive to compare Roland's and Deroin's political, feminist commitment with that of their contemporary, Flora Tristan. Ostracized from her own class by the illegitimacy of her birth, Tristan sought class solidarity in the union of all workers. She did not participate in the early Saint-Simonian women's associations, since she valued their attachment to the messianic role of women but dissented from their economic and political programme. She petitioned for the re-institution of divorce, abolished in 1816 under the Restoration, arguing that marriage should be based on genuine affection and esteem, not on monetary or dynastic considerations. She was critical of contemporary socialist and radical groups' inability to alleviate working-class conditions, a failure which in turn impinged on the lives of working-class women. Though she had no faith in the franchise, she wrote petitions to the Chamber of Deputies as a way of gaining representation. She became convinced that the workers needed to establish their strength and autonomy as a class and should not enter into alliances with bourgeois republicans. She founded a first Workers' International, well in advance of Karl Marx, and, as Hélène Brion noted nearly a century later, deserved to be remembered as the founder of international socialism.

Nevertheless, Tristan's work on behalf of the workers' cause, coming as it did during the 1840s, lacked the collective involvement of Deroin and Roland who for their part did not seek her leading role as a female messiah. Tristan's feverish labours to persuade workers throughout France to help themselves through the creation of a working-class association, resulted in exhaustion and her early death in 1844. She did not live to see the revolution of 1848 which she had confidently predicted.

A consideration of these three figures allows us to gauge the importance of gender and socialist politics within labour history. Marx, who had hypothesized a largely homogeneous working class, ignored both the particular needs and the material reality of women within that class. Tristan, Deroin and Roland in their individual ways articulated their gender and class politics both in words and deeds. In so doing they rendered their example far more significant than the effectiveness of their isolated acts of protest would suggest.

MADELEINE PELLETIER AND HÉLÈNE BRION: A SECOND WAVE OF PROTEST

Hélène Brion (1882–1962) and Madeleine Pelletier (1874–1939) were contemporaries, friends, militant feminists, socialists and pacifists. One an infants' teacher and the other a medical doctor, they were products of the post-Commune Third Republic, women who had succeeded in entering the professions yet who contested its generally conservative social and political ethos. Nurtured in revolutionary politics, they refused to accept their inferior civil, political and sexual status. Their careers overlapped in their struggles to achieve social justice for women and for the working class, but their characters could not have been more unalike. Brion, enthusiastic, open, idealistic but also practical and energetic, was the more sympathetic personality. Pelletier, whose caustic intelligence made her few friends, retained the manners of her working-class origins, strengthened by a desire to appear authoritative or, as she put it, 'virile'. She was often defensive and suspicious and lacked the healing sense of generosity that characterized Brion. But they both were prepared to live out their feminist principles to the point of martyrdom. Brion was tried before a military court in 1918 for the crime of pacifism or 'defeatism', an occasion which she turned into a triumphant feminist declaration. Pelletier ended her life in a psychiatric hospital in 1939 after being arrested on an abortion charge. As a writer, Pelletier's analyses of the nature and extent of women's subordination are the most extensive and probing to have appeared in France prior to Simone De Beauvoir's. It seems very probable, from textual evidence, that De Beauvoir borrowed from her work, though without acknowledgement.[6]

Both women wrote and campaigned in a hostile and often dangerous climate. Their feminist concerns crossed many territories in the public sphere: socialism, syndicalism, education, Freemasonry and neo-Malthusianism. They identified a lack of historical consciousness about and by women as one of the profound causes of their inferiority. Without a collective past and consciousness how could women, as Hélène Brion put it in *La Voie féministe*, 'dare to be'? Even within the socialist movement where they were both active, Brion as Secretary of her local socialist section in the Pantin suburb of Paris, and Pelletier as an active militant for Gustave Hervé's revolutionary socialist group and then member of the Permanent Administrative Committee (CAP) of the Socialist Party, felt that socialists at best gave a token commitment to women's emancipation and at worst actively opposed it. But this history of suppression and neglect of women's contribution was not new. As Hélène Brion said:

> Workers you have never been just to those women who have helped you in your struggles. In the dawn of 1789, at the moment when a new era seemed to be

beginning for the world, they came to you full of confidence because you promised them liberty and they thought they would gain theirs. You rejected them.[7]

The issue of grounding women's experience in the historical record as part of
the effort to bring them into the public sphere was profoundly important to
both Pelletier and Brion. Thus Pelletier in 'The Question of Votes for Women'
began her article with an indictment of the betrayal by revolutionary leaders
of those very women who had contributed to the revolutionary process.
Similarly, Hélène Brion situated French women's subjection within the history of republicanism in order to show the contradictions between official
culture and private life. The sense that the French republicans had forsaken
their women comrades is a consistent theme running through Pelletier and
Brion's work. As feminists and socialists they saw themselves as upholding
the republican ideals of 'liberty, equality and fraternity'.

Brion's memoir on Flora Tristan was conceived as a recuperative effort.
She wished to gain recognition for the role of a woman as a founding spirit of
the socialist movement, a woman whose memory in 1919 had been virtually
erased and her contribution forgotten:

> Who remembers today her name, even among the most fervent devotees of inter-
> national socialism and feminism? Who dreams of doing her justice and putting
> her beside Karl Marx and above him in the glory that belongs to the first founders
> of that great movement for workers' emancipation? No one. And it is in order to
> repair that injustice that I have wished to write this pamphlet, hoping that a little
> of the workers' recognition lavished on Karl Marx will go to this woman, his
> precursor in the socialist movement, and that the cause of truth and feminism
> cannot but gain.[8]

Hélène Brion struggled to redress this kind of historical amnesia regarding
women. Not an academic historian, she was nevertheless passionate about
history. Her mammoth and unfinished 'Feminist Encyclopaedia' (the despair
of subsequent scholars for its lack of conventional method), composed of
newspaper cuttings, photographs, postcards and hand-written articles, was
part of a one-woman effort to overcome centuries of neglect. The 'Encyclopaedia' was conceived as a biographical directory of prominent women, and
was also to contain a geographical feminine organization, describing the lives
of women in the various French *départements*. Significantly, the issue of
women's nomenclature and hence their identity preoccupied her, as is evident
from a note added in July 1950 to the 1912 Preface:

> I committed a serious error when in listing women in this book I did so by the
> names of their husbands or their fathers. I soon realized that the only name which
> is proper to a woman is her first name; too many women in any case sacrifice even
> their first names on the altar of holy matrimony and instead, for example of Mrs

Lucy Thing, call themselves Mrs Robert Thing – so great is the slave mentality still existing in women.[9]

Hélène Brion and Madeleine Pelletier's desire to record women's history was equally a manifestation of their ambition to enter the process of history. Their campaigns for women's suffrage, their activism in socialist politics and Hélène Brion's trade union work were all part of an historical consciousness in the broadest sense. For them and for feminists of their generation, the public sphere was the arena where history was made. This is starkly illustrated in Madeleine Pelletier's anecdote about her childhood. Telling her mother that she planned to become a great general (no doubt modelled on Napoléon) her mother replied: 'Women are not generals, they are nothing at all; they marry, cook and raise their children'. Little wonder that Hélène Brion began and ended her 'The Feminist Path' with the injunction: 'Women dare to be'. The perception that women are nothing at all, an existential perception of the nothingness of the traditional feminine destiny, was one that both women repudiated.

Organized French feminism in the *Belle Epoque* was a predominately middle-class movement.[10] Madeleine Pelletier and Hélène Brion both belonged to bourgeois feminist groups while actively engaged in working-class political groups. They attempted to bridge the class/gender divide between socialism and feminism, which many socialists in particular saw as an either/or choice between socialism and feminism. Pelletier became Secretary of a feminist group, *la Solidarité des femmes* (1906–1914), coinciding with her period of greatest activity within the Socialist Party, first in Jules Guesde's Marxist faction and then moving further Left to Gustave Hervé's revolutionary socialist group. Hélène Brion was a member and then General Secretary of the FNSI (*Fédération nationale des syndicats des instituteurs*), a left-wing trade union affiliated to the CGT (*Confédération générale du travail*) and Secretary of her local socialist section of Pantin. Both women joined the Communist Party after the First World War and both left it between 1922 and 1925.

Pelletier in her 'Memoirs of a Feminist' and Brion in 'The Feminist Path', indict their socialist and trade union colleagues for their anti-feminism, arguing that Proudhon's legacy of misogyny within syndicalism, as well as being a betrayal of socialist principles, impoverished both movements. The failure of French syndicalism and socialism to attract a substantial female membership reflected the restrictive practices of the former, dramatically illustrated by the Couriau Affair,[11] and the overwhelmingly masculine atmosphere at socialist meetings where women felt ill at ease. Though Hélène Brion and Madeleine Pelletier succeeded as active participants in this male world, they were acutely aware of the ways in which women felt excluded. Socialists labelled feminists as 'bourgeois' and 'reformist' and therefore opposed both to the working class and to revolution. Given these tensions, one can see that socialist feminists were torn in two directions. Many socialist women renounced the feminist movement altogether, for example, Clara Zetkin, Rosa Luxembourg and Louise Saumoneau. Those like Pelletier and Brion who attempted to maintain loyalty to both, inevitably found themselves in conflictual positions.

Syndicalism and Pacifism

As a primary school teacher entering the profession in 1905, Hélène Brion immediately joined the FNSI and the SFIO (*Section française de l'Internationale ouvrière*), or Socialist Party. As employees of the state, French teachers had previously been represented by *Amicales*, or teachers' associations. These were apolitical and did not contest the ideological terrain of the Third Republic. The FNSI, however, affiliated with the trade union federation, the CGT, and thereby allied itself directly with the working class. Many of its members by their class origins were workers or rural labourers, though by their educational attainments they represented a cultural elite. Through her membership of the FNSI, Hélène Brion had identified herself with a working-class political movement and served it faithfully throughout her career in the teaching profession. Her feminist strictures against trade unionists or syndicalists must be seen as issuing from a loyal member of the movement.

This class and trade union solidarity influenced her on the question of pacifism. While the Socialist Party and the trades unions were, as part of the Second International, opposed to national or 'capitalist' wars, hence the idea of uniting the proletariat across national boundaries to avoid war, for the most part they were also committed to revolution. Socialism was therefore not pacifist in the sense of necessarily believing in non-violence. However, the FNSI in particular had a long-standing pacifist commitment and had campaigned from as early as 1901 against the requirement to glorify war and nationalism in the teaching of history in schools. The union had also enraged the patriotic Right when in 1912 at its annual conference at Chambéry, it voted the *sou au soldat*, to give financial support from the union to serving conscripts, in order to maintain their loyalty to the International while serving the nation. This was interpreted as seditious and anti-patriotic.[12]

When France and Belgium were invaded by Germany in August 1914, the issue of national defence for most socialists took precedence over a more theoretical commitment to internationalism. The hoped-for solidarity of the International fractured along national lines and socialist deputies throughout Europe voted war credits in their national parliaments and embraced 'patriotism'. The SFIO was no exception, joining what was termed the *Union Sacrée*, the national coalition to resist Austro-German aggression and to pursue the war. Jules Guesde, the Marxist leader whose faction Pelletier had first joined in 1906, became a government minister.

It is difficult to exaggerate the traumatic effect this reversal of positions had on many thousands, if not millions, of committed socialists who had believed that with the creation of the Second International capitalist wars had become impossible. Like the Socialist International, the international feminist movement with its strong pacifist tradition underwent a similar metamorphosis, with most suffrage groups in Britain and France backing the war effort.[13] The detailed 50-page summary police report, *Vote des femmes* (1915), now in the French National Archives, in which the anonymous writer effectively congratulates the government on having little to fear from feminist groups in terms of anti-war propaganda, though prior to the war feminism had been explicitly associated with pacifism, accurately conveys the shift in opinion which occurred in France.[14] However there were a number of impressive minority rebellions: among others, those of Louise Saumoneau, Gabrielle Duchêne, Gabrielle and François Mayoux, Louise Colliard and Hélène Brion. In hindsight, what was perhaps most significant was the anxiety engendered in government circles by this tiny handful of pacifists, a minority even in their own political groupings.

Political Repression

Like the conservative republicans in the Second Republic and Louis Napoléon who transformed the Republic into the Second Empire, Clemenceau, who came to power in November 1917, fearing outbreaks of strikes and mutinies, inaugurated a period of severe internal repression. Twenty-three socialist or pacifist sympathizers were executed in this period, evidence, in the state of stalemate which the war had reached, of the government's fear of popular resistance. But in 1914 and 1915 it was indeed the case that the majority of French feminist organizations did overwhelmingly support the war, as Madeleine Pelletier caustically noted in her 'Memoirs'. She preferred, she said, to close down 'Solidarity', rather than see it function as part of the war effort. ('I had not carried on feminist propaganda for eleven years in order to come to the point of knitting socks.'[15])

To campaign for peace, or to talk of negotiation in a country invaded by a foreign power, seemed to most French people to constitute capitulation if not betrayal. Yet the complete reversal of public opinion on the war issue was remarkable and particularly marked in France. The patriotic fever and spy mania which Madeleine Pelletier described in her 'War Diary' is amply attested to by other witnesses. The unflinching opposition to war of trade unions and socialist circles, as well as of most feminist groups prior to the war, was transmuted almost overnight into fierce patriotic optimism. Gustave Hervé, the revolutionary socialist and pacifist whose group Pelletier had joined when she found the Guesdist faction too moderate, became a fervent patriot in 1914 and changed the name of his paper from *La Guerre sociale* to *La Victoire*. Virtually all newspapers printed misleadingly optimistic news from the front; the government operated a rigorous state of censorship. The word 'peace' was considered to be seditious and not allowed to be printed.[16] In this climate, the few resisters against the war, such as Pierre Monatte's *La Vie ouvrière*, the Metal Workers Union under Merrheim, the FNSI, the Committee for the Resumption of International Relations and the International Committee of Women for Permanent Peace (groups whose membership in France tended to be as small as their titles were long), were beleaguered but courageous exceptions to the bellicose mood. Socialists opposed to the war met in two 1915 conferences in Switzerland, the Berne conference in March, noted above, and the Zimmerwald conference of 5–8 September. The severity of political repression in France as in Germany make the clandestine struggles of war resisters particularly remarkable.

By contrast, bourgeois feminist groups in France not only embraced the war effort, most were hostile to the attempts by English, American and Dutch feminists who convened the Women's Peace Conference in The Hague in 1915 to promote peace. From the French perspective, the German military gains on French and Belgian territory meant that suing for peace was tantamount to accepting defeat. The Hague conference's final communiqué attempted to respond to the genuine difficulty which nationals of invaded countries would have faced in suing for peace. Rather than arguing about the causes of the war it looked towards the establishment of a world order in which peace would be guaranteed, though it evaded the question of on whose terms peace would be achieved.

The 1915 Women's Conference for Peace at The Hague has been taken as a litmus test of pacifist/feminist commitment, but for French women this view may be deceptive.[17] It is certain that French women would have been refused passports (as were many British delegates) had they tried to attend. Louise Saumoneau, the militant socialist but opponent of bourgeois feminism, 'declared that even if she had received an invitation, she would not have attended the congress, for positioning herself on the ground of the class struggle, she could not commit herself to women who represented the bourgeoisie.'[18] Saumoneau formed her own anti-war mini-group, entitled 'Committee of Feminine Socialist Action for Peace and Against Nationalism' and attended the 1915 Berne Conference of Socialist Women. She was imprisoned for two months in 1915 for distributing copies of the Berne Manifesto in Paris. Before the war, Hélène Brion had debated the issue of socialism versus feminism with Louise Saumoneau in a series of articles, arguing against the separation of socialism and feminism.[19] Saumoneau, however, remained implacably opposed to the feminist movement on class grounds. Brion, though she did not attend, followed the Hague conference of April 1915 closely, keeping a detailed series of newspaper cuttings on its proceedings.[20]

At the outbreak of the war, Hélène Brion's and Madeleine Pelletier's positions were complex. Neither can be said to have been unambiguous pacifists. Pelletier had a long-standing commitment to revolution and believed that women should do military service in the interest of sexual equality. Nevertheless she opposed the war. Hélène Brion, who had become National Secretary of her union in 1914, initially followed its majority line and accepted the *Union Sacrée*. However, by 1915 dissident voices in the FNSI began to make themselves heard, particularly those of Marie Mayoux and Louis and Gabrielle Bouët. Marie Mayoux's *Appel aux instituteurs*, a pamphlet which became a classic pacifist text, was one of those for which Hélène Brion was to be prosecuted for distributing. At its annual conference in 1915 the FNSI voted for an anti-war position, arguing that trade unionists should make active propaganda for peace, effectively a seditious proposal in the context of French state repression of all 'anti-patriotic' points of view. Brion, having accepted her union's pacifist campaign, became an active propagandist for peace.[21] There is some irony, however, in her prosecution for pacifism or defeatism in 1917–1918[22] as she had been a late, though ultimately loyal, convert to the Mayoux position. Her trial by a military court or *Conseil de Guerre*, a highly unusual procedure for a civilian, was one of the *causes célèbres* of the war years.

Hélène Brion's pacifist involvement was strongly influenced by her experience among the poor of her Paris suburb, the Pantin district, where she saw the acute deprivation which the war brought to non-combatants. She helped to organize the *soupes populaires* or soup kitchens for the women and children, distributed coal, sometimes pulling the cart herself, sawed wood and peeled vegetables. Her first-hand knowledge of seeing the misery and shortages inflicted on the civilian population by the war certainly contributed to her pacifist convictions.[23] Ironically, her very energy and enthusiasm in poor relief became one of the allegedly 'excessive' character traits to be held against her in the press campaign prior to her trial.

Repression, then, was the harsh reality for political dissidents at this period in France. Madeleine Pelletier has left her personal record of the war, her 1914–1918 'War Diary' published here for the first time. In the early part of the war, Pelletier, having unsuccessfully attempted to serve in the army medical corps (she was probably rejected partly because of her 'masculine' appearance), retired to Paris where she read for a degree in chemistry and stayed out of trouble. Like Brion she was under police surveillance and was suspected of spying[24] but, unlike Brion, she did not campaign publicly for an end to the war, though she is recorded by a police spy as attending a socialist meeting and arguing in favour of pacifism and internationalism.[25] Her attitudes were in any case ambivalent. She had enraged Gustave Hervé when in 1910 she had recommended military service for women on the grounds of sexual equality; she rejoiced that during the war women had broken down employment barriers and were earning good wages, yet the erosion of civil liberties and the return to 'barbaric' attitudes and the rise in war hysteria contradicted the hopes she had nurtured of the evolutionary progress of feminism.

Feminist Education

Madeleine Pelletier and Hélène Brion were further linked by their interest in education. Like Jeanne Deroin, Pauline Roland and Flora Tristan, they believed that educating women to function as citizens was central to the feminist project. As a practising teacher, Brion contributed to the journal *L'Ecole émancipée* ('The Emancipated School'; 1880–1914) which campaigned for a more liberal teaching regime, against the patriotic and militaristic teaching expected of state school teachers and in favour of co-education and the teaching of practical as well as academic skills.[26] The *Ecole émancipée* was part of a broader movement of the Left arising out of the Dreyfus case campaigning for anti-nationalist and anti-clerical education. Within this libertarian climate, feminists in the teaching profession founded the *Groupe féministe universitaire* and published feminist articles in the *Revue de l'enseignement* (Teaching Revue) campaigning, for example, for equal pay for men and women teachers. Madeleine Pelletier, though not in education herself, influenced feminists of this group like Marie Guillot.[27] Their campaigns were not, however, unopposed on the Left. Thus a syndicalist teacher, Muller, could write in the *Ecole émancipée* of 18 March 1911 in a classically Proudhonian vein: 'The married woman has no place in the laboratory, nor in the Chamber of Deputies, nor above all in the factory.'[28]

Education for women and about women was at the core of both Pelletier and Brion's feminist concerns. Pelletier's analysis of girls' gender education in passivity and compliance was imaginative and original, though some of her recommendations for teaching girls independence were draconian.[29] The issue of dress reform (comfortable and practical clothes for women and girls) entered centrally into this debate. Pelletier and Astié de Valsayre were the first feminists in France to give the wearing of masculine dress a political configuration, arguing that to adopt male clothing was to challenge the male monopoly of power. They were mocked and derided by both socialists and feminists.[30] Pelletier and Brion considered that if women were to be genuinely responsible for themselves, they must throw off their culturally induced passivity and modesty. As Hélène Brion said in writing of the neglect of Flora Tristan: 'We women seem to be ashamed of ourselves. For us there is a kind of immodesty in knowing let alone celebrating the talents or the ideas of our own sex.'[31]

Another way in which Madeleine Pelletier ran across the grain of mainstream feminist thought of the period was on the issue of women's sexuality and their moral obligations in relation to reproduction. Women's education, she believed, must include sexual education for their own pleasure and well-being. The concept of the *mère éducatrice* was the primary model of feminine virtue and usefulness since Rousseau and had been incorporated into mainstream feminism. It allowed women to argue that they needed civil and political rights in order better to fulfil their maternal duties. Pelletier's demands for sexual liberation (though she herself remained celibate) for women's autonomy and for the dissolution of the family grew out of libertarian, anarchist and neo-Malthusian thought, but she was original in shifting the focus from the needs of men or of the working class to practise family limitation, to the needs of women themselves. Pelletier believed that women derived great joy and strength from their children, provided they had the means and the health to look after them.[32] However, no one, she thought, should be forced to bear children against their will.

It is almost certain that Pelletier herself practised clandestine abortions. Though abortion had always been illegal, it was, as Pelletier argued in her pamphlet, widely practised and juries were on the whole unwilling to convict women found guilty of seeking abortions. She fell foul of the severe laws passed in 1920 and 1922 against propagandists for birth control and abortionists. In the repressive inter-war political climate, she became the victim of pro-natalist legal proceedings when in 1939 she was arrested, found too ill to plead (by reason of a stroke suffered some time previously), and was incarcerated in the psychiatric hospital of Perray Vaucluse, south of Paris, where she died within six months. Her detention in an asylum must be regarded as punitive.

Hélène Brion was also an advocate of birth control. At the time of her arrest in 1917 at the height of pacifist repression, she was found to have copies of neo-Malthusian leaflets in her flat, a detail which contributed to the press campaign of character assassination against her. 'Malthusianism, defeatism, anti-militarism, anarchy, these were the key ideas which motivated Hélène Brion.'[33] Given the declining French birth rate, birth control in the political climate of the first half of the century was understood as anti-patriotic and seditious.

Hélène Brion and Madeleine Pelletier, like Flora Tristan, Jeanne Deroin and Pauline Roland, represented minority voices even within their own movements, let alone within society at large. Their lives were overshadowed by police surveillance, by the fear or the actuality of arrest and incarceration and by the splits, feuds, rivalries and jealousies which characterize minority movements operating under conditions of great stress. Pelletier particularly became the victim of such pressure while indubitably contributing to her own social ostracism. Hélène Brion, possessing a more confident nature, retained cordial links with a variety of feminists and syndicalists throughout her life. Typical of this spirit of camaraderie is a letter she wrote to François Mayoux, dated 4 September 1922, after he had been expelled from the Communist Party:

> What the devil have you done you terrible pacifist warrior? I certainly hope that there will be a few of us who will send you a certificate of civic merit, for which you won't give a damn as such, old anarchist that you are, but where you will find the stamp of a warm affection, which is much more worthwhile.[34]

The long campaign to win women's votes proved fruitless, as the feminist alliances forged at the turn of the century failed to sway the French Senate which turned down women's suffrage on three separate occasions in the inter-war years (1922, 1928 and 1931). Even in the 1950s Hélène Brion was concerned that though there were finally women in parliament, there was no feminist movement worthy of the name in France.

Reading Madeleine Pelletier and Hélène Brion today, nearly a century after they and their foremothers and sisters began their campaigns to give French women the rights enjoined for all of humanity under the French Revolution of 1789, one is struck by the extent to which they articulated the tensions and contradictions arising between progressive political philosophies and gender politics and how clearly they grasped the psychological dimension of women's subordination. To read them now is to be reminded that women have a history of courageous struggle, which, as Hélène Brion said of Flora Tristan, must be remembered as a matter of justice and as evidence that women matter in the historical record. Tristan, Deroin, Roland, Pelletier and Brion, though leading lives of poverty and obscurity, rescued their personal and political struggles from historical oblivion by the act of writing. Writing was their major form of witness to the fact that women's voices could reach out to a 'humanity' which so often excluded them. The selection of published and unpublished writings collected here testify to the particularity of their experience and to the continuity of the feminist and socialist project in which they were engaged. These exceptional but combative figures turned their energies both to understanding their history and to changing it.

NOTES

1. For an analysis of the post-revolutionary construction of gender difference and its effects on defining citizenship, see Geneviève Fraisse, *Reason's Muse: Sexual Difference and the Birth of Democracy*, translated by Jane Marie Todd, Chicago, University of Chicago Press, 1994, pp. xiii–xviii.

2. See Claire Moses and Leslie Rabine, *Feminism, Socialism and French Romanticism*, Bloomington and Indianapolis, Indiana University Press, 1993.

3. The Third Republic did not immediately succeed the defeat of Louis Napoléon's empire. In the aftermath of Napoléon's military defeat in 1870 there came a further episode of civil disturbance and brief revolutionary government known as the Paris Commune. The conservative national government, led by Adolphe Thiers, ruthlessly crushed the Left in May 1871, executing hundreds or deporting political activists including Louise Michel. In the few years that followed a moderate form of constitutional government emerged as a compromise between monarchists and republicans in a regime which lasted nearly seventy years and became known as the Third Republic. See David Thomson, *Democracy in France since 1870*, Oxford, Oxford University Press, 1969.

4. Pierre Joseph Proudhon (1809–1865), early French socialist and anarchist, argued against the sanctity of property ('property is theft') and in favour of the total liberty and equality of individuals. His anarchism was opposed to a powerful state but he did not extend his libertarian views to women who, as he remarked memorably, had a choice of roles, either as housewife or whore.

5. *L'Atelier*, a labour newspaper, referred to Flora Tristan as 'O Connell in petticoats' for undertaking a speaking tour of France for her Workers' Union. See *L'Atelier*, 2e Année, no.9, mai 1843, p. 71.

6. Compare: Simone De Beauvoir, *The Second Sex*, translated by H.M. Parshley, Harmondsworth, Penguin, 1983, pp. 18–19 and Madeleine Pelletier, 'The Question of Votes for Women', p. 3 (see p. 148).

7. Hélène Brion, 'Feminist Message to the Committee for the Resumption of International Relations', p. 1 (see p. 221).

8. Hélène Brion, 'Preface', July 1912, July 1950, 'Feminist Encyclopaedia', Bound MS, Bibliothèque Marguerite Durand, Paris.

9. Hélène Brion, 'Flora Tristan: The True Founder of the International', *Epône: l'avenir social*, 1919, p. 1.

10. See: Steven C. Hause with Anne R. Kenney, *Women's Suffrage and Social Politics in the French Third Republic*, Princeton, Princeton University Press, 1984, pp. 191–7; and Felicia Gordon, *The Integral Feminist, Madeleine Pelletier 1874–1939*, Cambridge, Polity Press, 1990, pp. 77–100.

11. See Chapter 7, p. 215.

12. Huguette Bouchardeau, *Hélène Brion La Voie féministe*, Paris, Syros, 1978, pp. 32–4.

13. Steven C. Hause with Anne R. Kenny, *Women's Suffrage and Social Politics in the French Third Republic*, Princeton, Princeton University Press, 1984, p. 191; and Steven Hause, 'Women who Rallied to the Tricolour: The Effects of World War I on the French Women's Suffrage Movement', *Proceedings of the Annual Meeting of the Western Society for French History*, 6, 1978, pp. 371–81.

14. '*Vote des femmes*', AN F/7/ 13266.

15. 'Memoirs of a Feminist', Chapter 8, pp. 235–48.

16. Alfred Rosmer, 'The Fight Against War in France during the War', in Julian Bell (ed.), *We Did Not Fight*, London, Cobden Sanderson, 1935, p. 295.

17. Steven C. Hause with Anne R. Kenney, *Women's Suffrage, op. cit.*, pp. 191–7, Richard J. Evans, *Comrades and Sisters*, Brighton, Wheatsheaf, 1984, pp. 124–30.

18. '*Vote des femmes*', p. 43.

19. Charles Sowerwine, *Sisters or Citizens? Women and Socialism in France since 1876*, Cambridge, Cambridge University Press, 1982, pp. 132–4.

20. Newspaper clipping, 28 April 1915, Dossier Brion, Bibliothèque Marguerite Durand, Paris.
21. See Alfred Rosmer, *Le Mouvement ouvrier pendant la guerre*, Paris, Librairie du travail, 1936, pp. 306–11 and Charles Sowerwine, *Sisters or Citizens*, *op. cit.*, p. 147.
22. See Chapter 7, pp. 189–209.
23. Henriette Sauret, '*Hélène Brion, Héroine de la paix*', unpublished MS, Dossier Brion, Bibliothèque Marguerite Durand, Paris.
24. See 'War Diary', Chapter 8, pp. 248–58.
25. See Police Report, ANF7 13961 which reports on a meeting of 10 June 1915 at 76 Rue Mouffetard and another on 22 January 1916 at the Café Voltaire.
26. Thierry Flammant, *L'Ecole émancipée*, Paris, Les Monédières, 1982, pp. 54–6.
27. See Chapter 8, pp. 248–58.
28. *L'Ecole émancipée*, *op. cit.*, pp. 189–90.
29. *L'Education féministe des filles* (The Feminist Education of Girls), pp. 167–77.
30. Christine Bard, *Les féministes en France. Vers l'intégration des femmes dans la Cité, 1914–1940*, Doctoral Thesis, Paris, University of Paris VII, 1993, pp. 393–4.
31. Hélène Brion, 'Flora Tristan', *op. cit.*, p. 22.
32. See: 'Right to Abortion', pp. 177–84.
33. *Le Matin*, 18 November 1917.
34. Marie and François Mayoux, *Instituteurs pacifistes et syndicalistes*, Chamalières, Editions Canope, 1992, pp. 317–18.

2.   Flora Tristan's campaigns, 1835–1844

HISTORICAL BACKGROUND

Flora Tristan's campaigns for workers' associations, largely concentrated between 1835 and 1844, provide a link between the utopian socialist movements of the 1830s and the feminist socialists' attempts to influence the new but short-lived Republic of 1848 to 1852. Tristan's activism may be located within the larger context of political opposition to the July Monarchy.

This political opposition was composed, firstly, of the moderate republicans, the least dangerous to the regime and regarded as the most respectable. However, though they took part in the parliamentary opposition, republicans rapidly became disillusioned with the Orleans government. Through their newspaper, *Le National*, they campaigned for an extension of the suffrage to give greater political power to the middle classes but did not wish to extend these rights to labourers, peasants or women. Secondly, more in sympathy with workers, but equally opposed to women's political and social rights, were the small groups of Jacobins or radical republicans who flourished mainly in Paris and in some provincial towns. They believed in universal male suffrage, freedom of the press and a centralized republican state which would impose the equal rule of law for all. Their newspapers were *La Tribune* from 1830 to 1843 and *La Réforme* from 1843. They were less concerned with social questions than with completing the work of the revolution, and they were prepared to have recourse to insurrection if necessary to defend the principles of national sovereignty, law, equality and liberty.

Because of the tradition of political instability the authorities kept a very close eye on political activists. Included in the eyes of the authorities as dangerous revolutionaries were social reformers, followers of the philosophers Fourier and Saint-Simon. Etienne Cabet, Victor Considérant and Pierre Leroux, founders of newspapers, communities, schools and associations, were the main leaders of this unofficial opposition. Many of these socialists, including Flora Tristan, concerned themselves very little with the suffrage question. For them, democracy was simply a means to an end to secure for the poor a degree of material welfare that would enable them to live decently. These social reformers sought to cultivate links with the urban populace to find support for their reformist agenda. They believed that it was vital to abolish exploitation at work and to provide education for the workers in order to end poverty and create social stability and contentment. It was in this forum that the critique of the Civil Code as a basis of the organization of the family was the most developed. However, these social reformers rejected the more libertarian suggestions of Fourier and distanced themselves from the communal experiments of the early Saint-Simonians.

In 1835, when Flora Tristan began her public protest, the possibilities for political expression had considerably diminished. Since the July Monarchy had abolished freedom of association and freedom of the press, direct political action by republicans had virtually ceased. On the other hand, as poverty continued to increase, the intellectual critique of capitalism strengthened. Nevertheless, direct action by workers to combat exploitation was severely repressed, as demonstrated by the suppression of workers' riots in Lyons and Paris during 1834.

CONTEXTUAL INTRODUCTION TO FLORA TRISTAN

Biography[1]

Flora Tristan's early family circumstances do much to explain her later search for equality and justice for the oppressed. She was the illegitimate daughter of Tristan de Moscoso, an army officer from a wealthy and powerful Spanish Peruvian family, and Thérèse Laisney, a French refugee from the 1789 Revolution. They had met in Bilbao and after a religious wedding ceremony settled in a comfortable house in Paris where their daughter was born in 1803. The happiness of Flora Tristan's early childhood was shattered in June 1807 by the death of her father who had failed either to legalize his marriage or to regulate his business affairs with his brother, Don Pio de Tristan. The Tristans' situation was further complicated by the war between Spain and France. Their Vaugirard property was confiscated by the French government and the Tristan family in Peru refused to recognize Thérèse Laisney as her husband's rightful heir. Five months after her husband's death, Thérèse gave birth to a son in October 1807, who was only to live for nine years. Throughout her childhood, Flora's mother regaled her daughter with stories of her noble father and their lost wealth. In 1818, at the age of 15, Flora, who had received no formal schooling, was found work as a lithograph and painter's colourist. Not long after, on 3 February 1821, she married her employer, André Chazal. By 1825 she had borne two sons, the elder of whom died in 1832, and was pregnant again. In March of that year Flora left her husband and went with her children to stay with her mother.

Her marriage had been a disaster. Although divorce by mutual consent had been introduced during the revolutionary period and modified by Napoléon, it was outlawed under the Restoration Monarchy of 1815. Since neither of the spouses had an independent income they were unable to come to a satisfactory separation arrangement. Furthermore, according to the Napoleonic Civil Code established in 1803, the husband and father, in this case Chazal, had complete authority to determine where his wife should live, to have custody over his children and to benefit from his wife's earnings. It was legally possible, however, to establish separation of property. This was what the Chazal couple requested and were granted in 1828. Nonetheless, the court settlement did not prevent acrimonious exchanges which followed their separation and continued unresolved until 1838. Meanwhile, in an attempt to improve her financial situation, Flora Tristan placed her children in care and took up employment as a lady's companion. Chazal continued to pursue her, claiming his rights over his children. In desperation Flora decided to go to Peru to seek support from her father's family. Fearing ostracism as a separated wife, she went alone, posing as Mademoiselle Flora Tristan. She set out on 7 April 1833 and arrived in Aréquipa, at her uncle's home, the following September. Her attempts to secure legal recognition as the rightful heir of Mariano de Tristan were entirely unsuccessful. She was rejected by her father's family and returned, defeated, to Paris in January 1835. However this adventure did reveal another possibility to her, that of becoming a writer. Her powers of observation took shape in the material for a book, *Pérégrinations d'une paria* ('Peregrinations of a Pariah') published in January 1838.[2]

The return to Paris marked the beginning of Flora Tristan's career as a political activist and writer. She sought contacts with Victor Considérant, Charles Fourier and their followers, met Robert Owen, attended meetings organized by Eugénie Niboyet for the *Gazette des Femmes*, met Saint-Simonians and succeeded in having her first publications – extracts from *Pérégrinations d'une paria* – included in the *Revue de Paris* in September 1836. However, the stormy relationship with her husband continued. In 1837 Chazal was imprisoned for a short period, accused of incest by his young daughter whom he had forcibly removed from boarding school. In December 1838 Chazal shot and wounded Flora. He was condemned, in February 1839, to penal servitude for life. Thanks to her husband's trial, which received sensational press coverage, Flora Tristan's works, *Pérégrinations d'une paria* and *Méphis*, sold well. However, this publicity also had its adverse effects. Don Pio, the head of the Tristan family in Peru, had her work, *Pérégrinations*, burnt in public, because of its condemnation of the corruption of Peruvian society. In addition, Don Pio ended the small allowance which had been allotted to her. Flora Tristan was erased from political memory in Peruvian

history until the 1920s.[3] In the 1970s she was finally acclaimed as a precursor
by the radical women's movement in Chile.[4]

After her husband's imprisonment, Tristan lived in Paris, moving in literary and political circles and holding meetings in her small apartment in the
Rue du Bac. She became a well-known figure in both Paris and London
among the followers of Saint-Simon, Fourier and Robert Owen and other
radical groups such as the Chartists. However, she was not satisfied with the
ideas of contemporary philanthropists which, she believed, effectively excluded the poor from participating in schemes for social improvement:

> Men and Women workers, listen to me. For twenty-five years the most intelligent
> and devoted men have spent their lives defending your sacred cause; In written
> works, speeches, reports, dissertations, investigations and statistics, they have
> indicated, established, demonstrated to the government and to the wealthy, that
> the working class is, in the present state of things, physically and morally, in an
> intolerable situation of poverty and suffering; ... Workers what can be added now
> to the defence of your cause?...In twenty-five years hasn't everything been said
> and repeated in every way to reach saturation point? ... Well, the time has come to
> act and it is up to you and you alone, to act in the interest of your own cause.[5]

After completing her only novel, *Méphis*, in 1838, Tristan rejected fiction as
a medium of social reform. Neither were her relations with the newly formed
working-class groups such as the *Atelier* and *La Ruche* more satisfactory. The
leaders would not accept her criticisms of their mode of life and there was
some objection to her insistence on female emancipation; an extract from her
Tour de France will give some idea of Tristan's difficulties as a preacher to
the constancy of workers:

> The chapter on women was read. – It was listened to with much less attention, that
> was to be expected. – The audience was tired, and besides, this chapter said
> relatively little compared with the other. – When the reading was finished Vinçard
> asked to speak again. – This time he wandered completely off the point. He said
> that he was opposed to the inclusion of this chapter because, it was said in it that
> the worker went to the cabaret, and that this was going to renew the attacks the
> bourgeois class made against the working class. – I tried in vain to tell him that I
> was only talking about husbands, that I was not questioning the existence of
> cabarets, that he was digressing from the question. – Impossible, he would not
> hear of understanding anything. – This time again everyone agreed with me – and
> said he was wrong. – Only one, the carpenter Roly asked to speak and said, in a
> very emotional and angry way, that he was strongly opposed to its inclusion
> because I insulted men and women workers. I began a debate with him; he
> admitted that workers went to the cabaret but he said: 'amongst ourselves, we can
> admit our faults but we must not have to put up with outsiders coming to take us
> to task – on the contrary, we should hide them from the bourgeois; and we must
> not print in a workers' journal written by workers the painful and terrible things
> that Mme Flora has just thrown in our faces.' 'So Monsieur you would like me to

cure you without seeing your sores.' – 'Yes Madame.' – Opinions were divided, several agreed with him, others, the majority, strongly disagreed. – Vinçard, two others and Mlle Cecile Dufour said that I had mistreated women of the people too much – that they were not as rough as all that, – that they were tender towards their children and other sentimentalisms. – A woman, as silly as a goose, took the floor to say that I humiliated women by asking for rights for them, by saying that they had divine rights. – This poor woman was so inept that she could not go on. – This whole discussion was very heated. – The result of the ballot was 9 white over 3 black. It was not because of women's rights that there were three against but solely because of the cabaret issue etc., etc. – As I was leaving a woman came to me and said that she thought I had not demanded enough for women. – I exchanged a few words with her which proves that she is very advanced.[6]

Exasperated by the political wrangling of militants and the paralysis of the Saint-Simonians in their wait for the woman messiah, Flora Tristan's increasing sense of urgency about the need for action inspired her to start an association of all workers herself. Other ideas of a similar nature were in circulation at the time. Gustave Moreau and Agricol Perdiguier had proposed comparable schemes to promote working-class unity in order to combat the two great evils of poverty and ignorance.[7] Tristan's plan combined the existing worker ideas of solidarity with her own agenda for female emancipation. This was to be both a movement of self-help and self-emancipation, free from the interference of republicans, communists, democrats or other opportunists, and it was to include women in the fundamental demand of the right to work for all:

> I come to you to propose a *general union* among working men and women, regardless of trade, who reside in the same region – a union which would have as its goal the CONSOLIDATION OF THE WORKING CLASS and the construction of several establishments (WORKERS' UNION palaces), distributed evenly throughout France. Children of both sexes from six to eighteen years of age would be raised there, and sick or disabled workers as well as the elderly would be admitted.[8]

She set out with almost fanatical missionary zeal on a tour to contact workers in provincial French towns but died in Bordeaux before completing her tour, at the home of the Saint-Simonians Charles and Elise Lemonnier, just as she was achieving some success in raising political awareness among workers of both class and gender issues.

Writing as Protest

Looking back over Flora Tristan's career, it is clear that Peru was the turning point for her militancy. After her rejection by her father's family, she no longer tried to conceal her circumstances as a separated wife, as she had done previously, but expressed her unhappiness in the 'Petitions' and in the pamphlet, 'On the Need to Help Women Travellers', as an example of the wider problem of women's oppression. Henceforth Tristan exploited her own experience as politically necessary for liberation:

> Women, whose lives are tormented by great misfortunes, should make their troubles speak; they should expose the hardships they have endured as a result of the position laws have imposed on them and prejudices they are imprisoned by; but above all they should name names. ... Who better than they would be in a position to reveal the iniquities which take place concealed from public derision? ... In fact every individual who has seen and suffered, who has had to struggle with people and facts, should make it their duty to tell the whole truth of the events in which they were an actor or a witness and name those about whom they have a complaint or praise to make; because I repeat, reform can only take place and there will be no integrity or freedom in social relationships without the effect of such revelations.[9]

Writing became a major form of political activism for Flora Tristan until her death in 1844. By 1842 she had become totally committed to the cause of the Workers' Union. At the same period, she developed her ideas of social solidarity towards women, first sketched in 'On the Need to Help Women Travellers'. This principle was extended to a larger social group – the exploited masses – when Tristan mooted the notion of an alliance of interests between women of all classes and the working class. Her works, *London Journal*, published in 1840 and 1842, and *Workers' Union*, published in 1843 and 1844, express this concept very forcefully. During her tour of France she visited more than 20 towns, keeping a journal in which she recorded the depth of alienation of the working class and the success of her campaign for change. She capitalized on her encounters with leading activists and civic dignitaries, whether illustrious or modest, to illustrate her criticism of their apathy or misguided opinions for failing to support her. Gradually, as she realized that the union of all women and workers was not as imminent as she had hoped, Tristan revised her ideas of class collaboration through gender solidarity. She saw the economic exploitation of the urban working class as foreshadowing an uprising in which she would have no part. The February insurrection of 1848 which brought about the downfall of the July Monarchy occurred three years and five months after she had collapsed and died in Bordeaux.

Her last project was to revert to the role of commentator, as she had been in her *London Journal*. Her study of the condition of the working class in France was published in 1973 as *Le tour de France*.

Like many socialists and utopians of the period, Flora Tristan analysed the links between the exploitative structures of marriage and of capitalism. Though her own marriage had been unorthodox, by any standards, she was not in favour of public rebellion in her sexual relations, neither was she directly involved in revolutionary political events, as were Roland and Deroin. She had recourse to the Saint-Simonian idea of the woman messiah because she sought a justification for her leadership role. She championed the rights of the proletariat, those whom she described as the most numerous and most useful class of society, both to work and to education. Though she did not live to see such ideas realized, these two key principles were briefly implemented by the revolutionary government in February 1848. Like Roland and Deroin, Flora Tristan experienced material hardship[10] and police surveillance. Like Roland she was often ill and died prematurely. Illegitimacy, the impossibility of divorce with its consequences of physical and mental abuse for herself and her children, pushed her into protest sometimes of a marginal and solitary nature. Women's groups had faded after 1835, but even so Tristan's natural inclination was to lead as a lone campaigner. She was frequently at logger-heads with other socialists, though dependent on them for contacts during her tour of France. For Flora Tristan, economic liberalism was the class enemy, male despotism the cause of women's oppression, and society's double stand-ards of morality condemned girls and women to remain in ignorance and dependence in marriage.

Flora Tristan's message of economic equality for men and women and her messianic zeal ensured her place as a significant figure in socialist and feminist history. In the early months of 1848 when the republic was at its most radical and most socialist, Flora Tristan was honoured by the workers and a monument was erected in her memory at a ceremony attended by thousands. The following eulogy by M. Maigrot, a carpenter from Bordeaux, sums up her life:

> Madame Flora Tristan was the apostle of the workers; for us she braved the sarcasm, lies and even indifference of those who have not yet understood the importance of her message. Those of us who had the good fortune to know her and hear her, know what a fervent love of humanity, what confidence in God, what faith in the future inspired her heart and voice. She is dead, gentlemen, but the work she began will not perish with her. The seeds she planted in the breast of the people will bear fruit. May she live again in us! Let us show that we can follow her example and be strong, patient, active and courageous. Let us understand, as she did, the irresistible power of peaceful association. Let us all be brothers! Let us create among ourselves the union which she advocated; and when, with the help of God, the great day of the association will dawn for all men and women, we will inscribe among the great benefactors and benefactresses of humanity the hallowed name of Flora Tristan.[11]

However, in spite of the recognition of Flora Tristan's efforts by revolutionar-ies in 1848, she subsequently faded into political oblivion after the repression of the socialist experiments of 1848. Like Madeleine Pelletier, Flora Tristan was not an easy personality. Her singularity did not appeal to George Sand.[12]

Most important of all, the disappearance of women's emancipation from the political agenda after the failure of the 1848 revolution effectively repressed her memory. Significantly, her rescue from historical oblivion began in feminist, syndicalist, pacifist circles at the beginning of the 20th century. Hélène Brion was the first person in two generations to publicize Tristan's ideas, in her brochure *Flora Tristan: the True Founder of the First International.*

INTRODUCTION TO TEXTS

Text 1   'On The Need To Provide Hospitality For Women Travellers'
Text 2   'Petition for the Restoration of Divorce'
Text 3   'Petition for the Abolition of the Death Penalty'
Text 4   Published and unpublished correspondence (three letters)

The brochure 'On The Need To Provide Hospitality For Women Travellers'[13] was Flora Tristan's first substantial publication. Although it only contained a modest plan to give women greater physical mobility, in it we see her concentrating specifically on action for women as an oppressed social category. The work is particularly significant in recognizing that women shared oppression throughout society, though they experienced it in quite distinct ways according to their class. The greatest problem for the mobilization of women, as Flora Tristan was to discover, was that their dispersal into different classes prevented them all from associating or identifying with the proletariat. Her critical reference to the philosophical alienation of utopians, paralysed by their desire to build a new Eden, was a reference to those such as Fourier whose ideas were impossible to put into practice. Yet Flora Tristan shared Fourier's optimistic belief in the steady progress in civilization. The subjugation of women prevented progress of this 'selfish' civilization based on individual greed. Associations based on mutual self-help could provide economic and physical security for women travellers and enable them to enjoy the cultural advantages which travel opened up to men.

One of Flora Tristan's first significant pieces of writing was a petition for divorce, sent to the Chamber of Deputies. The request for divorce was one of the fundamental and persistent demands from women following the 1815 decision to rescind the right to divorce, a right which had been established by the Revolution but was already severely curtailed under Napoléon. Flora Tristan appealed to the deputies of the July Monarchy to distance themselves from the previous monarchy of 1815. The anti-clerical nature of the 1830 uprising which had overthrown the Bourbon monarchy had raised the hopes of those campaigning for the restoration of divorce.[14] In her petition, Tristan evoked the historic process of the evolution of political regimes, which had resulted in new attitudes to the question of marriage and the status of women. Paradoxically, though appealing to anti-clericals, she also availed herself of religious arguments in her plea. In the event, though a series of bills to restore the Napoleonic version of divorce passed through the Lower House between 1830 and 1834, they were all rejected by the Upper House.

After her attempted assassination by Chazal, Tristan presented a petition for the abolition of the death penalty to the Chamber. In it, she associated the high level of crime with the high level of unhappiness in family life, thanks to existing marriage laws. Producing figures to back her argument, she insisted that most criminal offences were related to domestic strife. With regard to the death penalty itself, she argued that the state did not have the right to take life. A principled opposition to the death penalty remained an anomaly in French political thinking for another century at least: abolition did not occur until 1981. Flora Tristan's opposition appears both far-sighted and courageous.

The selection of letters which follows demonstrates the overriding importance of letters as a means of political communication in the 1830s and 1840s for those political activists who sought to establish a network in France and abroad. Like Pauline Roland, Flora Tristan was a prolific letter-writer, some of whose correspondence has been preserved. Through these letters we can glimpse aspects of her personal life, particularly her preoccupation with her children and her network of political acquaintances. We have included here an unpublished letter to her brother-in-law about the future career of her son. In contrast to this insight into family tensions, Tristan's letters describing her political contacts in the Parisian circle of socialists, or encouraging disciples in Lyons, are more self-confident and hopeful.

TEXT 1   ON THE NEED TO PROVIDE HOSPITALITY FOR WOMEN TRAVELLERS[15]

'Help one another', Christ

Superior geniuses have aptly described our age when they called it an age of social transition and of regeneration for the human race. The bases on which the *ancien régime* of the Middle Ages was founded have disintegrated, fallen apart for ever, and a new society is seeking to build itself out of its ruins. From all sides unanimous voices can be heard resounding, demanding new institutions which can adapt to the new needs, a voice calling for co-operation, working together in one accord, to relieve the masses who are languishing in misery, unable to help themselves; because, divided, they are weak, incapable even of struggling against the latest efforts of a decrepit civilization on the point of extinguishing.

A whole class, making up half of the human race, is among these unhappy creatures which our civilization is condemning to live in distress; and the men who have a conscience feel that the condition of women must be improved, the condition of that part of humanity whose mission is to nurture peace and love within Societies.

It is naturally recognized that society as a whole, and particularly women, feel the need to improve the general state of affairs, and to change social habits which are no longer suited to the development which the point of progress has reached. But the fault of our time is the desire to generalize too much. In this way, we lose sight of the means of achievement; we dream up perfect systems, but which can only be put into effect in two centuries' time.

My aim here is not to create another brilliant utopia, by describing the world as it should be, without giving some indication of the route which could lead us to fulfil this wonderful dream of a universal garden of Eden.

I would like gradual improvements, and it is within these sights that I envisage only one part of humanity and its hardships. I think that if everyone wanted to follow this approach, by working towards different improvements, to a specific task, soon the dawn of redemption and happiness would break.

I want to concern myself only with the lot of women travellers without straying from this category.

To women who have no knowledge of the unhappiness of this position from their own experience, to men who will never know, no matter how hard they may try, how awful it is to find oneself as a woman, alone, and a stranger abroad; it is to all these that I am speaking and appealing. My ideas are dictated by the best intentioned philanthropy, my ambition is sacred; also, I hope, my divinely inspired words will have an impact on all sensitive hearts, on all noble and generous souls. For some time, I have travelled alone, and abroad. As a consequence, I am aware of how cruel this ordeal can be. I have found myself a stranger in Paris, in towns in the provinces, in villages, on the high seas. I have journeyed through several counties of England and its huge capital. I have visited a large part of America, and what I am saying is only as a result of the impact this experience has had on my soul, because we can only talk with authority about things of which we have first-hand experience.

In order to create a true picture of the hardships to which a travelling foreign single woman is exposed, I believe we should begin by showing her situation in one of the biggest and most popular capital cities, the centre of civilization, and Paris can provide me with more than I need to chill to the marrow everyone who has the ability to understand the misfortune of such an unhappy position.

I will start with Paris then, this Paris which for so long has achieved fame on a European scale for the affability of its inhabitants, and my accusations will be all the more forceful since, until now, no other town has been able to rival it.

If, sometimes, I seem to go into what appear to be minute details, it is because a combination of little discomforts taken together cause real hardship, and are all the more galling, since they continually recur.

The woman traveller, who has boarded a coach at the border, during the three or four days needed to travel the distance from there to the capital city, will already have had to endure a thousand sneers, a thousand instances of lack of hospitality or even of politeness. Instead of finding in her travelling companions or in the various hostelries where she will have had occasion to stay, the considerations and attentions which should normally be due to foreign women on all occasions, she will have encountered nothing but selfishness and curiosity on the one hand and complete indifference on the other. When at last she does arrive, she is exhausted, unwell, and yet she has to worry about finding a place to stay. She disembarks from this massive stage coach, dazed by the noise still resounding in her ears, and the cries of the coachmen and the messengers fighting over who will carry her belongings. The valets of the fancy hotels who want to lead her off, against her will, to the best *Hotel de France*, or the most magnificent *Hotel d'Angleterre*, must confuse her even more. Also, all this din which she is not used to, of bustling or indifferent people whirling around her, throws her into a kind of terror which is most distressing and upsetting. It seems to her as if some mishap is already threatening to turn her head; her bosom swells, her eyes fill with tears, and she sighs: 'My goodness! What will become of me, all alone in this city where I am a stranger!'. That is the effect Paris produces on a woman who arrives there for the first time alone, with no letter of recommendation. If the woman traveller had someone to welcome her on arrival, many of these discomforts would be diminished, but if the opposite happens, which is too often the case, as soon as she arrives in the famous *Hotel d'Angleterre*, she will be received with a certain air which I cannot describe. You can be sure that she will be greeted with the words: 'Madam is alone' (with the emphasis on the word 'alone'), and after her reply to the affirmative, the valet or maid will be told to direct her to the worst room of the house. She will only be served after everyone else, and goodness knows in what manner! However she will be made to pay 10 francs more for the poor quality room than a man would be made to pay. It will be the same for all the rest, and it happens everywhere. So much for physical hardships; let us look at the others.

If this woman traveller receives a male relation in her room, a fellow countryman or a businessman, it will be decided immediately, in the spirit of Christian charity which is practised in furnished hotels, that this woman traveller has come to Paris with dubious intentions. The mistress of the hotel will suspect it; the people living there will have no doubt of it, and the servants will swear by it. I cannot tell where these practices which exist in almost all furnished hotels come from, but they are exactly the facts that I am relating here.

These, then, are the hardships common to all women who travel alone; but I must divide them now into several classes, in order to study more closely their respective but equally unfortunate positions.

Let us look first at the position of women who undertake travelling for an educational or pleasurable purpose. It is to this class above all that the most distinguished and the most interesting women ever to be found in a city like Paris can be met; they could enrich and embellish society, as much by the abilities, as by the resources of the upper class to which they normally belong. However, what kind of welcome do these women receive? If they have a recommendation, they will be invited to dinner, to take tea or to a ball, but nothing more. It will be very difficult for them to meet people because they have no channels of communication. How will the woman traveller who has come to visit Paris as a place of interest for art and science manage to satisfy her noble curiosity? To whom can she turn to have useful contacts? Who will be able to help her achieve the aim she set herself, to use the time that she has sacrificed to make this journey? It is an insurmountable problem. No doubt a guide for foreigners will inform her of the days and times public monuments are open to visitors, but will a foreign woman, who may be rather shy, have the courage to visit these places only frequented by men, who are not used to seeing unaccompanied women, and because of this will look at her in a curious way? And if she does have the courage to do this, when she finds herself in one of these public places, seeing the way she is stared at, she will be completely intimidated, and will not dare to address one single question to anyone. She will have to renounce the purpose of her visit, because she will be forced to return home knowing neither the name nor the use of the thousands of objects which she would have been so interested to learn about. Alas! I am afraid that many a cold-hearted person would say to me: 'Well if your foreign lady finds herself alone, she should hire a guide'. First of all I would reply by saying that very few foreign women can afford the price of one, which is quite considerable; then our guides in no way resemble the original guides, the famous *ciceroni* of Italy.

There, it is a duty they perform with zeal, because they identify with the monuments of their town whose glory they believe they see reflected on themselves, whereas here, it is a duty which at best is carried out in an honest way. Many of the foreign women who come to Paris can hardly even visit one-twentieth part, and even then how do they do it? In a cold, sad and uncomfortable way, therefore they are quickly discouraged and their illusions vanish. They simply feel ill at ease physically and morally, but in a way which they cannot define, and the idea of leaving this great and beautiful city, this superb Paris, so highly praised, becomes their one and only desire.

Let us look at another class of equally interesting women. A large number of women come to Paris for reasons of business speculation, court cases or other matters of this kind. They have no one to guide them, and are obliged to entrust their business interests to total strangers by whom they are all too often duped. Lack of business experience, which is normally the state of women's education at present, makes them easy prey for exploitation by rogues and schemers of all kinds; they are victims of their generosity, and their isolation causes them a lot of trouble, often even the total ruin of their family in whose interest they had set out on this journey. How much sorrow comes their way! Deceived, irritated, ruined, they curse Paris and its inhabitants who were incapable of stretching out the hand of friendship to the unfortunate woman traveller who had come to look after her rights and who has to leave without one person coming to her defence, or one person to feel sorry for her.

Finally we come to the third class, the most numerous and the most interesting one, and which seems to suffer from all those mishaps which would render it worthy of the greatest compassion.

That cities have always been condemned, given that vice and infamy abound there and that everything can be concealed, mingled and swallowed up there is only too true. What is also true is that there is also to be found virtue, weeping and dying ignored, despair crying plaintively and wringing its hands, and calm and resigned unhappiness. I know perfectly well that if a poor young girl from a small provincial town has been seduced, dishonoured and abandoned in her misfortune, this unfortunate creature has no other option to hide her shame, than to go and sink into this immense abyss, where everything is ground down into the same shape and assumes the same colour. Here, too, the unhappily married woman who is permitted by our present institutions to live separated from her husband but not to divorce him, which would restore happiness to both and maintain general order, comes to seek refuge. Here, too, the woman traveller for whom misfortune or calumny has forced her to leave her native land, comes to seek refuge. It is just when their hearts are choked with anguish that the loathsome condemnation of their fellow creatures, perhaps a thousand times more guilty than they are, adds to their distress. Then they take refuge in the crowd within these cities, looking for the freedom to cry unnoticed in the shadows, and to hide their pain and sorrow there. It is for these women especially that this Paris which, so often in their rural homes had been depicted to their young imaginations with such vivid colours, it is to these women that this brilliant Paris seems horrible. How cold and empty this crowded city seems to them! For this class of traveller, their stay in Paris in a rented furnished hotel room, is a thousand times more terrible than facing the Tartar in his most hideous attire.

It is conceivable that displaced women who find themselves in such a position as I have described will always be without pecuniary resources because a young girl who has been deceived would not have been abandoned if she were rich. The maligned woman traveller would not have been obliged to leave home if she had money. Only the weak and unhappy are misled. Very few rich women find themselves in the cruel obligation of obtaining a separation from their husband, because of the custom they have of living a separate existence from him from the very beginning. Thus these displaced women are nearly always in need, and often face destitution.

However, it is these unhappy creatures who more than any other require a helping hand to come and offer them some support. How many of these young women living in neglect waste their lives, alone, in small dark chilly rooms, and die in the springtime of their lives. Not one ray of hope shines for them on the horizon, and sinking under the weight of their grief they end up by becoming prone to an unhealthy nervous sensitivity, an extreme irritability which, in the long run, affects even the most robust health. The scorn and the isolation to which they are exposed make them curse life, and the slightest lack of comfort, even the mildest of sardonic looks, are for them like daggers which stab deep into their breast. A friend would be more necessary to them than space for birds born to fly in the air, than sun for plants growing in the earth, but this friend so often dreamed of is nowhere to be seen, and if sometimes the shadow of one appears, it eludes them as quickly as a brilliant meteorite on a summer night. Oh! Grief overflows in their hearts, like a stream when the snow thaws. Where could they meet a person who could understand them, to whom they could confide in completely, and find some peace by giving vent freely to their grief? Could they speak to a stranger passing by chance? But do you not tremble at this word chance, in a city that is like a huge cesspool? Well! even if we do suppose that after many fears, many bitter anxious thoughts, they have enough courage or despair to risk their whole future to chance, we wonder where they will actually meet this stranger. Alone in their room, they are unaware of what is going on in the huge desert they come to hide in; in the same way the stranger who is passing by in the muddy street where they live is unaware that there is, at the end of the passage of the small hotel in front of him, a young girl or a young woman, perhaps from the same province, who is in the greatest need of his help.

The fact that people born for one another find it impossible to meet causes many hardships which have become overwhelming in the present state of our society. Oh! beloved fellow countrymen, living in the homes built by your fathers, who are comfortably off, surrounded by your family, by your friends, your pleasures, in a word, by all that can make life's happiness, for goodness' sake spare a thought of compassion and pity for creatures who breathe as you do, who feel like you, but who suffer a thousand times more than you do. You who do not know what it is like to have left your native land. Have you ever thought that there were some of your compatriots, perhaps some of your friends, who were strangers in a faraway place, where the climate makes them ill, where customs are strange to them, irritating them at every moment, and in fact whose language was foreign to them, which meant they were deprived of all resources and consolation? Oh brothers, that is terrible! that turns your heart to ice in fear and terror. Ah! let us have pity on the lot of these foreign women who find themselves in an unhappy position, let us love them, and help them as best we can. Many dare not say anything to you, they avoid all company, not from pride, but from fear; unhappiness makes people shy. This position of a woman alone, foreign, without an income, without support, is so awful that I am not even going to try to describe it. No language has a strong enough expression to be able to convey similar hardships. Only truly good and compassionate hearts are capable of penetrating the depths of this abyss of pain.

Many of those unfortunate women have brought a broken heart to Paris, but are pure, entirely virtuous, with simple moral standards, the right ideals and sound qualities. They only wanted to do good, and do it completely, but society which has rejected them, which treated them with suspicion, this same society, instead of treating them like sisters and helping them, opened all sorts of pitfalls. Instead of helping them accomplish their duty with the scrupulous correctness that they should have applied, society has shown them the path of vice, disguised in the most attractive brilliant colours, the path of vice, as the only way open to them. Society has mocked with a diabolical smile, their repugnance for this course of action and has given them a cruel alternative: either to degrade themselves in their own eyes or perish in destitution, maligned by the same seducers who would like nothing better than to get rid of them, and the same barbaric unworthy society, prouder of its cowardly triumph than Lucifer is of his beauty, with no regard to propriety, without pity, then used all its evil ingenuity to find ways of closing all escape routes, so that the victims could find no way of being able to escape from the abyss into which they were thrown. That is the present state of affairs: an unhappy victim falls and everyone throws themselves on her to trample her underfoot; not one person stretches their hand out to help her recover.

Alas, if we curse our brothers, if we let them perish in distress, who will come to our aid, when we are in a state of affliction one day? Men who have gone astray, remember that the hurt we do to others will rebound on us and our children.

It is a duty which must resound in the very depth of your heart, a sacred duty to come to the assistance of so many thousand suffering creatures who implore you and who succumb under the weight of their grief. Recall in your conscience the saying of Christ which must be the basis for all morality. 'Do unto others as you wish to be done to you'. Ah! Immerse yourselves in this sublime doctrine and do not leave for one moment longer, to languish in an ocean of distress, so many women who could be saved by your efforts! Do good, you will experience an ineffable joy, joy which is the prize and which will raise you up to God.

As for provincial towns, we can be sure that the lot of foreign women is no better than in Paris. In first rate towns they find the same isolation as in the capital, the same selfishness, the same lack of concern, and lack of politeness. As for other places, if they are less corrupt, indifference there is replaced by an indolent curiosity. If in large towns no one cares about foreign women, in smaller ones they are the topic of conversations, but as for a genuine concern, they find it in neither place. If a single woman, on a journey, wants to visit something interesting en route, she can only do it with great difficulty and in the sure knowledge of then being the subject of all the gossip of the village notables.

Finally if we talk about the spa towns, of thermal establishments, it is in these places that the position of a woman traveller alone is the most difficult. It is there that idleness allows more time and inclination to worry about other people's business and there she is also the butt of slander. If a woman tormented by some illness has the courage (and this word is not exaggerated) to go alone to the thermal waters it turns out that charitable people of whom there are many will have no scruples about doubting her honesty; others will affirm on hearsay alone that she is running after wealth. She can expect to hear suggestions from young people who will poison her heart and increase her pain instead of finding the relief from it she came to seek. I will say no more.

I will soon be publishing a work on England which has the special aim of giving an account of the way foreign women who travel in that country are received, details of which would be out of place here (I would say simply that the lot of single foreign women in that country is a thousand times worse than in France).

And as for America, it will be seen when I have the small account of my trip to these countries published, that the further they advance in European civilization the more they lose their former hospitality. This virtue seems to disappear with culture, like trees in an age-old forest, and it would be dreadful if the traveller wondered one day (a day which is not far away, if things continue at the same rate), what had become of the rural standards of our forebears, this natural hospitality, this kind-heartedness of the New World which had enchanted him in reading the accounts of travellers from past centuries. But I will draw a curtain over this image of these hardships, of the selfishness. I would even say of the barbarity of modern civilization that there are few changes to be made in the picture that I have drawn of France to make it appropriate for other nations.

But enough talk which appeals to the emotions: those who are sensitive will have already understood me. In our positive century, an appeal must be made to the intelligence. I must be careful not to be confused with these metaphysicians who only think on the lines of reason; I must try to ensure that my theories are not associated with moral utopias which are rising up everywhere and crashing almost immediately because their authors lack foresight and logical minds. Besides, since the masses are purely calculating and reason with figures in their heads and with a cold arithmetical method speculate on the chances of their happiness to come, I believe you must talk to people in their own language, so I am going to develop for them a picture of the material disadvantages which result in the poor welcome given to foreigners and the enormous advantages there would be in welcoming them in another manner.

It is certainly true that foreigners make up a great part of the wealth of cities and good relations between nations are a way to advance progress rapidly. We know the immense advantage for the whole of Europe that resulted from the Revolution. Our victorious armies, under the Republic and the Empire, travelled throughout many lands, established close links everywhere, and taught people to love one another, to no longer mistrust one another as in the past, and to profit from reciprocal knowledge.

At present we see that the English no longer despise what comes from the Continent; the Italians are no longer suspicious of any science developed beyond the Alps; and the French too, whom happy circumstances have pushed into the lead in progress, understand their mission of spreading civilization throughout the world. Consider what advantages trade, sciences, arts, industry have gained. Truth is no longer the exclusive right of those who discover it, but it is published and propagated. Nations are rivals in a noble ambition, and railways, canals, suspension bridges are being built everywhere. Our neighbours over the sea have made great progress in machinery construction but we are following them along the same path, because close links have been established between the two countries. Foreign languages are being studied, and written works are being translated immediately from one nation to another to share the light of genius in all countries.

But it would take too long to enumerate here all the advantages of travelling, of maintaining continuous links between nations and hastening the moment when so many rival nations will succeed in being just one family.

Women also play an active part as travellers and if they are unable to be useful to the sciences as much as men are, their powers of observation make their usefulness very pertinent to the area of human behaviour. But what do we do to attract them or to bring them to our city? As can be seen from the picture which we have just traced, women from the provinces and foreign countries are certainly not going to encourage their friends or fellow countrywomen to travel, to undertake journeys which from their own account have made them suffer so much. That is a fact which I have noticed myself, that a lot of women who had come to stay for long periods in Paris have left after a while without having seen or learnt anything, disgusted at the loneliness of this city and cursing the day they left their comfortable homes.

Parisian women for their part hardly ever visit the provinces and for the same reason. However let us look at the real advantages for society that these short trips would produce. Women feel that a new era is beginning for them that they too are called to take part in the sanctuary of education. The greatest misfortune for women comes from their idleness from the fact that because of their poor education they can only follow frivolous and ephemeral occupations. Parisian women would no longer be ignorant of their own country as most of them are; they would find and be able to acquire for themselves virtues which they neglect in their own lives but which provincial women possess in their homes, for instance domestic economy, common sense and frankness. This observation would lead them to reflect seriously on the incredible frivolity of a great number of Parisians. Provincial women for their part would return home with a more sophisticated education, be more affectionate and more advanced in progress.

Villages would bestow the purity of their moral standards upon towns and they in exchange would give of their culture. In short, tremendous benefits would result which would have an equal impact on all classes of society. It is unnecessary to discuss those women who would be travelling in foreign countries because the advantages I have just indicated would be even greater and on a much bigger scale. Thank God we are already all French without distinguishing between provinces, and these travels, this reciprocal hospitality would bring the long awaited day much closer when we will all be human beings, brothers, no longer able to distinguish ourselves by the names of English, German, French, and so on.

But when an evil is recognized, when we have found a remedy for it, the means to apply it must be sought and it is with this intention that I am proposing a new organization. Let us take a look at history and we will see that at every epoch, when part of society suffered and felt the need for change, organizations suggested reforms. These were intended as mutual self-help associations, to assist afflicted or persecuted brothers, because when we are individuals we are weak; only in a union can we find the strength, the power and possibility of doing good.

Take for instance persecuted Christians who created societies to come to the assistance of those victims of tyranny because of their faith. Look at persecuted Jews later in the Middle Ages: they too formed associations which spread throughout the world which, bringing from them the invention of letters of exchange, brought about co-operation and progress, trade and civilization. Look at the Crusades, the organization which formed in Europe to assist the faithful in the East. Finally, read the history of Protestantism and you will see that in Germany and England and wherever there was persecution practised firstly against them by Catholics, and then by them against Catholics, organizations grew up in order to help the unhappy victims of one or other of the sects.

We could say as much for all the periods of great political revolutions. All we have to do is show the pages of the history books to find a thousand examples.

Well is not our time comparable to other critical times where a great change is imperceptibly occurring? Do not women suffer? Is it not a sacred duty to come to their assistance?

Let us begin with a firm hand by raising the banner of self-help; let us create a truly worthy, truly hospitable organization and let us relieve some of those who suffer, who will bless us for having rescued them from distress. Our example will be followed, our voice will have an echo in all generous souls; of that we are in no doubt. Our heart will experience this pure divine joy, which only philanthropy and virtue can know. I will outline now the basis on which the proposed society rests and the statutes which I believe we ought to assign to it.

Statutes for the Society of Women Travellers

Motto of the Society: Virtue, Prudence, Openness

Article 1   This Society will have men and women as equal members.

Art. 2   To be admitted, proof must be supplied of address in the same vicinity as the Society.

Art. 3   No one under the age of twenty-five may be admitted.

Art. 4   To gain admittance, three members must present the candidate, and give every guarantee of good character and good intentions towards foreign women.

Art. 5   Each female member must pay for costs of the establishment, 30 francs per annum, payable six months in advance; each man, 60 francs.

Art. 6   No one can be admitted for less than a year.

Art. 7   The office will consist of firstly, a President (man or woman, local or foreign, as long as they reside in the locality). The President will be appointed, like all the other office holders, by ballot, with a relative majority of the members present, and for 1 year; after which they could be re-elected, if the Society considers them suitable.

Art. 8   Secondly, a Vice President for the same period, who will be asked to replace the President in case of absence.

Art. 9   Thirdly, three secretaries, who will be appointed only for three months; they could resign and be replaced but at their own expense, and only after agreement from the Society.

Art. 10   Six members will be appointed for three months, who will form what could be called the *External Committee*, which will be in charge of receiving the foreign women, listening to their requests, to establish if they are entitled to join the Society, and even to introduce them to the Society; to obtain for those who have come to do academic research, all the information they might require: for those who wish to become artists, contacts with artists: for those who are foreign to France contacts with their compatriots, if they wish: for those who have come for a job to strive to find a suitable one for their situation and also to help in any way possible: those who have come for a business matter such as a court case, a medical consultation, etc., etc. The members of this External Committee should come to an agreement with several managers of furnished hotels, so that, with a letter of recommendation, they will receive the foreign women who will go to them for accommodation with all the consideration due to a foreign woman. They should also give letters of recommendation whenever requested, so that travellers can find another society in whichever country they go to, like a kindly mother who will welcome them with open arms. In short these six External Committee members will have to ensure with the greatest care that the foreign women enjoy in all respects all the benefits that the Society has undertaken to offer them.

Art. 11   The Society will have a general assembly on the first day of every month. The aim of the meeting will only be to discuss the interests of foreign women. Each person should contribute ideas for improvement in favour of foreign women. Proposals for improvement put forward to the general session will be referred to a commission, in order to be examined in detail, to advise on the means of putting them into effect.

Art. 12   In the case of exceptional circumstances, for instance where a woman traveller has a secret to speak about, or wishes to speak in confidence about her position, which I will not elaborate on here, the President, the Vice President, a secretary and two members of the Society must meet in secret committee to hear her case and to discuss among themselves any useful way of helping her.

Art. 13   The Society should hire premises near the centre of the district where most foreigners normally meet. The premises should consist of a first room where the office will be, a second, where there will be a library, including all French and foreign newspapers, a third which will be a reception room, where meetings for social gatherings may be held, and finally a large salon for the full sessions of the Society. It could also be used for parties, concerts, lectures, and so on. However, entrance to this room should always be free, unless charity concerts, balls or other social functions are given to raise money for impecunious foreign women.

Art. 14   The Society, having no vested interest to prove to the public that its intentions are honourable, should make a statement of all expenditure incurred in running the establishment. The statement of all the monthly costs will be posted in the first room, so that everyone may be left in no doubt, that the Society for Foreign Ladies has had no intention of making it a commercial enterprise, a notion that it utterly rejects as being incompatible with the spirit by which it is directed.

Art. 15   Each member will be entitled to the use of the reading room and reception facilities. On the days of the general assembly, each member will be allowed to bring three people to the reserved seating area. The same applies when there are lectures, concerts and charity balls or other parties.

Art. 16   Each member will be required to wear, on the days of the meeting, a wide green ribbon, edged with a red selvage, with a silver medal on which the motto of the Society will be engraved on one side, and on the other, the following words: 'Society for Foreign Ladies'. The ribbon will be worn with as much ceremony as the one for the Legion of Honour. Each member will be required to wear on all occasions, men in their buttonhole, women on their chest, a smaller ribbon in the same colours as the full-sized one.

Art. 17   Each member in whatever place he finds himself, will be requested to give aid and protection to all foreign ladies who come with a request for assistance, recognizing them by the badge they are wearing, which shows their membership of the Society for Foreign Ladies.

Art. 18   Should the case arise where the Society has to complain about a foreign woman, it should be done in a public session, naming the person[16] and outlining the facts, but these must be treated with the utmost confidence.[17]

Art. 19   Foreign men and foreign women could subscribe to the reading of the newspapers at a price determined according to the numbers of subscribers.

I think I must point out that my statutes are perhaps not quite complete but obviously this is only a plan; it will be completed with the assistance and participation of those who wish to join in this effort. The spirit which has inspired these statutes guarantees prudence and discretion of the Society to all foreign women, essentially important points. Moreover, the foreign women who find themselves in a delicate and particularly difficult situation could even confide in us with the complete assurance[18] that they will be able to find in each member of the Society, a friend, genuinely interested in relieving their difficulties. They could look for assistance, advice, protection, knowing in advance that they will encounter in the heart of every member of this noble association, a true desire to serve them in every way, and a positive willingness to look for every means to succeed.

In short, they will not be alone in this immense Paris, where I would like to establish the centre of our first association; they could speak of their distress to good and compassionate people who would welcome them with gentleness and interest, and who would look for every means possible to revive their demoralized spirits with hope and calm.

These then are the moral advantages which our Society would give to foreign women, advantages which would virtually cause the distress which afflicts them now to disappear. We will open our arms to them, we will shed tears with them in their grief, we will pour oil on the troubled waters of their hearts, and we will be greatly rewarded for the trouble we have taken by this pure and simple joy which is experienced after carrying out a good and praiseworthy action. I realize perfectly well that the accomplishment of my plan will be difficult. As soon as one wants to do anything out of the ordinary, there are many obstacles with which to contend. But I feel strong and I will not fail in the task I have set myself. As soon as it is formed, the Society should be able to ensure that really good and charitable people are associated with it, capable of serving humanity. In a word, I will follow ardently the spirit of the Society which will only have one thought, only one and the same aim, to improve the lot of foreign women.

Now I will reply to the many people who object that it is impossible to do what I am suggesting, because everywhere, especially in Paris, there are many women to be found who are not all they should be, and the objection is how can this sort possibly be admitted to good company? If I was not short of space I could discuss the philosophical and moral aspects of this question in a general manner. It would be easy to show that almost always the cause of evil is in society itself rather than the individual wrongdoer. Society which rejects from its midst without any pity or pardon the individual who has committed the slightest fault, places that person inevitably in the cruel necessity of continuing along the path of vice. There are very few, very few indeed, who are endowed with that almost superhuman energy which makes man capable of being able to rise above society and scorn its contempt, contenting himself with the purity of his conscience, or to repent of his fault. 'Bring back the stray sheep', said our Saviour, and he spoke the truth because man, by nature, is not wicked, and cannot be happy doing wrong, but our society has made him unhappy and pushed him into corruption. Many of these stray creatures, victims of our egotism, could become excellent citizens, whereas at present they are dangerous to society. But this vast question cannot be discussed in this brochure. Later if I feel able I will try to develop it thoroughly. Let us suppose that in the early stages, some women come forward to ask for help from our Society, using false names, bogus problems, with the intention of taking people in wherever they get an introduction to society. Well even if this should happen, neither the members who present her nor the people who receive her will find themselves compromised in any way, because they will not have received her as a personal acquaintance, but as a foreign woman, and on this recommendation she will be given the consideration and care which her position merits.

If one of these women were dishonest, to speak plainly, if she were a schemer, the good company who will have received her will not be responsible; she will be accorded hospitality, and if she does not respond by praiseworthy actions, she will be expelled from the Society with public condemnation of her misdemeanours. Anyway, I will outline the duties of every foreign woman towards the Society and hope that the cases arising where there is fear of being deceived will be very rare indeed. The woman who would wish to benefit from the so-called Society for Foreign Ladies should be convinced first of all that she is applying to a completely honourable, philanthropic association, whose ideas, actions and aims are noble, generous and inspired by virtue. She should think that alongside virtue goes *strictness*, scrutinizing constantly behaviour, actions and even the very words uttered. She should realize that courage and self-denial, which are the inspiration for the commitment to alleviating suffering, to protecting the weak and innocent, to consoling grief, are only to be found in characters who are relentless when it comes to vice, lies and deception. Moral precepts will be established for our Society, and more severe laws than any code has been able to publish until now. We will have as a motto, written in large letters above the door of the premises where the meetings will be held, the following three words: *Virtue, Prudence, Openness. Virtue*, to me, means total devotion to humanity, reasonable indulgence, pardon for all faults which are not incurable, since they have not penetrated the heart. The word *prudence* will be used to remind us that in our century, men are very much inclined to deceive their fellow men, and we must be on our guard against all traps. It will be useful to remind us of the care and discretion needed for shy foreign women, who are asking for assistance. And finally *openness* will impose the imperative duty of denouncing vice, intrigue and nastiness in public. Yes, our Society will offer to foreign women a place of refuge, of consolation, of sweet joys: but if they were not worthy they would have to appear before a final board, who would make a public condemnation, which incorrigible evil deserves. After this profession of faith, I believe it is impossible for any woman to be brazen enough to come to us under the veil of hypocrisy.

Each foreigner, by applying to the Society, will be required to give her real names (if she has an assumed name, she could keep it for public use if that suits her), the reasons for leaving her country, her place of residence and what her means of existence are: all under the seal of secrecy if she prefers. It is useless for a woman traveller to apply outside of these conditions, and I am convinced that sensible and virtuous women, far from finding them too severe, will be happy with the guarantees that they provide. Let us follow the sacred impressions of the heart; let us expand the Society along these lines and we will be on the path of progress. The unhappiness of our age stems from the fact that men have no fixed belief. The melancholy which begins by producing a thousand new fantasies and dreams in their heads, then leads them naturally to materialism and egotism which dry up the heart and have people cursing their very existence.

But I have before me the most beautiful and sacred religion: love of humanity. There, there is no incomprehensible system, no superstition, no undetermined aim. The good of the masses is also that of the individual, and the banner of this religion can unite all others, because it is in the spirit of Christ.

Let us be altruistic and bring relief to women, because women are poetry, art in the human race, and without poetry, without art, nothing is perfect. Far be it from me to dream up a purely metaphysical system, but man is both a physical and spiritual creature, and he will never be happy until he can act according to the needs of both sides of his nature. The benefits which would result in this association I am offering will extend to all classes of society. Women will become better informed, less frivolous, greater, more loveable. Men will improve, become stronger and more powerfully able to do good, because happiness increases two-fold. Moral strength is weakened by suffering just as physical strength is sapped by poor health.

Then the reign of virtue will spread over the land; I hope to see this sensible demand for freedom realized, a desire which makes all generous and sublime hearts beat so ardently. Yes, only virtue and love can unite the masses, and from their unity an invincible force will be born. Also, dare I say it, the realization of our project will reveal man's potential when he wants to lean on virtue. Man who loves becomes God's equal: how shall I put it, can do more than God himself. If he wanted he could unite in one single belief[19] under a single hope, this universe, so vast, so beautiful, which is his inheritance but which is torn by divisions and hatreds. My brothers, let us renounce all odious rivalry, all family or national egotism; our firm and constant willpower has us looking for happiness, which until now was only a dream, in love[20] and unity. Let us work to one common accord and we will find it. Fellow men, I insist that we can do more than God; let us spread our philanthropy universally, and we will just be the one and the same family. Were we not human beings before being English, Italian or French?

The limits of our love must not be the hedges around our garden, the walls which enclose our town, the mountains and the seas which are the frontiers of our country. Henceforth our country must be the world. Jesus said: 'You are all brothers'. Let us ensure that the difference of our customs, of our habits, as with each climate, instead of being a motive for disagreement and continuous hatred, becomes a school for improvement where each person can seek perfection. Fellow creatures, let us love one another, and happiness will be instilled in our hearts but, above all, may we never utter a word of contempt, because whoever says Racca (fool) to his brother will be cursed by God.[21] Let us go boldly towards the noble aim of perfection which we all see and which, by dint of hard work and perseverance, we can reach. Man will then be worthy of his creator when he will have done as much with his love, just as God has done with his infinite power, creating the universe out of chaos! Chaos expelled from the universe, the universe in harmony: his mission will be accomplished. Noble and fervent souls, sensitive and generous hearts, who understand what is sacred and holy in virtue and charity, it is to you that I am directing this appeal.

I am counting on you, I am calling you with all my strength so that you can come to my assistance to carry out this project. Yes, I am in no doubt that my voice will find a sympathetic audience because there are still people among the crowds who are dedicated, whose elevated minds understand the sacred duty we must all fulfil, to do good according to our means. I do not want to limit myself to showing what must be done; but I will devote my life to working to the objective I have set.

France, my beautiful country, so enriched by the new ideas which are in a ferment there, will reply with a resounding echo to the appeal I am sending. France wants nothing better than to move to perfection; that is why I am happy to be able to indicate the path open to her. The prince, whom the victorious people appointed on the day of its glorious revolution, this prince who rules us, who nobly endured a long exile, will understand better than anyone the praiseworthy thought which my long sufferings have suggested. It is to him that I am sending my first appeal, as the king of a generous nation, who possesses sacred feelings, as a man who has the misfortune to find himself a foreigner, and however high a position he might have is just as capable of suffering, because the impenetrable will of God strengthens his authority in one day of suffering, on the world leaders, just as on the ants that crawl around in the dust. After the prince, I will find other men who like him have suffered exile and unhappiness, and have returned with this noble generosity which has always been the most precious quality of a Frenchman, and finally, women who owe this duty to themselves to contribute as best they can to such a useful work, as urgent for their own gender as for the whole human race. If my project is carried out, as I have every reason to hope it will be, I will bless God for overwhelming me with bitter hardships for ten long years, because these same hardships have given birth to this project which could be so useful to the cause I want to serve, the cause of humanity.

Note: Anyone who wishes to join the Society for Foreign Women, and who wishes to get in touch with the author of the plan for this Society, will find the address at the printer's.

Print works of Mme Huzard (*née* Vallat la Chapelle), 7 Rue de L'Eperon.

TEXT 2   PETITION FOR THE RESTORATION OF DIVORCE[22]

To the Right Honourable Gentlemen

Sirs

It is my wish that you do not see merely a personal grievance in the petition I am humbly presenting to you for the restoration of divorce. The widespread and harmful effects of the indissolubility of marriage are obvious to one and all. God granted continuity only to a very small number of our affections and we wish to impose immutability on the most vacillating of them all! Domestic bliss and public morals evaporate under this unnatural institution. It is needless to indicate that harmony between spouses, as in all kinds of association, can only result from a relationship of equals, that the hideous union of despotism and servitude perverts the master and the slave and that such is our nature, that dependence obliterates all affection. These moral truths must be familiar to you gentlemen because he who has not been nurtured by them would not be worthy of the votes of his fellow citizens.

Gentlemen, our glorious revolution had freedom of thought as an aim, and it was greeted by acclamation from the people. All governmental regimes which it established were destined to prolong and to encourage the development of this divine liberty which encompasses all other freedoms. It continued the work of Christ, recognized independence of affections as a natural consequence of freedom of thought, and granted it also a legal recognition, leaving the yoke of the Pharisees to those who consented to continue wearing it. Divorce by mutual consent or by the will of all of the parties was introduced and voluntary separation was followed by legal separation, so the lawmaker was no longer constrained by the absurd situation of having to recognize fictitious paternity. This myth, inseparable from that of indissoluble marriage, is enough to indicate the powerlessness of legislation to prevent irregularities which arise from the repression of freedom of affections, irregularities which are made obvious daily by the growing number of illegitimate children.

Despotism merely requires obedience. Napoléon would have liked to have legalized divorce as a restricted privilege. Not daring to abolish it he made it conditional on terms offensive to any self-respecting family and often impossible to fulfil. It made it the almost exclusive right of the husband and decided its effects in an immoral and arbitrary way. Then the *Chambre Introuvable*[23] came to power and the Coryphaeus declared that the law was irreligious. It most certainly is irreligious in the sense that it substitutes the will of one man for the general will, but in the eyes of these gentlemen the atheism of this law lay in its alienation from the Catholic dogma. It had to be brought back into the fold and the elected representatives of this reactionary party suspended the divorce law and removed from the Code the only solution to that extreme unhappiness resulting from the servile clauses which the same Code encapsulates. They threw themselves in this direction with a blind temerity by making already existing marriages permanent instead of optional as had been the case; they made their law highly retrograde, thus opposing the principle of freedom of religious practice which is written into the Charter. Who would have thought in July 1830 that this barbaric monument of the Gothic assembly would still be in place in 1837? Twice the lower House has voted to abolish it, twice the Peers of Charles X have voted to maintain it. With one foot in the grave, these old codgers are still defending the moral standards of their day.

This antisocial law has borne fruit. Today in France there are more than 30,000 broken marriages and the annual figures on recognized illegitimate children prove the increasing number of people who remain very attached to a possession which nothing can remove, which equally traps forever any young man seduced by love or ambition; the same goes for the young girl forced into marriage by her parents; it punishes the error of a moment by lifelong torment, and filial duty by perpetual slavery. It is not possible for the moral standards which ensue from this state of affairs to be fitting for the most important customs of the century and the rate of progress which the present generation is experiencing. You will recognize, Gentlemen, along with all the journalists, that without divorce, religion and morality are powerless to create legitimate moral standards, and that prosperity and domestic bliss are dependent on this legitimacy: that the union of spouses would unquestionably be more permanent with the possibility of legal separation, and that this desired effect cannot be achieved by imposing penal clauses and by granting all powers to the husband. Protestant countries have allowed divorce. Are moral standards there any lower than in the countries where binding marriage contracts maintain the civil state of marriage whereas the spouses have in fact separated?

Gentlemen, I have had bitter experience of the unhappiness which an unbearable marriage contract entails. Forced to leave my husband, although I had no income, while still young I had to provide for my needs and those of my children by my work. Rarely are women able to cope with such a burden.

Very few receive an appropriate education for a profession and when they are left by a husband without any means of support, or are compelled to leave him, the law is responsible for illegal relationships they may have because this law forbids them from contracting legal unions where their children would have the protection of a legitimate father.

Gentlemen, in a work which I have recently published and wherein I pay tribute to the House, I have revealed some of the difficulties to which women are exposed when they are in my position. Personal interest is not what moves me to approach you. I have been inspired by love of my fellow creatures, convinced as I am by my own experience that family happiness cannot thrive without freedom. Christ said: 'What God has joined together do not separate'. Could not the precept be completed by adding: 'Do not join together what God has separated'?

As a consequence of the above I solemnly ask the House to reintroduce divorce and institute it on a reciprocal basis and with the will of one partner, just as those laws had been established before the Napoleonic Code.

I remain, honourable Gentlemen, your very obedient servant.

Flora Tristan,
100 bis Rue du Bac, Paris
20 October 1837

TEXT 3   PETITION FOR THE ABOLITION OF THE DEATH PENALTY[24]

To the Right Honourable Gentlemen of the Chamber of Deputies

May God protect France!

Sirs

When we think that, every year, more than 6 000 culprits leave prison or the penal colonies where, for the duration of their sentence, they have trained as pupils or teachers in the art of crime: when we think that out of 25 million proletarians more than three-quarters have never had any means of learning any trade, any industry, and are reduced by this to living from the precarious employment of their labours: when we think that every year 500,000 individuals, men and women, are yoked to one another forever, that 250,000 young girls go from family serfdom to conjugal slavery; at the very thought of all these elements of social dissolution, we utter wholeheartedly with the King's instructor '*May God protect France*!'.

So far we have only managed to preserve society by removing those who attack it. No criminal is reformed by our penitentiary system and the deplorable results it produces go a long way to explaining why the legislator is so hesitant: he is afraid of compromising public safety if he abolishes the death penalty and, by his refusal, recognizes his helplessness to prevent the causes of the crimes committed and to establish penalties which would reform.

However, Gentlemen, the ever constant growth in crime no longer permits inaction; the judicial question is crucial to other questions of a social nature, because the number of breaches of the law are a measure of the progress or perversion of society and I think that it is an imperative duty, for an assembly which considers itself to be legally invested by power from the people, to take an interest in it before any other matter.

The first duty, the great social need, is to guarantee bread for all. From this obligation derives the need to set up apprentice schools. Security for everyone is parallel in importance to this first duty of society towards its members. If women were to enjoy the same civil rights as men, if professional training of children were guaranteed by the state, then three-quarters of court cases and hospices for abandoned children could be done away with.

Aggression of the individual against society is such madness that it only occurs when hunger or exasperated feelings provoke it. Unhappiness or lack of a job or skills are the chief causes of attacks against property, but the majority of murder cases or assassination attempts have motives other than theft.[25]

Infanticide has its cause in the monstrous prejudice which condemns an unmarried young mother, and two-thirds of the cases of poisoning and assassinations are caused by jealousy, the feelings which result from the indissolubility of marriage and woman's servitude.

Organized according to their function, all creatures when they issue from God are whole. But social institutions modify them in many ways and create their vices and their virtues. Society therefore should not feel the need to have any injury avenged, because infractions only occur where these laws impede creation, or because the culprits have not been trained to observe them.

A child throws and breaks the objects which it does not know how to use. Societies in their infancy will destroy people when they do not know how to utilize them. There is no wild animal which cannot be tamed by some suitable treatment and there is no person who cannot be taught to obey rules as long as the rule is not unnatural. Those who have let themselves be perverted by circumstances of their particular environment will be cured by the influence of other circumstances of the opposite kind; even the most vicious creature, who has broken many laws, can become a useful member of society by a moral and healthy routine appropriate to his nature and to the changes which his environment have imposed on him.

Damage done to property can only be repaired by work. Work and education are also the means to reform the culprit. As for crimes of passion, it is the laws which have repressed individuals which must be held responsible.

Crimes and offences of all kinds can most certainly be understood to be against everything included under the generic term of persons and of property, but the code has instituted a special class of crime, against the state. Without an exceptionally strong system of justice, despotism cannot act as an arbitrator. The legal courtiers of Napoléon provided him with the most flexible and the most awful weapon in the shape of the Civil Code, so far as vague definitions of offences and the frequency of the imposition of the death penalty are concerned.

Gentlemen, what advantage has there been for society to have the application of the death penalty? ... Have crimes diminished? ... No, most certainly not. We see men brazenly face death for a scrape of bread, to satisfy their hatred, their love, to avenge an insult, and we would still like to believe that the death penalty can ward off infringement of the law.

Far be it from me to suggest that safeguards for society be removed, that the sheep remain exposed to the wolf's jaws, the victim to the hatred of her assassin. No doubt the murderer should be put in a position where it is impossible for him to try again to hurt his fellow men, and when cupidity, hatred or madness drive someone to commit murder, there are not many signs of healing that can reassure the legislator. The murderer must always be separated from society but therein lies the limit of our duty, and it is pointless going further simply from a sense of insecurity.

From an economic point of view, the death penalty is an absurdity since it deprives society of individuals who would have been useful in a rational regime, and when we consider how insufficient the education and apprenticeship systems are for the people, and when we analyse the code of servitude which dictates the organization of family life, the death penalty seems to be a revolting atrocity. Finally, from a religious point of view the question was judged a long time ago: God is the only one who has the right to decide on the length of what he granted in the first place.

'Thou shalt not kill' said the divinely inspired shepherd, thirty-two centuries ago, at the foot of Mount Sinai. Jesus said: 'You shall not kill, you shall not bear false witness, and love your neighbours as you love yourself'. And the precepts of these two commandments are implanted into men's consciousness.

Gentlemen, the law cannot isolate itself from the basis of all religion, love of God and of one's fellow men. Outside this sphere it becomes oppressive, loses the people's respect, can only be enforced by violence and to enact it, policemen, gallows and executions are needed.

According to the considerations outlined above, I humbly beseech the Chamber to abolish the death penalty immediately.

I remain your obedient servant

Flora Tristan

Paris, 10 December 1838
Printed by Madame Huzard, 7 Rue de l'Eperon.

TEXT 4   PUBLISHED AND UNPUBLISHED CORRESPONDENCE

Letter 1[26]

Paris, 11 October 1835

M. Charles Fourier
9 Rue Saint Pierre
Montmartre

Dear Sir,

I have just discovered that you took the trouble to come and see me twice; I am most grateful for this gesture and feel deeply embarrassed at not being at home when you called. For the last two months since I moved from the Rue Chabannais I have had so much disruption and problems over family matters that it has been impossible for me to find a spare moment to go to give you my new address. Every day I go even further into the sublimity of your doctrine and I feel more keenly than ever the pressing need to mix with persons who profess it. Unfortunately I no longer know anyone, now that M. Berbrugger seems to want to settle for good in Algiers. I wanted to ask you to introduce me to M. Considérant about whom I have heard great praise and to two or three women who share our ideas. I do not move in society much, which I have never liked, and my melancholy, disagreeable and unsociable disposition makes it difficult for me to make friends. I have only one aptitude and that is work, the earnest desire to be able to make myself useful, to serve the cause which we love with such purity, Ah! If only you would employ me! I will be eternally grateful to you.

If I may be so bold as to beg you to come and see me; I was forced to come and live in this district but I hope to move back closer to you before long. I am always at home on Wednesday all day, but other than that I go out very little and in the evening one is always sure to find me at home.

Farewell, Sir, you have my deep respect and esteem.

Flora Tristan

42 Rue du Cherche Midi (opposite the War Office)

Letter 2[27]

To Mr Antoine Chazal [brother in law] 20 Rue de l'Ouest

12 June 1841

Sir,

I am not writing this letter for myself as you might imagine, but on behalf of and in the sole interest of your nephew Ernest Chazal.

After everything that has happened, it is my duty as a mother to prevent further misfortunes, and to do whatever it costs, everything in my power to avoid my son also doing any harm...

Having no personal fortune and believing that a trade is the surest path to wealth, I had to and I wanted to make my son a worker. With this aim, as soon as his father was consulted, I put Ernest in a good boarding school where he learnt languages, a little bit of drawing and maths; in short he received a sufficient education for a craftsman. Two and a half years have gone by; Ernest is nearly 17. For three months I have been urging him to choose an occupation as I do not wish to cross him in his choice, but the problem is that Ernest is displaying an extreme distaste for all trades. However, about six weeks ago, he decided to go into a printers to learn the trade of typesetter. But he has already written to me that he has given up this notion and furthermore he informs me that he wants neither that nor any other trade as it does not suit him to be a worker.

This refusal to work at a trade on the part of a child who knows very well that his mother has not got the means to feed him to do nothing, or to give him a so-called liberal profession, this refusal is serious and is of the kind to give rise to the most serious anxiety about the future of this child, because in our social order every individual who does not want to work becomes, inevitably, a bad lot, a vagrant, a criminal.

You know Sir, that for seven years this unhappy child had before him the most pernicious examples; that he heard his mother slandered and insulted every day for seven years. It is impossible even if he was born an angel for him to resist being corrupted by such contact. He must be seen then as a victim and not as a *culprit*; he is bearing the inevitable consequences of his upbringing and the milieu where he lived. It is therefore our duty to come to his rescue. Ernest who left me when he was 7 years old does not know me; he does not obey me, and I have no authority over him; how could he respect and love a mother he was taught to scorn? That would be a contradiction and children have too much common sense to make such mistakes.

You see Sir that the position of your nephew is an unhappy one. His vanity, the high opinion he has of himself, and the illusions of his age prevent him from realizing the implications, but I do. I know people and the things of this world, I dare not stop to think about it, it terrifies me so much. That is why I am letting you know all about this. I acknowledge my powerlessness to rescue this child and request that you would save him from this disaster that I think he is heading straight towards.

If you wished, you could be useful to him. Well placed as you are, and with the help of your contacts, you could have him go into either the civil or military or administrative services; such a position would flatter his self-esteem and from then on, probably, he would behave.

Whereas if he remains in the state where I wish to place him, and I repeat, I can only make him a mere worker, his mind will become frustrated, his frustration will turn him to despair and then to violence, and perhaps in the end, he too, we might see him stand one day in the dock...

Until now we have kept Ernest away from bad company. But he will come back to Paris, and then it will no longer be possible to keep him away from all nasty company, from bad advice.

This Sir, is everything I had to say to you in the interest of your nephew. I hope that you will find in your heart the motivation to be useful to the son of your brother.

Flora Tristan

64 Rue de Grenelle
Paris

Letter 3[28]

List of books that Mad(ame) Blanc should read

Lyons, 6 July 1844

You should begin by getting a grip on public affairs.

Ideally it would be a good idea to find out about the development of political events in Greek and Roman times, and the first centuries of the monarchy in France: but that would take too long – when I have the time, I shall do a summary for you so as to let you know about all the reasons that no historian could give you. You begin then with the history of the '89 revolution – it is vital to understand it perfectly and for that you should study the newspapers and writings of the time. So read the *Moniteur*, the *Père Duchène* and all the little newspapers of this period – the works of Marat, Robespierre, St Just and etc. etc. etc. You must go to the town librarian who will give you all these works – you must manage to find the right way to ask him yourself or through the recommendation of well-known persons to give you permission to read at home. You will read much better this way, more and more quickly, and best of all you can take notes – when you read seriously you must always take notes in a little exercise book so as to be able to keep written 8- or 10-page summaries of the work you have just read from the notes which give you the essence of the book. You must be able to do your own summary in broad outlines, but precise and exact, in order to be able to say in a few words what the essence of the book is.

You must not forget to read the political memoirs of Mad(ame) Roland. – When I am back in Paris I shall send you a detailed list.

You will continue with the *Moniteur* so as to have an exact idea of this phase of the Empire – then when you are up to 1817 or 1818 you will take the *Constitutionnel* – in 1822 you will still read the *Constitutionnel* and you will add to that works of the period of B. Constant, Manuel, Foy, etc.

It is also in this same period 1822 that you should begin the great study of socialism – the journal of the Saint-Simonians – the *Réparateur* – Saint-Simonian books, and you will follow this Saint-Simonian school without a break.

Let us stop here, dear child. After you have done this work, I will outline the rest for you.

You feel that I want to teach you with the greatest care; consequently I must know if you have understood what I have got you to study. So after every reading you must send me a summary of what you have done – I will read it, and I will tell you if you are in the right yes or no – and the reason for the yes and no. In this way we will be sure that the work will be well done.

I am not asking you to do any light reading such as poetry, novels or plays etc., that is useless. When you are tired of reading, you will stop reading anything for a fortnight to a month; it is the only way to rest. You must write very little because you must understand before writing. Get into the habit of asking yourself the reason for everything. Persevere in your search and you may be sure that you will find it. If you want to amuse yourself by writing, here is a very good way – ask yourself often these kinds of questions – what is goodness? and what is evil? – strength and weakness? – happiness and unhappiness? – and so on – all the opposites.

It is absolutely essential that you abandon routine ways of thinking – the masses confuse terms – goodness and weakness for them are synonymous – if you want to force yourself to work on this aspect of your education, in each of my letters I will ask you two questions; it will be a kind of essay which I will get you to do: in school your teacher taught you to write words: now you have to make yourself understand the meaning of words.

If you want to work seriously you will find me a tireless teacher. You can ask me as many questions as come into your head. I will always make it my duty and real joy to reply.

Flora

NOTES

1. Of the five women in this Reader the life of Flora Tristan has been the most documented, beginning with the biography published by a disciple immediately after her death (Eleonore Blanc, *Biographie de Flora Tristan*, Lyons, chez l'auteur, 1845) and later by the socialist historian Jules Puech (*La vie et l'oeuvre de Flora Tristan*, Paris, Marcel Rivière, 1925). Since the 1970s she has been a fascination from literary, political, sociological and artistic viewpoints. See Bibliography for further titles.
2. A recent French edition of *Pérégrinations d'une paria 1833–34* (Paris, Maspéro, 1979) omits the Preface and Introduction of the original 1838 edition. The translation of the Preface and Introduction can be found in Claire Goldberg Moses and Leslie Wahl Rabine, *Feminism, Socialism and French Romanticism*, Bloomington and Indianapolis, Indiana University Press, 1993, pp. 204–17. For a translation of the 1979 edition see Flora Tristan, *Peregrinations of a Pariah*, translated, edited and introduced by Jean Hawkes, London, Virago, 1986.
3. See Introduction to Luis Alberto Sánchez, *Flora Tristan: Una mujer sola contra el mundo*, Lima, Mosca Azul Editores, 1987.
4. See Magda Portal's paper in Stéphane Michaud (ed.), *Un fabuleux destin: Flora Tristan*, Presses Universitaires de Dijon, 1985.
5. Flora Tristan, *Union Ouvrière*, une édition de Daniel Armogathe et Jacques Grandjonc, Paris, Des Femmes, 1986 (reprint of third edition published in Lyons, 1844, first published in 1843). See also English edition, *The Workers' Union*, translated by Beverly Livingston, Urbana, Illinois, University of Illinois Press, 1983.
6. See Flora Tristan, *Le tour de France*, Paris, Maspéro, 1980, pp. 30–31.
7. The contribution of women to the wealth of ideas in circulation has yet to be fully appreciated in the history of the working class. This is acknowledged by Jacques Rancière, *La nuit des prolétaires*, Paris, Fayard, 1981 and to a lesser extent by Roger Magraw, *A History of the French Working Class*, 2 vols, Oxford, Blackwell, 1992.
8. Flora Tristan, *Union Ouvrière*, *op. cit.*, p. 142.
9. Flora Tristan, *Pérégrinations d'une paria*, Paris, Arthus Bertrand, 1838. Introduction, p. xxviij (*sic*).

10. Because of the gender imbalance in archival sources, records of the personal and professional circumstances of Roland, Deroin and Tristan are scarce, which is often an impediment to exact and sound debate about their ideas. For instance, one historian has queried the extent of Tristan's personal assets as if this detracts from her integrity as a political militant: see Francis Ambrière 'Qui était Flora Tristan', in *1848 Révolutions et mutations au XIXe siècle*, Bulletin de la Société d'histoire de la Révolution de 1848 et des révolutions du XIXe siècle, no. 9, 1993, pp. 21–35.

11. Speech by M. Maigrot, carpenter from Bordeaux, cited in Eleonore Blanc, *Biographie de Flora Tristan, op. cit.*, pp. 75–6.

12. George Sand had contributed generously to the publication subscription for *Union Ouvrière* opened by Flora Tristan in 1842. Nevertheless, she was critical of Flora Tristan for forsaking her daughter, Aline, during her tour of France. However, Sand was not sympathetic either to the ideas of Jeanne Deroin or Pauline Roland in 1848 and refused to take part in the female suffrage campaign organized by Deroin. Flora Tristan was also sceptical about the question of democracy for women and workers, although for different reasons. For an account of the tensions between Flora Tristan and George Sand see Stéphane Michaud, 'En miroir: Flora Tristan et George Sand', in Stéphane Michaud, *Un fabuleux destin: Flora Tristan, op. cit.*, pp. 198–209; and Sandra Dijkstra's PhD thesis, *Tristan and the Aesthetics of Social Change*, San Diego, University of California, 1976, published in a revised edition as *Flora Tristan: Feminism in the Age of George Sand*, London, Pluto Press, 1992.

13. In translation *étrangère* can be a female foreigner or traveller: Flora Tristan had been both.

14. For further discussion of petitions for divorce see Francis Ronsin, *Les Divorciaires: Affrontements politiques et conceptions du mariage dans la France du XIXe siècle*, Paris, Aubier, 1992; and Roderick Phillips, *Putting Asunder: A History of Divorce in Western Society*, Cambridge University Press, 1988. Divorce was finally legalized in 1884, although the terms were not as generous as the Revolutionary version between 1792 and 1803.

15. *Necessité de faire un bon accueil aux femmes étrangères*, par Madame Flora Tristan, Paris, chez Delaunay, Palais Royal, 1835. See also Flora Tristan, *Necessité de faire un bon accueil aux femmes étrangères*, édition présentée et commentée par Denys Cuche, Paris, L'Harmattan, 1988.

16. On no account must the confidentiality of the name of the person be betrayed (Flora Tristan).

17. This clause will be one of the most important sections of the oath which each member must take before admittance (Flora Tristan).

18. See Article relating to Secret Committee in the Statutes (Flora Tristan).

19. By belief, I do not mean one single and same religion, but the same and single thought, that of doing good; Muslim and Jew are equally appreciative of virtue just as are Christians (Flora Tristan).

20. I think I must explain that I attribute a much wider meaning to the word 'love' than has hitherto been the case: I mean love of humanity, love of good, love of virtue (Flora Tristan).

21. Words of the Bible (Flora Tristan).

22. *Pétition pour le rétablissement du divorce à Messieurs les Députés le 20 décembre 1837*, Paris, Imprimerie de Mme Huzard, 1838.

23. First elected Chamber under the Restoration Monarchy of 1815.

24. *Pétition pour l'abolition de la peine de mort à la Chambre des Députés le 20 décembre 1837*, Paris, Imprimerie de Mme Huzard, 1838. Tristan appended the following short letter to the Chamber with her petition:

To the Right Honourable Gentlemen, members of the Chamber of Deputies

Sirs

I am pleased to present a petition for the abolition of the death penalty. I have had it printed so as to distribute it to all members. I thought it would be more convenient for you to read than a manuscript.
I remain your respectful and obedient servant.

Flora Tristan

100 bis Rue du Bac, Paris
19 December 1838

25. Mr James de Lawrence, the author of remarkable works, in his introduction to *The Empire of the Naïrs*, established that in England, out of three murders, one was committed by a man or woman to escape from marriage, another by a young girl who kills her child, or by a lover who kills his pregnant mistress; in order to avoid being forced into marrying her by the officer of the parish; and only a third of murders could be attributed to avarice, hatred, vengeance and unhappiness. Mr de Lawrence gathered a quantity of material from observations in Germany and France which could prove that this proportion of diverse causes of murder was about the same in every country of Europe where divorce was not permitted. Mr de Lawrence pointed out that he was not the first to reveal the crimes which ensue as a result of the undesirability of marriage. Before the French Revolution, a pamphlet appeared entitled: 'The Call for Divorce by an Honest Man', in which we read that during the year 1769 the Tourelle Court in Paris delivered a verdict on twenty-one cases between husbands and wives for crimes of poison, assassination, and so on. Some time ago, the Marquis of Herbonville in the Upper House, spoke thus: 'Crimes of husbands against their wives and wives against their husbands are so numerous that the poison seems to be an ingredient of the nuptial banquet, and the dagger an ornament of the marriage bed' (Flora Tristan).
26. Published in Jules Puech, *La Vie et l'oeuvre de Flora Tristan 1803–1844*, Paris, Marcel Rivière, 1925, p. 70.
27. Unpublished letter, Fonds Puech, Castres.
28. Unpublished letter, Fonds Puech, Castres.

La femme libre

Le père Enfantin

Flora Tristan arrested by the police and taunted by passers-by

3. Jeanne Deroin, Pauline Roland and 1848

Jeanne Deroin and Pauline Roland were deeply involved in two fundamental developments for French feminism: the Saint-Simonian movement and political and revolutionary politics. Along with other women who had been active in the early phase of Saint-Simonianism, they strove to take a role in the major events of the 1848 revolution in order to ensure that women's demands would be central to the republican and socialist programme. They believed with a religious intensity in a democratic social republic wherein women's political, economic and civil rights would at last be recognized. The texts included in this chapter make the intellectual and rhetorical case for such equality.

CONTEXTUAL INTRODUCTION TO JEANNE DEROIN (1805–1894) AND PAULINE ROLAND (1805–1852)

Biography[1]

Jeanne Deroin was born on 31 December 1805 in Paris and died in London on 2 April 1894. From a modest background and with no formal schooling, she became politicized in the early 1830s when she took part in organizing a collective venture by women to publish a newspaper, which went through several changes of title – including *La femme libre* and *Apostolat des femmes* – before becoming the *Tribune des femmes*.[2] Through meeting Pierre Leroux[3] and Auguste Blanqui[4] she became familiar with the Saint-Simonian religion, and from the writings of Fourier[5] and Cabet[6] she learned about new socialist doctrines. In 1832 she married a fellow socialist, Desroches, a bursar at an old people's home by whom she had three children. A laundress by trade, in the 1840s she succeeded in qualifying as a primary school teacher, obtaining a teachers' certificate though with some difficulty, as she was barely literate at the time. She subsequently set up a school for children from poor families.

Jeanne Deroin is associated with two important developments for French feminism. Firstly, she challenged the ideological limitations of the Saint-Simonian movement. Jeanne Deroin was not part of the Saint-Simonian hierarchy of men and women who dominated the movement. Rather she questioned the authoritarian basis of much of the new doctrine. Secondly, she strove to participate in the major events of the 1848 revolution in order to ensure that women's demands were included in the republican and socialist programme. In both areas she demonstrated an enthusiastic faith in women's participation in a future egalitarian society. Her hopes for a New Order based on social and gender equality were, needless to say, not realized. One of many martyrs to her convictions in this period of repression, she paid the price of exile for her public and private acts of rebellion.

Pauline Roland was born in 1805 in Falaise, a small town in Normandy.[7] Her father, a postmaster, died in 1806, a year after his daughter's birth. Pauline and her elder sister, Irma, were brought up by their widowed mother, who carried on her husband's business after his death. She was ambitious for her daughters, hoping that they would find professional employment, and had them educated by private tutors. As an impressionable girl, already chafing at the restrictions of Norman provincial life, Pauline Roland fell in love with her tutor, Desprez, a Saint-Simonian enthusiast. It was he who was responsible for converting her to the new religion's doctrines of a socially and sexually liberating future for women. Roland's letters from this period, especially to Agalae Saint-Hilaire, a Saint-Simonian 'Mother' charged with recruiting new members, convey her emotional involvement, both with the movement's ideals and its disciples.

Pauline Roland's relationship with Desprez was short-lived. Obliged to earn her own living and anxious for financial independence, she set out for Paris to join the main Saint-Simonian group, through which she hoped to find emotional support and the chance to work. This she was able to do, if precariously, through journalism and teaching. In Paris she put into practice the movement's doctrines on an individual's rights to sexual fulfilment, by entering openly (and to the scandalized disapproval of her supposedly liberated Saint-Simonian fellow disciples) into a series of sexual relationships. At the age of 30 she had a brief affair with a journalist and fellow Saint-Simonian, Adolphe Guéroult, by whom she had her first child, Jean, born in 1835. No sooner had she conceived, than she fell in love with another Saint-Simonian, Jean Aicard, by whom she was to have three further children: Marie, who died in infancy in 1839; Moise, born in 1839; and Irma, born in 1844.

Both Enfantin and Agalae de Saint-Hilaire profoundly disapproved of her decision to have children outside marriage, and accordingly withdrew their protection and friendship. Nevertheless, Roland asserted her rights as mother to take on the sole care and maintenance of her children. In order to support them, she turned to writing, did research for a new encyclopaedia, submitted articles to *La Revue indépendante* and produced educational material for schools. She also gave private tuition.

Roland's relationship with Aicard foundered over financial pressures as well as the latter's involvement with another woman. Roland focused her affection on her children, arguing that she alone had rights over and obligations towards them and that their father had none. Without independent financial resources and in a social climate where single mothers were stigmatized, it can be said that Pauline Roland displayed courage if not wisdom in her ethical choices.

For the remainder of her life, she maintained a precarious existence, earning her living by teaching and journalism, writing for newspapers of the fringe political movements of the 1840s. For a short period in the 1840s, she helped run a school and a newspaper for Pierre Leroux, a former Saint-Simonian who had founded a utopian community at Boussac. With the outbreak of revolution in 1848, Roland, like Leroux, returned to Paris to take part in the events there. The toast which she proposed at a socialist banquet in December 1848 gives a flavour of the messianic social hopes which she cherished for this soon to fail revolution:

> Let's drink to public education, equal for boys and girls! Through socialism, the new religion, we must solemnly establish the foundation of marriage, the basis of the family. Perfect equality is the very essence of love and marriage. Public education is necessary to establish this equality. With the same public education for children of both sexes, oppression of woman by man is impossible. With the same public education, infidelity and intrigue will disappear from the world, because for a man every woman becomes a sister, a single one can be both a wife and a lover. With the same public education, inequalities will disappear between husband and wife, inequality whose reason for existence is the inferiority of physical, moral and intellectual education which women receive. Let us drink to equal public education for girls and boys which should bring to families the realization of that sacred motto, Liberty, Fraternity, Equality.[8]

Background to Political Developments of the Second Republic, 1848–1852

Though short-lived, the Second Republic and its politics can be divided into four phases. The first, from February 1848 to June 1848, comprised the most optimistic phase, marked by attempts by the first provisional government at social reform and granting freedom of political expression. The second period, from June 1848 to December 1848, marked the shift in power to the conservative republicans, who sharply reduced political freedoms. The third period, from December 1848 to December 1851, saw the newly elected Bonapartist President, Louis Napoléon, gradually erode parliamentary power as he prepared to take over the state by a *coup d'état*. Finally, from December 1851 to December 1852, Louis Napoléon consolidated his power, eliminating his political enemies, and the Second Empire was born, the consequences of which are illustrated by the texts in Chapter 4.

February 1848 to June 1848

Although the nascent republican socialist and feminist opposition groups of the early days of the July Monarchy had lain dormant in the decades preceding the 1848 uprising, they rapidly re-emerged in the euphoria of February of that year. In the first four days of the insurrection, it was mainly student groups which led the disturbances. Subsequently, republican leaders intervened after the demonstrators had succeeded in winning over the National Guard and toppling the Orléans monarchy. The provisional government of the Republic, proclaimed from the Hôtel de Ville, included Jacobins and socialists, but was predominantly composed of moderate republicans. As a concession to the Left, this new government created national workshops in an effort to alleviate unemployment and set up a commission to study the conditions of the working class. This *Commission de Luxembourg*, chaired by Louis Blanc, had no powers, however, to implement changes.

Immediately following the February revolution of 1848, political clubs sprang into existence, and radical newspapers were permitted to appear, reflecting the hopes that many on the Left cherished for a new era of social justice. One notes in the writings of the revolutionaries a messianic belief in the dawn of a new era. It was then that Jeanne Deroin, anxious to contribute to political debate and to assert women's right to associate freely, founded the *Club de l'émancipation des femmes* (Club for the Emancipation of Women) with Désirée Gay, Adèle Esquiros and Eugénie Niboyet. Through the Club, Deroin campaigned for women's right to vote during the election campaign of March and April. It held its first formal meeting on 11 May 1848, adopting the new name of *La Société de la voix des femmes* (Society for Women's Voice) with its own journal, *La Voix des femmes* (The Voice of Women), founded by Eugénie Niboyet. Jeanne Deroin wrote articles for this paper until it disappeared on 18 June 1848. From 18 June to 5 August 1848 another paper, *La Politique des femmes* (Women's Politics), appeared weekly, to be followed by *L'Opinion des femmes* (Women's Opinion) edited by Jeanne Deroin, a monthly publication which ran from 28 January to 10 August 1849.[9] Through the columns of her papers and in political meetings Deroin argued for socialist and feminist ideas, exhorting fellow militants, including Proudhon, whether they were conservative, republican or socialist republican, to listen to feminist demands. In April 1849 Deroin stood as the first woman candidate in the legislative elections, though her candidacy was declared unconstitutional.

By April, the tenuous alliance between Jacobins, women and workers had begun to dissolve. In elections held in April 1848 for the constituent assembly, manhood suffrage had been declared to be 'universal suffrage', effectively excluding women.[10] The election result proved to be a triumph for moderate republicans who won 500 out of 900 seats. The monarchists (known as the Legitimists and Orleanists) who had renamed themselves the Party of Order, won 300. The Jacobins, however, won only 100 seats.

June to December 1848

The outcome of the April 1848 election was a blow for the Left, composed of revolutionaries like Blanqui, who considered that the restless Parisian crowd had a custodial role to safeguard the course of the revolution: the socialists who wished to introduce further economic and social reforms, such as the right to work and free state education, and socialist feminists who wished to include all women in the right to work, education and the vote. After the elections, a failed attempt by the left-wing radicals to take control of the revolution, by intruding into the Assembly on 16 May and violent demonstrations in June, resulted in the closure of political clubs. Indeed from June 1848 onwards, the moderate republicans and the Party of Order considered the alliance of Jacobins, workers' leaders and women as dangerous and subversive.[11] Police surveillance of political activists increased. A decree of 28 July 1848 abolished the autonomy of clubs, forbade secret societies and required prior authorization for political meetings. By August 1848, freedom of the press was once again restricted.

Meanwhile, the peasants and the middle classes had rallied to the conservatives after the attempt by the moderate republicans to impose tax increases. As time went on, the moderate republicans grew weaker in power, although it can be argued that republican ideology continued to develop because the Jacobins decided to collaborate with the socialists.[12] There were two major left-wing movements: the Mountain and the Democratic Socialists or Democ-Socs.[13] However, although the feminists active in this camp were convinced socialists, the reverse was not true. Within the democratic socialist and republican camp, nowhere were the divisions more apparent than on the subject of women's rights. Out of all the deputies in the Assembly in 1848, there were only four socialists: Pierre Leroux, who had employed Pauline Roland in his community project in Boussac; Victor Considérant, who had championed Flora Tristan; Louis Blanc, who led the attempt to institute a social programme for the workers; and Joseph Proudhon, who actively campaigned *against* women's emancipation and had argued *against* their presence in politics since the 1840s.[14] Of these four only Considérant and Leroux favoured women's political enfranchisement.

December 1848 to December 1851

In 1848, the Constituent Assembly decided to institute Presidential elections by direct suffrage with a non-renewable mandate of four years. On 20 December 1848 the successful Presidential candidate, Louis Napoléon Bonaparte, won 75 per cent of the votes cast, largely from conservatives and the peasantry. From this point, Bonaparte gradually reduced the power of the legislative assembly and further divided opposition political groups until he was able to seize power for himself. The Left lost a number of leaders, arrested after civil disturbances, who chose exile as a better alternative to imprisonment. In spite of political repression, however, to the conservatives' dismay, in the legislative elections of May 1849, the Jacobins won 180 seats. In June 1849 there were further disruptions by the Parisian crowds over France's intervention in an Italian uprising. As in previous cases, leaders of the protest movements fled abroad to avoid arrest. Throughout 1849, although political action was becoming more dangerous, the defence of the Republic became the chief preoccupation of the increasingly splintered groups of socialists, feminists and Jacobins.

By June 1850, the work of political repression was nearly complete. The conservatives in the Legislative Assembly reintroduced residential voting qualifications, thereby disenfranchising the propertyless and the poor, extended bans on political clubs, further reduced the freedom of the press, banned the right to petition and reintroduced educational concessions for the Catholic Church with the *Loi Falloux*.[15] On the Left, meanwhile, the Jacobin republicans had become firmly anti-clerical; Jeanne Deroin and Pauline Roland, on the other hand, maintained their religious faith and maintained that the 1789 Revolution was a continuation of the work of Christ. This utopian religious sentiment strongly pervaded Roland's philosophy and increasingly clashed with the republicans' anti-clericalism.[16]

Though subject to increasing restrictions, small groups of socialists and feminists continued to debate in public and to develop ways of campaigning for the implementation of a social republic through workers' associations. Once the ban on political clubs was imposed, they turned to building up groupings of workers – fledgling trade unions, in fact – to defend their social and economic rights. For the feminists, the move to the formation of associations constituted another opportunity to combine republican, socialist and feminist beliefs into one active movement. Jeanne Deroin and Pauline Roland led the association movement to defend workers' rights against exploitation by employers and argued for the right of all classes to education. On 6 February 1849, the Association of Socialist Primary School Teachers was launched at a meeting at Perot's home.[17] Jeanne Deroin, Gustave Lefrançais, Perot and Pauline Roland were among the founding members. Disillusioned by the limitations of the provisional government's social programme and its failure to alleviate widespread hardship and poverty, they encouraged self-help associations and sought to overcome the fundamental weaknesses of divided and poorly funded organizations. With the latter end in view, Deroin founded a union of 83 associations, reminiscent of Flora Tristan's Workers' Union.[18]

The aim of creating unity among the organizations represented was furthered when, on 5 October 1849, delegates of 104 associations unanimously adopted a proposal to form a Union of Workers' Associations, sometimes referred to as the Union of Fraternal Associations. Pauline Roland served on its central commission as a representative from the teachers' union. Five committees were set up for production, consumption, finances, education and law with a credit voucher system for transactions for members in order to avoid the need for money. While the Union met with approval from other socialists, such as Auguste Blanqui, it was viewed with flattering suspicion by the police. Its career came to an abrupt end when, on 29 May 1850, 80 police officers raided the Union's offices in Rue Michel le Comte. Jeanne Deroin was among those arrested and charged.[19] It was at this time that Deroin wrote to the National Assembly (which by then had voted to close the women's clubs) protesting about its proposal to restrict for men and abolish altogether for women, the right to present petitions of a political nature.

Roland and Deroin continued to be faithful to the ideal of an egalitarian republic, where universal rights would be assured for all and women would claim their legitimate place. For them the measure of the extent of socialism and republicanism was the acceptance of women as equal citizens in every sense. They believed that the revolutionary events of 1848 were an historic moment for women. However, their support for the Republic was not uncritical. They attacked the limitations of a republicanism which excluded women from civic participation. Jeanne Deroin was not as deeply religious as Pauline Roland, but she was equally attentive to the question of a new moral order as well as to the idea of women's suffrage as an inalienable right. Both demonstrated their determination to advance the cause of women by declaring their intention to stand as parliamentary candidates. They saw their candidatures as a challenge to the state to recognize that women were excluded from the newly won, 'universal' suffrage and to the republicans who supported this exclusion of women. Deroin's and Roland's electoral campaign sparked off a fresh debate among the Left about the role of women in society. Joseph Proudhon condemned their actions, but he was not alone. Emile de Girardin also expressed antagonism to the notion of the right of women to work, to vote or to take part in politics and was challenged by Pauline Roland.[20] These socialists associated the role of women with the conservative view of marriage enshrined in the *Code Napoléon*. Given that it was Proudhon's version of socialism which became most popular within workers' protest politics in the France of the Second Empire, his continued influence constituted a severe blow for women's emancipation.

Only recently has the extent and nature of women's participation in the politics of the Second Republic been widely recognized. Labour historians have not tended to analyse the discrepancy between the weakness of the organized socialist republican movement contrasted with the sophistication of feminists' ideas of republicanism and socialism. In retrospect, one can see that feminist demands were successfully sidelined by the dominant socialists, led by Proudhon and Marx. This exclusion from socialist and labour history and theory ran parallel to the overt state repression which this generation of feminists experienced.[21]

JEANNE DEROIN'S ELECTION CAMPAIGNS OF 1848 AND 1849: INTRODUCTION TO TEXTS

Text 1   Election campaign petition
Text 2   Election campaign poster
Text 3   Election campaign brochure

The texts which follow include a petition from March 1848, an election poster pasted up in the Seine *département* in April 1849, a declaration of principles of the 'Democ-Socs' and a campaign report during the election campaign for the Legislative Assembly of the new Republic, all of which demand equal political rights for both men and women. The Constituent Assembly of the previous April had voted by a majority of 899 to 1 not to grant the suffrage to women (on a motion proposed by Victor Considérant). The Assembly also voted against the restoration of divorce.[22] The principle of equality of education for boys and girls was lost with the *Loi Falloux* in 1850. With many politicians opposed to the cause of political and civil rights for women – out of the 900 seats for the Constituent Assembly, there were fewer than 60 socialist republicans and fewer than 300 republicans, with the rest being monarchists – the agenda for reform collapsed.

However, in April 1849, Jeanne Deroin, still cherishing hopes of radical change, embarked on the more daring enterprise of asking the newly formed election committees to give her an official status as a candidate. By this tactic she hoped to bring the debate on gender equality into the open. Although she found very little support for her cause, the fact that Deroin had access for a short time to the press meant that she could make her views public. So her five-page brochure produced in 1849, which called for the formation of an association to support women's franchise in a class and gender alliance, represented her success in articulating the issue of women's suffrage and emancipation. This work contained a mixture of idealism, in its desire to see a complete application of republican principles, and practicality, in its efforts to organize an electoral campaign. In her election campaign report, Jeanne Deroin described her confrontation with male socialists in April 1849, when she attempted to secure her eligibility to stand as a candidate. She was required to appear before various male gatherings to persuade them to adopt her nomination as an official candidate. Remembering that for a woman to appear on a public platform at all would certainly have been contested as scandalous by many of her male colleagues, Deroin's courage in standing up to persistent heckling is to be admired.

At first glance it might appear that Jeanne Deroin was more concerned with the principle of equal eligibility than the general question of women's suffrage. However, her tactical, political instincts were sound. Had women been accepted as candidates for the first Legislative Assembly elections, they would have secured the inclusion of women's suffrage from the very inception of the new regime, ensuring that the question of women's suffrage became a priority with republican and socialist democratic allies alike. Her account illustrated the mechanisms by which women were excluded from the democratic process. They were not taken seriously by men who held political power or potential power; even the non-propertied men had power over their women. So although the Republic was potentially egalitarian, it nonetheless failed to live up to its promise. At the core of this failure was the refusal of the Left to confront the issue of gender equality. Jeanne Deroin's experience is significant because it focuses on the issue of the invisibility and exclusion of women from either the idea or the process of democracy in mid-19th century France. The potential alliance between feminists and socialist republicans failed to actualize the principles of the fragile Second Republic in 1849, thereby excluding women from the public sphere for several generations. This denial by republicans of women's inclusion in the concept of democracy at the moment of enfranchisement of all men was to have a long-lasting effect on the position of women on the Left in France. The contradiction which socialist feminists faced was that within republican–socialist discourse of equality of citizenship there existed an unspoken inequality and exclusion of the female citizen.[23]

TEXT 1   ELECTION CAMPAIGN PETITION

Petition sent to the government in March 1848 and to the French People.[24]

> If, when you were called, you were a slave, do not let that bother you; but if you should have the chance of being free seize the opportunity (St Paul).[25]

Once upon a time, a council met to decide the following important question namely: whether women had souls.[26] The reply in the affirmative by a majority of three votes meant that women were at this point declared by the holy council to be the equal companions to men. This encouraging example taken from history compels me to ask you please to state your opinion on another question the importance of which you cannot deny. Should women enjoy social and political rights, and should they be recognized as men's equal, in every function which does not by its nature need the exclusive prerogative of strength? I will not question your honest decision and I will not blame you for having hesitated before deciding. For if women were fully aware of the providential event which must change the face of the earth (the revolution) they would start to prove to the world that they wish, more than ever, to attach themselves to the movement of great and sacred causes (revolutionary socialism). Before their rights could be proclaimed you insisted that women should understand our great revolution, and that they should be convinced in advance that God would not allow such a miracle to be achieved permanently for only half of the human race. Very well, like those holy women who believed in the infinite power of Christ before seeing any proof of it, here we are before your assemblies, representatives and people! We come, because we believe! If the motives of our faith could be a work of edification for women and the weak of the earth, may we express them as follows:-

You say that our glorious revolution was made for everyone, well, as we are half of the human total, how could we not believe?

You say that the sacred motto liberty, equality, fraternity, will be applied in all its aspects? Well, as our share should be proportionate to our needs, to our abilities, how could we not believe?

You say that this sublime motto is one and indivisible; well, recognizing this like you, and recognizing furthermore that each of its terms is also indivisible, there cannot be two liberties, two equalities: that liberty, equality, fraternity of man are obviously those of woman – how could we not believe?

You say that royalty is called upon to transform the whole world and that the time has come for a new and sacred era of the sovereignty of the people as King; well, the populace is composed of two sexes as royalty is itself, so maximum sympathy should be gained for your noble wish. In order that it crosses every frontier, into every part of our country, beside the sovereign people as King, it is vital to proclaim the people as Queen or even better include both King and Queen in the sovereignty of the people. The people therefore being you and being us, how could we not believe?

You say that those forms of legal incompetence which existed under previous laws are no longer an obstacle to eligibility to vote; well, this declaration, which entails the right of eligibility, gives us the right to take part in the election, the right we all want, how could we not believe?

You say that only corporal punishment, exile, prison sentences or certified madness are legitimate reasons to deprive a citizen of civil rights; well, as far as we know, the women's qualification does not fit into any of these categories, and therefore, according to all these proofs, the same electoral right belongs to women, so how can we not believe?

See how our faith was to be tested by many trials, and how we ourselves have understood that the idea of universal justice will not be shown to be in vain!

And furthermore while women have not been lacking in any of these great ideas and have found recognition in their own eyes, at the same time they have been degraded by their social position, dependent, lacking dignity, deprived of educational resources and of varied and honourable work. They have been able, simultaneously, to show their true value and to predict and make certain their future role by demonstrating numerous and notable exceptions [to their traditional role]. In short, women, in spite of all the negative circumstances against them, have associated themselves with the glories and the misfortunes of France, with her heroes as well as her martyrs. Imagine what their potential would be when their chains have been broken!

By henceforth associating women with men in the immense human task, you will advance further the great work of creation, since these words: 'It is not good for man to be alone' will always resound painfully on this earth. Do not be misled; nothing can be achieved for the general good until man's beloved companion, brought to life by the divine breath, is created as a social being. Do not doubt it; by the solidarity of new and natural links which you will establish between man and his companion, will be established a marriage *par excellence*, a social marriage with a triple dimension – material, intellectual and moral – to face the tasks of the future. In fact it was especially about this marriage, the regenerating force of the world, that Christ must have said: '*What God has joined together let no man put asunder*'.

Paris 16 March 1848.

(Extract from a previous article in the Fourth issue of *L'Opinion des femmes*.)

TEXT 2   ELECTION CAMPAIGN POSTER

Jeanne Deroin: To the Electors of the Department of the Seine[27]

Citizens:

I come to present myself as a candidate for your votes because I am dedicated to establishing that great principle: civil and political equality for both sexes.

In the name of justice I appeal to the sovereign people against the denial of those principles, which are the basis for our society's future.

If, by exercising your right, you call upon a woman to take part in the work of the legislative assembly, you will establish our republican principles: liberty, equality fraternity, in their entirety, for all women as well as for all men.

A legislative assembly entirely composed of men is just as incompetent to pass laws to govern a society which includes men and women, as an assembly composed of the privileged would be to discuss the interests of workers, or an assembly of capitalists to uphold the honour of the country.

Jeanne Deroin
Director of the newspaper *L'Opinion des femmes*

TEXT 3   ELECTION CAMPAIGN BROCHURE

To the Fraternal Association of Socialist Democrats of both sexes for the Political and Social enfranchisement of women.[28]

Declaration of Principles

In the name of God and of the solidarity which links all the members of the great human family:

We affirm that women have the same right as men to liberty, equality and fraternity.

Liberty for a woman, as for a man, consists of the right to be able to develop, and freely and harmoniously to exercise all their physical, intellectual and moral faculties, with no limit other than respect for each person. All freedoms are interdependent; you cannot undermine one of them without affecting all the others.

Equality is for women as it is for men the right and the duty to take part in all social activities according to their faculties and abilities.

To split humanity into two unequal parts, to refuse women their rights to freedom and to equality is to undermine this principle and to sanction the right of the strongest and the most privileged.

Fraternity is the exercise of freedom and equality for all men and women: it is the respect of the rights of all members of the great human family, it is the devotion of all for each one and each one for all. To refuse women their rights to freedom and equality is to perpetuate antagonism; it is to scorn respect for others, human dignity and the principles of fraternity and solidarity which are the basis for universal harmony. Humanity consists of both men and women; the law drawn up by men alone cannot satisfy the needs of humanity.

The law of God, the rights of the people and women are treated with contempt; women, children, workers, all are oppressed and exploited by partial, oppressive and imprudent laws to the benefit of the mightiest and those privileged by birth and wealth. We affirm in the name of the sacred law of solidarity that no one has the right to be completely free and happy so long as there remains one solitary oppressed and suffering person.

We affirm that social reform cannot be carried out without the support of women, half of humanity. And in the same way that the political enfranchisement of the proletariat is the first step towards their physical, moral and intellectual enfranchisement, the political enfranchisement of women is the first step towards the complete emancipation of all the oppressed.

That is why we are calling upon all women and men who have feelings and intelligence, all those women and men who have the strength of their beliefs, the strength of their convictions and who never hesitate to implement them, so that they can come to our assistance in order to enter the true path of social reform, by opening the doors of the city to the last of the pariahs, women, without whom the work of our social redemption cannot be accomplished.[29]

Amendment to the Report of the Socialist Democrat Committee of Voters[30]

We have been reliably informed by several members of the Committee that the name of Madame George Sand[31] was put on forty lists and that her candidacy was taken into consideration. This fact establishes a precedent which should be published in the interests of the social cause and it is for this purpose that we have sent the following protest to the Committee:

To the Citizen members of the Socialist Democrat Committee.

Citizens:

The report of the Committee is incomplete and says nothing on a matter which must be made public: the acceptance of the candidacy of Madame George Sand. It represents the voice of your conscience; why do you stifle it?

Men who fight in the name of freedom and equality cannot wish to maintain a privilege which is at the source of all tyranny and all social inequality.

The silence of the Committee on this subject would give the enemies of socialism reason to suppose that social democrats, by initially opposing its implementation, reject the principle of civil and political equality of the two sexes. But this principle is at the basis of socialism. Without its application, no social reform can be complete and long-lasting, because it contains within it the absolute and complete eradication of all privilege and class prejudice.

That is why I am asking the Committee to declare solemnly that it accepts the principle, and that the exclusion of the name of a woman on the list is based on the same grounds as for the other candidates. If I cannot obtain this declaration, the duty to which eminently revolutionary and social task I have dedicated myself requires that I protest loudly at the silence of the Committee and the conclusions one could draw from it.

I must insist and remonstrate in the name of the principle I stand for that the decision of the Socialist Democratic Committee can be founded neither on sex privilege, nor on unconstitutionality nor on the difficulty of applying the principle.

I will therefore publish the following protest and I will support it with my deep convictions and ardent and unfailing perseverance.

In the name of God and of humanity, all sincere socialist democratic men and women proclaim the civil and political equality of both sexes and affirm that the decision of the Committee to exclude the name of a woman from the list of candidates from the legislative Assembly elections can only be founded on sexual privilege, since all our principles of freedom, of equality and fraternity, the basis of individual, family and social life, include in them the abolition of all prejudices, of all privileges, of all royal power, even that of the man in the family, since they accept no human domination founded on divine right, not even that of a man over a woman.

Neither can this exclusion be based on respect of the Constitution since the Constitution is founded on the principles of liberty, equality and fraternity. Therefore, it cannot be in contradiction with these principles. The Salic Law was annihilated along with the throne which depended on it.

Finally, this exclusion cannot be based on the plea that the idea is inopportune, since it is precisely during the elections that it is important to demand women's right to take part in the work of the legislature. This Assembly will be unrepresentative and inadequate if women are not represented, and its chief task, the revision of the Civil Code, will not be complete or permanent because, by themselves, men cannot impose laws on a society of men and women, which is founded on the right of the strongest, a blatant violation of our principles. It is never too early to enter the path of progress, and the admission of women to civil rights is the first step to take to achieve the reform which we are earnestly advocating.

Such a reform would be the most effective way to make everyone understand the need for co-operative associations.

No law for the future can be drawn up and confirmed without the participation of women, half of humanity. As the political emancipation of the proletariat is the first step towards the complete emancipation of all the oppressed, so is the drastic extinction of that most deep-seated of all privileges, the realization of our sacred principles: liberty, equality, fraternity, for all women as well as for all men.

PAULINE ROLAND'S CAMPAIGN FOR EDUCATION: INTRODUCTION TO TEXTS

Text 4   'To Primary School Teachers from the Association of Socialist Schoolmasters and Schoolmistresses'
Text 5   'Education Programme of the Fraternal Association of Socialist Schoolmasters and Schoolmistresses'
Text 6   'The Right to Work'

After the closure of women's clubs in July 1848 and their electoral campaign of May 1849, Pauline Roland and Jeanne Deroin continued to work on other collective ventures. Their paths had crossed in earlier journalistic activities; this time they worked together to unite women in various trades into associations and then to combine them into one umbrella organization. At the moment when political action had been closed off to women, these unions or associations were an effective substitute in practical politics, though this episode of women's activism has tended to be neglected in labour history.[32]

Pauline Roland and Jeanne Deroin wanted to ensure that sexual equality figured as a central plank of trade unionism. They saw education as the key to changing mentalities to ensure lasting change for women. They both had first-hand experience of teaching the working classes in voluntary schemes throughout the 1840s. In the spirit of self-help associations, they believed that teachers had a vital role to play in devising the fast developing education system, instead of waiting for the clergy or the wealthy to reinforce the existing system to maintain privilege. Although the need for primary school education in every commune had been recognized in principle by the Guizot Law of 1833, girls were excluded from the provision; education was neither to become free nor secular until the Jules Ferry Law of 1880. In 1849 the commune school was often staffed by religious orders which were not required to have teaching qualifications, unlike the state school teachers. Although the number of schools was increasing, buildings were inadequate, teachers' training and pay were poor and there was a huge discrepancy in the funding for children of primary school age who far outnumbered the children of the much better endowed secondary school sector.

Like many other teachers, Pauline Roland responded warmly to a call by a schoolmaster, Perot, in *Le Peuple*, 6 February 1849, calling for a meeting of teachers to campaign for better pay and against the threat of competition from religious schools. Pauline Roland succeeded in persuading like-minded colleagues to seize the opportunity of forming a socialist teachers' association as a means of returning to the values of February 1848, under attack by conservatives. She threw her enthusiasm and energy, and also her professional experience gained from running a progressive school in Pierre Leroux's socialist community in Boussac, into the association. At Boussac she had already implemented socialist educational theories, emphasizing class and gender equality and the importance of consulting the collective views of teachers.

The Association of Socialist Schoolmasters and Schoolmistresses which was formed following Perot's initiative did exhibit conflicts of interest among its members in relation to its role as a labour movement. The group's initial aims had been to defend pay levels and working conditions in their profession. Pauline Roland, however, directed and broadened its agenda, but in doing so limited the Association to a relatively small group of men and women committed to a more idealistic socialist programme, among them Jeanne Deroin, a young teacher Gustave Lefrançais who became Roland's close friend, former Saint-Simonians Doctors Guépin and Ferdinand, Pierre and Jules Leroux, one of Proudhon's associates Jules Viard, Alphonse Pecqueur, Pierre Dupont and his wife, and Perot.[33]

The *Association des instituteurs, institutrices et professeurs socialistes* (Association of Socialist Schoolmasters and Schoolmistresses) published two major documents on 30 September 1849. The first consisted of an appeal to all teachers to save the Republic. Rather than concentrate on material issues, Roland urged teachers to fight for the uneducated masses, dependent on teachers for enlightenment and leadership. In the past, teachers had been too hesitant to rally to the new regime but their social origins and enlightened views dictated where their loyalties should lie. Roland's idealistic appeal mentioned none of the practical benefits of the Association for members, such as its system of self-funding insurance schemes.[34] The Association's second document was an ideological treatise on education which glossed over members' differences in their interpretation of socialism. Arguments had abounded on the question of religion and atheism. From the content of both texts it is clear that Roland's version carried the day. In the name of revolutionary solidarity, staunch anti-clericals, like Lefrançais and Perot, allowed generalized religious statements to be included, in particular a profession of faith in similar vein to the Catholic credo. The programme itself included detailed pedagogical prescriptions on which the members did agree, centring on the interaction between the individual, the family and society. No longer would there be class inequality of education provision, with poor children having access only to primary school education. No longer would there be pressure on individuals to specialize too early. A fully integrated approach would replace distinct primary and secondary systems, giving pupils the opportunity to develop their full potential in a continuous process from the cradle to the age of 18. While the crèche was acknowledged to be useful for mothers, it had pedagogical and social benefits for all parents and its uniformity of application would abolish class differences. Education would thus provide a means of cementing society into harmonious unity instead of maintaining divisions and class conflict.

Overall, the texts by Pauline Roland included in this chapter deal with two major issues relating to her concept of a democratic and egalitarian society: education and work. The excerpt from the *Education Programme of the Fraternal Association of Socialist Schoolmasters and Schoolmistresses* outlines the education befitting a citizen of the new Republic, an education which was to begin in earliest infancy: not separating the child from its parents, but allowing children to develop in a genuinely social setting. While Roland's ideas seem to owe much to Rousseau's theories of organic child development, her notion of a humanist education for all, but one which did not neglect life skills: her view that children should freely develop their capacities and not be motivated by fear: the notion of parental involvement in the education process and the idea that one of the central functions of education is to overcome arbitrary social inequality and to value children for what they are capable of becoming rather than for the social class to which they belong, allow one to see why her memory is still honoured in France by the numerous schools named after her.

The second issue included here in Pauline Roland's text, a polemical reply to Emile de Girardin written from Saint Lazare Prison in 1851, defending women's right to work (men's right to work being a basic socialist premise), effectively demolishes the functionalist argument that women's destiny is purely reproductive. The debate on women's right to work had raged throughout the 1840s with the fiercest opposition coming from within the Left.[35] Roland asserted women's right to full economic participation in the community of work. Having worked while bringing up her children, Roland argued that paid employment was vital both as an economic right and as a means to develop a woman's full potential, which the duties of motherhood alone could not provide. Given the economic basis of the socialist analysis of class relations and the idea of 'the right to work' as fundamental to the proletariat, Roland's argument was hard to refute logically, though it was to be largely ignored by socialists for some two generations. Madeleine Pelletier's article, 'Women's Right to Work' (see pp. 156–62) is evidence that almost the same arguments needed to be deployed to male socialists some 50 years later.

TEXT 4   TO PRIMARY SCHOOL TEACHERS FROM THE ASSOCIATION OF SOCIALIST SCHOOLMASTERS AND SCHOOLMISTRESSES[36]

Citizens and brothers,

The causes of the February Revolution were simultaneously moral and material. The people finally rebelled against the monarchy in the name of morality, outrageously violated by Louis Philippe and his agents of corruption, who immediately took flight. As for the concrete power of this Revolution, it would be folly to deny it after two years which have just passed and during which there have been protests everywhere against an exploitative regime which has been in government for too long.

The workers' associations are heading towards the accomplishment of this second part of social transformation. In spite of the setbacks which the defenders of the old order have imposed, these associations will soon show, we hope, what intelligence and work united in fraternity can achieve. But besides this predominantly industrial reform, there is another no less important moral reform. This one can only be achieved through education, which alone will preserve the generations to come from selfishness, with which the monarchy has more or less poisoned everyone's heart, in order to govern us with greater security.

Some men and women primary school teachers, whose commitment is even stronger than their knowledge, thought that it was time to do something, and they formed an association to this intention. Their programme is simple and can be summed up in a few words: to give everyone without distinction an equal education by abolishing this division of state schools into primary schools and secondary schools: a fatal separation, which will maintain class distinctions which the Republic is trying to abolish; to give a moral education which would be the development of these three terms: Liberty, Equality, Fraternity. That is the aim. As for the means, they have their goodwill and the strength which gives them faith in the future of Humanity. So far as intelligence is concerned, although their own is insufficient for such a huge task, they are hoping, and they have no doubt about it, to find among their brothers, men who will support this.

Before beginning the mission it has set out for itself, the Association of Socialist Primary School Teachers felt it would be lacking in fraternity towards you if it did not inform you of its existence and its aims. It hopes to find numerous supporters and friendly support.

Until now primary school teachers have remained aloof from the Revolution. Whether through indifference or fear of being persecuted, and we are sure that it is more the latter motive, they have virtually aided the monarchist reaction.

Instead of uniting fraternally in solidarity, they have become isolated from one another, shutting themselves into the narrow confines of a misunderstood self-interest. So what has happened? The people who had counted on them to be its guides believed them to be indifferent to its cause, left them and abandoned them; the royalists then took advantage of this mistake to weaken their influence in the villages and insulted them in all kinds of ways. Only recently a former member of the provisional government tried to disgrace the commune primary teachers by writing to ask for their mass dismissal.[37] As for this latest insult, if at any rate it can be called one, on the part of such a person, it was promptly answered by one of our comrades: the matter is no longer of any concern to us. We thought that it was time to call a halt to this state of affairs, and, waking up from our apathy, to ask the People to hold the flag of socialism up ourselves which we should have been the first to raise. We thought that the time had come at last for teaching to become a true vocation, and the primary school teacher to become the priest of the new world with the task of replacing the now power-less Catholic priest in leading men to the way of truth. But as we can only achieve this aim of uniting under the banner of the social and democratic republic, the Association of Socialist Primary School Teachers is not only proposing to give a democratic education to children entrusted to their care, but also to establish a close solidarity among all those who would like to unite to bring victory to justice and equality.

Therefore we are addressing you, fully confident of your goodwill and your affection for the people whose children you are, with these words:

Brothers, we too have a revolution to achieve; we too have a stone to add to this great edifice whose foundations the people laid in February. Let us unite for such a great task and let us not fear the obstacles we must overcome. The ignorance of some, the wickedness of others will not succeed against us. Let us enlighten the hearts of the first (the People) and the second (the monarchist reaction) will soon be confused. Government persecution, poverty, depriva-tion await us perhaps, what does it matter? A new era is open to us, and the People are waiting for us to lead so that they may follow us; let us act in such a way that it will not be able to accuse us one day of cowardly treachery. Help us then brothers, help us, and we will more easily conquer this world of ignorance, selfishness and corruption which is set against us. It is our isola-tion alone which gives it strength; if we fight against it together it will not withstand us, and we shall soon enter the temple of Fraternity.

Let us hope you can answer our call.

Greetings to everyone in the present and confidence for the future

On behalf of the Association:

G. Lefrançais; Pauline Roland; Perot
Paris, 30 September 1849

N.B. Membership can be sent (franco)[38] to the provisional headquarters of the Association in Paris, 21 Rue de Bréda at the home of citizen Perot, primary school teacher.

TEXT 5   EDUCATION PROGRAMME OF THE FRATERNAL ASSOCIATION OF SOCIALIST SCHOOLMASTERS AND SCHOOLMISTRESSES[39]

Declaration of principles

In the presence of God and of Humanity, we democratic socialists are associating together with the aim of making available the benefits of a Republican education to all children and all adults, male and female, who would benefit from this training. Before uniting together for the work of education and settling the bases for it, we feel the need to agree completely on the principles in whose name we intend to act. As a consequence, we have jointly written the following profession of faith:

We believe with all our mind, with all our heart, with all our strength, in God, the source of all life.

We believe in the Unity of the human race, in Solidarity, in Fraternity among all men.

We believe that Humanity contains within it as equal members all individuals who make up the human family.

We believe in the perfect equality of man and woman, in perfect equality among all human beings.

We believe in the perfectibility of man and humanity, in their constant and infinite progress.

We believe that there is no salvation for humanity other than in a voluntary association which is religious, perfectly free, fraternal and egalitarian among all men.

We believe that all nations are sisters and should consider themselves as different members of the same family.

We believe in the sovereignty of the people; the Republic is in our eyes the only form of legitimate government. It must fully realize LIBERTY, EQUALITY, FRATERNITY.

We believe in the sanctity and eternity of the everlasting family, a special organization which must survive in a harmonious way within the great human family to which it is joined.

We believe that there should no longer be any wealthy or poor, neither privileged nor disinherited, neither superiors nor inferiors, in fact no other hierarchy than the one necessary for the task of the different functions which we recognize as entirely equal among themselves.

We believe that since all men are equal and brothers, they all have an equal and inalienable right to the development of their physical, moral and intellectual abilities.

We believe that each one has a duty to everyone and everyone has a duty to each person.

We believe that each person has the right to work, that each one has the duty to work within the limits of their strength and ability.

Finally, we believe that the Republican motto LIBERTY, EQUALITY, FRATERNITY contains the word and the rule of life, and we will promise never to do anything, say anything, proclaim anything detrimental to achieving this sacred motto: to have it understood, loved and practised by everyone and we swear to base all our teaching as well as all our life on it.

Programme

Chapter 1 – preamble

Education has always been the subject of contemplation to religious souls and whether it be in antiquity or in modern times, the greatest thinkers, no matter what doctrine they adhered to, have been concerned with this grave matter.

Since Plato and Saint Augustine to Rousseau and his sons the Montagnards of 1793, it is possible that no doctor, no philosopher, no statesman worthy of this name exists who has not left the world either a workable plan, or a utopia, or some practical essay on education. But has not everything already been explored relative to this important question? We do not believe this is so. Is current practice good or even adequate? We do not think so either.

When the veil which separates us from that eternal truth, towards which we gravitate unceasingly, is removed, when a new dogma revealed to the world instils itself into Humanity, everything changes, everything must be redone because every dogma in itself contains a new religion, every religion has a moral, every moral a civilization. In fact a new civilization demands, imposes a whole system of education perfectly in tune with this civilization for those generations which will at the same time contribute to its development and be controlled by it. This system which changes and renews itself with every great evolution of Humanity does not overthrow the old system any more than the new religion overthrows the one it has just replaced; it develops it, stretches it and if it seems to kill it in the end, it is only to transform it. To be good and solid, it must take and search for part of its elements; true progress is attained at this cost.

A new doctrine, the development of a doctrine brought by Jesus eighteen centuries ago, was revealed to the world by the French Revolution. This doctrine basically contained in the Republican motto: Liberty, Equality, Fraternity, is therefore embodied in the French People to such an extent that it would be impossible to wrench it from its heart without taking its life away. From this renovating doctrine is bound to spring a new religion and civilization, and it is the duty of every primary school teacher to examine what the educational principles are that must be given to a human being in the new career which is opening up before him.

In the societies of antiquity founded on inequality of birth and on the theocratic principle, education only provided for a restricted number of castes, its only aim was to train kings and priests under whom the rest of humanity were to act like a lowly kind. In the Greek and Roman Republics, education, accessible only to citizens, was mostly warlike. It developed physical strength and even intelligence but as for less intimate matters, it took no account of the emotional faculties of the human being. Besides, this education, although it has been extended to a greater number of individuals than it had been in Antiquity, was divided between and different for the aristocracy and for the plebeians; it excluded the mass of slaves, who only received the benefits of education if it would make them more suitable for service to their masters.

Under the influence of Christianity, education, starting from the premise of humanity's dualism between mind and matter and condemning the latter, gave itself the task of ruining the body for the benefit of the mind. As a reaction to the exaggerations of pagan life, this was no doubt very impressive but it was not the truth and could not form the basis for the people's education. One had to wait for Christianity to become a political force for it to generate a whole civilization before founding the University of the Middle Ages. And if starting from the fundamental principle of the fraternity of human beings, education provided by Christianity could theoretically be extended to everyone without distinction of caste, it is obvious that since work was carefully kept at a distance, this education was the lot of a very small number.

Today, work is as sacred as art, as science, there cannot be the *liberal professions* on one hand and servile professions on the other. Today, all men, destined to live at the same time, in Liberty, Equality and Fraternity, on the earth which belongs to them, which they have a duty to embellish, to improve, to make more and more agreeable for their use: everyone has the right to receive an education which entitles them to the respect of their abilities and the duty to seek to implement in its highest and healthiest state their education which will enable them to fulfil the vocation to which each one among them is called.

In the new era into which we are beginning to enter, education will not have to consider anything other than the value of individuals, their intrinsic value, their own abilities. To have each one achieve harmoniously within society the highest stage of development of which they are capable, from a physical, a moral and an intellectual perspective, through which human life expresses itself: to form people, and all people, capable of living in accordance with the Republican motto: that is the aim that education should be putting forward for itself. But to get to that stage, society must be constituted in a sane manner.

Since Catholicism, the great religion of the past, has died, since its leaders have ceased being inspired by democratic principles, by principles of progress which were its strength for so long, anarchy rules in education, which is completely deprived of leadership. In the different systems produced since then, and we do not exempt those which have started up in the nineteenth century, we find at every step all the opposing antagonisms which our atheistic society has created.

'Education should be provided by the family only.' says one, 'education belongs solely to the state' says another. One answer will do for both so we reply: Yes, the family's rights in the child are inalienable, its duties towards it are immense, inescapable and no one can free themselves from that; but if one is a member of that family, one is also a person, and as such, one has rights and duties towards society, which in its turn has rights and duties towards the individual. Education, therefore, must be given simultaneously within the family and in state schools with the individual, the family and society in mind.

But the best schools are not necessarily colleges or boarding schools. Institutionalizing schools, destructive of family life, should be completely rejected, in the same way as an exclusive system of private tuition. The Republic gives the same education to all children who are born within it because only a common education can form real citizens. However, after spending eight to twelve hours in school per day in the state schools, children should return to their families who have been educated morally by the progress of the Republic's laws and moral teachings, furnished with a generous hand to adults as well as to children, and who will help, instead of contradicting as is the case today, the action of communal and public education provided by society.

The education of the future will comprise: the development of the body in general and of each of the senses in particular, instruction contained in the word gymnastics which should train one for several industrial professions: an instruction of the heart, including moral development and artistic development: finally intellectual training, taking in the whole domain of human science, by a teaching accessible to all, within the limits of their abilities and which constitutes Republican education. In the present system, two types of education exist: one tends to turn people into encyclopaedias, the other claims to specialize the individual for a trade.

The first of these systems will never be anything but a utopia, because from the outset, all branches of industry, art and science should be made available to all. I am far from claiming that every person can study everything but we should not conduct education policies in such a way that we manufacture a mathematician, a cook, an engineer or a pianist, in fact an instrument instead of a person. Education must be directed in such a way as to develop in each child a certain universality which expresses its humanity. At the same time education must make individuals capable of specializing in one or several artistic or scientific professions. Now that we have tried to outline what the aim and the procedure for education should be, we will say, with reservations for the teaching of adults, that education, properly speaking, should in our opinion take a person in hand from birth onwards to the age of eighteen, the date of legal emancipation and the true coming of age in a healthy society.

This period of eighteen years, at the end of which education gives to society a citizen, a state servant, an adult in place of the child it had been entrusted with, divides naturally into six periods of three years each from the crèche to vocational schools inclusive. But before developing this new programme of teaching and showing its practice, let us say a few words about the present university system.

The training organized through the university system is based on liberal individualism and not on social equality. It perpetuates the division of society into two classes, the proletariat and the bourgeoisie, by its teaching: for the children of the poor, a primary school system: for the children of the bourgeoisie, a secondary school system. This division of its programme forces the education authorities to parcel out the study of the different branches of knowledge in such a way that they become practically unintelligible for the pupil obliged, after having lost precious time in primary schools, to recommence alone and on another level. Even if his mind is strong enough to undertake such work, his education will be faulty and incomplete. Another consequence, no less disastrous, of this division of studies is the production of a crowd of semi-literates who, finding themselves pushed through a lack of enlightened guidance towards professions which are unsuitable for them, become incapable of doing anything whatsoever, and give a semblance of justification to the protagonists of obscurantism.

Socialist education, however, being based on Equality, will direct the individual's education according to their abilities without taking into account their family position, so that when the education system hands over the child to society, the child will not be an expert in such and such a specialism, but as a person whose mind will have received all the development of which it is capable and who will be competent to fulfil adequately the work towards which their abilities will have directed them.

Chapter 2   First period comprising birth to 3 years of age

The crèche   Poor and underprivileged, relying on its own resources, it is not yet possible for socialism to set up schools at all levels; it is even difficult at present to found schools for adults and children, combined with professional training, as we propose to do. Nonetheless, we still believe we should give the complete and detailed plan for republican democratic and socialist education as we understand it. We are submitting for the scrutiny and appreciation of all our brother socialists this programme which is the fruit of conscientious thought and discussion. We shall begin, therefore, with an explanation of the CRÈCHE.

A serious question not only of education but more importantly of public morals arises with this one word: crèche. Those calling themselves *defenders of the family* are combating the creation of this first stage of communal education and have invented pure sophisms simply to prevent, if not to destroy, the first attempts of existing crèches today. At best they admit that the help given to mothers, which is the only way the crèche is envisaged at present, is only beneficial to the poor, and prejudice against it is so strong that as soon as a family is wealthy enough to pay for a distant and unknown wet nurse, the child is dispatched and deprived for one or several years of its mother's milk and affection.

In wealthy families, it is rarely otherwise: the monstrous selfishness of women from the so-called superior classes, their incurable laziness, has them discharge the sacred duty which providence has imposed on them on a stranger, whom they treat as a servant. Aristocratic motherhood, by those who take wet nurses in residence, has no other result than to rear the child in inequality and isolation without reinforcing family ties in any way. In this case as in the other, the nursery is always relegated away from the parents. This demeaning and mercenary hiring of wet nurses is an integral part of domestic service, the scourge of our social order, affecting rich and poor children alike.

In the present state of things, we maintain that if the crèche became compulsory for all, within the limits which we have assigned to public education, the child would be restored to its mother and, by the same token, instead of being weakened, precious family ties would be strengthened. But to give all children back to their mother's breast, even during the time the child is at the breast, women must not be completely absorbed as nurses. Motherhood is a duty of woman, a sacred duty, a religious one even; but at no time should it be considered her only duty.

To these general considerations, particular considerations of education should be added, which cannot be partitioned off in diverse categories distinct and different from one another. From one end to another of human life, everything must be in harmony and there are no grounds, as the Republicans wanted to do in '93, for separation of the early years of childhood from the general plan for education in order to contain it entirely within the family, or to take the child away from the family with the aim of overdoing the development of the citizen.

In socialist education, the crèche represents the first of the great periods which properly speaking divide education; it takes the child from the moment of birth to the end of the third year.

The aim of education is to train men (and when we say men we mean human beings without distinction of sex), members of one family, free citizens, as equals and as brothers. It is important that as soon as it has taken its first steps, the child can develop its own personality, that it should receive the attention of its family, that it should be surrounded by its affection: but it is important also that society should exercise over the child its inalienable rights and fulfil all its duties towards it. The division of time which during the course of a human life should be shared out so that individual liberty can be preserved, family life respected, and finally so that society loses none of its rights, would ideally be for the child to spend eight out of every twenty-four hours at the crèche. The mother could follow it there, become a paid carer and stay there all the time with it. As much as possible, the carers should be nursing mothers and fathers. It is more important than one would think to keep single people away; celibacy inspires souls either with a merciless strictness or dark glowing passions, far removed from the calm and sweetness which should surround childhood.

As the education of the early years is carried out, above all things in the environment in which the child is placed it is of the utmost importance to have around it devoted, loving and intelligent carers. Crèche education which in essence already contains all aspects of life can be summed up in three words: Hygiene, Morality and Teaching. Let us look at the importance of these different aspects of the first stage of education.

Children's bodies must be considered first, robust health being one necessary condition of normal life. Diet is only one part of children's hygiene; the temperature, the airiness of the room they occupy and clothing are no less important. Now it is obvious without needing to prove it that it is easier to combine all these points of good hygiene in the crèche than within each family.

Nursing mothers as well as the carers entrusted with this first stage of education must become devoted to developing in the children right from the cradle the sentiments of Liberty, Equality and Fraternity. Far from submitting the pupils, as they do in the old system, to absolute obedience which can only make slaves of them, socialist education must, from the outset, closely watch out for the expression of willpower and, instead of repressing, make every effort to ensure its free expression. All moral aspects of education are exerted in an indirect way; the child remains absolutely passive at this point. Music, which possesses to the highest degree moral power, allied to the religious character of the carers, retains the most influence at this stage of education. In gymnastics, the third part of crèche education, one must devote oneself particularly, not only to developing muscular strength and the whole body, but also to expanding each sense to its highest point of normal development: that is, sight, by the attentive contemplation of objects, and if the eye is defective, by gradual exercises intended to decrease the defects: hearing by frequent listening to music and to the attention given to various noises: as for touch, smell and taste, education must concentrate on having them simultaneously develop subtlety and soundness which these senses possess in the natural state and not have them perverted as they are nowadays by shameful refinements or annihilate them as the Christian ascetics wished to do.

We cannot repeat it often enough: education must be devoted to developing the body as much as the heart and the mind, since this aspect of life is equal to the others: since work, through which it manifests itself above all in the life of humanity, is one of the great aspects of this existence. In the crèche the children can begin to learn languages other than their mother tongue. All carers and nursing mothers must speak perfectly and fluently one or more foreign languages and teach the children orally, only speaking to them in those languages. As children's questions arise, every effort should be made to give them real scientific notions, never to tell falsehoods in place of truth, which would have the double disadvantage of giving children wrong ideas which have to be rectified later on and weakening in their minds the moral authority of those who are responsible for initiating them in life.

In the crèche everything is a game; nothing should be considered as work; however the greatest regularity should reign there, in the order of various exercises, as in the order of the meals, and even as much as possible of sleep, not for the children collectively, but for each one as an individual. Regularity of habits is an introduction to the feeling of duty which from a very early age should dictate the lives of human beings.

And finally the greatest peace, the greatest gentleness, a true serenity should abound within the crèche because the children should only experience harmonious feelings, capable of inspiring a taste for order, one of Beauty and Nature's manifestations.

TEXT 6   THE RIGHT TO WORK[40]

Disclaimer from the Editor

The condition of women has too much influence on society for anyone not to be aware how important an issue it is and we are unequivocally on the side of those who have the highest regard for this subject.

But while we do not hesitate to grant women this eminent a place in the moral order, at the same time we think that they are in a secondary position because of the way social factors have evolved. We think that moral perfection depends essentially on physical well-being; it is poverty which destroys society.

Questions about the condition of women therefore seem inopportune today, and irrelevant to fundamental social and political issues. One can nonetheless say that the woman question still appears inappropriate to those institutions not directly involved with women. That is why we are not inclined to enter this domain very often. However, we thought that there was a certain appropriateness in deviating momentarily from our custom when a woman prisoner and, what is more, an intellectual woman – not that this makes any difference – asks to speak in favour of her sex. While she is responsible for her own beliefs we consider that it is still appropriate to publish them. We present Madame Pauline Roland.

Adolphe Chouippe

Has woman the right to freedom? A simple question

Sent from a woman prisoner, addressed to Citizen Emile de Girardin, editor of the *Bien être universel* (Universal Well-being)
Saint Lazare Prison, April 1851

It is exceedingly difficult for newspapers and pamphlets to come through prison bars and they do so with some considerable delay. Rumours from outside usually arrive distorted and false, and when they bring to prisoners a piece of news to which they would like to respond out of sympathy or other feelings, the news is so old that it is irrelevant in the outside world. But when a prisoner realizes how quickly time passes, even in the case of quite a minor slander or a rude insult, he ignores it because no one will know any longer what he is talking about outside the small circle which separates him from life.

Is it because of this that we are determined to respond to our enemies who, among other unkindly remarks, have heaped insults upon us, we who are jailed because of a feeble gesture of revolt? To be honest, these enemies do not seem really dangerous for various reasons: they are on the side of reaction. Reactionaries are not in the limelight; they speak a strange antediluvian language which we no longer hear in the new world to which we are proud to belong. In fact their stupidity is worse than their offensiveness and in our country what is stupid has no chance of succeeding. They can spout all their errors in peace because their speeches have no authority whatsoever.

But that is not the case for you, Citizen. You claim you are a man of progress and of practical progress, aspiring somehow to the role of Robert Peel, a socialist, if I am not mistaken. Many democrats gave you their vote in the elections; your newspapers are like ours; you are a pamphleteer and above all a polemicist of the highest distinction: in fact you are an eminent intellectual. Any mistake you make has every chance of spreading: it must be refuted quickly. Therefore I was very sorry that for reasons I have previously outlined, I was unable to write to you earlier on the question of women working, an issue often discussed in the press, and which you are presenting rather daringly to the proletariat. I must say, to me it seemed rather irrelevant whether or not the literate and the bourgeois readers of the press were suspicious of such and such a question of morality and politics: the future of the world does not lie in their hands. Rather it is in the hands of the workers to whom the *Bien être universel* is addressed, and there it is useful to discuss seriously the question of these principles.

Well, Citizen, in the first issue of this newspaper which reached here yesterday, I read, signed by yourself, in bold letters, in an article which supposedly passes for a manifesto, the most outrageous remarks ever produced in my opinion about the role of women since the famous axiom: housewife or harlot, which I submit should be housewife *and* harlot.

Allow me, then, to send you some observations and if, as I like to think, in what you write about my sex you are motivated by serious moral considerations and by love of truth, deign to give some attention to a woman who finds herself in prison for believing that work is the right of every human being, that woman is a human being just like a man, equal to him, and having more or less the same rights and the same duties.

Let us examine your words and reply in good faith; you are liberal-minded enough to be able to admit for once that you were mistaken.

I quote from your words exactly:

'The first and supreme function of a mother is to bring into the world healthy strong and robust children, to nourish and educate them. It is therefore up to men to work, to the woman to look after the household. She must only do what she can without leaving the maternal home when she is a daughter, the conjugal home when she is a woman, her children's nursery cradle when she is a mother.'

That is the law of a woman's life in all its simplicity as you would decree it, Citizen Emile de Girardin, if tomorrow, God willed you to be summoned like Bérard or Armand Marrast to devise some constitution or other for us. You give us the right to idleness which we do not want, by holding us in perpetual dependency, which we equally reject, because as the popular song says:

Work is freedom.

But let us continue.

Has woman a soul? asked the doctors of Mohammedism and as a certain Bishop from the Council of Mâcon had asked before them, where, according to Gregory of Tours, the question was quashed under the general reprobation of his colleagues.

Has woman her own life or is her life a mere appendix of man's life?

Is she a free, equal person, existing as a member of humanity, independent of the functions assigned to her? As a human being has she the right to acquire as much in her own interests as in the interests of society of which she is a member, all the physical moral and intellectual development of which she is capable?

That, Citizen, is the moral question in three lines – jotted down carelessly, allow me to say – you have resolved it in the negative. If the matter had been raised in some Council of Mâcon, you would not have been allowed to continue, and I strongly doubt if you would have been any more fortunate if you had posed the question in a congress of doctors of theology of the new faith which you claim to follow.

Here let me relate an absolutely true story, whose protagonist is one of the most illustrious physiologists of our time, Doctor L__ . One day in Montpellier, this expert was about to examine an aspiring doctor. He asked him what the role of woman was in humanity's existence.

'To charm our lives by making herself loved, then to reproduce the species and breast feed her children,' the candidate replied immediately.

'Is that all?'

'Yes, Sir.'

'That is the whole role of woman?'

'Without a doubt.'

'Young man, have you a mother?'

'Yes, Sir.'

'What is her age?'

'Fifty.'

'Well, well, then you should drown her,' the doctor vehemently replied. And in truth if your system were to prevail he would have been right.

But seriously to continue the debate.

There is no denying the possibility of motherhood for a woman, and the sacred law of nature which entrusts children to her tender care. Certainly it is socially desirable that the children she brings into the world receive a healthy education from her – to which you would add a healthy soul... .

Certainly children should be breast-fed by their mother wherever possible and in every case the mother should be near the cradle. She has to educate the child by agreement with the father and with society. But in all honesty does this take a whole lifetime? Many women have no children. The average family size is three per household. If one extends nurture and early education to the limit, the only part of education you deign to entrust to the mother, that would give women ten years of active life, in a life which lasts some sixty years. The rest of the time will be spent adorning herself, knitting stockings, playing the piano, cleaning saucepans or playing a game of whist. Thank you for your munificence, Citizen, we prefer real work to that boring idleness and we assure you that the household can only improve when it is no longer our sole concern.

Besides, Citizen, even if women should accept the lot you wish to impose on them, is it by confining them to the role of a baby machine which is dangerously close to becoming a harem or more like the lot of a slave, even if you were to make her the healthy reproductive machine that you describe, the robust nursing mother, the sensible teacher, is that what you want for your sons? Some examples from ancient history could clarify this point.

Athenian women lived in the heart of a gynaeceum, and there is no doubt in my mind that the dreadful corruption depicted by Plato and Plutarch, as well as Aristophanes, came to the most intelligent people on earth because of the absence of women in all transactions of civil and political life. For models of womanhood, the cradle of the civilization gives us only Xantippe and Aspasia, the avaricious housekeeper and the shameless courtesan.

On the other hand the Lacedæmonian girls took part in gymnastic games and even in combats between the adolescents of the austere city, Sparta, leading up to the games. The Spartan ideal of mother and citizen, if not of woman citizen, is still remembered to this day.

Finally let us look at some of the features of the portrait of the virtuous woman in the book of proverbs attributed to Solomon.

'Who will find a valiant woman because her price is beyond many pearls. Her husband's heart is assured in her. She does good every day and never does any harm. She obtains wool and linen and makes what she needs with her own hands. She is like a merchant's ships; she brings back her bread from afar. She looks at a field and purchases it. She plants the vine, as the fruit of her hands. She girds up her loins and strengthens her arms. She makes clothing and sells it; she makes belts which she gives to the merchant. She oversees the running of the household and does not eat the bread of idleness.'

I know, Citizen, that you see no disadvantage to women being as Solomon describes, since he seems to keep them confined to the household. However, to be consistent, you would have to reject several of the verses I have quoted. Furthermore, I would say to you that I have too much faith in the sacred law of progress to satisfy myself with an ideal dreamt up twenty-eight centuries ago, any more than with the virtue of the Spartan women.

The life of a modern woman should be superior to both because the progress of humanity has benefited women as well as men. And if we have gained in value we should also gain in rights.

I shall summarize, therefore, and in answer to the four proposals put forward by you and quoted at the beginning of my letter, I reply:-

Woman is a free being, equal to man whose sister she is. Like him she must fulfil duties towards herself by maintaining her personal dignity beyond all reproach, by developing in virtue, by making her life not from the work or love or intelligence of another – even if that other is her father, husband or son – but from her own work, her own love, her own intelligence. Like the man she must fulfil family duties which are the sweetest recompense of other labours, but which cannot completely absorb her, and the same goes for men. It happens all too often that they fulfil no other duties to the family than that of a breadwinner.

Finally woman is a citizen by right, if not in fact, and as such she needs to become involved in life outside the home, in social life, which will not be a healthy one until the whole family is represented there.

That, Citizen, is my response to your first proposition. As for the second and third, which in real terms are only one, I would say:- Woman is entitled to work as is Man, and to have productive, independent employment which will emancipate her from all dependence. She has the right to choose her work herself as well as a man and no one can legitimately confine her to the house if she feels she is called to live otherwise. Finally, as soon as a woman comes of age, she has the right to arrange her life as she wishes.

The paternal home should be a refuge for her, not a prison from which she can only escape by going to another prison. The conjugal home is her dwelling, her property, as it is that of the man and within the same limits. She is not obliged to stay there any more than he is if her conscience calls her elsewhere. In fact, since her arms are her children's natural cradle, she may take them where she thinks fit. One cannot imagine anything more beautiful, and more honourable in the future than a woman, thus discharging all her duties, expending all her virtues, satisfying all her loves and taking part in industrial and civil life as a full human being.

All that, Citizen, had been discussed some twenty years ago in Saint-Simonianism and it seemed so good to me that the cause of female emancipation was won, that when there was fierce debate to win equality of the sexes, I was inclined to laugh saying that there did not seem much point in breaking down already open doors. Citizen Proudhon and you yourself have shown me, alas, that the struggle still goes on.

I am weak and almost defenceless before such illustrious opponents, but I have faith, remembering the struggle between David and Goliath. Whoever fights for truth does not need arms. The war can last a long time, however, and such a debate cannot be resolved in a few lines. Will you accept the battle for which you alone can provide the terrain? That is the question I address to you today. I await your reply and whatever it is I remain yours fraternally,

Pauline Roland.

NOTES

1. No exhaustive biographical works devoted solely to Jeanne Deroin exist. A recent publication discusses her political development, but sheds little light on the missing details of her personal circumstances. See Michèle Riot-Sarcey, *La démocratie à l'épreuve des femmes. Trois figures critiques du pouvoir 1830–1848* (Désirée Gay, Jeanne Deroin & Eugénie Niboyet) Paris, Albin Michel, 1994. Jane Rendall gives her a brief mention in *The Origins of Modern Feminism: Women in Britain, France and the United States, 1760–1860*, Basingstoke and London, Macmillan, 1985, pp. 291–300.

2. For further details see Claire Goldberg Moses, *French Feminism in the Nineteenth Century*, Albany, State University of New York Press, 1984, pp. 60–87, in which Moses sees a common focal point of feminism to be its rejection of marriage. For further details on the development of these newspapers see also Laure Adler, *A l'aube du féminisme: Les premières journalistes 1830–1850*, Paris, Payot, 1979.

3. Pierre Leroux (1797–1871) is less known today for his own ideas but in his time wrote articles, supported activists, ran a commune, and organized a number of activists' publications. A former mason and typographical worker, in 1824 he turned to journalism and founded *Le Globe*, a thrice-weekly literary review before developing it as a liberal daily in 1830 and later transforming it into a Saint-Simonian publication in 1831. After breaking away from the Enfantin-led Saint-Simonians, Leroux founded the *Revue encyclopédique* and moved closer to the republican position defending those prosecuted in 1835. From 1836 to 1843 he ran the *Encyclopédie nouvelle* and in 1841 the *Revue indépendante* with George Sand until 1848. A progressive in social matters – he favoured women's enfranchisement and opposed the *Loi Falloux* – he repudiated all violence and challenged Proudhon's economic ideas on property. As a socialist member of the first Assembly and part of the Left republican movement he was forced to leave France for exile in England and Jersey in 1851, returning in 1860 to obscurity and poverty. The Commune government paid homage to him in recognition of his devotion to the cause of the working class.

4. Auguste Blanqui (1805–1881) also wrote for the paper *Le Globe* during its Saint-Simonian heyday. A communist and revolutionary activist, he believed that political violence was justified as parliamentary suffrage was not sufficient to achieve and ensure an egalitarian society. As a result of his involvement in insurrection he was arrested, tried and sentenced many times, spending a total of over 40 years behind bars or in exile right up to his death. He was revered by many as the symbol of resistance to monarchy and conservatism. See *Actes du Colloque Blanqui, Blanqui et les blanquistes*, Société d'histoire de la Révolution de 1848 et des révolutions du XIXᵉ siècle, Paris, SEDES, 1986.

5. Charles Fourier (1772–1837) was an influential individual with many followers, the most important being Victor Considérant, and admirers such as Flora Tristan, but did not engage in militancy himself beyond writing. A rather remote figure with a horror of political violence after his arrest and brief imprisonment in 1793, he was a commercial traveller and an unsuccessful businessman who wrote about practical ways of establishing collective communes or phalansteries. His writings contain advanced views on sexual freedom although his followers rejected many of his ideas as too eccentric or libertarian. See Susan K. Grogan, *French Socialism and Sexual Difference: Women and the New Society, 1803–44*, Basingstoke and London, Macmillan, 1992, pp. 20–66.

6. Etienne Cabet (1788–1856), a utopian socialist theoretician, developed an ideal commu-

nist society named 'Icarie'. He made several attempts to found experimental commune groups in France and later in St Louis, USA, where he died.

7. There are two biographies of Pauline Roland, one by a lifelong militant on the Left in France, a member of the Resistance and historian, Edith Thomas, *Pauline Roland: Socialisme et féminisme au XIXe siècle*, Paris, Marcel Rivière, 1956; and the other by a feminist militant and novelist, Benoîte Groult, *Pauline Roland ou comment la liberté vint aux femmes* (with illustrations), Paris, Robert Laffont, 1991. The latter is not a rigorous historical piece of original research, contains neither bibliography nor index, but features many socialist men with whom Pauline Roland was remotely connected.

8. *Le Peuple*, 10 December 1848. Quoted in Edith Thomas, *Pauline Roland, op. cit.*, pp. 116–17.

9. The former Saint-Simonian Olindes Rodrigues was among those who assisted financially with the publication of the first issue of *Opinion des femmes*. For further details on the production of women's newspapers in 1848 see Evelyne Sullerot, 'Journaux féminins et lutte ouvrière (1848–1849)', in *Société d'histoire de la Révolution de 1848*, Paris, CNRS, 1966, pp. 88–122.

10. For a discussion on the exclusion of women from universal suffrage see special commemorative issues of *French Politics and Society*, **12**(4), Fall 1994, pp. 1–76; and *Modern and Contemporary France*, NS3, no. 2, April 1995, pp. 127–57, 199–202, 208–12. See also Actes du Colloque d'Albi des 19 et 20 mars 1992 *Femmes, Pouvoirs*, sous la responsabilité de Michèle Riot-Sarcey, Paris, Editions Kimé, 1993. For accounts of the struggle from a masculine suffrage perspective, see Raymond Huard, *Le suffrage universel en France 1848–1946*, Paris, Aubier, 1991; and Pierre Rosanvallon, *Le sacre du citoyen: Histoire du suffrage universel en France*, Paris, Editions Gallimard, 1992.

11. Members of this supposed alliance were referred to as 'reds' by their enemies as this colour was associated with the costume of one particular radical club. In the same way in popular discourse blue came to represent the conservative republicans and white monarchists and Bonapartists.

12. John Plamenatz, *The Revolutionary Movement in France 1815–1871*, London, Longman, 1952, p. 82.

13. 'The Mountain' referred to a group of radical republicans in the Second Republic who revived the name of this 1789 revolutionary group in the National Assembly (referred to by Roland as the Montagnards of 1793) because of the position of their elevated seats. The term 'Democ-Socs' or *démocrates socialistes* described a loosely organized body of moderately left-wing republicans of bourgeois origins who were condemned by later generations of socialists for failing to withstand the reactionary Party of Order and repression of the Republic. See Maurice Agulhon, *The Republican Experiment 1848–1852*, Cambridge, Cambridge University Press, 1983.

14. For references to this debate see Susan Groag Bell and Karen M. Offen (eds), *Women, the Family and Freedom: The Debate in Documents*, Stanford, California, Stanford University Press, 1983, vol. 1, 1750–1880, pp. 280–85.

15. The *Loi Falloux*, 1850, while ostensibly democratizing educational provision by extending primary education to girls as well as boys, gave girls' education over to the Church. Religious orders were not required to have teacher training, whereas lay teachers were so required. See Sharif Gemie, 'Docility, Zeal and Rebellion: Culture and Sub-cultures in Women's Teacher Training Colleges, c.1860–c.1910' in *European History Quarterly*, Vol. **24**, 1994, pp. 213–44; Richard J. Evans, *The Feminists*, London, Croom Helm, 1977, p. 125; Patrick Bidelman, *Pariahs Stand Up*, London, Greenwood Press, 1982, pp. 14–17; and, generally, Françoise Mayeur, *L'Education des filles en France au XIXième siècle*, Paris, Hachette, 1979.

16. In his account of their meetings, Gustave Lefrançais recorded how he disagreed fundamentally with Roland on this matter. See *Souvenirs d'un Révolutionnaire*, texte établi et préparé par Jan Cerny, Bordeaux, Edition de la Tête de Feuilles, 1972, p. 96.

17. See Edith Thomas, *Pauline Roland, op. cit.*, pp. 116–26.

18. On 23 August 1849 the delegates of 83 associations met and formed a provisional com-

mission with five members: Jeanne Deroin, Delbrouck, Blaizon, Solon and Descheneaux. See Michèle Riot-Sarcey *La démocratie à l'épreuve des femmes, op. cit.*, pp. 254–69.

19. See Chapter 4, p. 95.

20. Emile de Girardin (1806–1881) converted to socialism in 1849 and ran a newspaper, *La Presse*, which championed the workers' cause. He won a parliamentary seat in the June elections of 1850 but was forced to leave France after the *coup d'état* of 2 December 1851. He returned during the Second Empire, having made his peace with Louis Napoléon.

21. John Plamenatz, *The Revolutionary Movement in France 1815–1871, op. cit.*, p. 71. For other accounts of 1848 without women see Maurice Agulhon, *The Republican Experiment 1848–1852, op. cit.*; Roger Price, *The French Second Republic: A Social History*, London, Batsford, 1972; and Roger Price (ed.), *Revolution and Reaction 1848: and the Second French Republic*, London, Croom Helm, 1975.

22. For a comprehensive account of this defeat see William Fortescue, 'Divorce Debated and Deferred: The French Debate on Divorce and the Failure of the Crémieux Divorce Bill in 1848', in *French History*, **7** (2), 1993, pp. 137–62.

23. For a lively discussion of the equation between religion and women's conservatism see James McMillan, 'Religion and Gender in Modern France: Some Reflections', in Frank Tallet and Nicholas Atkin, *Religion, Politics and Society in France since 1789*, London, The Hambledon Press, 1991 pp. 55–66.

24. 'Les femmes au gouvernement et au peuple français', in *Opinion des femmes*, no.4, 1848 reprinted in, *Campagne électorale de la citoyenne Jeanne Deroin, pétition des femmes au peuple*, Dépôt central de la Propagande Socialiste, Rue Coquillière, Paris 13, 1849.

25. First letter to the Corinthians, chapter 7, verse 21.

26. Reference to 'The Legend of the Council at Mâcon' which in AD 586 debated the question as to whether women had souls. See Geneviève Fraisse, *Reason's Muse, Sexual Difference and the Birth of Democracy*, translated by J.M. Todd, Chicago, University of Chicago Press, 1994, p. 141.

27. *Aux électeurs du département de la Seine*, Paris, Imprimerie Lacour, Rue St Hyacinthe-St Michel, 33, et Rue Souflot, 11, 1849.

28. *Association fraternelle des Démocrates Socialistes des deux sexes, pour l'affranchissement politique et social des femmes*, Paris, Lacour Printers, 1849.

29. 1°   Are members of the association all the women and all the men who accept our declaration of principles and who are committed to supporting as far as their faculties and abilities allow, the promotion, teaching and the realization of these principles?
2°   One can be a member of the association as an apostle, promoter or subscriber.
3°   Three commissions direct the role of the association: one is an apostolic commission, one is a promotion commission, one is an administrative commission.
4°   The apostolic commission is composed of men and women who devote themselves to the task of developing teaching and speaking up for the principles contained in our declaration, in all public meetings or in publications.
5°   The commission for promotion is composed of all men and all women whose task will be to collect membership and to establish a centre for correspondence in all the *arrondissements* of Paris and in all the *départements*.
6°   The administrative commission is composed of twelve members elected by subscribers; it will look after all the administrative details; a set of rules will settle its attributions.
7°   The subscriptions will be intended for: transforming one monthly journal into a weekly paper, the publication of works approved by the apostolic commission, the payment of travel costs and all necessary expenditure for the promotion of the principles.
Signed on behalf of the members of the apostolic Commission

Jeanne DEROIN, Jean MACÉ, HENRIETTE artist, DELBROUCK, Annette LAMY, Eugène STOURM.
The members of the propaganda commission will send membership and subscription lists on the first of each month to the head quarter of the apostolic Commission and to the office of the newspaper *l'Opinion des femmes*, 29 Grande Rue Verte.

30. 'Rectification du compte-rendu du comité démocratique-socialiste des électeurs', in

Campagne électorale de la citoyenne Jeanne Deroin, pétition des femmes au peuple, Dépot central de la propagande socialiste, Rue Coquillière, Paris 13, 1849.

31.   For an account of George Sand's hostile reaction to this move see Michèle Riot-Sarcey, *La démocratie à l'épreuve des femmes, op. cit.*, pp. 203–10.

32.   Workers' collective organizations came into their own in 1848 after unionism had become common parlance in labour and social discourse during the July Monarchy. See William H. Sewell, Jr, *Work and Revolution in France: The Language of Labor from the Old Régime to 1848*, Cambridge, Cambridge University Press, 1980; Roger Magraw, *A History of the French Working Class, Vol.1, The Age of the Artisan Revolution 1815–1871*, Oxford, Blackwell, 1992; Mary Lynn Stewart McDougall, *The Artisan Republic: Revolution Reaction and Resistance in Lyons 1848–1851*, Kingston and Montreal, McGill Queen's University Press, 1984; and Marcel David, *Le printemps de la fraternité: genèse et vicissitudes 1830–1851*, Paris, Aubier, 1992. If the same authors have barely recognized the effect on women's mobilization in certain sectors of the workforce, rarely are the female leaders Pauline Roland or Jeanne Deroin mentioned.

33.   For biographical details see Chapter 4, pp. 140–41.

34.   See Roland's letter to Lefrançais, Chapter 4, pp. 108–10.

35.   See Bell and Offen, *Women, the Family and Freedom, op. cit.*, pp. 180–226, 456–81. For further reading on the debate within the Left on women and work from a feminist angle, see Katherine Blunden, *Le Travail et la vertu: Femmes au foyer: une mystification de la Révolution industrielle*, Paris, Payot, 1982; Louise Tilly and Joan Scott, *Women, Work and the Family*, New York and London, Routledge, 1978 and 1987; and Patricia Hilden, *Working Women and Socialist Politics in France 1880–1914*, Oxford, Clarendon Press, 1986.

36.   *Aux instituteurs, l'Association des instituteurs institutrices et professeurs socialistes*, Paris, par la société typographique de Paris, Imprimerie Schneider, Rue d'Erforth, 4, 1849.

37.   See the *Conseiller du Peuple* by A. de Lamartine, September issue, 1849 (Pauline Roland).

38.   A French term indicating a sale by correspondence, rather than in person. It is used when the rate is different from that used for sales in person as it includes an element of postage.

39.   *Programme d'enseignement de l'Association fraternelle des instituteurs institutrices et professeurs socialistes*, Paris, par la société typographique de Paris, Imprimerie Schneider, Rue d'Erforth, 4, 1849.

40.   'La femme a-t-elle le droit à la liberté?', *La Feuille du Peuple*, 25 April 1851.

4.   Jeanne Deroin and Pauline Roland: prison, deportation and exile, 1851–1852

CONTEXTUAL INTRODUCTION

Jeanne Deroin and Pauline Roland paid a high price for their political and feminist convictions. Louis Napoléon's successful *coup d'état* of 1851 had ushered in a period of severe repression. Freedom of the press, of public assembly, of association in self-help 'unions', and of both men's and women's clubs were brutally curtailed. The texts in this chapter relate to Deroin's and Roland's imprisonment and subsequent exile. Arrested on 29 May 1850 in a raid on the 'Fraternal Association of all Associations' (an amalgamation of some 83 workers' associations founded by Deroin in 1849), at their offices at 37 Rue Michel le Comte, Pauline Roland, Jeanne Deroin and Louise Nicaud, the other woman arrested, were sentenced to six months' imprisonment.[1] At their trial, they were interrogated about their marital status and accused of subversive activities against the state, both by virtue of implicitly criticizing the Civil Code in their refusal to use a married name (Deroin) or to enter the married state (Roland) and for fostering workers' associations.[2] They were condemned on the basis of their private as well as their public lives.

The workers' associations, which had been formed with the aim of achieving social change through mutual self-help without recourse to violent revolutionary means, were construed as deeply subversive by Louis Napoléon's government, as were women's clubs and newspapers. The police report detailing Roland's 'associationist' activities, singles her out as 'fanatical':

A society has just been created under the name of the Fraternal Association of Socialist Democratic Primary and Secondary Schoolmasters and Schoolmistresses. This society, the provisional headquarters of which are at Bréda, the home of Perot, schoolmaster, has among its main founders the same Perot who has a boarding school at the address cited; the woman, Pauline Roland, who before the February revolution ran an educational establishment together with M. Pierre Leroux in a small village in the Creuse, at present residing at no. 33 Chemin de la Ronde at Barrière Blanche, and a man, G. Lefrançais who calls himself a schoolmaster. The latter, aged about twenty-five, has been unemployed for a long time and is dependent on his father who is a worker. Perot has around thirty pupils in his establishment who pay very badly, so he does not seem well off. He appears to be on intimate terms with the woman, Pauline Roland, who is a widow. After the February revolution this woman, who shares all the political and socialist opinions of Pierre Leroux, came to settle in Paris where she writes for the *Tribune of the People*. This woman is absolutely devoted to the socialist cause. She should be counted among the most fervent and the most fanatical of its supporters.[3]

According to official figures, 26 884 people were arrested or charged in France on the occasion of the insurrection of December 1851 against Louis Napoléon's *coup d'état*, when he declared himself Emperor on 2 December. Of these, 169 were women. Not all those arrested were sentenced, but over 6 000 prisoners in all were condemned to transportation to Algeria.[4] Deroin's and Roland's experiences of the regime's savage repression and their response to it throw valuable light on the beleaguered resistance of the minority Left. Their treatment as women dissidents may help to explain the social conservatism of many subsequent French feminist movements. As Mary Wollstonecraft's character was vilified after her death in order to discredit her political radicalism and feminism in a largely successful effort to render her example anathema to 19th-century women, so French women of the 1848– 1852 period who contested the social, political and gender roles which had been allotted them, received punishments which served as a warning to women thereafter.

Deroin and Roland did not desist from political activity in prison. Deroin wrote to the Legislative Assembly in February 1851 protesting against the regime's restriction on the right to petition the National Assembly, one of the few political rights, as we have seen with regard to Flora Tristan, that women possessed under French law. Roland wrote letters to socialist colleagues, read voraciously, and organized classes for women prisoners. After serving her prison term, Deroin emerged to find that her husband, Desroches, who had held a post as bursar in an old people's home, had been dismissed because of his alleged socialist sympathies and suffered a complete breakdown. Deroin's three children, who were cared for by friends, had been placed in homes far from Paris. Though aware that she was under continual police surveillance, Deroin resumed her teaching duties. In December 1851, after the *coup d'état*, she organized support for victims of political persecution, gathering aid for families of prisoners. Realizing that she faced almost certain further imprisonment, she fled to London in August 1852 and remained in exile there until her death in 1894. In the 1850s she produced three editions of a 'Woman's Almanac' of which extracts are printed in this chapter.[5] In London she lived by giving lessons. In 1880 former exiles from the Second Empire interceded with the government of the Third Republic to obtain a pension of 600 francs a year for her, which she used for the care of her mentally handicapped son.

Though she ceased active political involvement in the last years of her life, Deroin was well known in English socialist circles. In 1894 no less a figure than William Morris gave her funeral oration.

Jeanne Deroin's memorial to Pauline Roland remains a testimony not only to a remarkable and courageous individual, but to a generation of political idealists who suffered imprisonment, transportation and death for their beliefs. Women, excluded from the polity, were far less likely to be politicized than men, but those like Deroin and Roland who committed themselves to socialist militancy and to feminism were remarkable exceptions in a France where gendered conformity for women was largely successfully enforced. But as Victor Hugo argued in his speech at Louise Julien's grave (26 July 1853), women were now worthy of becoming citizens. They had fought on men's terrain and shared the worst deprivations normally allotted to male political dissidents. Formerly, Hugo observed, they had represented the soul of the family:

> But at this time of adversity, their attitude changed; they said to us 'We do not know if we have a right to share your power, your liberty and your greatness. But what we do know is that we have the right to share your misery. To partake of your suffering, your despondency, your destitution, your distress, your renunciation, your exile, your abandonment if you are without asylum, your hunger if you are without bread, that is the right of women and we claim it.' O my brothers! and see how they follow us into combat, accompany us into banishment and precede us to the grave![6]

Hugo's tone, as befits the occasion, is elegiac and rhetorical and women might well object to their gender yet again being assigned a continuing role as the bearer of men's suffering. Yet it is significant that Hugo was convinced that women's participation in revolutionary and other political events would lead in the 19th century to the proclamation of the rights of women as those of the 18th century had the rights of men.

The letters of Pauline Roland written to a friend, Gustave Lefrançais, imprisoned before her in 1848, and her letters from prison and from Algeria testify to her political and religious faith in the human family. For her, socialism and feminism were integrated in her religious belief. Her Christianity was not that of doctrinal Catholicism, but a faith that Christ had come to succour the poor and the destitute. Her somewhat unorthodox but passionate religious faith sets her apart from later generations of socialist feminists like Madeleine Pelletier and Hélène Brion, who were profoundly anti-clerical and who tended to accept Marx's dictum that religion was the opium of the masses. In her letters, Roland reveals herself as warm-hearted, concerned with improvement (what books should Lefrançais read) and when she writes of her own difficulties, these are largely in connection with her concerns for her children.

Like Jeanne Deroin, Pauline Roland served a six month prison sentence, first in La Conciergerie and then in Saint Lazare prison.[7] She was re-arrested on 6 February 1852, having refused to disassociate herself from her colleagues, Deroin, Perot and Lefrançais for their and her involvement in the Socialist Teachers Association, and was imprisoned again in Saint Lazare (the prison for common prostitutes) until her deportation to Algeria on 23 June 1852, where she remained for five months.

Victor Hugo expressed her situation and her resistance to systematic degradation in these lines:

Cinq mois elle subit le contact des souillures,
L'oubli, le rire affreux du vice, les bourreaux,
Et le pain noir qu'on jette à travers les barreaux
Edifiant la geôle au mal habituée
Enseignant la voleuse et la prostituée.[8]

For five months she experienced this degrading life,
The neglect, the frightful laugh of vice, the warders
And the black bread thrown through the bars.
She transformed this prison accustomed to evil,
Teaching the women thieves and prostitutes by her example.

Roland's letters, often humorous and ironic and lacking in self-pity in spite of the terrible conditions under which she was imprisoned, show her determination to continue to serve others by organizing classes and readings for women prisoners. Though she made light of her personal situation, the effect of her incarceration on her children seems to have been unbearable to herself and to them. Her account of little Irma's dejection is particularly moving. Madame Bachellery, a fellow associationist and one of her correspondents, escaped imprisonment and took over the guardianship of Irma. Anne Greppo and Claudine Hibruit, her other two correspondents in this collection, were fellow prisoners.

The extract of a letter written to Mme Bachellery gives a dramatic account of Roland's removal from Saint Lazare on 22 June 1852 to face transportation. The nuns, in charge of the women prisoners, came late at night and woke Roland with the news of her sentence: 'Are we leaving for Algeria?', I said, 'Alas! Yes, you poor woman'. Even the trip across Paris, undertaken on foot with their warders, served as a way of humiliating the ten women chosen for this ordeal. To be seen as a woman under police escort was to be identified as a prostitute. 'We had to endure the gibes and insults of the ignoble gentlemen to whom we were handcuffed.'

The ten women deportees, along with some 210 male political prisoners, set sail for Le Havre on 23 June 1852 whence they transferred to the

'Magellan'. They lay out on open decks with no shelter. Their destination, Algeria, at this period served a similar function for the French government as did Australia for the British, a place to dispose of a burgeoning prison population and of the poor of mainland France. There were three different categories of treatment available to political prisoners when transported to Algeria: imprisonment in forts or work camps, release on parole in villages, or the right to become a settler and to work the land. During her stay, Pauline Roland fell into the first two classifications. The ten women prisoners arrived at Mers El Kebir and were transferred to Fort St Gregory at Oran, where they were locked up under terrible conditions. From Oran, they journeyed by sea to Algiers where, on 13 July, they joined five other women political prisoners at the Convent of the Good Shepherd, a penal institution designed for the reformation and conversion of prostitutes. Here, as in France, Roland took an active role among the prisoners, attempting to combat the culture of guilt and mortification encouraged by the nuns.

> Matter is as divine as the spirit. Do you really believe that God is interested in your insignificant prayers, your acts of mortification, your special head-dress and habit and the fish you eat on certain days of the year? We redeem the flesh, we have a religion of action. God would prefer to see us improve the economic, social and spiritual state of the world.[9]

Unsurprisingly, perhaps, she was considered a bad influence. The Mother Superior, fearing Roland's effect on her charges, begged the authorities to remove her. On 22 July, Roland left St Gregory for Sétif, journeying by mule across the mountains. There she was released on parole and found a menial job in an hotel which enabled her to live. Meanwhile, in France, Roland's case had aroused public concern. Béranger and George Sand both protested on her behalf and the Sétif Governor, in his turn, was anxious to be rid of her. He urged her to sue for a government pardon. Pauline Roland, however, who considered she had committed no crime, who claimed solidarity with other political prisoners and who in any case wished to defy the regime which she despised, refused. Victor Hugo's tribute to Roland in *Les Châtiments* (1853) reflects the extent to which Roland had become a symbol of political repression. Help was even forthcoming from one of her children. Her son Jean, who had won first prize in a national Latin examination, took advantage of the public platform at the award-giving ceremony to make a plea for his mother's release.

On 9 October, the Governor of Sétif, apparently desperate to force Roland to apply for a pardon, re-interned her. She was transferred to a prison in Constantine where the other prisoners demonstrated on her behalf. She was eventually placed in solitary confinement at Bône and there she received news of an unsolicited pardon. Without a general amnesty for political prisoners, Roland still feared re-arrest on her return to France. However, she decided that she must return for the sake of her children. The homeward journey proved almost as gruelling as the journey out. The crossing to Marseilles took six days. Roland's health and strength, already gravely undermined by her imprisonment, finally failed her and she died of pleurisy shortly after arriving at Lyons on 16 December 1852. She was 47 years old. Pauline Roland had literally burned herself out in her devotion to the socialist future of humanity in which she believed so passionately. Of her three children, Moses died in childhood. Jean and Irma, however, lived on to become teachers, a choice which would have pleased their mother.[10]

Pauline Roland became a *cause célèbre* in her own lifetime. From the point of view of a reactionary state, she represented danger both as a private and a public example. Her refusal to marry, her determination to bring up and educate her three children herself, her espousal of socialist educational principles, her enthusiastic support for workers' associations were all evidence, as far as the Second Empire was concerned, of her subversive tendencies. In character, Pauline Roland was generous, incautious and an impassioned advocate for the oppressed. In her short life she ran the gamut of political experimentation, from Saint-Simonianism to mainstream socialism. Her commitment to improving women's condition was profound. In one of her last letters, she implied that she was being punished less for her acts than for the tenor of her whole life in which she had never accepted the constraints of gender or class definition. She bore testimony to the refusal of one woman and potentially all women to be victimized.

Like Jeanne Deroin and Flora Tristan, Pauline Roland espoused a form of messianic Christianity. These women enacted concretely the imagery and vocabulary of proselytism and martyrdom. Deroin in her last years planned to write a 'Women's Gospel' in which socialism and Christianity would be reconciled. As Pauline Roland discovered in Algeria, the Church was not swayed by their faith. The nuns at St Gregory's found her intensely problematic because she focused on present redemption rather than guilt and future salvation.[11] Roland's faith was above all a faith in human possibility.

The repression meted out to Deroin and more forcefully to Roland testifies not only to the political threat they posed, but to the fact that they undermined gender conventions. Even to argue for equal citizenship for women (Deroin), for a non-gendered education (Roland) or for equality in sexual relations were ideas which appeared profoundly disruptive of post-revolutionary stability and were held to recall the worst excesses of the Terror. Terrified of social upheaval, the reaction of French conservatism against unsatisfied republican demands was that of repression. The state's fears of social unrest were mirrored by popular opinion when in 1848 and 1849 the republicans lost heavily in the elections. Those socialist republicans who argued for an extension of rights to either the propertyless or to women were in a weak electoral position.[12] Given this overwhelmingly conservative political climate, Deroin's and Roland's faith in a socialist future seems all the more remarkable. Their attempts to liberate their own sex and the working class, which to them seemed self-evidently virtuous, were construed as profoundly destabilizing of the social order.

Louis Napoléon's regime succeeded in crushing dissent until the Commune of 1871. The terrible events of the siege of Paris also had their revolutionary heroine, Louise Michel. Her generation looked back to the failed promises and hopes of the Second Republic. The continuity of the French revolutionary tradition and of women political activists which Michel represented also inspired Madeleine Pelletier and Hélène Brion a generation later. On 12 May 1894 *Commonweal*, the English socialist journal, published a poem of Louise Michel's to commemorate the May uprising of 1871. Remembering the fallen, Michel served a warning to those who believed in the efficacy of unremitting state control to repress dissent. Her vengeful spectres of revolution were a far cry from Pauline Roland's generous vision of a human family:

'The Commune', 'The Spectres'

> *Nous reviendrons foule sans nombre,*
> *Nous reviendrons par tous les chemins,*
> *Spectres vengeurs sortant de l'ombre,*
> *Nous reviendrons nous tenant les mains,*
> *Les uns pâles dans le suaire*
> *Les autres encore sanglants*
> *Les trous de balles dans leurs flancs*
> *La mort portera la bannière.*

> We will return in a countless crowd,
> We will return along the ways,
> Vengeful spectres from out death's cloud,
> We will return linked hand in hand,
> Some of us pale in the winding sheet,
> Some still bleeding, we will return
> With open wounds where the bullets beat
> And Death shall carry the flag.

Roland's Algerian letters describing conditions of the prisoners, focus largely on the generality of hardship rather than on her own difficulties. In all her time in prison, Roland refused any privileges that might have been granted her as a political prisoner. She was characterized by generosity, warmth of heart and a feeling of solidarity with her fellow sufferers. She surmounted her early dependency on Enfantin and the idea of the Saint-Simonian 'Father' to commit herself to political action and to serve as an example of resistance against arbitrary power. Ironically, she could be said to have become that 'Mother' whom Enfantin had claimed could not be found, the mother of the genuinely human family. Though she may have sought martyrdom, she bore it with extraordinary fortitude. Jeanne Deroin's 'Almanac' with its tribute to Pauline Roland insisted on her selflessness and the power of her example. Though couched in the rhetorical style of the period, Deroin's judgement does not seem exaggerated. Victor Hugo, the major French poet of his day, also exiled by Louis Napoléon's regime, opened his poem on Pauline Roland with the following estimate of her character:

> *Elle ne connaissait ni l'orgueil ni la haine;*
> *Elle aimait; elle était pauvre, simple et sereine;*
> *Souvent le pain qui manque abrégeait son repas.*
> *Elle avait trois enfants, ce qui n'empêchait pas*
> *Qu'elle se sentît mère de ceux qui souffrent....*
> *Elle apercevait Dieu contruisant l'avenir.*
> *Elle sentait sa foi sans cesse rajeunir;*
> *De la liberté sainte elle attisait les flammes;*
> *Elle s'inquiétait des enfants et des femmes;*
> *Elle disait, tendant la main aux travailleurs:*
> *La vie est dure ici, mais sera bonne ailleurs....*
> *Tendre, elle visitait, sous leur toit de misère,*
> *Tous ceux que la famine ou la douleur abat,*
> *Les malades pensifs, gisant sur leur grabat,*
> *La mansarde où languit l'indigence morose;*
> *Quand par hasard moins pauvre, elle avait quelque chose,*
> *Elle le partageait à tous comme une soeur;*
> *Quand elle n'avait rien, elle donnait son coeur.*
> *Calme et grande, elle aimait comme le soleil brille.*
> *Le genre humain pour elle était une famille*
> *Comme ses trois enfants étaient l'humanité.*[13]

She knew neither pride nor hatred.
She loved; she was poor, simple and serene;
She often knew want of even life's bare necessities.
She had three children, which did not prevent her
From considering herself the mother of all those who suffer....
She saw God building the future
And constantly felt her faith renewed.
She stirred up the flame of sacred Liberty;
She made children and women the centre of her concern;
She would say, holding out her hand to the workers:
Life is hard here, but will be better one day....
Gentle, she would visit under their miserable roofs,
All those struck low by famine or poverty,

Morbid invalids lying on their pallets,
Garrets where gloomy penury languishes;
When, by chance, less poor than usual she had anything to give,
She shared it with everyone, like a sister;
When she had nothing, she gave her heart.
Calm and tall, her love was as generous as the sunshine.
For her, humanity was a family
Just as her three children were humanity.

In his poem, Hugo constructed Roland as a heroine of and for the people. Beyond the rodomontade, his verses carry the ring of truth.

TEXTS BY PAULINE ROLAND

Letters from Pauline Roland to Gustave Lefrançais
Letters from Pauline Roland to Anne Greppo
Extract of letter from Pauline Roland to Mme Bachellery
Letter from Pauline Roland to Claudine Monniot (Hibruit)
Letter from Pauline Roland to Madame Bachellery
Letters from Pauline Roland to Claudine Monniot

LETTERS FROM PAULINE ROLAND TO GUSTAVE LEFRANÇAIS

Letter 1

Paris, 7 April 1850

My dear child,

What did you think of your old friend, when she did not write to you? The fact is that I had hoped to see you from one day to the next, and finding that in a letter one says so little, and so badly what one would like to say, I put off communicating by this means until today. Thank you my child for writing to me as soon as you were able. That shows me that you are in no doubt about my affection, useless affection alas, which I would love to prove but cannot. I saw your excellent mother, whom I found to be a worthy mother of a republican, a noble courageous woman faced with this great sorrow, a thousand times more heartrending than the material difficulties that we all have to confront.

My dear child I am not wondering what you are guilty of doing; I know you are not, nor do I know what you are accused of being, any more than our friend Carle and those arrested with you.[14] The *Journal des débats*[15] has completely fantasized about this, it is more stupid than ill-natured which is not saying much. These people do not believe that it is possible to be upright in the search for good without worrying too much about daily bread. The fact that we are poor makes them conclude what Caesar thought about Cassius' lean and hungry look. May heaven have pity on them! Forgive them as we forgive them! Your mother told me that you were asking for books. What would you like me to send you?

I also wanted to make arrangements for your food. I even asked Blairon to send you some roast meat. I do not know if he did. Write and tell me all about your conditions even though I hope that you will only have to stay a few days in prison. I would want you not to have to suffer too much physical discomfort if that is at all possible.

Farewell my dear child, shake Carle's hand warmly for me, and trust in the deep and lasting love of your old friend,

Pauline Roland.

Letter 2

Paris, 9 April 1850

My dear child (or rather my dear friends, because this letter is for Carle as well as for you),

Tomorrow Wednesday at midday, I will be at the hearing to ask for the visitor's pass required from Mr Fillon. You would have seen me on Saturday if your parents had not come to warn me that this permission would not yet be granted.

Your letter was delightful, but I have even less courage than you to write letters which will be read by the police. It is not because I am afraid of showing my feelings and bearing my soul. I would reveal all that willingly; and what they would see there would perhaps change their hearts which God's light might illuminate some day. But I have an insurmountable loathing at being obliged to communicate expressions of belief, of friendship, of intimate dialogue even, under the eyes of those whose job it is to find guilty meanings in what is most sacred in life.

I have a deep spiritual love for you; that is what I can say. You are there in my heart very near to my own children, and what I suffer and want for them, I suffer and want for you.

Our colleagues are doing their utmost at the moment, being the kind of people they are, and everything will turn out for the best, because God wants the triumph of virtue and justice.

I do not really know which books to bring you; I shall risk the Corneille; then when I see you, we will see what you need. I do not know what you have read, that is my problem. Well we shall talk about it, and in the meantime the republican soul of Corneille will fly to yours. Farewell dear child, farewell Carle, my noble young friends I shake your hands both in a comradely and in a motherly way.

Your old friend,

Pauline Roland.

We are sure to be able to cater for your needs: do not worry about that. If you do not see me tomorrow it is because I have not obtained permission to see you.

Letter 3

no date

My dear child,

Yesterday I obtained a pass to see you and Carle from Citizen Fillon, but this morning just when I was getting ready to leave for the Madelonettes,[16] going past the police station I realized I had lost the pass, how, I do not know. Even if I apply for a new one I will certainly not arrive on time to get it. Tomorrow we have to settle the matter of the person who we are pretty sure got you arrested by a concocted denunciation. So I will not be able to see you yet. Your case comes up on Monday and I foresee that to be able to shake both your hands I will have to wait until Wednesday. On that day we will surely see one another, because I have no doubt that Mr Fillon will give me a duplicate pass.

What I learnt about your plan for your defence on Monday filled me with joy. It is truly religious, it is simple, it is noble and good, just as it behoves the apostles to speak of their brothers, even when these brothers, still blinded by ignorance and prejudice set themselves up not as judges but as enemies.

Faith! hope! courage! The future belongs to us, because what we want is the reign of justice and truth. It is the will of God! I hope that you are well, that you see your family regularly and that that is a relief for you. Our dear Carle is less fortunate because he is more alone. May this letter bring him a token of my esteem and my deep friendship.

As for me I am really miserable and even a little ill because of my problems. The question of my little girl, which should be settled tomorrow, does not seem to be getting sorted out the way it should. Well, God's will be done! And no matter what happens not one word of complaint will cross my lips.

Farewell my noble and dear child, shake the hand of our friends in the Madelonettes for me. All those who suffer for justice and truth are our friends. I shake both your hands.

Your old friend,

Pauline Roland.

Best regards to our friends.

Letter 4

Paris, 3 May 1850

My dear child,

I really am unfortunate. On Wednesday I went with Perot[17] to the public prosecutor's office to obtain permission to see you. The prosecutor didn't come. Today I went back. He was not on duty. Tomorrow I have my classes to teach when he is available. Moreover neither on Sunday nor on Monday am I free to see you. Will I see you on Wednesday? I dare not build up my hopes. Yet I am most unhappy, and I admit that it is heartbreaking not being able to see you. I discovered at the public prosecutor's office that Carle had got out and when I arrived home I found his card with the words '*case dismissed*' scrawled on it in pencil. As for you, you are being kept in, for that unfortunate gun no doubt ... . Well it will be a matter of only a few days I hope. Then we will meet again and begin working with renewed courage and God will come to our help as he does to those devoted to the good.

Some days ago, I was subjected to a little home visit [by the police] which put my papers in a state of great disorder, and will delay the publication of my letters on the Association, a publication which I was going to begin at last, and for which I had an agreement with a publisher.

It is a great blow to me. I hope at least that there will not be any further delay in returning my papers to me. I have been deeply saddened by this arbitrary act against a poor woman who has done no other wrong than to love the Republic deeply and seek above all else, Justice and the Kingdom of God.

I will have my little wolves at home for these two days' holiday, and your last letter led me to hope that you would complete the celebration. There will be one of my children missing this time again: but we will think of one another won't we?

I have recent news of François[18] who is in Savoie, where he is about to leave to give himself up. Otherwise he is well. He shakes your hand. Viard[19] is doing another newspaper, I have just received the second issue. He was kind enough to reproduce my latest article on the caterers. Finally Guepin's[20] book is about to be published; and I have finished the unending job that I had to do. I have the first ten pages which I am very happy with. That is all I think except that I really love you like a mother, and that my children embrace you cordially, Jean and the little girl especially.

Farewell then, my child, everyone loves you, misses you and shakes your hand.

Your old friend,

Pauline Roland

Letter 5

Paris, 9 May 1850

My dear child,

Perot still could not obtain a pass to see you and neither could I. I am going to try to get one for Sunday but it is no longer Mr Fillon who gives them, and I do not know whom to ask. However, I shall go on Saturday to the *Palais de Justice* to ask for one.

I saw your worthy mother the day before yesterday, and I asked her, in case I should not see you again, to tell you how much I am suffering from your absence. I do not know how to and cannot write to you as I would like, the idea that my letters are being handled by strangers inhibits me and arrests everything, even my train of thought. It will not alter my affection for you, you can be sure of that.

Everyone sends love and wishes you were among us. On Sunday we had a meal with Carle; myself and the children and the Perots. We had just been listening to the wretched Thierry[21] who had asked to be heard, not with the intention of vindicating himself but with the aim of persuading us to erase the word 'expelled' from the article that we are going to publish in the newspapers. The editorial decision was maintained unanimously. I can think of no deeper humiliation than the one that this wretch showed in front of us. I was the one who read the accusation which I had drawn up. He was standing right in front of me, trying from time to time to raise his eyes but unable to bear my look. Since he couldn't get us to change our minds he tried threats. He would sue us for libel, he said. Today the same article will be sent to the following papers: *Voix du Peuple*, *République*, *Démocratie*, *National* and *Presse*. Here is the gist:

'The association of [blank] and [blank] hereby gives notice to democrats that according to the two consecutive decisions taken unanimously on Sundays 21 April and 5 May 1850, Mr Albert Thierry has been expelled.'

We will probably sign the note in the names of Perot, yours and mine. We have decided that your name should continue to figure alongside ours in all public declarations of the association. It goes without saying that you will receive the items.

The headquarters will be transferred to Carle's place, where meetings will be held. The sale of Perot's day school has forced us to make this change. Our poverty prevents us from renting a permanent office.

Farewell my dear child, I love you from the bottom of my heart. My children embrace you.

Pauline Roland.

Letter 6

Paris, 29 May 1850

My dear child,

I do not know if you heard what your guard said to me, about the frequency of my visits. What he said prevents me from going to see you today, and I do not know how to go about getting an extended permission from Mr Roux Dufort. I will still try anyway and no matter what happens you can count on it that in a week from today, I shall spend as much time as possible with you. I hope that there will not be as much of a crowd as on Sunday and that we will have a cosier chat together which is what we surely both need.

I have requested the first volumes of ecclesiastical history from the library and I hope that they will be given to Perot who is willing to take charge of them and take them to you. See if you need anything else and I will fetch it; I wrote a letter to Citizen Delonne posted on Monday in which I urged him either to take what you need or else to leave it off here. I am waiting for his reply. The same goes for the various small amounts belonging to the association, which I am trying in vain to recover. This and the absolute state of destitution I find myself in explains why we are sending you nothing. I am not excusing myself; but I want to tell you that I have lived on 3 francs 50c. last week and I have to live on the same this week. I would not complain only it concerns more people than myself.

I shall not talk to you about politics. My heart is broken, and I feel humiliated when I see the current problems and universal cowardice. My gut feeling is that we are plunged back again about twelve years into the subservience that February [1848] had tried to and did rescue us from. We will have to work strenuously on the conversion of souls because a real victory can only come from that, one which is not destroyed the day after a conquest. Let us begin with ourselves. Let us seek justice and truth. Let us educate the few children entrusted to our care to be worthy citizens of this Republic of God whose reign will finally come some day. Yesterday I received an excellent letter from our friend Gautrin. He hopes to come to Paris, because he longs for a life of devotion to the cause. I think that we have made a great gain there even though he does not seem to be as much of a revolutionary as we are. For all sorts of reasons, I am inclined to believe that we are of that persuasion because that is our nature.

And now farewell my dear child, I do not want to say how much I miss you; that would increase the pain of your captivity. It is really because my heart has adopted you as a son, and I am so used to having you near me, to scold you like an older brother of my son Jean. Those days will return no doubt; but what is the good of separation of people who love one another? I will not send you the pages of Guepin's book because I am in dire need of them for an urgent job. As for the rest I have just read what our friend has written on the first five centuries of the Christian era. I do not know if it is accurate but it goes entirely against my feelings. The chapter on Pélage, which was inspired by a few words that I had told him on the matter, according to what the doctor wrote to me, seemed abysmally weak to me. Will all those Christian sources, which would illuminate so clearly the path to socialism if they were well known, never be dug out without bias, without prejudice? Try then my child, to study history seriously. Your just but passionate soul can give you immense enlightenment I'm sure. I studied very badly and now I do not know how to and no longer want to do it. In fact, apart from my ability to teach young children to read, I no longer feel good for anything but retirement. But from there could I not still show the way to those starting their career?

Farewell then my child, take heart, not to be able to withstand prison, I know you well enough to believe that it is not necessary to exhort you to endure that, but to be able to withstand the moral and physical pain of life which gets too much to bear internally and externally. Have the courage to endure loneliness, the absence of any religious attachment, the real cause of all our troubles and our greatest difficulty. I who am so weak and prone to discouragement like a child, I who am so shamefully ill prepared for life, am crying out to you to have courage. This word courage, coming from me, is nothing more than a cry of my weakness to yours. Let us unite to resist.

Farewell, I embrace you affectionately,

Your old friend,

Pauline Roland

Letter 7

Paris, 14 June 1850

My dear child,

I ran as fast as my old legs would carry me to the *Palais de Justice* to see you in court on Wednesday and above all to shake your hand as you passed: a useless endeavour. Your case was over, and I looked in vain for Citizen Malapest to find out the result. A lawyer whom I stopped in the corridor because he was blond, told me that he thought that the sentence had been upheld, just as I had been anticipating.

Lunched in the *Palais* ... ,

It is impossible for me to say truthfully that I know all the roundabout means. I had to leave without finding out anything of interest to me. Then I went to the Madelonettes, where I stayed and waited for you, as long as they were prepared to tolerate my presence. The black maria brought back other prisoners and I went sadly home, heartbroken, not knowing when I would see you, because double prison bars threaten to separate us. If you have gone back into the Madelonettes, our friends must have told you that I am implicated in the Rue Michel le Comte case. Like the former gallant knights I have given my word to give myself up as a prisoner as soon as the prosecutor summons me.

My interrogation lasted three hours; the public prosecutor was quite agreeable. I think I was, too, having felt within me no other desire than to have truth triumph.

I have no worries at all about the outcome of this matter because if men are the judges, God would not allow the sacred cause to perish under the error of their judgement. For those who have this living faith, this profound belief, what is suffered physically is of little importance. My children are all really well settled, the three of them. They will come and see me on visiting days if I am kept a prisoner, and I hope that the place where they will receive the lessons I will try to give them will reinforce this teaching and their mother's character. I am not saying that I am resigned to it, I am indifferent. That is the truth. I feel fine no matter where I am as long as I can strive to have God's will triumph everywhere.

Write to me quickly to tell me of your whereabouts. If it is at St Pélagie prison I will try to see you on Sunday, before the meeting. I shall be in despair if you are in the Madelonettes because the meeting is to take place at 1 o'clock. Yet I need to see you and have so much to tell you. I cannot write these letters which I know are sure to be read by the clerk.

Still I need to talk to you about Miolan. I gave him an appointment for Friday the 7th, as we had agreed; I left him a letter because I had to go out very early but he didn't come for it. Since then I have found an apprenticeship box-maker. He would have his board and lodging there in a family of fine decent people. I would have written to him myself about it if our friends in the Madelonettes had not suggested to me that it might be better for someone else to do it. I'm sending you the poor kid's mother's address:

Mme Mialon, 29 Quai Napoléon.

Needless to say that I shall do everything in my power to help him.

If you are taken back into the Madelonettes I will go and see you again on Wednesday, but I will leave early to chat for longer with you.

The children are well and so am I and all our friends. Perot has gone to the country, I do not know when he will be back. Goodbye dear child, I send you a warm embrace.

Your friend,

Pauline Roland

Fraternal greetings to our friends; because wherever you find yourself you are bound to find some. My friends from the Madelonettes told me to write to the Conciergerie. If you are no longer in the Madelonettes tell me when it is possible to see you.

Letter 8

Conciergerie, 4 January 1851

My dear child,

I have been a prisoner in the Conciergerie for two days; our plea was rejected this morning. Therefore at this moment I have only five months and twenty-nine days to do. I am not completely used to my new home, which looks out on to the Rue de Provence, with the precious advantage of having no smoke, which could be attributed to the total absence of stove and fireplace. On the other hand it is true that it is very cold, but is that surprising for the month of January? Anyway I am only here provisionally and will return or rather go to St Lazare one of these days.

But since I have begun describing my cell let us complete this little tour round my room. It is less fun but no less philosophical than the other. It will be the *other* which will bear the cost of this one, because *my person* is absent. Only a beast would dwell within walls three metres thick.

Louis IX was a great King. You know my profound admiration for this monarch but what an architect! Sure, the brave and dignified king was not responsible for his place having been transformed into a prison, and for a poor old woman coming to replace vigorous armed soldiers. So I am not blaming him.

I have three beds which gives me ten mattresses and as many bed covers. I have taken one off to make a carpet and no one has said anything. I have just transformed this carpet into a footmuff and I am still cold. The cell is freezing. A superb tiled floor has replaced the parquet floor. The vaults are of stone. Ah! My child if you get yourself arrested make sure it is in the middle of the summer!

I have two tables too low to write on and three chairs too high, so that with my short sight my neck is twisted. Two boards complete the furniture along with a bucket. Contrary to what you might believe the latter is not there to provide for my aristocratic tastes, I found it in the apartment. I did not find any light and my candle (luxurious!) is there stuck on the table with a drop of wax. I cannot hear the clock chime and am going to make the evening last as long as this candle does which I think measures five hours. I am relating this and telling you about all my little discomforts to forget the bigger ones. My popery did not prevent me from crying like a child yesterday when I found myself alone separated by prison bars from my children and all those I love. I went through two or three hours of real agony. Our precious association has me worrying as well. Perot has promised to do all he can to save it but ... well for these things we have to trust Providence. Even Proudhon[22] himself would not be able to accuse us of being in the wrong for doing that, considering the state of powerlessness we are reduced to.

Speaking of Proudhon, his window is opposite mine. But do not worry, not only are we not devouring one another but we will not even catch so much as a glimpse of one another. The authorities have had put on his window one of those handsome shades in a funnel shape with which you are familiar.

I saw your parents the other day and have been told that you are in prison once again. I can easily understand why you have come back to such a delight.

Ah! I have just arranged something I am delighted about. I have put a chair on its side with a pillow on top of it and here we have a perfectly comfortable seat. I have decided about the furniture. If I am here for several days, tomorrow I will have a sofa. I am waiting for the director's reply before turning one of my beds into a sofa. Forgive the trivialities.

But farewell my dear child, you have had enough of all this nonsense. For you outside, it will waste your time but it will save mine. All I want now is to be able to embrace you warmly.

Your old friend,

Pauline Roland

Your parents were well on Friday but they had no news of your sister. My children are well and send their love. Viard should write to me.

Letter 9

Paris, 17 January 1851

My dear child,

I have received no letter from you other than the one dated the 21 December which your mother handed to me and I have it before me now. I have news of you regularly from her because ever since I came into prison, she has been looking after me the way she looked after you. After reading your last letter the day before yesterday I wrote off to De Berry at once. I told him to write to you immediately if he found you anything and I gave him your address. I will press him on this when I see him again, but when will I see him? We have two hours in the parlour, one on Tuesday and the other on Friday. Apart from that matter I am very comfortable here, and I am working hard. True, I have a room to myself and Mme Nicaud lets me off cooking completely.

My health is excellent, and I am normally in good spirits although my companions, who are rather a dull and lifeless lot, leave it up to me to keep the conversation going. We meet three times a day for meals, first at coffee, then at lunch after which we read the paper aloud together while others sew, finally in the evening between six and seven for supper. After supper, reading. Schiller is on the programme at the moment. We are locked up at nine o'clock. I work from then until midnight or one. I get up at daybreak and begin by doing my cleaning and ablutions. You can see how much time I have for working.

I have done an article on the Rue de La Vrillière where I raise the question of luxury and that of republican politeness. I have at this moment the first of these moral issue letters I was telling you about. It is addressed to my son, about the duty of a man and a socialist. I have to stop because of an awful pain in my tooth which I used to cut something when I was doing some mending. You will know that a letter about religious feeling is on its way to you. For Mme Greppo I have one on solidarity. Mme Bachellery wants one. I do not know what to do it on. Besides she would consider it to be argumentative. We shall see.

Mme Bachellery who brought me my Mimi [Irma] today informed me that she has made it up with them [the Greppos?]. Admittedly I did the right thing not to get angry with them. If that was the case no doubt she would be forcing me to patch things up today.

Write me a long letter, my dear child, and remember this: the friendship of your old friend is indestructible. It is past midnight. My teeth (what a striking metaphor) continue to hurt me. Goodnight then,

Your adoptive mother, Pauline Roland

Letter 10

Saint Lazare, 27 January 1851

Dear child,

Your letter which reached me yesterday informs me that you received the one I wrote from here on the 17th but not the one I sent from the Conciergerie dated on the 4th. Have you received the one which I had sent via your mother? I have not received a reply. In all, since your departure I have only received two letters. I am not reproaching you with anything my child, I am stating a fact, that is all. And now I am going to reply as best as I can, the best in here means as accurately as possible.

My confined existence has been altered somewhat over the past few days. They have stopped our evening reading, locking us up at half past seven. You know that it is against my principles to ask for the aristocratic privileges of a political prisoner. My companions who are more submissive than I am, from all points of view, do not complain whatever happens and these things change according to the whims of those in power guarding us, without any prior warning. Yesterday I nearly missed my supper because of a verbal decree, and it was only thanks to the serving girl on duty who protested I think, that I was not locked up in my cell with only a jug of water with me and not even a crust of bread. But what does all that matter? I think as little as possible about all these small discomforts and I find prison is quite bearable.

I see my children on Sunday in the parlour with the lawyers, in the presence of the warders, but I am separated from them by a screen. One hour is the time allotted for our hugging and kissing which the weeping of poor Mimi interrupts every time. The poor little thing breaks my heart. Those tears fall so silently but so bitterly that I feel as if each one is burning my heart. Jean is harder, but is also sad, only my Moses is his usual self, affectionate, smiling and calm. Anyway to obtain this singular favour of seeing my children for one hour on a Sunday I had to write directly to Mr Carlier. I had actually asked, one, to see them on Sunday, two, to have them in my room. The parlour is all I got; why would require too many explanations. Carlier returned my letter to the governor telling him to do whatever was possible. The director claims to be a socialist republican, his generosity went this far. Moreover I had written about Justice and even mentioned the matter of a poor unfortunate woman locked away in prison! I do not want to ask for any favours. I do not want to owe anything to these good republicans who are more anxious to run with the hare and hunt with the hounds than to act according to their title. Today these people are not a threat. When they do become a danger and it is time to rise and judge them, I want to do so in complete and absolute freedom. You know that through Béranger[23] I could obtain almost anything I want, but you also know what would be reported in the *Moniteur*.[24]

Anyway this time in prison will not be wasted and I hope to leave here with more observations which will further inform my proposed work on the education of prisoners. The mother superior seems to be a remarkable woman, even if she is blinded by a Catholic mentality. At one point I was just about to have a chat with her on improving the running of the establishment but an unfortunate incident beyond my control prevented me. However, we shall see.

François is well. Charassin[25] says that he is afraid that he is becoming so comfortable down there that when the time comes for his release he will forget to leave. And there you are back in prison yourself, my dear child. I beg you for the sake of the affection I have for you, do not be annoyed by this teasing. De Berry is still looking for something for you. Tell us what you want him to find or if you want to stay where you are.[26] What you were saying about those men down there does not surprise me, no doubt we are arguing among ourselves; but we all need indulgence, intelligence, love, to convert them. Besides are we any worthier? For my part I must say I am deeply humiliated at my lack of goodness when I examine myself thoroughly. You and some friends end up giving me illusions about myself but deep down I am still not worth much, I know. Yet you and others tell me that my affection is a great comfort to you. I do not want to despair of myself.

Let us not talk of these physical discomforts of prison which we can succeed in ignoring. It is true that I am talking about it in comfort since I have just arrived and I am in a special category, pampered with the privileged, looked after by my friends. But I certainly suffered in the Conciergerie. I think I was cold and hungry and discomfort got the better of me during the first night. But what does all that matter? I think we have been softened by Christianity. We should force ourselves to return to ancient stoical values.

I do not know if the Association will reply to you. Perot came to see me twice. I have had no word from the others. Yesterday I sent my vote to the new commission. Desmoulins[27] or Perot, whom I was counting on seeing tomorrow will let me know what is happening. Dearbeyrette must have left for Ahundi by now. I intend to write to him very soon. But I shall have to slow down my letter writing mania. This letter is the hundredth one that I have written since my entry into prison (no more no less). Around five per day, and I see I have planned to write another eleven. Certainly I intend to reply to you promptly. Send me either an article or notes on the Dijon associations. You could do that in the form of a letter to me and I will definitely have it inserted in *La République*.

I only have news of Viard through you. Farewell my dear child. I shall send your messages to all my little ones next Sunday. I embrace you from the bottom of my heart and hope that you will see to your stomach ache. I am in excellent health but I am not putting on weight. It looks as if this thinness is incurable. I have an itchy head again. An awful stove pipe goes over this poor head and they have supplied me with plenty of wood.

Your old friend,

Pauline Roland

It is past eleven o'clock. I am going to bed so I can get up at daybreak.

I sleep very badly, perhaps because I go to bed late. Never before midnight, sometimes at two o'clock. I must do something about that. Write to me directly if you are not afraid of the censorious clerks. My letters all arrive very carefully opened. I receive very few but I see a lot of people.

Letter 11

Saint Lazare, 25 March 1852

I am impatient to reply to your letter, my dear child, and would have written much earlier if I had not been in the embarrassing position of not knowing where to send my letter.

Do not pity me too much for the misfortune which has befallen me, dear child. First of all, never have I been so calm as during this captivity and never have I been more convinced that there is good to be done everywhere. As I get older I am no longer troubled by the fits of anger which made me suffer so much in the past. I am no longer so intent on what I can achieve. Although my thirst and my worship of the infinite are as strong as ever I feel better because I can be patient as I have eternity before me to achieve it. Surely I will be in God's care wherever providence places me? What should I fear then?

When I returned from my interrogation and discovered that I was going to be transported, my first thoughts were for you. I prayed to God to calm your anger at what you would call an injustice. My poor child, they say that my first reply to the Judge sealed my fate. I do not believe that. Here it is anyway:

'Did you take part in the December uprising?'

'Physically no! In my heart I was completely with it.'

I myself think that my opinions have been condemned along with my friends and a little of this poor name which had already taken part in another revolution.

Apparently I was supposed to have been arrested early in December but they thought I had gone abroad. All the while I was quietly teaching and spending my spare time helping those who had been hit. Some day I will tell you all about my arrest which happened quite cheerfully in the middle of a fry-up, cooked and eaten in the presence of the police who declined to share in it. Then my triumphant return to St Lazare after 13 days in police cells. All this was rather farcical.

I have asked permission from the War Office to take my children with me. My information about the sanitary conditions of the country are such that I will just leave Moses here, provisionally no doubt. Jean is very good in all this, calm, firm, already a citizen and an upright man. Mimi is still sad, sweet and loving as you know. Moses is keeping well, sweet and gentle as you know. I see them for two hours every Sunday, François twice a week. But that is about all. Jean and François have examined my file. Deportation with second degree, that is, colonization. Ten years I think. Several women have been condemned in a similar way.

If I am taken away unexpectedly, I would have my children brought out later when I am settled. Until then my friends and providence will take care of them. I assure you, my child, that whatever happens to me, my courage will be equal to the ordeal. We shall meet again, I believe, in this life and if we were not to find one another in this one we have loved one another enough to meet in the next.

Anyway I think that they cannot carry out the order to deport women, at least not yet. Seemingly there are no facilities whatsoever to receive us. They are talking of exile and prison there, would you believe. That is the very last alternative I would want. I cherish my beloved France so much that I would prefer anything on this dear earth, poverty, misfortune, prison, even death, rather than exile.

You know that all my friends have been hit. My God, all those arrested were my friends. Legrand is in Brest if not in Algeria. We were in police cells at the same time. I was able to shake his hand briefly and share my meagre funds with him. Ferdinand is well but terribly sad. He will write to you if I am not mistaken. Your good mother was able to see me once. She is still the best friend, the devoted angel you know her to be. She is the one who brought me my packet for the journey just in case I have to leave unexpectedly. My friends have provided me with a small sum of money deposited at the Court office. So now I am ready.

In the meantime I have been working as hard as I can for the past five days since I got a cell to myself. I am very busy, absorbed with the history of our first revolution and with my beloved Plato.

Farewell, I embrace you as a mother.

Pauline Roland

Cell 5

LETTERS FROM PAULINE ROLAND TO ANNE GREPPO[28]

Letter 12

Saint Lazare, 15 April 1852

My dearest friend,

I received your letter with the greatest pleasure. I was thinking that perhaps you had not received mine, and although I do not attach much importance to my prose, I was annoyed to think that those few lines that spoke of my affection for you should have been wasted.

Mme Huet[29] and Claudine[30] remain here with us. The first thinks she is to be transported: at least she says so at times, while at other times she states that the military court has decided on an exclusion order for her as it did for you.[31] Her friends are taking very active steps to obtain her release and they may well succeed. As to Claudine, she does not know nor does she even wish to know what is to be her fate. She has been really suffering the last few days, and I am very anxious about her. She heard yesterday from Hibruit who is well. I can truly say that like you, my noble friend, every day I hear news of the misfortune of some of my old friends of whom I have very few here now. For some of them, exile has entailed the most awful catastrophes. L__ has seen his wife actually go insane. Oh, my God! my God! why can I not fly to help so many unfortunate friends? Like you I deplore the fact that some of our group are forced to depart even farther away from our beloved France, which I always look upon as destined to regenerate mankind. But the emigration of those new religionists who are setting off for New America via England, reminds me of the voyage of the Puritans, which took place under very similar circumstances more than two centuries ago. The Puritans of the seventeenth century founded civil, political and religious liberties, on the other side of the Atlantic. In the same place our brothers will sow the holy seed of Equality and Fraternity which contains a religion in itself, that is to say a whole new civilization. It will magnificently radiate that sacred formula of the sweet words of Christ uttered long ago: 'Love each other as brothers'. And we ourselves, dear friend, are about to be transported to Africa, to that land from which, more than once, has shone forth a luminous ray of civilization. Are we too not the humble apostles of the new Gospel? God be praised, if our sufferings, if even death itself which we may meet in such a murderous climate, are the price to pay for the little good we may do.

To fulfil our daily mission in all simplicity by doing all possible good around us, that is what we have to pray to heaven for, that is happiness, no matter what those false teachers may say, who wanted to teach us to look for that happiness elsewhere.

Nonetheless, my friend I must admit it, although generally calm and prepared for everything, my heart is broken at the thought of my beloved children. I have kind friends, but scarcely anyone who comprehends life exactly as I do myself, can care properly for my beloved orphans. I would wish to arm them not against life but for life, to prepare them early for the rejection of our apostolic creed, which will be a necessary reaction for a long time, according to some at least, in this world in which vanity and ambition dominate. If my hand were withdrawn, how could that tender mould be impressed on those beloved creatures whose affection for their mother has rendered so pliable, too pliable perhaps.

At this moment, my son especially gives me cause for worry. My beloved child in whom I have never seen anything other than noble instincts, might fall into any one of those selfish weaknesses which society too easily condones. Will he preserve his purity far away from me? Will he preserve his openness of heart, or will he not be forced to 'make his way', as they say? Will they not impart to him those notions which I have guarded him from, as if from a poisonous germ? Will they not persuade him that he should seek his fortune in order to carry out the duties of a son towards an exiled mother, his brother and sister?

Dear friend, everything that is the envy of other parents is what I fear. In this world where one cannot find a place without displacing others, my first duty is to ensure that my children hold no position, that they remain poor. Let us maintain that simplicity of life to which daily labour should suffice, whatever that labour may be.

If you see A__ beg him to tell P__ that I frequently receive letters from his daughter, and that I am very pleased with this dear child whose character is equal to her situation. He ought to know that D__ is an internee in Corsica. I think that that derisive reduction in his sentence may be changed into exile. Should we be taking steps to that end? Let them write on the subject and I will do my utmost.

A week has elapsed from the beginning to the ending of this letter. You have no idea what I have to do here. There are twenty-two of us, a quarter of whom can hardly write. I am the general secretary of the association. I also have much to do for myself, having to prepare for my children and myself in case of a sudden departure. At last things seem to be in order. I will have a little rest, and if they let us remain here, I mean seriously to recommence the long-neglected historical work for which I have a contract signed with the house of Didot; I do not know whether I have ever mentioned it to you; it is a history of women of France. Meanwhile I am reading the Gospel and Plato, which I used last year, during my imprisonment. It is a good and fortifying study to which I need to add very little.

Claudine and Madame Huet embrace you with all their heart. Our other ladies salute you most cordially. As for myself, you know how I love you and those belonging to you.

Pauline Roland

PS My affectionate compliments to the exiled ones who know and are fond of me.

Nothing, absolutely nothing to report about my case.

Saint Lazare, 23 April 1852

Just as I was finishing this letter, four new companions from the Loiret arrived, three of whom are mothers of families and the fourth a young girl of twenty one.

So many victims! God have pity in the end!

Letter 13

Saint Lazare, 13 May 1852

Dear friend,

It seems ages since I heard from you last, and yet I wrote you a letter on the 22nd April, which perhaps you have not received. The gentlemen of the police appear to be particularly greedy for my correspondence. For this reason, a few days ago, they confiscated a letter of mine from Barbès which I would have been happy to have received. Moreover, after having separated us from each other, for our good, these good people might furthermore be tempted to prevent us from writing for our own well-being.

I am taking advantage also of the opportunity of sending you my letter by a less direct but more sure route. How are you out there? The festivities now being celebrated are making us frightfully sad here.[32] Those cannon shots fired as signs of rejoicing appear to me as if they are striking the open breast of our dear and holy Republic, already so frequently injured. And yet we have truth on our side! Let them do as they will against us, our duty is to ensure and to activate the triumph of truth, by assisting Providence, which surely wants to ensure its triumph.

For my part, my friend, I have no other desire than to serve the holy cause, and I smile with pity when I think of those who imagine they will chain us here, whereas they are only giving me the rest I needed to recover my strength, as I was exhausted by my illness of December. What are they going to do with me and the other women confined here? They do not know themselves and I believe they are forgetting us. Maybe we will be here for a long time yet. Relying on that eventuality, I am preparing for work, which is up to now, what I have been unable to do, because of my accommodation. Nearly all the women which you have known here have asked for pardon, but this has got them nowhere. Four are exiled: Mme Frond, Catherine and Rey (Allier) are free, and Mme Bietry (Allier) is interned a hundred leagues away from her home. At present there are twenty-four of us: Mme Fouffé is condemned to eight months' imprisonment, six to Algeria plus, that is to say two in Algerian prisons; eleven to Algeria minus, that is to say, transportation to Algeria on parole, five administratively detained it would appear, one condemned to Cayenne. There are five of us, absolutely resolved to ask for nothing: Augustine Bean, Claudine, Mme Huet, Jarreau (Cayenne) and myself. It appears that Maupas[33] is furious with me. Much good may it do him. Really I am not afraid of him; the wretch can only kill my body.

Let me know if you can think of anything important to be done there for developing the social idea, for realizing the future community on a small scale. I have come round to thinking that it is the small groups converted here and there who will convert the world. More than ever I am convinced that revolution and social renovation can only be accomplished by the conversion of souls. If they send me to Algeria, I will do all in my power to act according to these principles. If they exile me, I will preach the new Gospel by all the means that God puts in my hands and we should all do likewise according to the limits of our strength. All that is still very little, for in spite of the exaggerated accounts they made of our people, counting millions of Socialists for our France alone, we are scarcely more numerous than the Christians during the first century.

We are as yet very much preoccupied with a thousand petty personal details, which take precedence over the general situation. I am writing to you all about this, because I too am obsessed in this way, and no matter what I do, I cannot keep myself busy with anything else, and yet I too have my big personal preoccupation. I do not know what will become of my poor children for whom my friends can do very little, scattered as they are, and scarcely any one of them knows how to survive in the land of exile or in transportation. My Moses is sick, and I am seriously worried because my friend S__ on whose kindness towards him I can depend, will very likely be forced by the state of his health to leave his institute. On the other hand the uncertainty in which they hold me prisoner is preventing me from making an energetic appeal to any one of my acquaintances who is still free, which I would have every right to do, if I were more harshly or severely treated. In the end God, the protector of the widow and the orphan, will surely come to their aid. The excellent Mme Bachellery wrote to tell me not to be anxious for my daughter, but I know how difficult her situation is. I feel very remorseful, leaving her so burdened, but God will come to her help too.

Write to me, my friend, and always address your letters to J__ who will convey them to me. Do not forget that you are by far the woman that I love and esteem the most.

Again, farewell, your friend

Pauline Roland

EXTRACT OF LETTER FROM PAULINE ROLAND TO MME BACHELLERY, 52, RUE DU ROCHER

Letter 14

[No date]

... It was Tuesday 22 June 1852. As usual some friends, faithful visitors to the bleak prison, had come to greet us. All were calm, almost cheerful. There was a rumour that Mr Bonaparte had promised Uncle Jerome that women would not be transported. There would be a general amnesty on the 15th August setting us all free and if anyone had been accepted she could freely choose the path of exile. However, we did not share the confidence or the joy of our friends; we had just heard another fateful rumour. The rumour was the death of a hero of democracy. The noble and heroic Barbès was supposed to have been killed in his prison by a policeman![34]

The period after dinner was a long agony for us. Once they locked us up I decided to write to Belle Isle to find out the truth, the whole truth. No sooner had I gone to bed at ten o'clock, than I heard footsteps in the corridor and a disturbance. It occurred to me that we too might be killed. I arranged myself in my bed to die decently dressed. Then I extinguished the light and slept the sleep of a child which God sends the prisoner as a refreshing balm.

I had been sleeping for two hours when my door was opened with a great racket. Two pale nuns, each holding a candle as if they were funeral candles stood by my bed and urged me to get up. 'Are we leaving for Algeria?' I said.

'Alas! Yes, you poor woman.'

'Long live the Republic!' I arose immediately. But a cry of horror struck my ears. I assumed it had been uttered by one of my companions. I ran to each of their cells. They were all steady and smiling. It was a young nun who had involuntarily let out this exclamation and who no doubt will have been punished for it. Soon some men arrived and the prison director, oblivious of the emotional upheaval he was creating, went from room to room calling out these words to each of us as if he had learnt them by heart: 'Ladies, get ready, you are leaving for Algeria. At one thirty you will leave the prison. I have only just received the news an hour ago, otherwise I would have told you earlier.'

We hurried, raced around half dressed, in haste to prepare our packages, not one of which could leave the prison without the humiliating formality of a search. We shook hands, some wrote to bid a last goodbye to their children, to their friends. Then, afraid we would be separated from one another, we divided up the money a few of us had in our possession. All this time the men went from cell to cell mingling as they pleased with the nuns, without a single one of them having any regard to the laws of propriety being violated. The jailers do not consider a female prisoner as a woman. The important thing for them was to get these wretched women away on time whom the new Council of Ten had condemned, operating as it did in dark secrecy like the odious Venetian court had done long ago which history has long since condemned as an aberration.[35] One of our companions, only just recovering from a serious illness, was summoned to leave with us. Two women held her up by the arms, and the warders excused her from standing for the roll call, no doubt for fear of seeing her fall in a faint. The tallest woman, still quite young, remarkably beautiful and quite famous, now seemed prostrate by age and suffering. Strands of white hair strayed from her black hat. She was the very personification of torture endured, a living protest against the iniquity of deportation!

At last we were ready. We went down into the dungeon where they locked us up for a while again in that famous cage from whence once before they extracted us to be delivered up to General *Comte de Goyon*. This time it was not such an eminent person, we had come simply to perform the derisory formality of the release which would only be a transfer. ... Led by their mother superior, the nuns came to settle up the little accounts of labour done for the prison by some of us, and the work was inspected so closely, so scrupulously examined that they deducted about half of the wages from women without any other resources! Moreover to do justice to these *saints of God*, we must add that they uttered not a word of consolation or sympathy, neither did they offer as much as a glass of water to these poor sacrificial victims about to set out for exile along a route fraught with danger. No doubt this would have seriously broken the iron commandment, the first article of which seems to be: 'Thou shalt not love'.

Oh Christ! You for whom these women carry a disfigured image on their breast, would you ever have guessed that in your name, they would banish love and pity from their souls, and change into stone this heart which God gave to every woman to make her an angel of mercy and consolation? Noble Theresa, you emitted this sublime cry as you contemplated the tortures of Satan: 'Poor creature, he does not love me!'. What would you have said about this decadence of your daughters?

However, since it was daybreak the prison commander decided to change his mind and allow us our ration of food. He had it brought to us and in spite of our reluctance stuffed as much as he could into the small numbers of baskets in our possession. Henceforth we no longer belonged to Saint Lazare. We were handed over to police custody, to numerous sergeants who bustled in armed with bludgeons. They had picked the biggest and the strongest of these brave knights from the Rue de Jerusalem. Impressive-looking pistols peeped out cheekily from their pockets kept half open intentionally. What an ignominy it was to have to walk arm in arm with them to the pier for Le Havre!

It was pouring. Nearly all of us had only our slippers on, and no coats; we were very poorly dressed. In vain we asked for a cab for which we offered to pay. We eventually succeeded in ordering one single cab for the patient and a cart followed with our luggage.

In broad daylight they would have locked us up in the awful black maria. But the streets were empty so they could drag us along on foot. In fact we only met one or two workers who stared at us trying to figure out the meaning of this silent procession which was neither a funeral nor a wedding. Some rich person's coach returning from a party perhaps on the Champs Elysée splashed us at the Chaussée-d'Antin. Further on we collided with a tramp stretched out in a doorway. As well as that we had to endure the gibes and the insults of the ignoble gentlemen to whom we were handcuffed.

As we went on to the landing stage by the cargo entrance we saw three lines of bayonets shining in the first light of dawn. It was the line-up of the representatives of ancient chivalry, the support of French honour, who, I had been informed, rifles at the ready and trigger released, had come to supervise ten women going on board, after which France could sleep in peace! They shoved us into two wagons where the inevitable police town sergeant received the order bellowed out to take note of everything we said. Numerous police officers placed in other wagons were to accompany us, some to Brest, some to Algiers.

But what were we waiting for? Why did they throw us into these wagons which were not due to leave before four in the morning? We were waiting for none other than our brothers, fellow deportees – two hundred and ten men in all, who had been brought from the Bicêtre prison to leave with us.

They stared at us in surprise. Some of them wondered who we were. Nobody really knew. The bravest took the risk of raising their caps, but on the whole they skirted around us with that worried look of the mice that the good La Fontaine described when they had to recognize Rodilard covered in flour. Of course our friends expected a trap. In fact much later we learned that the police had cleverly manoeuvred to inspire them with this suspicion. They had been hoping they would hear hurtful insults heaped on us!

We would have liked to have been given something from the hand of a brother in the same way that Christ received the sponge dipped in honey and vinegar on Golgatha from the hand of an unknown soldier.

Once the loading was complete, the skipper blew his whistle which was the sound for us of the final signal of exile and we went off full steam ahead for ... the sea.

Pauline Roland

LETTER FROM PAULINE ROLAND TO CLAUDINE MONNIOT (HIBRUIT)

Letter 15

Sétif, 11 August 1852

The post from Algiers has arrived, dear and good friend. I was counting on it bringing a letter from you especially since I had written a long letter to you myself from Bougie which ought to have reached you by the 4th or 5th of this month. I was hoping for at least ten letters, at least as many from Paris as from different parts of Algeria and I did not receive a single one. I am not blaming my friends, you know that anyway, but I am suffering so much from this cruel silence.

A fortnight since our parting, dear good friends, during this fortnight I have endured tough physical torture but this torture was nothing compared to my moral suffering. Why was I forced to leave you my poor sisters? Why? But to all these gentle 'whys' no other response than an inflexible 'because'. So it is better to avoid asking why as much as possible.

Tell me about yourselves. Would all those who can write without too much trouble write to me as often and as much as possible. Leaving you all for me was leaving my family and France all over again. ...

If you want to get to Sétif you should come by Philippeville not via Bougie and arrange to travel overland and on stretchers. The journey by Bougie was a real torment for me. I thought I was going to die on the way and when I got here, I could not move for days. None of the weariness of the route so far had prepared me for this. Mme__ and you my Claudine would certainly not survive it. Imagine the hill up to Fort Gregory going on for thirty leagues in a heat of forty degrees, in the splitting sun, without a tree to shade under, and all that on the back of a mule on a packsaddle chafing you from the start. It was impossible to walk after nightfall because of the Kabyles, and for a night's rest nothing but the bare ground in the open air, in the midst of the guards or Arab tribes. I would not have wanted to miss the opportunity of going on this journey which I found very interesting but I would not wish it on any woman.

From the second day on my hands and face were swollen along eight or ten lines from sunstroke and all covered in huge water blisters as if coals had been run all over them. My brain was affected by it for some days and I do not know how I did not fall ill. Now my skin is peeling as if after a burn and new blisters are coming up and thanks to the mule I could not sit down for a week. So if anyone is coming here they should be very careful. They should take plenty of supplies for the journey because there are hardly any on the way. There is just bread and wine available only in two places, one six leagues from Bougie and one about six leagues from Sétif. The trip lasts three or four days. There are some watering holes here and there, but that is all.

Farewell friend and friends! May God keep you and protect us all.

Your sincerely devoted friend

Pauline Roland

LETTER FROM PAULINE ROLAND TO MADAME BACHELLERY

Letter 16

Sétif, 12 August 1852

I was unable to write to you while I was prisoner good and dear friend. The eyes of these jailers, who inevitably came between you and me, filled me with complete loathing. Furthermore I have not had one minute's solitude since I left Paris on the 23rd June until my release on the 28th July on parole, as I was always kept in shared accommodation with nine to fifteen other women who, with the exception of one, were all perfect strangers to my way of thinking, although perfectly well meaning towards me.

Well, since the day I anticipated what was in store for me, I found it impossible to attend to my poor children without collapsing into a dreadful state of anguish which brought on outbursts of nervous fits. I can admit this to you and a few select souls but I cannot make it common knowledge.

I am writing positively about my situation, going into great detail in letters sent off with every post, to my son and our friend François [Ferdinand] and I am asking them both to keep all my friends informed, among whom you rank first and foremost. I hope they are doing so, and if not I authorize you to claim this right. Furthermore I am writing, and I will finish, I hope, under the title of *Memoirs of a Prisoner of War* a tiny episode of a great struggle in which I got myself involved. I shall only talk to you about intimate details and also about those which personally concern you in this letter.

First my daughter, my poor little Irma, whom I love more than I thought it was possible! May God bless you for having placed you on the path of my life, noble and saintly woman, for preventing me from falling into despair, even into remorse at having thrown myself into public life without wondering if my maternal duty would be equally fulfilled. May God reward you friend for taking in the orphan and making less bitter the taste of this chalice of gall which I must drink in its entirety. Bring up my daughter in strength, simplicity and republican virtue. Poor little one! What sorrow, what loneliness surround her cradle! And yet what smiles, what affection, what family qualities surrounded her until now! Her mother seems to be destined to be deprived of the same precious family atmosphere because of her faith! Bless you again noble and saintly woman!

When will I be able to earn anything in Algeria? God knows. By granting me my so-called freedom that is actually internment, the clerical influences have expelled me to a rock where I am chained like Prometheus long ago and threatened with the vulture of hunger. I was told formally that I have been put here to stop me from doing anything because – I do not know by what Machiavellianism – they still insist in regarding me as an excessively dangerous person. I have to struggle against punishment meted out from sheer hatred and which tortures my soul all the more since you have all spoilt me by exceeding kindness, by constant friendship. If it was just my own life I was fighting for I would wrap my head up like the ancient Caesar and calmly wait for death as a delivery and as a step towards a better world.

But I owe it to my children. I owe it to this truth for which God deemed me to be the humble apostle. So I shall fight on for the triumph of this sacred truth. I shall fight but with love for the same unfortunate people who believe they hate me and who use lies and subterfuge to conquer justice, those weak souls who will not win!

I do not know how it is, dear friend, that every step I take in this painful life convinces me even more of the righteousness of our cause, of the truth of what we proclaimed. Everywhere I see ignorant women, slaves because of that very unawareness of the slavery of men. The Gordian knot is definitely still there. We have been right for twenty years!...

I saw my poor fellow women deportees, in whom every aspect of the condition of European woman seemed to be personified. I had just studied the nuns and French courtesans in Saint Lazare prison. In Algiers I saw together in the same convent the nun, the penitent, the adulteress, the young girls brought up to become nuns, penitents or adulteresses. In Kabylie I saw women as beasts of burden and the odalisques of a rich harem. I slept near the former on bare ground, without even a bowl to drink from, near the latter on gold and silk, with a solid silver basin to wash myself in. Everywhere, friend, I thought of you because everywhere I felt that the future of the world depends on this question: the provision of a republican education for women.

What is to become of me? I do not know and frankly it matters little to me. The important question about that is this: do every day in simplicity all the good that every opportunity presents; do not try any longer to change the world in such and such a way but only try to do one's duty as the case arises.

A few days ago in the harem of a *kaid* this duty seemed to me to enlighten and especially love these poor women, my sisters, tarnished by a degrading slavery. I would have loved to have been able to send you a magnificent child of six years as physically developed as my daughter, but who will (alas!) be sold as a slave in a few years. I could not speak the language and it is difficult to study Arabic.

I wanted to meet the *kaid*, but was unable to, even though they promised to let me see him, but I might not be staying in Sétif, and there again it might take a month only to discover that I cannot leave there. We shall discuss these poor Arab women again, my friend.

In the meantime, farewell: excuse this scribble rushed along with the pen, embrace all our girls for me. Please give my daughter the enclosed note and tell Perot that I shall write soon. I have not said anything to you for Mr Bachellery. This letter is for both of you. Having met a blessed union in my life I am careful not to separate a happy couple in my heart. Farewell then dear friends. The six hundred leagues which separate us will never divide us.

I love you.

Pauline Roland

LETTERS FROM PAULINE ROLAND TO CLAUDINE MONNIOT

Letter 17

Sétif, 1 September 1852

My dear Claudine

I was expecting word from you by the previous post, but it has not arrived. I am not complaining, it is enough to love as I do for one not to believe that those who are loved have to return every favour they receive.

Our friend D__ has written to say you are interned in Algiers with your friend. I congratulate both of you. He wrote to say that I was free to return to France. I am waiting for official word and I do not know what I shall do if it is true. We have spoken so often about this in the past that you must know exactly what I feel about this news. It certainly is not joyful ... . Some people are very hard to please and I am one of them. I have never been sadder, more tortured than I am at present. And I cannot adequately explain the thousand legitimate reasons for this sadness, for this turmoil. The citizen in me is torn one way, the mother in me another, the woman another. The thousand ties which link me to life and which correspond to the fibres of my heart are all equally painful.

May God's will be done and may his name be blessed.

Will I ever see you again my friend? God only knows, and if we do not see one another again in this life, will you remember me well enough to recognize me in another? I sincerely hope so. I shall ask to go via Algiers if I am to return to France but will I be given this permission? Will I go back to France?

I shall let you know the way I decide to act when the official notice of my release, and a letter from my son which I am expecting on the 20th of this month, lets me know if I am to accept my liberty, to try to settle in Africa or to go over to England to suffer there with my friends.

Now this is what the citizen in me would like:

Send me by the next post an exact record of the political status of each of our companions in captivity, that is to say let me know who is to be interned and where, those who are to stay in prison and those who are being sent back to France. If you cannot make this list yourself, have someone else send it by the next post.

A letter from Paris also informed me that the sum of over one hundred francs is being sent for the needs of women deportees. This is not an official fund but has come from a collection of some women who hope to make it a monthly subscription. Please let me know how it should be distributed. The letter which contains it must have been sent from Algiers to Bône, from Bône to Constantinople, and most likely it will be sent to me by the post of the 4th. Several letters have arrived by this route. I am going to claim the money. If it reaches me before I leave, and if by the 10th I hear from you, I will distribute it as you decide. If I am obliged to leave without seeing or hearing from you I will send it to you to dispose of as best you can.

Farewell, my friend, I will never stop loving you.

Pauline Roland

Letter 18

Sétif 2 September

... As long as a woman is to be deported, I must be and want to be that woman; as long as some men are sacrificed to the Moloch of fear, women must share in the martyrdom. I do not know what has become of my companions, apart from two whom I know are interned in Algiers.

For the matter of my own personal security the following point must be considered: my imprisonment and deportation are no simple accidents, they are the consequence of my whole life, of the position I hold in the party. The order for my release was obtained by a kind of moral pressure from my friends, from journalists and from my son's success. This material change of circumstances has changed nothing fundamentally. If I were to return to France, I would be arrested on the first day back without doing anything, when it suits the authorities, and this time by virtue of the decrees of the regime under which we now live. I would be sent straight to Cayenne. A new kind of enemy has emerged to pursue me, the Jesuits. They will deal the blow unless the other lot do so more promptly. ...

Pauline Roland

THREE TEXTS BY JEANNE DEROIN IN EXILE

'Obituary for Pauline Roland' (*Almanach des femmes*, London and Jersey, 1852)
Introduction to *Almanach des femmes*, 1852
Introduction to *Almanach des femmes*, 1853

OBITUARY FOR PAULINE ROLAND BY JEANNE DEROIN[36]

(Deroin included two of Roland's letters written from Africa as part of the article)

PAULINE ROLAND
Pauline Roland has passed away!

She died by succumbing to the cruel horrors of transportation to Africa. The martyrdom of this holy and noble woman adds to the shame of our adversaries. It forms the last jewel in the crown of the new emperor of France, in that crown made of crime, blood and mire!

She died just as she reached French soil. The last struggle she withstood was to be fatal for her. She was deeply shattered by the decline of her native land, which she looked upon as a personal disaster. Ordered to return to those beloved children whom she already called orphans in her letters, she was on her way home, without having made any concession unworthy of her noble soul, of this we are certain, to devote herself once more to the sacred cause of truth and justice!

She expired and was too late to receive the comfort of the parting embraces of her beloved children. It would seem that this heavenly soul, unable to contemplate the humiliation of her fellow citizens, sought refuge in death rather than accept this long overdue release granted by a corrupt authority.

These thoughts come to me through the intimate knowledge I have of the tender but heroic feelings of this distinguished sister, whose society I valued so much during our shared captivity in Saint Lazare.

Alas! The unforgettable recollection of these moments, when our minds would meet and meditate together over the same ideas, is all the more painful as I write these sad lines in regretful homage and veneration to our friendship.

While in this prison, she devoted herself to relieving the moral and physical troubles of the unfortunate victims of social hardship who usually inhabit this depressing place. That noble woman exerted herself with a praiseworthy perseverance to stir a sense of moral dignity in these lost souls.

She had devoted her life to spreading the ideals of socialism and she ardently pursued the implementation of our principles, which she defended in her writings with a remarkable talent.

At this moment I am so overcome with sadness that I cannot do justice to an appreciation or a summary (as it ought to be done) of the numerous works where she developed the highest ideals on the social question. I will only recall that she helped to form the Association of Socialist Schoolmasters and Schoolmistresses which has been dissolved by the tyranny of Bonaparte, the rules of which, developed in an admirable programme that she prepared, will form the basis of education in the future.

Before 1848 Pauline Roland had been a member of the association founded by Pierre Leroux at Boussac. The friends with whom she then began a new life were strongly united to her by ties which death alas! has severed too soon.

Later, after February [1848], she was elected, by the general meeting of delegates, as a member of the central commission of the Union of the Associations. This ultimate proof of her esteem and the sympathy for the working classes was destined to expose her to the reactionary violence of the authorities who saw in all these efforts of social transformation evidence of the imminent emancipation of the people.

She was then pestered by police visits to her home. Her precious manuscripts were confiscated. As a result of the charges brought against the Union, she was summoned for trial, where we appeared together accused as criminals. For three whole days she exhibited that great energy and dignity of character of which she alone was capable.

She had only just left the dark prison of Saint Lazare and rejoined her children when, six months later, she was arrested after the 2nd December. Her friends had often pleaded with her to leave France. But she was as much attached to France as a daughter to her mother! She imagined that she could only heal her country's woes and get rid of her country's servitude by her personal presence even if it was at risk to her own life. Perhaps she did not fully perceive that to serve Humanity and to be useful to France, she should not have deprived her country of her noble qualities by dying.

She insisted that there were victims to be rescued from the fury of the reactionary government and that she could console and comfort those families scattered by death, imprisonment or exile.

Pauline wished to fulfil her sacred duty by encouraging the enthusiasm of those who had escaped proscription, to induce them to help their unfortunate brethren. But one day, soon after the arrest of her heroic and worthy friend Anna Greppo, she was arrested the very evening she had insisted on visiting her in prison.

During her cross-examination, when they accused her of having taken an active part in an insurrection in Saint Martin's square, this sincere republican replied: 'I was not personally but "mentally" present'. Interrogated at Saint Lazare by General Goyon, she continued to show the same firmness of principle. Consequently, she was transported to Africa. This at least spared Pauline and her associates the farce of a trial.

Two of her letters, inserted in the *Presse* and in the Belgian paper *Nation* describe some of the sufferings she had to endure. We consider it is our duty to reproduce these letters at this sad time, simply to prove the courage of our friend and the ignominy of her executioners.

We read in the *Presse*: 'What crime has the woman committed who wrote the two letters which have been sent to our office?'

Letters from Pauline Roland to Mme Bachellery

Fort St Gregory, 9 July 1852

I cannot allow the post to leave without writing something, if only a few words. The strange fashion in which we are held here means I have not had a minute's peace, nor the power to collect my thoughts.

I am quite well and my courage remains unshaken, that is the most important thing for you to know. We are now at Fort Saint Gregory, situated opposite Oran, just as the Valerian Hill is to Paris, only up on a steeper hill.

The officers of the ship the 'Magellan' thought that in a spirit of brotherly hospitality, we would be allowed to remain in the pretty village of Miserghin and later be interned in some inland town we might choose, but nothing of the sort. On our arrival at Mers-el-Kebir, we were handed over to the military authorities and locked up in Fort Saint Gregory.

There we had to sleep on straw, with no other diet than army rations, black bread but no wine or coffee. Add to this the great advantage we have as prisoners of only having one common sitting room and a very small yard.

I can say nothing about the country which I have only seen from the top of the army van which transported us to the fort and nearly broke our necks in the process. The road which leads to it is cut out of a perpendicular rock and is on the edge of a precipice. At one time even our coachman and guides, the Zouaves, were frightened. The horses stumbled: I turned my head away and many of my friends uttered such a cry of despair that our escort allowed us to ascend our cavalry on foot. This was indeed an awful scene. During the whole of our journey the weather was very bad. Before I regretted not having been permitted to bring my little girl with me, but now I thank God that she did not witness such horrors.

Algiers, 16 July 1852, Convent of the Good Shepherd

We arrived at Algiers on the evening of the 12th, after a most stormy passage of two days, during which we remained lying down upon the deck with no bedding other than a sail canvas for a mattress and a sailor's blanket. Indeed it is three weeks since we slept a single night in any sort of a bed or had a single good meal. In fact it is amazing that ten unfortunate women, nearly all of whom were weak and sickly when they left Paris, have been able to survive the sheer fatigue and the mental tortures to which we have been exposed.

I am happy, however, to state that in matters concerning the navy, everyone both on board the 'Magellan' and on board the 'Euphrates' which has transported us from Oran to Algiers, has given us every mark of kindness and of respect. But noone was expecting us, nobody was ready to receive us, and we were thus compelled to share the hardship of a sailor's life. On board the 'Euphrates' one of the officer's cabins was offered to me. I refused, as I did not wish to enjoy a privilege denied to my companions.

When we landed at Algiers we were escorted to the Convent of the Good Shepherd, but then our situation as prisoners became more painful than anything we had ever known, as you will see. We are kept here together with five female prisoners from the *départements* of the Mediterranean coast (Var, Hérault, Gers); in all fifteen women, all sharing one single room as our home which is almost completely filled by our 15 pallets so that there is only enough room left for a long table where we eat together. So as to form an even better idea, add to this a yard just double the size of our room, without any tree or anything to shelter us from the rays of the burning sun.

I know not if that is what Mr Guizot[37] intended, when he fanatically insisted on imprisonment with deportation, but such a sentence is intolerable, it is true hell.

Farewell, do send me some news especially of my dear children as I have not heard from them since I left France three weeks ago.

Pauline ROLAND

In this account of the sufferings which were to lead our beloved sister to the grave, a few words testify to her pure and disinterested conduct.

One of the officers' cabins was offered to her: 'I refused it,' she says, 'as I did not wish to enjoy a privilege denied to my companions'. The life and death of this noble woman are embodied in these words. She accepted transportation and all its stern severity. She rushed to martyrdom, and this martyrdom crowns with dignity the whole work of her life as she understood it. May this glorious example inspire real maternal love within the breast of every mother and of every woman. May they all understand that, through the law of solidarity which binds all beings together, they are mothers of every child, not just their own but of those of their sisters, they are spiritual and moral mothers.

We would also suggest that the Republic would have been saved if all who claimed to cherish a love of truth and of justice within their heart had imitated those who preferred prison, exile, deportation and even death itself to the dereliction of the most sacred of duties they owe to themselves and to humanity. Tyranny triumphs much more easily by the moral cowardice of slaves than by the force of weapons. But by her example Pauline will fortify the apostle of the new faith and add new recruits to their ranks. Nations will learn that to vanquish tyranny one needs only expose the disgust and horror it inspires.

Pauline! your noble life will not be wasted! Whether you are holding communion with God or have assumed a second existence among humanity upon earth with renewed power, we can never forget your image. We still see you, we still feel your influence. You inspire us, you support us, you encourage us to persevere. Farewell! Farewell to your mortal remains, but to your memory, never.

Jeanne DEROIN

INTRODUCTION TO THE *ALMANACH DES FEMMES*, 1852[38]

These days an almanac should not just indicate changes in temperature and the position of the stars, but also variations and different mental tendencies and the progress of social truths which encompass the prophecy of a better future. We have tried to achieve this aim by highlighting the importance of some significant questions, the foremost of which are the rights of women to complete social freedom and equality, the organization of work and the abolition of the death penalty.

All other matters are directly or indirectly related to these three principles, and in particular the question of women's rights encapsulates them all.

From a religious point of view, to recognize women's rights is to incorporate the law of solidarity. This is the providential law of humanity, according to which all members of the human family are called to associate with one another and unite their efforts, so that there is no longer one single disinherited, oppressed or suffering being left on earth. To do this is to fulfil the will of God.

From a political point of view to recognize women's rights is effectively to abolish privileges of domination and exploitation.

From the point of view of the organization of labour, to recognize women's rights is to take the course of justice and truth, it is to sanctify work. Until now women and the proletariat have been considered as mere machines for production. Women, because they endure the pain of childbirth, are stigmatized by slavery and civil and political indignity, and the proletariat is deprived of the means of fully developing and exercising its most noble abilities. Therefore, this is why the fate of women and the proletariat are linked by providence, and women's rights are the basis of the organization of labour.

To organize labour is to relate the manufacture of all agricultural, industrial, artistic and scientific products to the needs of mutual consumption using machines where hand labour is insufficient. It is to guarantee to each member of the social family, from the minute they enter this world, the complete development of *all* their faculties by education, and the means to exercise the same faculties according to their free choice and real abilities by the advancement of the means of production. It is to guarantee to women who carry out the sacred role of maternity and to sick workers, to old people, to the ill and the infirm, the satisfaction of all their needs and all the well-being to which they are entitled. And only then will the death penalty be abolished, not only the death penalty inflicted by an executioner but also the death penalty inflicted by hunger and war, and the moral and intellectual death penalty inflicted by poverty and prejudice against women and the proletariat. There will no longer be any call for international conflicts or civil war. Ignorance and brutality, violence and cruelty, which are the vices of slaves and tyrants, will disappear from the earth.

Only then will truth become evident in freedom and questions of a moral and religious nature which divide us today be resolved. Through a deep conviction of the wisdom of Providence and of the sacred laws of nature we affirm that humanity can only progress in step with nature in the providential direction of progress with an infinite capacity for perfectibility when work for all will guarantee to each member of the human family, without distinction of sex or race, the complete development and free use of their moral, intellectual and physical faculties.

Solidarity, which includes liberty, equality and fraternity in their natural limits, is the credo of social religion. It is the powerful link which either fatally imprisons human beings in suffering, because they do not love one another, or will bind them together in peaceful happiness when they do love one another and are united to go forward together in the direction of progress.

INTRODUCTION TO THE *ALMANACH DES FEMMES*, 1853[39]

It is a year since the Almanac was first published and what terrible events have occurred during that time!

Yet everyone can appreciate the lesson to be learnt from these events. They demonstrate the degree to which the old society is corrupt. They show the immorality of its institutions, based on individualism, on privilege, on the right of the strongest. They prove that the old society can only survive by iniquitous methods. They have inflicted a mortal ethical wound on the Army, the Judiciary and the Clergy by transforming them into servile instruments of perjury and tyranny. Thus they show that the old society is rotten to the core and every effort it makes to reinforce itself is one more step towards its inevitable transformation.

For this reason, the apostles of the new faith are motivated to persevere, knowing that this is a sure sign that the triumph of justice and truth is imminent.

Furthermore it is a solemn warning to all those seeking an alternative way of life but who are not yet regenerated by the profound conviction of human solidarity and universal fraternity. They must see in these events proof that the sacred work of social transformation cannot be achieved by force, nor by feelings of hatred or of vengeance.

They must not forget that their enemies are their brethren gone astray, corrupted by vices of a social organization, the origins of which date back to barbaric times. But just as it is permitted for a brother to defend himself against the rage of an unenlightened brother, so too is resistance the right of the oppressed, and it is the most sacred of duties for all those who have a moral conscience, a feeling of human solidarity and justice. To allow the oppressors to accomplish their iniquitous deeds is to become their accomplices. To imitate their wrath would be to stoop to the same degree of immorality.

But until now the oppressed as well as the oppressors have only had recourse to the sword to cut the Gordian knot of the problem of social organization in the style of the deeds recorded by history of Alexander the Great, that bandit famous for horrible acts of slaughter and shameful death.

That is because until now man alone has determined the destiny of humanity and it is he who took the first step in the fatal move towards individualism, injustice and tyranny, by enslaving woman: his mother, sister and companion.

Woman bowed beneath the yoke or else she tried to shake it off by imitating man. Man alone has organized society and as a result he based all institutions on individualism and on privilege; he founded them on the right of the mightiest. Man alone interpreted all religious belief, he disowned the one true God, the principle of love, harmony and liberty; he created a God in his own image which he called the powerful God, the almighty and avenging God. Morality has thus been based on servile submission to the law of the strongest.

Until now, the relentless course of progress, the principle of life and activity of the universe, has stumbled painfully through a deluge of blood and tears. Individualism, tyranny, ignorance, poverty, all provoke revolutions. Selfishness, fear, ignorance of rights and duties, of truth and justice, lead to reaction. Reactions inevitably and fatally induce further revolutions. Humanity continually goes around in this vicious circle of fratricidal struggles and moral and material hardship.

But the time for the coming of Woman is imminent from whence humanity will abandon this destructive course of change through suffering, conflict and poverty to follow the happier course of peaceful and harmonious change through the intervention of the mother of humanity: Woman, regenerated by liberty.

Already, since time immemorial, she has uttered numerous protests but these protests were always isolated and lost in the obscurity of the Dark Ages. She awoke over sixty years ago from this dark sleep. At the end of the last century, Olympe de Gouges in France responded to the Declaration of the Rights of Man by a Declaration of the Rights of Women and mounted the scaffold proclaiming: 'Woman should have the right to rise to speak in the Assembly because she has the right to rise to the scaffold to be guillotined!'.

Around the same time, a daughter of Albion, Anne Lee of Manchester, protested against the reproduction of so many millions of disinherited paupers, destined for a slavery of poverty and ignorance, by founding the Shakers Association in America based on absolute continence [total abstinence from sexual relationships].

Since 1848, women's organizations have been mobilized in France, America and England. Women members of these organizations are demanding their political rights, so as to act themselves for the future welfare of their children and to safeguard themselves from the yoke of tyranny, poverty and ignorance.

This time the adversaries of progress have admitted the right of women to political equality by granting them equality in political persecutions. A large number of women were transported to Africa by the new government of France; many have endured prison and exile. Many even paid with their lives just like Olympe de Gouges did, in their dedication to justice and truth. Our friend and sister, Pauline Roland, was among these. We who have so often been edified by her life, now have the example of her death.

Neither the sight of evil triumphant nor the feeling of our personal sorrows will ever make us forget the powerful law of human solidarity. Encouraged by the virtue of our martyrs and by the ideal of justice which upheld them in their struggle and in their heroic sacrifice, we affirm that for woman it is a right and a duty to take part in the work of regeneration and reconciliation. We appeal to all brave and intelligent women. We exhort them to unite and work to preserve their children from tyranny, ignorance and poverty. To found a new social family and with this aim, adopting and raising children, is the only pacifist and sure way to accomplish progress. We call all women to accompany us in this direction, because it is certain to lead us to the realization of the kingdom of God on earth, that is to say to fraternity and universal harmony.

NOTES

1. For an account of Deroin's project to create a union of associations similar to Flora Tristan's 'Workers' Union', see *l'Opinion des femmes*, August 1849, cited in Edith Thomas, *Pauline Roland: Socialisme et féminisme au XIXe siècle*, Paris, Marcel Rivière, 1956, p. 141, and in Michèle Riot-Sarcey, 'De l'utopie de Jeanne Deroin' in *1848 Révolutions et mutations au XIXe siècle*, no.9, 1993, pp. 29–36.
2. See Claire Goldberg Moses, *French Feminism in the Nineteenth Century*, Albany, State University of New York Press, 1984, pp. 142–9.
3. Police Report on the Association of Socialist Schoolmasters and Schoolmistresses, 29 September 1849 (Archives Nationales F17 12528), cited in Evelyne Lejeune-Resnick, *Femmes et associations (1830–1880)*, Paris, Publisud, 1991, pp. 208–11.
4. Archives Nationales, cited in Maurice Agulhon, *The Republican Experiment 1848–1852*, translated by Janet Lloyd, Cambridge, Cambridge University Press, 1983, pp. 196–7.
5. *Almanach des femmes*, London and Jersey, 1852, 1853, 1854.
6. Quoted in P.J. Yarrow (ed.), *Victor Hugo, Châtiments*, London, Athlone Press, 1975, p. 278.
7. See Roland's letters to Gustave Lefrançais and to Anne Greppo, pp. 111–22.
8. Victor Hugo, *Les Châtiments*, 1853 XI 'Pauline Roland', ll in Yarrow edition, *op. cit.*, p. 158.
9. Cited in Benoîte Groult, *Pauline Roland ou comment la liberté vint aux femmes*, Paris, Robert Laffont, 1991, p. 218. For further details of her conditions as a deportee, see Pauline Roland, Arthur Ranc, Gaspard Rouffet, *Bagnes d'Afrique Trois transportés en Algérie après le coup d'Etat du 2 décembre 1851*. Introduction et notes de Fernand Rude, Collection Actes et Mémoires du Peuple, Paris, Maspéro, 1981.

10. For details about Roland's children see Edith Thomas, *Pauline Roland, op. cit.*, pp. 206–12 and Jean Maitron, 'Pauline Roland', *Dictionnaire biographique du mouvement ouvrier français*, Paris, Les Editions Ouvrières, 1964, première partie, tome 3, pp. 334–5.

11. This theme, a return to earlier religious Saint-Simonian idealism, is also evident in articles on Saint-Simonianism in Jeanne Deroin's *Almanach des femmes* of 1853 and 1854, *op. cit.*

12. See Roger Price (ed.), *Revolution and Reaction: 1848 and the Second French Republic*, London, Croom Helm, 1975, Introduction, pp. 60–61.

13. *Les Châtiments*, 11, in Yarrow edition, *op. cit.*, pp. 157–60.

14. Gustave Lefrançais (1826–1901) was arrested in April 1850 along with Carle on a charge of conspiracy. After three months' detention he was condemned on 12 June to two years' internal exile. Re-arrested in 1851 on a charge of possession of illegal weapons he was banned from teaching and forced into exile in London. He later returned to Paris and continued his political activities, becoming a member of the Paris Commune in 1871 and the International in Geneva where he was exiled after 1871. For further details see Jean Maitron, 'Gustave Lefrançais', *Dictionnaire biographique du mouvement ouvrier français, op. cit.*, première partie, tome 2, pp. 475–7.

15. *Journal des débats*, a newspaper of right wing tendency.

16. The Madelonettes prison was one of the several prisons used to hold republicans in Paris, the other ones mentioned in the letters being the Conciergerie, St Pélagie, Saint Lazare and Belle Isle in Brittany.

17. Perot, a founder member of the Association of Schoolmasters and Schoolmistresses, was himself arrested later and banned from teaching, along with Lefrançais, in 1850. Little is known of him subsequently.

18. Ferdinand François, a doctor and former Saint-Simonian, who took part in the Menilmontant community in the early 1830s before settling in Lyons where he contributed to the publications of the *Revue indépendante* along with Charassin. In 1849 he joined Pauline Roland's circle in Paris, became a fellow militant in the Association before returning to Lyons where he was arrested after the *coup d'état* of 2 December 1851 and imprisoned for four years. See Jean Maitron, 'Ferdinand François', *Dictionnaire biographique du mouvement ouvrier français, op. cit.*, première partie, tome 2, pp. 212–13.

19. Viard, a socialist journalist and former Saint-Simonian, worked with Proudhon on the paper *Le Représentant du Peuple* which he founded in 1847. Through attending meetings at Pauline Roland's home he became friendly with Gustave Lefrançais, encouraged teachers to join their Association and worked to create other workers' unions. He saw Lefrançais briefly in Dijon in December 1850 but was himself condemned to exile after the *coup d'état* of 2 December 1851. See Jean Maitron, 'Viard', *Dictionnaire biographique du mouvement ouvrier français, op. cit.*, première partie, tome 3, pp. 499–500.

20. Ange Guepin (1805–1873), doctor, Saint-Simonian, socialist republican and philosopher. See Jean Maitron, 'Ange Guepin', *Dictionnaire biographique du mouvement ouvrier français, op. cit.*, première partie, tome 2, pp. 309–11.

21. Thierry was accused by the Association of having denounced Lefrançais to the authorities.

22. Proudhon was vociferous in his criticism of the socialist feminists but this did not prevent him from being imprisoned for his journalistic opposition activities, although unlike Pauline Roland he later accepted Louis Napoléon's regime. See Edward Hyams, *Pierre-Joseph Proudhon, His Revolutionary Life, Mind and Works*, London, John Murray, 1979; and Jean Maitron, 'Pierre-Joseph Proudhon', *Dictionnaire biographique du mouvement ouvrier français, op. cit.*, première partie, tome 3, pp. 256–61.

23. Pierre-Jean de Béranger (1780–1857), a republican and socialist, was an influential poet and lyricist whose help Flora Tristan enlisted for her Workers' Union. This popular figure campaigned for Roland's return to France in 1852.

24. The newspaper *Moniteur* was conservative in outlook.

25. Frédéric Charassin (1804–1876), journalist, politician, elected deputy for a brief period during the Second Republic; he was expelled from France in 1852 and returned in 1862. See Jean Maitron, 'Frédéric Charassin', *Dictionnaire biographique du mouvement ouvrier français, op. cit.*, première partie, tome 1, pp. 387–8.

26. Lefrançais was by this time in internal exile in Dijon, unemployed and disappointed in fellow republicans whom he found too timid. See Gustave Lefrançais, *Souvenirs d'un révolutionnaire*, texte établi et preparé par Jan Cerny, Bordeaux, Edition de la Tête de Feuilles, 1972, pp. 150–90.

27. Auguste Desmoulins (1823–1891), a typesetter, journalist, disciple and son-in-law of Pierre Leroux, a Democ-Soc, campaigned for the creation of associations including the Schoolmasters and Schoolmistresses Association and Deroin's Union of Associations. After the *coup d'état* of 2 December 1851, his journalism was outlawed and he was condemned to transportation to Guyanne in his absence. In February 1852 he fled to Jersey to join Leroux from where he went to the United States to join Cabet in founding his utopian community, Icarie. When he returned to France in 1871 he continued his socialist union activism under the Third Republic. He corresponded with Flora Tristan in 1844. See Jean Maitron, 'Auguste Desmoulins', *Dictionnaire biographique du mouvement ouvrier français, op. cit.*, première partie, tome 2, pp. 75–8.

28. Anne Greppo, militant wife of Jean Louis Greppo, who was arrested in early December 1851. She took part in organizing workers' protests against the *coup d'état*. Arrested and condemned to deportation she was freed as the evidence against her was supplied by a secret police *agent provocateur*. See Jean Maitron, 'Anne Greppo (née Glattard)', *Dictionnaire biographique du mouvement ouvrier français, op. cit.*, première partie, tome 2, pp. 299–301.

29. Armandine Huet, friend of Greppo and Roland, took part in the December 1851 uprising, was arrested and sentenced to deportation to Algeria but her sentence was reduced to release on parole.

30. Claudine Monniot had already endured her companion, Jean Pierre Hibruit's, arrest and sentence to hard labour because of his involvement in previous insurrections in June 1848 and May 1849. She took part in protests during the December uprising of 1851 and was sentenced to transportation to Algeria.

31. Sentencing ranged from release on parole, internal or external deportation, or compulsory exile or transportation to a penal colony with hard labour.

32. Official festivities to celebrate the establishment of the Second Empire.

33. Charlemagne Emile de Maupas, politician appointed Prefect of Police in Paris by Louis Napoléon in October 1851. He led preparations for the *coup d'état* in December 1851 and was responsible for rigorous repression of republicans. He was Senator in 1853 then Prefect of Marseilles between 1860 and 1866.

34. This rumour was untrue. Barbès (1809–1870), a revolutionary who spent long periods in prison under the July Monarchy and Second Republic, was released from prison in 1854 and died in exile in The Hague in June 1870. Flora Tristan exchanged letters with him when she tried to see him in prison on her travels in 1844. See Jean Maitron, 'Sigismond, Auguste Armand Barbès', *Dictionnaire biographique du mouvement ouvrier français, op. cit.*, première partie, tome 1, pp. 147–9.

35. The Council was an emergency court or special tribunal which sentenced the 1852 insurgents.

36. *Almanach des femmes, op. cit.*, Second Year, London and Jersey, 1853, pp. 213–25.

37. François Guizot (1787–1874) a conservative politician, had served as First Minister under the July Monarchy and had unsuccessfully attempted to halt the republican meetings by suppressing the Banquets in January and February 1848, an action which led to the downfall of the Orléans monarchy. Exiled in Belgium and England he returned to France in 1849 but took little part in politics subsequently.

38. *Almanach des femmes, op. cit.*, London, 1852, pp. 7–11.

39. *Almanach des femmes, op. cit.*, Second Year, London and Jersey, 1853, pp. 8–15.

5. Madeleine Pelletier: feminism and politics

CONTEXTUAL INTRODUCTION

The three articles by Madeleine Pelletier grouped together here – 'Feminism and its Militants' (1909), 'The Question of Votes for Women' (1908) and 'Women's Right to Work' (1931) – are concerned with women in political or public life. In these texts, Pelletier both theorized and demonstrated the links between feminism, economic power and public political action. In analysing the problems faced by feminists of her generation to enter political parties and to gain voting rights for women, the issue of exclusion remains of the greatest importance. Women in France were excluded by law from civic participation, though as Hélène Brion pointed out in her 'Statement to the Court Martial' (1918), women were subject to the law's penalties. Women could join political parties, as Pelletier and Brion both joined the Socialist Party, but their voting rights within the party were limited. Furthermore, exclusion from the 'universal' suffrage granted to adult males in 1848 meant that political participation at the party level represented no more than token- ism. In 'Feminism and its Militants', Pelletier analysed the problems of organizing mass action by French women on the model of the British women suffragists. She lamented middle-class women's reluctance to engage in pub- lic political demonstrations. Pelletier identified women's gender training in modesty and submissiveness as a determining factor in shaping women's social and political timidity.

'The Question of Votes for Women' surveyed the women's suffrage debate from the perspective of French history since the revolution of 1789, and from the perspective of international feminism. Like Brion, Pelletier stressed the betrayal of feminists by the male revolutionaries of 1789. However, women's subordination, she suggested, was partly of their own making. Their lack of solidarity with other women, she argued, compounded their subservience to men. Women's particular form of 'moral servitude' was to live in intimate relations with their masters, so that they identified with their oppressors not with other women.

In her overview of international feminism Pelletier sought to portray femi- nism as a powerful movement, comparable to international socialism. Her survey included the United States, Britain, Germany, Russia, Spain, Italy, Finland, Norway, Sweden, Australia and New Zealand, from which we have included substantial extracts. The final section is of interest in showing how Pelletier countered anti-feminist objections to women's suffrage, particularly the alleged intellectual inferiority of women, supposedly scientifically proven by craniometry and anthropology.[1] Pelletier concluded that women's inferiority was not innate but stemmed from their cultural and educational limitations.

'Women's Right to Work', written two decades after the suffrage articles and during the Great Depression, focused primarily on women's emancipation through their economic independence in paid labour. Attacking the still prevalent idea that women should be supported by men, she equated marriage, as did other socialist thinkers such as Engels, with prostitution.[2] A capitalist economy reduced personal relations to an economic contract. Not only were women demeaned by being supported by men, they could never become fully functioning citizens in the public sphere if they were confined to the narrow range of the home. Pelletier offered a range of practical suggestions for the problems besetting working women, recognizing well before second-wave feminism that women in work effectively have two jobs. Her solution was to socialize domesticity; armies of paid cleaners and launderers would perform the majority of domestic chores. The tone of mordant irony in which she described domestic life suggests scepticism about altering relations between men and women. Pelletier recognized that women's increasing financial independence would have repercussions for the traditional family structure. Her emphasis of economic independence can be seen as complementing her discussions of political enfranchisement but also as reflecting the failure of the campaign for enfranchisement in France in the 1930s.

TEXTS BY MADELEINE PELLETIER

'Feminism and its Militants' (1909)
'The Question of Votes for Women' (1908)
'Women's Right to Work' (1931)

FEMINISM AND ITS MILITANTS[3]

French feminism, unlike English feminism, is not organized into one great party. Its groups are either very isolated or weakly united, but the progress in the concept of female emancipation is nonetheless very real. One can without exaggeration affirm that within a few years the co-ordinated efforts of women will succeed in gaining them their political and civil rights.

Opposing feminism, the first obstacles we find are male egotism and masculine pride. For most men today, a woman is still not an equal. They see in her an inferior creature, suitable for endless exploitation in the gratification of the passions, for the completion of their household tasks and for the reproduction of the species. If women wish to earn their living, they are pushed out of well-paid jobs, professions and trades and only left with minor posts and badly paid work. Nonetheless, heads of government, more broad-minded than the masses, have finally ceded bit by bit to the just representations of women that they should be able to eat without prostituting themselves. But it will be a long time before the general public acknowledges the changes that this legislation reflects.

Although women have been allowed to study medicine for the last thirty years, they are only today beginning to find enough patients. For many years penurious women doctors were obliged to undertake drudgery disdained by male doctors. With the same degree, they had to become midwives or masseuses in the rich quarters of Paris. The male doctors let them give injections, do bandaging and so on.

In printing, a trade where workers earn a good living, women were treated as pariahs. Men rejected them for union membership and they were obliged to accept work at lower wages and to replace men during strikes.

Last year, when the relatively lucrative profession of cab driver was opened to women, they received a volley of abuse from the masculine clan. The cab drivers (what masculine chivalry!) ambushed the women cab drivers at night and beat them up. They cut their horses' reins and tried to collide with their cabs in the crowded streets. These men, perfectly prepared to allow women to work twelve hours a day in order that they earn twenty-five sous in the rag trade, saw a peril for the institution of the family if women were able to earn six or eight francs as cab drivers with less difficulty.

As an objection to woman's paid labour, men put forward the notion of what they claim is her mission, decreed by whom I do not know, to be a housewife, that is to say, to be in a man's service. They also put forward the objection, this time without any silly mysticism, of competition. The professions, they say, are already full up; what will it be like when women have access? In reality this is a mistaken calculation, for whereas when a woman is supported by a man he must earn enough for two, once a woman is able to be self-sufficient, a man will only be obliged to look after his own needs. But ultimately, it is a matter of masculine pride. Men want to dispose of their own money and spend it on women as they wish. When a woman is young and pretty a man buys her: in exchange for satisfying all his lusts, even the most degrading ones, even the most unhealthy. He buys her expensive jewellery and extravagant dresses; when she becomes ugly or faded, he throws her over to starve.

Men think themselves superior thanks to their sex organ. The great Danton, when he and his friends were reproached with being *sans culottes* [revolutionary rabble; trouserless scum] replied: 'They will be even better able see that we are men', and everyone admired his reply. A man of the lowest intelligence, who is of the humblest station, believes himself to be the master of his wife and indeed of all women. Only a rich woman fills him with respect, though this respect may be entirely superficial. He believes that a woman only controls her own fortune via the men among whom she is lucky enough to live, but that he, though poor, is by reason of his masculinity, superior to the richest woman.

Among educated men, male pride is somewhat more restrained, forced as they are by their surroundings to hide it and also because they often meet cultivated women whose merits they are obliged to recognize. But they are far from considering women to be their equals. If they concede that women have the right to open their minds to the higher reaches of thought, in literature, in politics, in science, in philosophy, they still refuse to see women as anything other than their pupils, capable of taking in ideas, understanding them, but incapable of producing original ideas themselves or of achieving recognition for them ... .

Another even greater obstacle to the success of feminist demands, perhaps than masculine pride, is women's timidity in the manner of pressing their claims. Whatever her social station, every woman in her childhood and in her youth has been raised for servitude. She therefore brings a serf mentality even to the most daring of her demands. Women doctors, lawyers, teachers, painters, sculptors, novelists, etc. who should be ardent propagandists for feminist ideas, to whose efficacy they owe the positions they occupy, declare themselves, on the contrary, to be entirely detached if not opposed to feminism. Each strives to separate her own condition from that of feminism, by claiming to be a transcendent intelligence which has soared over all obstacles and also because she lacks the courage to support a minority opinion. The mentality of such women is similar to that of so-called blackleg workers or scabs who support the bosses against the men of their own class. But since the subjugation of women is more complete than that of the working class, the blacklegs of feminism are in proportion much stronger than the blacklegs of the trade union movement.

Until the last few years, the claims of women's groups were extremely vague. The members of these groups in any case were women who, having thought and written on these issues, were looking for a place to assert themselves, rather than to achieve any clearly defined aim. There were spiritualists there, seeking to make conversions, misunderstood philosophers, women interested in politics, wanting to exchange opinions. A common feeling, nevertheless, united them all. Belittled in society by men who alone make the laws, by journalists and by editors, they suffered from their disappointed expectations and bore little love in their hearts, as one may imagine, for that sex which had stood in their way. In their disillusionment, they set women against men, proclaiming themselves to be the most worthy sex ... .

But the mistake in the feminist generation preceding our own, has been not to understand the sterility of such a concept of feminism. Brought up in subjection, afraid of political agitation, afraid of action, they have delighted in useless rantings and ravings against men and in an equally useless exaltation of their own sex's virtues. Because M. Baschoffen [*sic*.] had shown that women's slavery had not been as general as anthropologists claimed and that in past civilizations women enjoyed great respect, they spent the whole of their meetings analysing this writer; matriarchy became identified as the whole of feminism.[4]

Thought to be fiery harridans in the eyes of people who only knew about them through the popular press, feminist activists were in reality very timid people. The notion of a woman's right to lead her own life without regard to the man with whom she may choose to share her life, seemed to them so outrageous that they did not hesitate to declare that those who demanded it wronged the cause. They could only conceive of themselves as housewives asking that the law protect them better against the selfishness and inconstancy of their husbands ... .

Feminists are constantly complaining of the physical discomfort that they experience from their impractical mode of dress, but nonetheless they do not have the courage to liberate themselves. A well-known German socialist, Mme Lylie Braun, wrote at length in her book *Woman* on the question of dress which she resolved in a traditional manner. With comic indignation she demonstrated the social dangers which feminism would unleash if women started cutting their hair short and wore starched shirts [like men].[5] This is a form of ancestral serfdom which continually reappears; woman, an instrument of man's pleasure, and esteeming herself as such, trembles at the very idea that any woman should have the criminal audacity to free herself to the point of making comfort and freedom of movement the priority, as men do, rather than considering the effect produced on the opposite sex.

In the presence of men, even emancipated women behave like little girls. They do not dare to express an opinion, or if they do, they do not emphasize it, the moment they are contradicted by a man. There are some who, noisily and constantly angry when they are in women's groups, keep quiet like well-behaved schoolgirls in groups where there are men present ... .

Until recently, there was only Mme Hubertine Auclert's feminist group which demanded the right to vote.[6] The other groups limited themselves to demanding their civil rights. Under pressure from '*Solidarité des femmes*', which was treated like an unruly child because it was too daring, other groups eventually rallied to the cause of women's suffrage. But many women still hesitate, fearing the danger of reaction, as though the Republic, which has given us nothing, could matter to us. 'Solidarity' with its posters and its meetings on the right to vote appalled most feminists thanks to their coward-ice in the face of action. When women are valued in society, their pusillanim-ity will add to the general good; they will help to prevent war; but at present this very pusillanimity renders a disservice to their cause ... .

Men have shed blood to win the right to vote. If it were necessary for women to use the same means, it is probable that they would never win it, not only because they would be afraid for themselves, but because violence in general fills them with horror. During the last parliamentary elections, I proposed to throw stones at the windows of a polling station, because given our small numbers, it is only illegal acts like this which can adequately attract the attention of the press and public opinion to those ideas in whose name we continue to act. As soon as I announced my determination to our activists, urging them to follow me on this path of action, three-quarters fled, appalled. The remaining quarter agreed to follow me but refused to act and begged me to restrain myself to verbal protest. They objected on the grounds that the stones might injure the voters. Certainly it is always unfortunate if someone is wounded, even slightly, but when one fights for an idea, one needs to think in terms of success. If success can be achieved without causing damage, it is obviously better, but if harm is necessary, one has to resign oneself to it and carry on ... .

Yet it is not only violence that terrifies women steeped since infancy in the idea that modesty and a self-effacing manner are suitable to their sex and that they should not put themselves forward or stand out in any way. The inoffen-sive tactics of the English suffragettes seem to the last degree improper to our activists. One day, in order to attract the attention of Members of Parliament to feminist issues, I decided to attempt for a second time my deed of 1906, namely to throw pamphlets proclaiming the right to vote into the Chamber from the Visitor's Gallery. I proposed this to fifteen of my most daring supporters – only ten accepted. Of the ten, four found some kind of excuse to cry off. Finally, of the six remaining who were daring enough to enter the Palais Bourbon carrying leaflets, only one threw the proclamations.[7] We need a whole educational process to reactivate female vitality, but this kind of educational reform is impossible for individuals who can only influence a minute number of people. When women gain entry to public life through having the vote, they will become individuals worthy of the name.

We should not forget either that it is also rare for men to hold burning convictions, to show the capacity to sacrifice personal peace and public esteem for their ideals. Among the thousands of workers who would have everything to gain and nothing to lose by a social transformation, how many socialists are there? Even among that limited number of socialists, how many active militants are there? And among the handful of active militants how many are personally disinterested? The hope of a parliamentary or municipal mandate, the hope of a post or a decoration is what peoples the political parties, the Socialist Party like the others. One should not be astonished, therefore, to find only a tepid activism among feminists.

In any case, in spite of the half-heartedness of active groups, feminist ideas are becoming increasingly widespread. Twenty years ago there were only a few rare regulars of feminist groups prepared to claim the right to vote and most people considered them to be eccentrics of no significance. Today, every salon features discussions on women's emancipation, which has its place as one of society's controversial subjects. If a referendum of the well-educated were possible, it is not impossible that the vote would go in favour of women. Feminist articles proliferate in journals and newspapers, and while it is true that my contribution on women soldiers unleashed insults and sarcasm in the popular press, a number of important publications have addressed this issue as it ought to be addressed. England has begun to resolve this question by creating a military nursing corps.

The evolution of ideas currently in progress should lead to a victory for feminism. But will not this evolution shortly be overthrown by a revolution? Would a revolution be good for feminism? One cannot be sure. Certainly it is encouraging to see women postal employees address crowded meetings and be listened to. But in 1789 women did that and more. They fomented riots and even led them; important missions were confided to them, but that did not prevent feminism being crushed as soon as women demanded general rights instead of particular privileges. Today a few women individualists succeed in making a place for themselves in left-wing politics, though not without struggles and setbacks. But masculine pride and anti-feminism is much stronger among these men than among the bourgeoisie currently in power. If the women activists of the revolutionary parties were more numerous, perhaps they would succeed in bringing about sexual equality in the event of a revolution. Yet they are so few that they would probably be silenced or crushed. We must conclude that feminism finds its greatest hope in social tranquillity. Yet how much longer will this continue?

THE QUESTION OF VOTES FOR WOMEN[8]

I

It was first during the Great Revolution [of 1789] that the demands of women for political existence were affirmed, though if one consults writings left by distinguished women well before this period, one finds that the elite of the female sex had protested against the injustice of their lot. But these protests, though frequent, were, nevertheless, individual and isolated. So it is, I repeat, that one must await the Great Revolution to find, as we say nowadays, a truly feminist movement.

In reality, among the great mass of women who attended clubs and took part in riots at that time, feminist ideas, namely the demand for the political and social assimilation of their sex with the male sex, were rather unclear. These women were above all revolutionaries. The events which swept everyone along carried them away as well. The starving populace thought that by bringing the baker, the baker's wife and the little baker's boy back from Versailles, the famine would cease.[9] Women therefore went along to fetch them, believing that they, the women, constituted part of the people and that remedying food shortages was as much their business as that of men.

But already at a more informed social level, specifically feminist demands had begun to appear. Throughout France societies formed which had as their aim the civic education of women and which as part of their platform claimed the right of women to be elected as representatives of the people.

But if the mass of women were eclipsed, a few, superior to their companions of both sexes, enjoyed a certain esteem that was not without influence. They debated with the leaders of the revolution and were sent as delegates to larger assemblies. Finally, a few, superior to the others, placed themselves at the forefront of events; such a one was Théroigne de Méricourt and such above all was Madame Roland ... .[10]

Though somewhat lost in the turmoil which destroyed both men and institutions, feminism nevertheless remained alive. Rose Lacombe, Olympe de Gouges, Aspasie Carlemigilli, demanded in their writings and speeches women's right to defend their opinions before the Parliament, of which sufficient notice was paid to expedite them to the guillotine.[11] Women's clubs opened, where women discussed current events. Naturally their opinion differed. Parallel to the revolutionary clubs, clubs of royalist women were formed; others had a politically moderate tendency. Women's organizations, in short, reproduced similar differences as among men and market fishwives sometimes exchanged blows in the name of these differences. Masculine pride was at stake. A great debate arose at the Conventions on feminism and the conclusion reached, expressed by Chaumette, was that the role of the woman citizen should be limited to mending patriots' socks.[12] A decree closed all the women's clubs.

Women tried to resist, but weakly. What could a few years of semi-emancipation do against centuries of slavery? Under the brutal heel of masculine egotism, this newly born feminism had to die, and die it did.

The revolutions of 1848 and 1870 awakened women anew. They were seen in the midst of revolutionary crowds, armed with rifles, sabres and daggers.

Women's clubs were formed and similar demands for political equality [as in the 1789 Revolution] were formulated. But each time feminism was but an episode soon to be blotted out and men's struggles for their own freedoms were the only ones to monopolize public attention.

The fact is that the moral servitude of the female sex is even deeper than that of the lower classes. A serf, once his work is finished, lives apart from his master. The worker lives separated from his boss. Clearly by spending their lives separated from the upper classes, the subordinate groups can only be the gainers. By living among one another, they become conscious of the links which unite them; they feel that they are among their own kind, whereas the others, those who are more handsome, stronger, better educated, seem to them different, like another race.

Between men and women no similar situation exists. The institution of the family gives them a life in common. The master cloisters the slave in his house. It is true that among her women friends, where she feels free, a woman will complain of male tyranny. Women forge between themselves a sort of tacit Freemasonry where ideas and feelings, unknown to men, are exchanged. Among themselves, they praise the feminine virtues, namely those of the weak, prudence, economy, patience and common sense, and contrast them to the ruinous carelessness and boastfulness of men.

But the link of solidarity is weak. Women pour out their feelings and sorrows to each other far more than they support one another. Unaware of the power which organization gives, each is only interested in herself. They entertain themselves among other women, but for material support they turn towards men and spend their lives searching for one, keeping him and getting the most out of him. Bad treatment and humiliations seem to them the disagreeable side of a natural situation. Unhappy in her home, excessively oppressed, a woman will certainly confide her inner rebellion to her sisters; but as soon as the storm has passed, she returns to the man whom she admires as a superior being.

At the beginning of their careers women are confronted by male egotism, more or less masked by hypocritical pretexts. If it is a question of a scientific career, women's brains are too small; they cannot understand scientific laws. If it is a question, less ambitiously, of driving a cab across Paris, a woman is not muscular enough, not agile enough; she drives badly; there will be accidents. Fortunately private interests open a breach here. The lower and middling civil servant, though anti-feminist with regard to other women, is a feminist for his daughter. Obviously he would like to marry her off, but cannot manage a sufficient dowry. Therefore he makes her study and once she has obtained her diplomas, he moves heaven and earth to find her a job. The cab driver would willingly send all women back to the kitchen and to their darning; but his own wife, driving her own cab, brings in three times the amount of money that she could have saved by staying at home. He becomes, therefore, the defender of women's right to work and stands up for his woman cab driver against the invectives and clenched fists of masculine competitors ... .

All girls and women forced to work through circumstance become the unconscious agents of the forward march of ideas towards feminism. A woman doctor treating the sick, the secretary transcribing commercial papers, the interpreter, the employee, the civil servant dealing with the public behind a counter, succeed in dimming, little by little, the image of the housewife and the courtesan. They are wives and mothers but only for a few hours every evening; all day long they are only workers.

One should not conclude from the above that women's economic emancipation is everything and that their intellectual, moral and political enfranchisement is of no importance. I have tried to show that women's economic situation is undergoing an indisputable evolution and that this evolution will be a factor in women's integral emancipation. However, this is not the only factor and if publicity on sexual equality, the arousal of more dignity and self-respect and, above all, the right to vote are not achieved, then women's emancipation will be far less rapid.

II

America was the first country to grant votes to women. Women have, in fact, enjoyed political rights there since 1865. The states where they have voting rights are Wyoming, Colorado, Utah and Idaho.

The effect of women's suffrage in those states has been to make political life less turbulent. Americans are not very concerned with a candidate's political label; their choice depends upon his moral stature. Thus in those states where women vote, politics has gained a great deal in respect of honesty. It is impossible for anyone to succeed unless he has an irreproachable past ... . Alcoholism and prostitution have very much declined in those countries where women vote. This is easy to understand as it is women who suffer the most from these social scourges. Regulation of prostitution, the arbitrary imprisonment of women who have not committed any offence and have only passed on to men an illness given to them by men in the first place, is monstrous in a civilized society. It is certain that in France, as soon as women have the vote, this custom which arises out of masculine selfishness, will be abolished.

Among the working classes, moreover, alcoholism leads to women's martyrdom ... . A woman retains her self-awareness and finds herself forced to cohabit in a narrow room with a vile brute who hiccoughs, who vomits on the floor and the furniture and who beats her and the children and who condemns her and her little ones to atrocious poverty, if in addition he does not kill her in an attack of delirium tremens. Consequently there is no doubt that in France, as in the United States, one of the first advantages of votes for women would be to check the spread of alcoholism ... .

In England, the question of voting rights for women was raised more than half a century ago by John Stuart Mill. From his early youth, Stuart Mill declared himself in favour of women's emancipation and argued that a society in which women had no part in government was tainted by injustice. Unlike most of our male French allies, who only bring a tepid support to the cause, Stuart Mill was enough of a feminist to fall out with Auguste Comte on the sole question of women's rights ... .[13]

England is the place where at least for the moment, feminism is at its most active. Not only do women hold meetings and form associations to support their cause, they also hold street demonstrations and on several occasions have attempted to invade Parliament. One can affirm that the English feminist party is the most powerful among all the similar parties in Europe and it leaves French feminism far behind. In appearance English feminism may appear a little ridiculous; we in France would with difficulty accustom ourselves to generals in epaulettes and shoulder straps, with caps festooned in gold braid, colonels, captains, leaders and deputy leaders of groups, speakers wearing the insignia of their rank. But French women would be wrong to criticize all this, given that as far as commitment and numbers are concerned, they, the French, have nothing resembling this. Whereas in France the different feminist groups compete with one another, and whereas within a given group the leader is hated and is an object of jealousy to most of the members who do all they can to undermine her, among English feminists these rivalries do not seem to surface. It is true that there are two big associations, 'Women's Franchise' [sic.] and 'Votes for Women' [sic.] but within each one the members are disciplined if not in their hearts, at least in their behaviour.[14] Certainly one can find absurdities among the suffragettes' methods, such as their affectation of maintaining their 'femininity' by putting military braid on a frilly white dress. To see them on the eve of their great demonstration of 21 June of last year [1908], running down the staircase of their headquarters, singing and laughing, one was reminded more of a girls' school getting ready for prize day than of a great opposition party proposing nothing less than to wrest power from government.

Yet in all this there was a harmony, conviction and devotion which was extraordinary. The most ordinary work of the humblest activist is noticed and praised in public by the leaders. If a suffragette is sent to prison, there are celebrations on her release and they award her a beautifully framed and illuminated diploma attesting her devotion to the cause. If she only pins a badge on her blouse saying 'Votes for Women', she is congratulated for her courage in facing up to the hostile comments of ill-mannered passers-by. They are still timorous women and their heroic acts are often on a very small scale but they bring to the cause whatever energy they can. How many activists in male political parties could truthfully say as much? Without a doubt, one can affirm that the state of mind reigning at the present time among the 'suffragettes' is unknown in France, not only in feminist organizations, but also in the much larger masculine political parties ... .

In Germany, the question of votes for women is also making progress. A suffrage party composed of women belonging to the German aristocracy has been formed and in addition there are numerous women in the SPD (Social Democratic Party). German socialists appear to be much more seriously in favour of votes for women than French socialists, who in reality are shameful anti-feminists. Nevertheless it would be desirable if German women socialists, insofar as they were feminists, could be a bit more independent of their party. At the recent Stuttgart Conference they rejected what they refer to as bourgeois feminism with an ostentatious lack of decorum.[15] If like a man, a woman has the right to be a socialist, she cannot, without betraying her cause, sacrifice her feminism to any masculine political party whatsoever. To be sure, German male socialists at Stuttgart did not display that contempt for women socialists that their French colleagues show. One of their leaders, Singer, chaired several meetings of the women's section. But it is nonetheless true that, universal suffrage not yet existing in Germany, German social democracy would without hesitation sacrifice women's votes for the votes of male proletarians. German socialists should understand that feminism cannot be in reality either bourgeois or socialist, for it is not a party of class but of sex. From a political point of view, a middle-class woman is in no better a situation than a woman worker. If, on the other hand, women workers gained merely the political and then the economic status of male workers, this would already constitute an immense advantage for them. Even the granting of limited women's suffrage to middle-class women alone would do more for German women workers than the male working-class vote, for in raising public esteem for women in general, women's work on the labour market would at a stroke achieve greater value ... .

III

Anti-feminists' objections to women's suffrage can be divided into two categories:

1. Objections of principle.
2. Objections on the probable results alleged to flow from such a measure.

Objections in principle are not aimed solely at votes for women; anti-feminists make them for all feminists' demands, no matter what they be. Such opposition is based both on a belief in the moral and intellectual inferiority of women and on a belief in a special and limited role that has been prescribed to women by nature.

A great deal of ink has been spilt over women's inferiority. Anthropologists, looking to science for their justification for women's alleged inferiority, as well as a justification for their hatred of burgeoning feminism, claimed round about 1860 that the female brain and skull were inferior. However, attention having been drawn by them to this question, other anthropologists took it up and demonstrated that it was nothing of the kind ... . The female skull of today is the model of the masculine skull of tomorrow if evolution continues to alter forms as at present. But this only means that the female skull belongs to a less muscular individual than a man and there is no conclusion to be reached as far as intelligence is concerned.

When people began to suspect a possible link between the weight of the skull and intelligence, it occurred to them to compare the two sexes on this issue. Since women, it turns out, have 100 to 150 grams less brain weight than men, scientists hastened to conclude their inferiority. As in the case of the skull, this conclusion was too hasty. It was subsequently discovered that if the brain grows by reason of greater intelligence, it also grows in proportion to physical development. Comparing the brain mass to the overall organic mass, the comparison was to women's advantage. In relation to her body development, a woman has a bigger brain than a man ... .

From all this, one must conclude that anthropology cannot answer the question of the greater or lesser intelligence of individuals of the two sexes. We must resign ourselves to impartial and patient observation. What does such observation of the two sexes show us? Intelligent women and stupid men; stupid women and intelligent men ... . The real inferiority of the average woman is not an essential inferiority, but a lack of information caused by a repressive education. The proof is that as soon as any prohibition is withdrawn against any form of intellectual activity whatever, the feminine mind quickly develops. Without mentioning those women who have made a name for themselves in science or in literature and whom one can consider to be exceptions, thousands of girls who have gained their doctorates at the university prove that the female mind is capable of understanding and assimilating what are, in fact, quite difficult subjects ... . Besides alleging women's inferior intelligence, the defenders of arbitrary male power make the objection that nature herself has prescribed that women should remain strangers to political life as to all public life and that they should limit their ambitions to the home. It is easy to see that this objection is quite senseless, given that Nature has never been able to prescribe anything to anyone. Because gestation takes place in the uterus and not in the male prostate, for example, does not give grounds for concluding, in my view, that it is impossible for someone possessing a uterus to vote. 'Your sex shackles you at certain times', man says to woman, 'therefore I am going to shackle you your whole life long'. One must concede that women are not pregnant or nursing their whole lives long, though anti-feminists have grossly exaggerated the debilitating effects of these physiological functions. I have known a number of women intellectuals who during the first six months of their pregnancy wrote novels and prepared their examinations as normal. Apart from reproduction, all the other constraints on women are not in the least natural; they are made by men to weigh them down. I cannot quite see why it is prescribed that women should mend clothes, cook and clean the house. Nature nowhere says that a woman should be her husband's domestic servant.

Yet there is a more serious answer to oppose those who argue for women's sexual weakness, namely that society does not have the right to decree, *a priori*, that anyone is incapable. A community in which individuals do not have the right to explore their potential as they wish is monstrously unjust and individuals have the right to retaliate as against an enemy.

Thanks to the progress that feminist ideas have made in the past few years, it is rare for this category of objection to be raised against women's suffrage in educated circles. Today people argue largely about the consequences, the peril which the votes of millions of women would suddenly bring to the Republic. Though repeated frequently, this argument is not any the less bizarre. What? The Republic refuses to give women the vote under the pretext that women might use it against the Republic? Well, why not do away with the Opposition altogether? Why not declare that the right to vote means the obligation to vote for those currently in power?

In any case, who was it who made women religious, if not men, who left them no other nourishment for their minds, forbidding all others. There is no natural reason why women should be religious; one is not born religious and royalist any more than one is born a socialist or an atheist. That sentimentality ascribed to women and which is in any case a sociological factor could be applied to subjects other than religion. One can focus one's passion on art, on science, on questions of social progress, on politics in general, and if this passion is sometimes harmful, thanks to women's difficulties in reflecting long and calmly, they perform a great service in bringing their energy to the world of action.[16]

WOMEN'S RIGHT TO WORK

Nov. 1931

'Live by working or die in the struggle', demanded the workers in 1848.[17]

I

This is a fundamental demand. From the moment that property is declared to be inviolable and it is forbidden to take the goods that another considers to be his by force; society, protector of the property-owning classes, should ensure that those who possess nothing can earn their livelihood by their labour.

This right, our present-day society is far from ensuring to men. For the past ten years, unemployment has been rampant in an endemic way and at present attains enormous proportions in a number of countries. Impossible to work, it is forbidden to steal, forbidden to beg. What is to be done?

We could have a revolution, and governments, educated by history, know it perfectly well. That is why the English and German middle classes are resigned to paying huge sums of money to support the unemployed. The problem of women's work has up until now been discussed in a somewhat different light. Society only recognized men. Women lived dependent on men, who, in principle, supported them.

In point of fact, there have always been women workers who were productive outside the family home. Seamstresses, laundry women, milliners etc. worked for a wage. But these were limited minorities. The great mass of women, whether married or not, were kept by a man – housewives or whores, as Proudhon put it. But not all women can be kept women. There are widows too old to wed again, single women who for lack of beauty, health, acquaintances or money have not been able to find a husband. To assist the plight of widows, Jewish law required that they should marry an unmarried brother-in-law. In France, they remain, like old maids, dependent on their family, if they have one … . It is a life of dependency and unhappiness. Petit-bourgeois relatives accept it as their duty to take care of the widow or the old maid. But the bread of charity is always hard. Reproaches, humiliations, derision, were not lacking towards the 'useless mouth' which was gorging itself at others' expense.

The situation of women controlled by men [for example, in marriage] though regularized, was far from being entirely happy either. A dog is happy when he has a good master who pets him and gives him delicious scraps. But the master is not always kind. There are those who, armed with a whip, are moved to strike rather than to give caresses. For women it was the same. A dog does not talk and women talk. This has helped them in many instances to improve their lot. When one speaks, one can lie, use cunning; one can manipulate a naive master or one who is blinded by passion. So it sometimes happens that the roles are reversed and the master becomes the slave.

Who commands when he loves
And what empire remains in the heart
Where love plants its conquering heel?

One of the reasons that women's emancipation is so difficult is that women's slavery is special; it is a sexual slavery.

Sexuality is very powerful. Freud has shown that it is far more powerful than was thought. By playing with her sexuality like a bait that she promises, refuses, withdraws, a woman can gain her ends and she knows it perfectly well. Bewitched, a man gives her his money if he has any, his influence, his honour etc. And Nana dances on his belly.[18]

But Nana is young and beautiful; no one is young forever and most women are never beautiful. Love does not last eternally, as we are constantly being told. The more the master was initially anxious to please and the more pressing he was, the more he becomes hard and indifferent [after his conquest]. For the male, the female has become a creature *who means nothing to him*. If he is married, the man will bear the fetters as best he can. If he has money, he revenges himself by keeping one or several other women. If he has none, he is obliged to be contented with his legitimate, insipid lot. His bad temper manifests itself in sulks, sneers, curses and blows.

Undoubtedly marriage is not always happy and women would like to be able to liberate themselves. But what are they to do? They have no fixed trade. They are housewives, that is to say, they know how to do a certain number of things poorly. They can cook, but not well enough to be a chef; they can launder, but a professional laundress would not accept them in her business; they sew, but do not know how to make a dress and cannot be employed in a workroom. Furthermore, there are often children. How can a woman earn a living for them when she cannot for herself?

Nana, it might be said, in a certain sense lives better. Her lovers are middle class and shower her with luxuries. But Nana will not always be young. If she has not saved her money, which is not usually the case since a number of parasites dupe her in every possible way, to what depths will she not sink? Market woman, rag and bone woman, beggar, she will go about covered in rags and vermin to the bistro to drink that little glass [absinthe] which brings a bit of forgetfulness. The hospital awaits her and at the end the dissection table, a terrible fate.

II

The coming of mechanization inaugurated the growth in women's employment. The same work which performed by hand necessitated masculine strength has become, thanks to the machine, within the reach of the weak. So capitalism cries out: 'Women, to work', 'Children, to work'.

Women rushed to the factory and agreed to work cheaply. How could they not? This work was a godsend. Formerly the household could scarcely make ends meet. Obviously the housewife cooked the cheapest food, did the washing and the mending. But her husband drank two litres of wine a day, he could not manage on less, not to mention the apéritifs. The pub is like a salon – that is where one meets one's friends, that is where one talks. Men cannot live locked up at home like bears between the missus who scolds and the screaming kids. The wife's wages bring happiness to the home. The rent will be paid regularly; a subscription will enable the wife to save money for a change of clothes. A wife who is houseproud can replace bare shelves with a dresser where her pots and pans can gleam ... .

Men try to banish women from the workplace. It is a question of competition. Women work at a lower wage, even if their productivity is the same as men's. Men behave like women's enemies and the latter respond in kind. If men can succeed in hounding women from the workplace, they do not hesitate to do so. They do not give a damn whether or not women have enough to eat. They refuse to understand that not all women can live by soliciting. But if men refuse women the right to work in their own workplace, they permit it in their capacity as husbands or fathers of daughters. Twenty francs a day is worth having; it plugs many a hole in the household budget.

The last war [1914–1918] opened up new horizons for women workers, as for women in general. The absence of men gave them an open field; their labour was demanded everywhere. Suddenly these slaves perceived the relative freedom conferred by money that one earns oneself, by the certainty that by knocking on the door of a factory, they could be hired and earn the fantastic sum of forty francs for a day's work. Halcyon days! Nothing but silk stockings, rabbit furs, costume jewellery, eau de Cologne. Women wore lipstick, and silk stockings to go to the factory.

When the husband came home on leave he found his wife looking jaundiced. What! Not only had the government taken him, they had taken his female as well. 'What fun can you have with a woman whose face is yellow and whose hands are lemon coloured?' But his wife shows signs of rebellion: 'What has come over you? Do not you know that I work in munitions? My yellow colour is from the melinite.'[19] As for mending those symbolic socks, she tells him where to get off. 'They have holes? Well, chuck them in the bin and buy some new ones'. The world turned upside down. Oh this war!...

The average worker of whatever sex, with the exception of a handful of anarchists, never asks himself whether what he makes in the factory will have a fitting destination. His only concern is his wages. Women were the same. They thought only about the forty francs a day which were an improvement on the seven francs fifty which the government granted them as an allowance. When the war ended, the men came back: the end of good times. In factories, on the trams, in offices, women were made redundant. Traditional life re-established itself. Certainly, apart from really unhappy marriages, women were pleased to see their husbands return. But nevertheless, they had developed a taste for the relative independence that work gave them. You could hear women conductors on the trams lamenting that they were going to be sacked. Obviously it did not occur to them to rebel, the time was not yet ripe, nor is it yet.

Nevertheless, the *status quo ante* was not re-established in post-war society. It is fair to say that the war precipitated women's economic emancipation. Administrative careers opened wider possibilities to women, especially since men, far from seeking employment in the narrow but secure bureaucracies as they had formerly done, spurned them for better paid posts in private industry. The baccalaureate which very few girls aspired to before the war became general among the middle classes, to the point that it became necessary, to the horror of arch-conservatives, to produce a common syllabus for secondary schools of both sexes. With a degree in Law, Art, or Science, many girls found jobs in government departments, in lawyers' and barristers' offices, and in factories for chemical products.

These jobs are not marvellous, but they allow one to live modestly without being a burden to anyone. If a husband turns up, fine, if not one can do without. Marriage, furthermore, no longer entails, *ipso facto*, giving up work. Women's wages have become necessary to the family budget, even among the lower-middle classes. The cost of living has risen six-fold and salaries are far from keeping pace.

The birth-rate obviously is affected by this new lifestyle. A child is very inconvenient. But ideas have changed. Formerly women submitted to maternity because they saw no way of avoiding it. Now contraceptive methods are known and one can predict that endless pregnancies will be a thing of the past.

III

Women's right to live like men by their labour is a question of elementary justice. They should not be obliged to live dependent on men. A woman will take a man; that is a natural need, but she shouldn't be forced into it by economic necessity. Proudhon's famous dilemma: housewife or whore, could only be defended by a man who wanted to limit freedom to the male half of the population. In a rational society, every individual, whatever their sex, should find their livelihood guaranteed by their labour. The battle of the sexes should disappear like all others ... . Though less in evidence because of being hidden, it is not for all of that less widespread. A rational social structure would suppress the struggle for existence; it is recognized that every man, woman and child has the right to live.

The nuclear family is very much weakened by the need for women to work. Until now it seems that work, far from liberating married women, has only crushed them since each must be both worker and housewife. The destruction of those prejudices which forbid men to help their wives with the housework is not a solution. In any case this would be a slow and uncertain business. What is needed is to transform work itself. Housework is comparable to small-scale artisanal industry of former times; a great deal of time was spent producing very little.

The one hundred ovens which cook the meals for one hundred households in an apartment block could be located in the basement and become one kitchen. A restaurant installed in the workplace can provide the mid-day meal. Alongside, one could have a common room for reading newspapers, chatting and so on. In the evening, the man and woman worker would go home to rest and to entertain themselves, not to work.

Houses for workers are beginning to be built, fitted out for modern life, but as with all reforms, this has been done timidly. A block of flats built for one thousand people should include:

1. restaurants
2. an infirmary for minor illnesses
3. a housecleaning team which cleans tenants' flats
4. a laundry and mending service
5. a crèche with a garden.

How bitterly narrow-minded people blame mothers for dragging their babies to the cinema. It is true that the baby will not enjoy the cinema. It is also not enjoyable for the spectators when he howls loudly. But the mother also needs to be entertained. If she has no one with whom she can leave her kid, she is obliged to bring the child with her.

The crèche provided with beds and a garden for playing etc. would liberate the mother. She can go to the cinema calmly to amuse or educate herself, knowing that her children are safe. Readers may think that these paradisial conditions will only be achieved under a far distant communism. We do not need communism for this. All these services can be paid for by the tenants and included in the rent, as today in a modern block of flats the heating is included.

Some writers have expressed the fear that once women's livelihoods are rendered secure through work, they would flee men and the latter would be unable to satisfy their sexual urges. This fear is groundless. Women's present-day attitude with regard to sexuality is artificial. Women have been brought up in the belief that the sexual act when it is not a question of marriage is immoral and shameful. Women put all their energy into repressing an instinct that society demands they destroy. In the past few years, however, there have been great changes in this regard in the estimation of these values and women dare to do what their grandmothers would never have dared. Novels written by women are full of disillusionment with the idea of virginity; they discuss the legitimacy of adultery and the rehabilitation of lesbianism as a replacement. Our mothers would never have dared to flaunt such ideas, seeking if need be consolation in religion. Work for women will not have the effect of distancing them from men. Young men and women are less separated than formerly and marriage is easier. It is true that marriage is not so long-lasting. People no longer marry for life. Divorce allows people to reclaim a liberty given up too easily. Should we deplore it? Not at all.

The family of former times was nothing but a façade. In the eyes of the world it presented a couple united if not by love at least by affection. In reality, the couple instead of loving one another, hated one another. The husband had mistresses and his wife champing at the bit put up with a home which she loathed because that home gave her a living. A woman who is independent economically more easily breaks out of a union which only renders her miserable. This is a good thing, not a bad one. Nothing should oblige individuals to lead lives which they hate.

The idea of competition by women for men's jobs is only the expression of petty egotism. A woman must eat and she should be able to do so by means other than that of prostitution. The war showed us that the distinction between men's and women's trades was one of custom, not a natural one. Women have shown that they can drive trams, carry sacks of coal, build houses and so on. One may object that it is not fitting for a woman to display a face blackened by coal or whitened by plaster. If people think like that it is because they do not want to renounce seeing women as sexual slaves, continually preoccupied with pleasing. It would be better for men, as for women, not to be soiled by hard labour, but women are no more debased by it than men. It has been said that work is freedom. There seems here to be a contradiction. It is a poor sort of freedom to be crouched over cloth, iron, wood or business letters to type, all day long. It is a beautiful day but one hardly notices, since the workshop opens on to a narrow, grey courtyard; the walls of the factory are black with smoke. The sunny streets invite one to go for a stroll; if there is freedom, it exists for those with private incomes.

Nevertheless, work does, to a certain extent, represent freedom because the money thus earned guarantees some degree of independence. For a young woman, paid work is freedom because it gets her out of the house. At the workplace she sees comrades; she exchanges ideas; her mind is broadened. Her life is no longer limited to her husband, children and a few neighbours. Her husband is boss and so is her employer, but his authority is less strict; an employer doesn't beat her; he is satisfied with reprimands or with dismissal. Finally it is easier to replace a harsh employer than to replace a husband who makes one's life hell.

Confined to her home, a woman develops a narrow mind full of pettiness. Outside her own circle, the only thing she is interested in is religion. The housewife constitutes a brake to social progress. Why have progressive political parties not recognized this long ago? No doubt they have understood it, but male egotism has been too strong. The idea of an individual's right to life and liberty is very recent. The most fiery speeches on liberty made by men during the Great Revolution [1789] only intended to celebrate masculine freedom. As a free citizen of the state, every man believed he had the right to dispose of his wife as he wished, since he believed she belonged to him. The Republic had been established in the country but the monarchy continued to hold sway in the family. The dogma of paternal and marital power continued to oppress women and children.

Slowly but surely democracy is gaining on the family, and its most powerful instrument will be the economic emancipation of women.

NOTES

1. For a discussion of Pelletier's involvement in craniometrical research see: Claude Maignien and Charles Sowerwine, *Madeleine Pelletier, une féministe dans l'arène politique*, Paris, Editions ouvrières, 1992, pp. 31–52, Felicia Gordon, *The Integral Feminist: Madeleine Pelletier, 1874–1939*, Cambridge, Polity Press, 1990, pp. 51–74; and Evelyne Peyre, 'Paris 1900: Une fervente de l'anthropologie', in *Madeleine Pelletier (1874–1939), logique et infortunes d'un combat pour l'égalité*, ed. Christine Bard, Paris, Editions Côté-femmes, 1992, pp. 35–50.
2. Frederick Engels, *The Origin of the Family, Private Property and the State in the Light of the Researches of Lewis H. Morgan*, translated by Alick West, from the German edition, 1891, London, Marxist-Leninist Library, 1943.
3. *Les Documents du progrès*, Rapports. I Progrès du Féminisme, July, 1909.
4. Baschoffen: Pelletier meant Johann-Jakob Bachofen (1815–1887), a classical scholar who developed the theory of 'Mother Right', a reconstruction of a history of matriarchy based on interpretations of myth and religion.
5. 'Lylie Braun' or Lily Braun (1865–1916), German feminist and socialist, forced out of the Social Democratic Party by Clara Zetkin who insisted on the rigid separation of feminism and socialism.
6. Hubertine Auclert (1848–1914), early champion of women's suffrage, became leader of '*Le Droit des femmes*' in 1876 and changed its title to the more radical '*Le Suffrage des femmes*'.

7. Caroline Kauffmann (1840–1926), feminist and advocate of the physical culture movement for women. She recruited Pelletier to '*La Solidarité des femmes*' and participated in various feminist protests, rare events in the annals of French suffragism.

8. *La Revue socialiste*, September–October, 1908.

9. 'The baker, the baker's wife...' is a reference to Louis XVI, Marie Antoinette and the Dauphin who were marched back from Versailles to Paris by Parisian women in October 1789. It was hoped the King would relieve the famine.

10. Théroigne de Méricourt, early feminist in the revolutionary period, was a member of the 'Fraternal Society of Patriots of the Two Sexes'. She took part in the October march to Versailles; however as a moderate Girondin, she was flogged by Jacobin women in March 1793. She subsequently suffered a mental breakdown and was confined to an asylum. Madame Roland (1754–1793), a republican *salonière*, had considerable influence in the Girondin circles. She was executed under the Terror.

11. Rose Lacombe: probably Claire Lacombe, early champion of women's rights during the revolutionary period. Olympe de Gouges, wrote the 'Rights of Women' (1791) in imitation of the 'Rights of Man', calling for complete equality between the sexes. A playwright and a royalist, she was guillotined in 1793. Aspasie Carlemigilli, a French revolutionary born in 1772, was executed in 1796. Interned as a lunatic almost from childhood, she left hospital during the revolutionary period and drew attention to herself by her exalted and eccentric behaviour. In 1795 she entered the Convention Assembly with the Parisian mob, struck the deputy, Ferand, and attacked another deputy, Camboules, with a knife. Arrested and tried on 19 March 1796, she did not deny the part she played in the assassination of Ferand and was condemned to death. (See *Nouvelle biographie universelle des temps les plus reculés jusqu'à 1850–60*, Paris, Didot frères, 1964.)

12. Chaumette, Pierre Gaspard (1763–1794), prosecutor for the Commune of Paris in 1792, was one of the founders of the Cult of Reason.

13. John Stuart Mill (1806–1873), English liberal and utilitarian philosopher, was greatly admired by Pelletier for his *Subjection of Women* (1869). (See Stefan Collini (ed.), *On Liberty with the Subjection of Women*, Cambridge, Cambridge University Press, 1989.) Mill corresponded with Auguste Comte (1798–1857), the founder of positivist philosophy, but finally broke with him over Comte's markedly conservative views on women's role in society.

14. 'Women's Franchise': Pelletier probably meant the NUWSS, the National Union of Women's Suffrage Societies, founded by Millicent Garrett Fawcett in 1897. By 'Votes for Women' she probably referred to the WSPU, the Women's Social and Political Union, founded around the turn of the century and dominated by the Pankhursts.

15. 'Stuttgart Conference': 1907. The congress of the Socialist International on 17 August, 1907 included the first International Conference of Women Socialists, directed by Clara Zetkin of the German SPD. Zetkin strongly opposed bourgeois feminism and argued in favour of women's but not feminist sections within the Socialist Party.

16. This is a good example of Pelletier's elitism. While considering women's alleged intellectual inferiority to be the product of sociological conditioning, nevertheless she thought that the vast majority of women were intellectually poorly equipped. They lacked training in concentration on intellectual issues. Pelletier saw herself as a rare exception.

17. Flora Tristan also used this motto attributed to the silk workers' uprising in Lyons in 1834.

18. Nana: Eponymous heroine of Zola's novel (1881) who became a highly paid courtesan and a byword for sexuality and corruption. (See Emile Zola, *Nana*, Paris, Librairie Charpentier, 1881.)

19. Melinite: used in the manufacture of explosives. Pelletier is describing a form of industrial contamination.

6. Madeleine Pelletier: the politics of sexuality

CONTEXTUAL INTRODUCTION

One of Madeleine Pelletier's strengths as an analyst of women's oppression lay in her capacity to make causal connections between seemingly disparate issues such as women's sexual ignorance, their social passivity and their unwillingness to enter the political arena. 'The Right to Abortion', 'The Feminist Education of Girls' (from which extracts are printed here), 'On Prostitution' and Pelletier's letter to Arria Ly, a form of feminist declaration, represent the breadth of her views on women's sexuality and education, and her conviction that women's control over their reproductive capacity was a key to their political emancipation.[1] Her letter to Arria Ly highlights a turn-of-the-century debate on separatist feminism. While advocating celibacy as a rational choice for women, Pelletier strongly dissented from Arria Ly's advocacy of separatism and her hatred of men.[2] For Pelletier, feminism was 'integral' in the sense that issues of private and public life were inextricably conjoined.

Pelletier's title, 'The Feminist Education of Girls' evokes the many works on the education of girls produced from the 17th to the late 19th centuries, influenced by Rousseau's *Emile* (1762).[3] Though Rousseau's education novel focused primarily on the ideal education of a young man, his heroine, Sophie, educated to be Emile's wife and companion, became the pattern for middle-class girls' education for much of the 19th century. Since Rousseau asserted that 'woman is made for man's delight', it followed that a girl's education should fit her to be a seductive partner, a useful companion to a future husband and the competent educator of his children. Similar views are found in Fénelon and Dupanloup, both of whom saw value in educating women to some degree, but not too much lest they lose sight of their 'natural' duties as wives and mothers.[4]

Pelletier's analysis of the need for changed educational provision for girls went far beyond questions of syllabus arrangement or the opening of examinations, schools and universities to women. Recognizing that children are taught in society, more than in schools, she analysed women's psychological as well as intellectual formation. How were feelings of inferiority or superiority engendered within social relationships? For Pelletier, 'education' represented the sum of all the influences bearing on a child. Well before De Beauvoir or sociological analyses of gender, Pelletier examined the way in which our sexual personality is constructed by the surrounding culture. It followed that the 'feminist mother', no matter how committed to feminist ends, could not hope to mould her child in an image totally contrary to society.

Pelletier considered education under three broad categories: education of character, education of intellect and sexual education. She linked the issue of dress to that of women's servility. Women's habits of false modesty and flirtatiousness (recommended as 'natural' by Rousseau), were conditioned by the elaborate and constricting styles of the *Belle Epoque*.[5] Women were literally caged by their clothes. This sense of constriction operated from an early age when little girls, thanks to their skirts, were prevented from moving as freely as boys. The child's peers and social custom created the psychological sex, or what is now called gender. Girls should dress in trousers and engage in all forms of physical exercise. Physical courage, which was held to be the perogative of men, could and should be taught to girls at an early age. Pelletier, the enemy of amateurism in education for women, thought that intellectual confinement for girls had succeeeded in restraining their minds as their bodies had been restrained by corsets. Their literary models should show heroic figures who could inspire a young girl to emulate them. After their formal education, women should seek careers, not as stopgaps until they married, but for financial and social independence. An early advocate of lifelong education, Pelletier thought that everyone should attain the greatest degree of intellectual development of which they were capable.

Sexual education was still a novel idea in a culture where 'innocence', virtue and ignorance were synonymous concepts and female virtue still equated with chastity. Pelletier, following through her ideas on the virtual indivisibility of the educational process, argued that a woman should look after her body, including its reproductive aspects, with the same care as she would look after her mind. She assumed girls would take responsibility for the choice of sexual relations and advocated celibacy as a reasonable option, though not for all. 'The Feminist Education of Girls' is an innovative text in its views on the social construction of gender. There are clear tensions, however, on the issue of 'forming' the child in a more or less authoritarian way, against a commitment to a more libertarian approach. This was also a tension that ran through all Pelletier's political theory.

Pelletier's *Le Droit à l'avortement: pour abrogation de l'article 317* (The Right to Abortion: For the Repeal of Article 317) appeared both separately and as part of a larger work, *L'Emancipation sexuelle de la femme*, from 1911 onwards. In the latter work Pelletier attacked the sexual double standard, advocated a single morality for both sexes, analysed the family as an authoritarian institution and advocated the right of women to reproductive choice.

'The Right to Abortion' was a key text, both for Pelletier's feminism and a radical contribution to feminist thinking on women's sexual rights. Pelletier drew on her experience as a medical doctor who had witnessed the results of badly performed abortions, as well as her eye-witness view of the misery brought to working-class families from unrestricted natality. A partisan of the neo-Malthusian movement to encourage birth control among the working class, Pelletier defended voluntary family limitation to her socialist colleagues and in articles for Gustave Hervé's *La Guerre sociale*. French neo-Malthusianism had its roots in working-class libertarianism and anarchism, represented by the leader of the Movement for Human Regeneration, Paul Robin, and to that extent Pelletier's political affiliations, first to anarchism and then to revolutionary socialism, allowed her to link birth control to class liberation.

Pelletier, reasoning from the basis of the 'Rights of Man', focused on the idea of personhood and on the rights of individuals over their own bodies (not to undergo torture, for example). At the root of all other forms of women's exploitation – economic, legal or class-based – lay sexual exploitation. She believed that women's emancipation would only be achieved when they, and not men, chose whether or not to reproduce, since women's bodies were uniquely engaged in, and in danger from, the reproductive act. The 'right to abortion' was a logical necessity for women's self-defence, not desirable in itself, but a last resort when contraception had failed. Women should not be seen as species agents but as individuals in their own right with the responsibilities and choices available to other free individuals. It was only when women had achieved sexual equality on the level of reproductive control and the right of desire that the underlying causes of political and social inequality could be addressed.

The article 'On Prostitution' shows Madeleine Pelletier in her most rationalist and uncompromising mode, joining a Marxist critique of prostitution to a call for women's sexual liberation. Like many feminists, she opposed regulation of prostitution and the enforced medical inspection of prostitutes. These inspections, carried out on women but not on their male clients, were ineffective as a prophylactic measure and a violation of civil liberties, since any woman could be arrested on suspicion of soliciting and subjected to forcible medical examination. Adopting a Marxist critique of sexual relations, Pelletier claimed a positive case for prostitution under capitalism. It was preferable to rape; at least a woman sold her sexual services rather than having them 'taken' without her leave. Pelletier mocked the double standard that society applied to women who sold their sexual favours, pointing out that class distinctions operated even here between well-paid courtesans and street walkers in slum districts. If sexual repressions were lifted and if women, like men, were free to express their sexuality, prostitution would disappear.[6]

TEXTS

'The Feminist Education of Girls'
'The Right to Abortion'
'On Prostitution'
'Letter from Madeleine Pelletier to Arria Ly'

THE FEMINIST EDUCATION OF GIRLS[7]

Chapter i: The Value of Education

It is often said and rightly so that nations have the governments they deserve. An oppressed people which did not deserve its oppression would rise against its oppressors and would render them incapable of tyrannizing over them. This truth applies not only to nations but to all groups. The proletariat certainly deserves the fate meted out to it in present-day society; if it did not deserve it, given the fact that it forms a majority of the population, it would have dispossessed the bourgeoisie from its power long ago.

The same is true of the two sexes. Marginalized by society, women as a group deserve the slave-like position that is accorded to them. They only know how to groan when the male yoke is too painful. If they showed greater dignity, if they knew how to organize themselves better, if they campaigned with greater energy, they would long since have attained political and social equality.

But it is pointless to rail against the oppressed for their lack of spirit; they are what they are. People make their own circumstances and circumstances make people; psychological and social factors are interdependent. Only rare and superior individuals have been capable of rebelling against their situation and inciting their brothers in servitude to rebellion. The masses are subjected to their condition, not even realizing that it can change. Nevertheless, in the long term, social evolution does occur under the influence of exceptional individuals. The common people finally freed themselves from feudal rule; the bourgeoisie triumphed over the nobility; women are in the process of emancipating themselves from their dependence on men.

The work of women's emancipation is above all else a collective struggle. It is the state which will free women by legislation, bringing to perfection by sanctioning it, the work begun by economic evolution. The right to vote and eligibility for public office will transform women's mentality and will change standards of behaviour. Ambition, which women only had through men, the son, husband or lover with whom they shared their lives, they will feel for themselves and under the impulse of this stimulating passion, an intelligent, courageous and restless elite will rise up from the mass of women and draw other women along with them. Being more highly valued, women will lose the timidity which renders them inferior; they will speak to men as equals.

Compared with social education, individual education has a very limited power. Thus it will never be possible to recommend the setting up of feminist schools. Obviously there are circumstances when one is obliged to accept the solutions available. If a wealthy feminist insisted on giving money to a school for 'the cause', one should not prevent her. No effort is absolutely useless, but the money would be better spent in campaigns for political agitation. Reforms for women's emancipation speak to the whole population; a school only addresses a small number of people and since its efforts are negated by society at large, the result is almost nil. It is a drop in the ocean... .

So it is without much hope that I write this little book, and what I expect from it is the opening up of discussion in feminist circles, rather than any genuinely practical result. For an individual's feminist education, which I try to map out here, will have few positive results. It is almost impossible to bring up a child with ideas which are in opposition to the immense majority in society. A feminist mother will have against her: her husband, her parents, her servants if she has any, her friends, her neighbours, the school, passers-by in the street – in short, all of society. Even were she to possesses the necessary will to resist all these, she would still fail because her child would abandon her to join the majority... .

Further, our hopes will not be realized unless our work makes feminist teachers decide to mould their pupils to these ideas. If private schools are useless, state schools, given their number, allow one to act on a scale that would be genuinely valuable. Reflect all you teachers that you have the entire feminine future of France in your hands. If you will it and and by your actions, in ten years all girls will be able to understand how iniquitous women's condition is and to demand equality between the sexes. Obviously schools and lycées are not everything and feminist propaganda disseminated there will be negated everywhere by familial and other influences. Nevertheless, something will remain, indeed much will remain.

It is true that one has to follow a syllabus as a teacher, but the syllabus only controls the subject matter taught. The educationist can, to a large extent, do with it what she chooses. What can prevent one in a history course, for example, from explaining the injustice of the Salic Law which excluded women from the throne. With regard to Joan of Arc, a teacher could show that it is not impossible for a woman to lead an army to victory. Instead of depicting the Good Woman of Lorraine as a sort of visionary, a teacher could show her as a most powerful feminist figure, a woman commander-in-chief.

Chapter ii: Training the Body and the Character

First of all, how should a little girl be dressed? The question at first glance may appear to be of minimal importance, but it is on the contrary a crucial one. Along with our physiognomy, our clothing is all of us that appears to public view. It is on the basis of dress that one judges strangers, and the impression made on others is also the impression made on ourselves. Soldiers are not made to wear a uniform or monks a habit for no reason. An army without uniforms would have little value and monks or nuns without habits would resemble lay persons. Expensive clothes make one feel proud and daring; they stimulate energy whereas rags induce humiliation, sloppiness and fear.

If, from an early age, you clothe your little girl in dresses loaded with ribbons and decorations, if you deck her in jewels, you will turn her into a flirt who thinks only of dolling herself up. Any effort you make subsequently to make her into a serious and dignified person will be in vain. Your daughter may listen to you with seeming deference, but her real education will be with her little friends with whose frippery she will compare her own. When her childhood is over you will have, if you are rich, nothing but a worldly doll. If you are poor, you will have something much worse, for your child will be determined to do anything in order to obtain the baubles that she craves.

The feminist mother should, therefore, try to dress her little girl like a boy. Masculine clothes will have the most beneficial effect on the child's character. Firstly, their cut permits her to execute any movement without indecency. Her mother will not need to order her constantly to 'pull down your skirt' – 'don't lift your legs like that, it's unbecoming'. Children have a need to move about incessantly and these constant prohibitions have the end result of creating fetters for girls from the earliest age. It goes without saying that one should not say, as some mothers, even feminist ones do: 'Little girls don't turn somersaults', or again, 'Hold still then, little tom-boy'. A mother who behaves in this way should not be surprised if her daughter becomes a woman, like other women, in spite of attending the lycée and gaining the baccalaureate ... . A feminist educator will take particular care over a child's toys, for these, to a great extent, contribute to moulding the mind and character. Dolls, doll's house furniture and kitchen cookers which teach the little girl from the cradle that she will become a housewife, will be proscribed. Instead the child will be given constructive games requiring patience and which accustom her to concentrate her attention. Girls may even be given military toys ... .

When watching over your children's games, it will often be obvious that boys, indeed even the girl's brothers, will try to humiliate the little girl by repeating comments to her that they have picked up about feminine inferiority. 'Women are useless' – 'Women aren't soldiers' – 'You don't know how to turn somersaults, one can tell you are only a girl'. Sometimes the 'stronger sex', instead of trying to humiliate the little girl, wants to excuse her but this is just as bad. 'Obviously, that was a pathetic somersault, but for a girl it's quite good.'

The mother must never hesitate to intervene in such instances. If the guilty party is her own son, she will explain to him why common opinion is mistaken. If he wanted to vex his sister, she will make him ashamed of his lack of feeling, of the abuse he has made of a power which he acquired through no merit of his own, but which society has given him purely by reason of his sex. Then she will punish him severely. If the child is not a member of the family, the mother should give the same explanations and then send him packing from her home for some time.

The mother should not restrict herself to defending her daughter; she should teach her to defend herself. She should tell her what answers to make, and if, in order to avenge her honour and that of her sex, the little girl cuffs these young anti-feminists, instead of being blamed, she should be congratulated. As a general rule, one should refrain from protecting one's child from other children. The girl must grow accustomed to defending herself and to giving as good as she gets. Educationists draw inspiration, as far as girls are concerned, from a moral model of passivity. Thus when children scrap, where girls are involved, teachers punish the defender as much as the attacker. Already weak by nature, women, by this foolish educational policy, are deprived even of the instinct of personal self-defence, which leads us instinctively to retaliate when we are attacked. The feminist educator should on this issue take the opposing view from that of tradition. She should train her daughter to defend herself and when she loses out in a scrap, far from pitying her, her mother should show her contempt ... . As a general rule, one should not constrain children without a reason. There are mothers who spend their time forbidding things, especially to their daughters: 'Don't wander off so far; close the door; haven't you finished jumping about; stand up straight; don't run about like that'. Mothers often hand out these orders for no reason at all, but simply to pass the time. To a great extent, a child has the right to its freedom and as long as it does nothing harmful, the child should be allowed to act as it pleases. There is one prohibition to which I have already made allusion and which a feminist mother should avoid. It is that which consists of telling the little girl to pull down her dress when it rides up in the course of her games. The child should wear pants under her skirt and indecency will not then pose a problem ... .

One of the fundamental points of character education, *the* fundamental point, even, is the struggle against fear. Courage cannot be manufactured; it is a natural quality and perhaps pusillanimity itself is a sign of superior intellect. Among primitive peoples, courage is very common. Simple people go into danger without thinking, impelled by their motives at the moment, by duty or the desire for power. Fear is the product of a highly developed imagination, which represents to itself the dangers to be undergone and exaggerates them. But one does not live in a vacuum and thus while working to develop intellectually, one must think about self-defence. Courage is our best weapon in the battle of life.

No one needs this weapon more than a woman. Education today, however, far from developing courage in women, represses it as not being suitable to feminine graces. The natural result is that women, incapable of defending themselves, look for a protector and often find only an exploiter. I have said that education cannot alone create courage where it does not exist, but education can limit timidity to a considerable extent.

One should first make a point of analysing everything which at first glance appears dangerous. This will allow one to eliminate imaginary dangers which will then no longer arouse fear. One should explain to a child that a mouse, even a rat or a spider, little creatures who ask for nothing better than to flee human beings, are not to be feared. For the same reason one should overcome the fear of the dark which is, one may say, general among children. The fear of thunder can be eliminated as well by explaining that cases of death by lightning are extremely rare, especially in cities. Obviously one should refrain from commenting on the crime reports in the papers in front of children. I remember the terror I felt as a child when, in the evening, after having heard read aloud the gory details of a murder, I had to go up or down our staircase which was unlit. Between the ground floor and the first floor there was a sort of storeroom where a shopkeeper kept his shutters. I trembled whenever I had to pass them. I imagined all kinds of murderers hidden there, ready to leap on me and slit open my stomach, as had been done to the women in the newspaper.

Nonetheless, reason alone is not enough to conquer fear. One should bring feeling into play by expressing admiration of courage and complete contempt for cowardice. But the best antidote against fear is habituation to danger. The railway engine driver does not worry about derailments. The anatomy student dissecting bodies every day does not think about dangerous infections. One should arrange dangerous-seeming situations to which to expose the child. She should be taken on a roller-coaster and a water chute and all other entertainments based on simulated dangers. In addition, physical exercises like fencing, shooting, swimming, horse riding and boxing are an excellent education in courage and endurance.

Along with courage, one should stimulate initiative. Some mothers cocoon their sons, but they are the exception. The majority conform to the tradition which ordains that boys be given their liberty. But for daughters, the social mores being the opposite, mothers take advantage of this by being over-careful with their daughters, showing a harmful concern. Society gives a young man all the facilities necessary to launch himself in life. For a girl, on the contrary, almost everything is closed off. What will it be like then, if, when starting life, one adds to the exterior constraints all those which flow from timidity and inexperience? To encourage a child's initiative is largely a matter of non-direction. One needs only to confront children with difficulties and to refuse to advise them. A first lesson in initiative would consist in not accompanying a child to school. After warning against the dangers of the street, she should be allowed to go alone. From the age of eight it is a good idea to accustom the child to take the bus alone or to go to the cinema alone, not too far from home. A little later the child may take short railway journeys and be sent to eat at a restaurant. All these little acts by which the child learns to procure what she needs by the sole assistance of the money she has in her pocket, will develop in her not only initiative, but also a feeling of the force of her own character. When she is about thirteen years of age she can go on short bicycle trips, learning to read maps in order to find her route. It will then be necessary to dress her as a boy and to furnish her with a revolver, which of course she will already have learned to use.

Self-effacing modesty is often preached to girls; this is to be expected. Destined to be subordinated to men, it is deemed unsuitable for girls to have a high opinion of themselves. But we, who want this child to become an independent woman, will not lean towards the side of humility. A dispropor-tionate pride is harmful and makes us antipathetic to others, turning them against us. But one must teach a girl to value herself and to make herself valued. She should become accustomed to holding her head high, her body straight, to looking at people frankly and to stating her own opinions frankly without worrying about whether her hearers agree with her or not. Timidity, like fear, is often the result of intellectual superiority. A stupid person rarely feels self-doubt. An intelligent person, by contrast, often doubts herself. Like fear, timidity weakens the individual; one should, therefore, combat it. Girls need to be taught not to show inner hesitation about the value of their knowledge or their opinions and to speak aloud as though they were sure of themselves. Ahead of them in life are many adversaries, and it is a good tactic to hide one's weaknesses from them.

Chapter iii: Intellectual Education

Until recently, those authors concerned with girls' intellectual development only applied themselves to the task of restricting it. I recall that M. Marion, a professor of education at the Faculty of Letters at the Sorbonne, used to say some ten years ago that the motivating idea behind girls' lycées was that they should not prepare girls for careers. Anatole France in *The Crime of Sylvestre Bonnard*, a novel about a girl's education, surrounds the child with flowers, but as for developing her mind, that is out of the question.[8] Herbert Spencer himself, so great a thinker in many respects, partook of the common opinions about girls' education. He only granted them the right to learn to cook and to charm.[9] Society's great preoccupation has always been to keep women confined. Barbarians confined them materially between walls, modern societies confine them within a whole system of legal and traditional snares, and in order to prevent any temptation to escape care is taken to confine their minds from an early age. A woman always knows enough, says an old but still current adage.

In the past twenty years, a great deal of progress has been made. Faculties of the university have opened to women, one after the other, but women are only tolerated there. Girls' secondary education continues to lead nowhere. Therefore, girls who want to gain their baccalaureate must fall back upon private instruction, organized by some means or other. As is to be expected, most give up; the only ones to persist are middle-class girls whose parents want to make sure of an honourable position for their daughters should their dowries be insufficient and they fail to find someone to marry. In all this there has obviously been progress. Formerly, a girl who did not marry remained an expense to her family, an old maid with girlish affectations, a childish mind, affected manners, bad tempered and sharp tongued.

In order to occupy the long hours of her aimless life, she had nothing but religion. Affiliated to *Les Enfants de Marie*, she carried a banner at religious festivals, attended all the services; the gossip of the sacristy nourished her mind, a secret love for the young and handsome priest consumed her heart. Today such a woman has a career, which is both more lucrative and more healthy. But a life in the public sphere is still only conceived of by many women as a last resort following a failure to marry. Furthermore the access to careers for women is only half-open. Men jealously guard for themselves the most challenging and most lucrative posts where there are good career structures. To women they apportion the menial jobs without a future where one only has the perspective of monotonous secretarial work to ensure an eternally mediocre and colourless existence ... .

Education should not be a stop-gap or insurance policy for women any more than for men. Whatever the sex, the individual has the right to intellectual development, to the full growth of his or her mind. There is never enough education available. It is not up to a teacher to set a limit on what his pupil can do; the limits of self-development are up to the pupil whose intelligence, faced with insuperable problems, at some point will come to a halt. A feminist should encourage her daughter's educational development as far as possible.

Feminist campaigns have had some effect within women teachers' circles. Nowadays there are a certain number who slip a few feminist ideas into the set syllabus. But one cannot depend on the teaching profession, because, being both women and civil servants, teachers at girls' lycées have two motives for being cautious. Through their natural timidity, and also thanks to their fear of their superiors, teachers only expound a watered down feminism to their pupils. To correct what seems to them an extreme point of view they will launch into a whole anti-feminist speech. Pupils do not know what to make of such a teaching strategy which has, in addition, the problem of perpetuating a weak and timorous character in girls, the most contemptible of all. A young feminist should know what she thinks and not be afraid to say it
... .

It should be the aim of feminists and of everyone to make the greatest possible intellectual development accessible because this applies to girls as well as to boys. One should not be put off by the perception of those barriers which society raises up in front of the poor but well-educated girl. Firstly such a young woman may succeed in finding a post in one of the liberal professions, which though not outstanding for women is better than the badly paid drudgery of manual work. If she does not succeed, and is forced to seek work in commerce or industry, she will bring to this work qualities of intelligence which will serve to advance her in her job and in her leisure time she can enjoy music, visit museums and appreciate nature. This may divert her from marrying a worker, but there is nothing very bad in this. On the contrary, I think that a woman should be educated for her own good, not for that of a man ... . It goes without saying that the entry into a career should not mark the end of education. That attitude is for crass souls who only understand the acquisition of knowledge as means of making money. Education is an end in itself and should continue all one's life.

Chapter iv: Sexual Education

Sexual education is now on the agenda. People are increasingly throwing off the old notions which suggested that it was moral to appear ignorant of sexual matters and good to be silent about the facts of life. How many girls used to get married still believing that marriage only consists in dressing in white in order to go to the town hall and the church accompanied by a husband? The revelation of the reality was always a disagreeable surprise and sometimes a terrible one. It often happened that the newly married young woman expressed indignation and complained to her mother. Her mother would preach resignation. 'Women,' she would say, 'are made to submit and to suffer; that is nature's way – and God's!' Many men did not consider women to be human beings, but rather instruments for pleasure which they had the right to use and abuse. Many men had and have few scruples (one can speak in the present tense, for the sexual education of women is still far from being an adequate preparation for marriage) about marrying when they were infected with gonorrhoea. After a few weeks of marriage, the wife would fall ill and take to her bed, knowing nothing of the cause of her illness. Hypocrisy and ignorance combine as accomplices to deceive her. 'Look,' say relatives and friends, ' how fragile the female sex is. This young woman has only been married for two months and she has taken to her bed.' The surgeon talks of an operation.

Neo-Malthusian propaganda drew the attention of progressive people to the sexual question. They came to the conviction that sexuality had nothing shameful about it and that one can deal openly with it as with any other question. But for men of progressive as well as of conservative views, women are only an instrument. Thus neo-Malthusianism was only concerned with the economic viewpoint and with the security of the single man. Nevertheless, among the neo-Malthusians one finds a few fair-minded men who think that women should at least be taken into consideration on sexual matters. But even in their writing, if women are something more than an instrument whose feelings one can ignore, they are far from being the equals of men. The most advanced works on sexual education restrict themselves to giving men advice on how to manage women. Women are depicted as human beings but inferior and weak. Men may do harm to women, therefore it is a moral act to restrain the male sexual impulse. Men should beware of seducing young girls because they may become pregnant and in this way ruin their whole lives.

A feminist worthy of the name does not want pity. The care of organizing her life falls on herself and herself alone. She should be aware of the dangers of sexuality in precisely the same way as she guards against illness and other dangers which surround her. But in order for her to be capable of this self-protection, her teacher, breaking openly with those prejudices which even the most liberal people only tackle with timidity, must undertake her daughter's sexual education ... . In order to take away any perverse character from sexuality, it is absolutely necessary to divest it of the mystery in which it is habitually shrouded. One should begin, then, at about the age of seven, to tell a little girl that children are not born either in cabbages or in roses, but from their mother's belly. As for inter-sexual relations which lead to procreation, these do not need to be revealed before the age of twelve. In healthy-minded circles it is rare for the child to be preoccupied with the subject before the twelfth year. Sexuality should be treated matter-of-factly as part of biology. There should be no shameful connotations attached. A chart should be drawn showing reproduction in plants, lower animals, birds and mammals and then it should be explained that Man belongs to this latter class and reproduces according to the same laws … .

How can one measure the value of sexuality from a moral point of view? Obviously, given the fact that I believe that women have like men a right to sexual pleasure, I cannot advise a feminist mother to draw inspiration from tradition. Having a lover is not an evil. What is an evil is to allow oneself to be supported by him because one then becomes contemptible by selling one's sexuality. Before thinking of sexual satisfaction, a young feminist should be in a position to earn her living, if she is poor, and to be intellectually independent if she is rich. One should point out that if sexual desires are satisfied too early, this can only disturb preparation for a career and throw a young woman off course for the rest of her life.

One must also explain how deep the gulf is between real justice and present reality. The inalienable right to sexual pleasure which women ought to possess is not accorded by society, and since we live in society one must take account, as little as possible, but still, take account to some extent, of social prejudices. For example, a girl's belief that she has the right to sexual pleasure must not make her the dupe of men and expose her to being rejected by society as part of a class of shady women, because today distinctions are scarcely made between a girl living in a free union and a kept woman. This conflict between true justice and social reality means that one should watch over the girl up to the age of twenty, while still leaving her a great measure of liberty. She should be restrained as much but no more than middle-class families restrain their sons. Reason is still very weak in a girl of fifteen or sixteen. In spite of advice and even examples, she may give way to the natural attractions of youth and lose, little by little, all the good habits of regular work and study. At twenty, a girl is a fully reasonable person; she can then be given her liberty with all its risks and dangers.

If a girl wishes to blot out the chapter of sexuality from her life, she should be encouraged in this path. Laws and customs enslave women and they can only really find a bit of liberty by depriving themselves of sexual love. Even in a free union, a woman is subject to the man who believes he is her master. In order to gain her independence, the young feminist must maintain a constant struggle in her household which may make life intolerable. Doctors who have written on the dangers of chastity have only considered men. Women do not have such an overwhelming sexual instinct. In convents, many nuns live to a very old age and in better health than married women. The nervousness of old maids is a product of idleness, not of celibacy. If they are frequently sad it is because celibacy has been imposed on them by circumstances in spite of their strong desire for marriage … .

On the other hand, the young woman may wish to find a place for sexuality in her life. What advice to give her then? That will depend on her social circumstances. If she is rich, she can marry, whereas a free union would place her outside her class. Marriage among the ruling classes is less enslaving than in the middle and especially the working classes. Obviously one should take precautions to guard her fortune, choosing the system of separation of property. If the man disappoints the young feminist's expectations, she can seek a divorce which is easy to obtain for someone with money.

In the lower-middle classes a free union does not have the same drawbacks as in high society. There is little entertaining; one does not need to fear being ostracized by one's milieu. One need not overly regret the breaking off of relations with a few families of minor civil servants, doctors or industrialists. To the extent to which one is educated one can gain access to literary and artistic milieus which are very liberal on the question of relationships outside of marriage. Among the working classes, free unions are not a problem; if need be, one can always say that one is married.

In general, a woman's well-being and that of her children should be ensured by herself, either by means of her personal fortune or by a sufficiently well-paying career. Under these circumstances a free union is preferable to marriage. This alone permits a couple either to remain united throughout their lives if they are harmonious, or to separate if both or one do not find in this relationship the happiness they expected.

THE RIGHT TO ABORTION[10]

The natural aim of sexual desire is the reproduction of the species. Partisans of final cause explanations say that Nature has rendered the sexual act pleasurable in order to persuade individuals to reproduce themselves. According to transformist theories … it appears that among the bi-sexual species, only those have been able to survive for whom the union of the sexes has been pleasurable. If bi-sexual species had existed in which the two sexes felt no attraction for each other, they have necessarily had to disappear. Nevertheless, if the initial act of reproduction is pleasurable, reproduction itself is painful and offspring are a burden. Animals have a very low intelligence and reproduce themselves in any case, being little more than blind slaves of instinct. But the human species … makes a distinction within natural law between the agreeable and the painful, and puts its efforts into avoiding pain in order to retain that which is pleasurable.

Far from being limited to marriage, love (sexual desire) greatly exceeds its bounds. From puberty to old age, men freely devote themselves to it outside the conjugal bond and in this freewheeling career devoted to sexuality, the concern for reproduction is completely banished. When a child arrives unexpectedly, it is seen as an accident, an unfortunate accident.

As long as women are considered as inferior beings, it is clear that sexual pleasure will be reserved for the male sex. Woman is only an instrument which a man uses in order to enjoy his sexuality; he consumes her like a fruit. In marriage and especially in maternity, however, a woman's moral situation is improved. While still an object, she is also, to some extent, an intellectual and moral companion; her role as housewife and educator of children masks her sexual role. But outside marriage woman again becomes the instrument of animal passions. Depending on the social milieu, women are bought dearly or cheaply, a man may even ruin himself for them, but they are always despised ... .

Women are not merely desired, however, they too desire. The sexual instinct cries out in them too. But society gives them absolutely no right to assert these desires. A woman can only satisfy her need to love by putting herself under matrimonial domination unless of course she prefers to sell herself; in that case abasement is added to domination.

When women began to reflect on their condition, when thanks to the careers opening before them, they discovered the possibility of ensuring their existence without the help of their family or of a man, they demanded, along with all other rights, the right to sexual expression. It is certainly the case that there is nothing sublime about the physiological act of love; nevertheless, sublime or not, if it is permitted to men, why should it not be to women? ... The only barrier which keeps women chaste is the barrier of morality and moral barriers are easy to break. Where there is a will there is a way.

In reality, however, the rules of these unwritten laws are not without their power. In practice, free love brings women all kinds of miseries, thanks to the generally unfavourable nature of public opinion. Men treat women disrespectfully; families close their doors to them. Nevertheless increasing numbers of women are making up their minds to enter into free-love unions. They are prepared to endure contempt in order to satisfy their senses ... . Sexual desire is therefore tending towards equality. It is no longer the unique blessing of men. Women want their share, and an active share. The feminine role, though the inverse of the masculine role, is not in any sense degrading.

Nevertheless, an obstacle, even more powerful for not being of a social order, but of the natural order, arises for women who wish to satisfy their sexuality without hindrance; this is the advent of children. The prospect of a child throws a woman who has emancipated herself by education or work into all the slavery of the past. How can one speak of equality in love when the man goes off freely, his needs satisfied, while the woman is responsible for maternity? Pregnancy turns sexuality into a real trap for a woman ... . She ceases to be an individual, conscious of her dignity, and falls into all the degradations of the seduced girl. A beseeching slave, she pursues the man who deserts her: she asks him for pity, like one defeated in battle.

In the future, when economic emancipation has been achieved, becoming a mother will not necessarily be a calamity for an unmarried woman. Pregnancy is tiresome and childbirth painful; but afterwards, the woman has the child who is a source of happiness. A man, after satisfying his passion, remains alone (*post coit animale triste*); a woman has her child, who by the joys that he gives her is a recompense for her suffering ... . Guarding her child, a woman forgets herself, and that is a good thing. The many troubles that weighted upon her formerly seem to have flown away. She is stronger. But even if a woman's wages allowed her to bring up one or two children alone, in order for maternity not to be a form of slavery, it should not be forced upon her. It is up to each individual woman to decide if and when she wishes to be a mother.

Voluntary birth control practices have been in common use for many years among the educated and prosperous classes. If rich people have fewer chilren than the poor, it is not that they are less prolific, nor that they abstain from sexual relations, it is because they have willed it. At the present time [1913], to the great consternation of conservatives, voluntary birth control is gaining ground among the proletariat. The men of this class, less energetic than the rich, refuse, in general, to make the necessary effort at a given moment not to make their wives pregnant. The neo-Malthusians have invented all kinds of appliances and products for women's self-preservation which have become an important industry in trade union and anarchist circles. But often the methods used fail. The workers do not use them properly. The need to have recourse to them methodically at each time of sexual intercourse is a burden; often they neglect them and the wife becomes pregnant. Nevertheless, neo-Malthusian propaganda has been effective. Not only does the trade union elite have relatively fewer children, but the mass of workers themselves begin to have fewer than formerly.

Though almost entirely successful if one applies them carefully, the means of avoiding pregnancy are nevertheless not absolutely foolproof. When a woman, either by negligence or ignorance, becomes pregnant and rejects maternity, a second avenue is open to her: abortion. Abortion is at the present time in general use in urban centres... .

Abortions are performed above all in Paris by agencies who on page four of newspapers carry out a scarcely disguised advertising campaign. As recently as last year it was possible to read advertisements such as these: 'Delays: infallible method' followed by an address but no name. The word

'Delay' raised an outcry. Legal proceedings followed; as a result at a given moment all these 'Delays' disappeared to be replaced by 'Midwife: complete discretion'.... . Sometimes abortion agencies swindle their clients. The operator introduces some instrument or other in the vagina. The client pays and leaves, satisfied. Nothing happening, she goes back to the agency; the farce is repeated; she pays a second time, and so it goes on. No one complains; and with reason.

Nevertheless, the majority of abortions are not carried out in these places: women have learned to abort themselves and they frequently do so. The medical means to cure 'Delays' are nowadays known to everyone and it can be said that at least in the big cities there is no woman who has not used them sometime or other. Mechanical means are also commonly practised; the long inter-uterine probes which one sees displayed everywhere in herbalists' shops make this very clear, for these instruments made of rubber or bone are not bought by doctors, who employ metal instruments which are easier to sterilize. Women, in any case, don't make a mystery of these practices. On the landings of working-class apartment buildings, at the baker's, the butcher's, the grocer's, housewives advise their neighbours on the means of abortion, women on whom brutal or improvident husbands have inflicted repeated pregnancies. Abortion is sometimes dangerous, but only because it is forbidden. The operation required is of the most minor kind. If Article 317 were abolished and if doctors were allowed to perform abortions within the first three months of pregnancy for women who wished it, there would be virtually no complications ... . The danger comes from the ignorance of practitioners. In the north of France I met a cheese merchant who boasted of inducing labour in women by means of douching equipment. She felt nothing but disdain for antisepsis. She said that safeguards of boiling and washing have been dreamt up by doctors purely to increase their importance. One shudders when considering the number of infections that this woman and her ilk, who are legion, can have caused ... . There are cases where complications are extremely serious. The douching pipette may be dirty but at least it is flexible, which cannot be said of curtain rods, knitting needles, hat pins, button hooks or pokers which women sometimes use to deliver themselves from a pregnancy. By committing these follies, they can precipitate a fatal case of peritonitis.

Abortion is no longer, as it formerly was, an exceptional act; it is, so to speak, the rule in all classes of society ... . Abortion permits lovers to be generous at small expense. That is why they insist that their mistresses make up their minds to have one. 'I loved you; you loved me', the young bourgeois says to the little working girl; 'We've had some good times together. It is true that I have made you pregnant, but I've paid for an abortion and now we are quits.' ... .

Abortion is not limited to unmarried relationships; married couples constantly have recourse to it. Sometimes the first pregnancy is aborted; it has come too soon. The couple wish to have a few good years in front of them to enjoy life; children are postponed until later. More often they only have recourse to abortion at the third or fourth pregnancy. While the first child's arrival was greeted with pleasure, the second accepted and the third greeted with resignation, the fourth is absolutely rejected. Civil servants, clerks, prosperous small shopkeepers are all determined to bring up their children well. They would like, if possible, for their descendants to gain a superior social rank to their own or at least to keep an equal rank. A skilled artisan does not, save in exceptional cases, have this preoccupation with education, but he wants to enjoy a good lifestyle. M. Bertillon, in his recent book on depopulation, claims that large numbers of children are not the cause of poverty.[11] This is wrong. The simplest arithmetic demonstrates that less money is required to nourish three people than six, and any observation of working-class homes shows everywhere the relative prosperity of those whose fecundity is limited and everywhere poverty where people have many children. A working-class household of one or two children has, on average, two clean rooms, comfortable furniture, sufficient clothes, linen and food. Such a household pays its rent, has no debts and even manages to save ... . Working-class families with many children are semi-beggars; the wife goes begging to the town hall, to the church and to charitable institutions. In order to get her rent paid, she feigns religious devotion and sends her children to church. She grovels for a few crusts of bread, for coal or for old clothes.

Thanks to abortion, situations which formerly could only result in tragedy are today much simpler. A friend of mine, a well-known woman writer, had for many years remained with her mother while awaiting marriage. She had about fifty thousand francs in dowry and she wanted an educated husband of her own social class. She did not find one, however, and at the age of thirty she took a lover. Intelligent, well educated and somewhat liberated from the prejudices of her milieu, she knew all one could learn about sex from lectures and conversations. She even knew about neo-Malthusian practices, but all this was, naturally, theoretical. The lover whom she took assured her that with him there was no fear of pregnancy. She believed him. Two months after their relationship began she became pregnant. She first thought of an abortion but the unsettling appearance of the people to whom she applied terrified her. She was afraid of dying bathed in her blood like the girl in Zola's novel, *Fécondité*,[12] and after a great deal of procrastination, she confessed everything to her mother. The mother, a middle-class woman with all the prejudices of her generation, threw her daughter out of the house in the middle of the night, and the poor unfortunate had to go on foot and penniless from the Etoile Quarter to the Latin Quarter where I live to ask me for hospitality.

Unfortunately I was not at home; she therefore went to another friend at *La Chapelle* whom she did find after having walked all night. A few days later, her mother sent her some money, but joined to her parcel was a flask of laudanum and a note advising her to drink it in order to escape her 'dishonour'. These pregnancy dramas are the epitome of banality by their very frequency. One girl in order not to be dishonoured commits suicide, another kills her child, another, a young worker, maid, or farm girl, dismissed by her employer, falls into prostitution. Thanks to abortion, these terrible *dénouements* diminish in frequency. They will no longer occur when the law, ceasing to make abortion a crime, recognizes that a woman has the right not to be a mother unless she chooses ... .

Infanticide is a crime. By the mere fact that it is born, the child should command respect, and it cannot be permissible to do away with it any more than it is permissible to kill an adult. The child's weakness, far from giving us rights over it, should, on the contrary, be a safeguard in a civilized society ... .

Logically, and according to natural justice, it is birth which should be the criterion of personhood. All children who are born should have the right to the protection of society. The unborn do not exist [as individuals] and the law has no jurisdiction over them. A pregnant woman is not two people; she is only one, and she has a right to have an abortion in the same way as she has a right to have her hair cut, to cut her nails, to go on a diet or to put on weight. Our rights over our bodies are absolute, since they extend even to suicide.

One should, however, emphasize the time limit for abortions, though more in the form of advice than by imposing penalties, which are always arbitrary since they infringe on a person's sacred rights over their own bodies. An abortion carried out at six months is a nasty operation. Once ejected, the foetus shows signs of life, it breathes, moves, cries. It only lives, it is true, for a few hours, but nonetheless, abortion in these circumstances already has the appearance of infanticide. A woman should be sufficiently sensible to know from the beginning of her pregnancy whether or not she wants the child ... . Some opponents of abortion argue that a woman who has accepted sexual relations with a man has a duty to carry through her pregnancy because she should be obliged to suffer the painful consequences of her pleasure. Fundamentally this is a religious idea. The Christian religions, believing that we are only in this world in order to suffer, teach that sexual pleasure is always a sin, for which the punishment is pain. Many people, even among those who seem to be free of any religious belief, are still imbued with this idea. It underlies many novels and plays. Nevertheless, life teaches us that it is a false idea. To undergo an avoidable misery in order to run after some vague future compensation is pure fantasy, a fantasy that renders life joyless to those haunted by it.

The only serious arguments against abortion are those of reasons of state. The continuing decrease in the number of births is a fact and many people are alarmed by it. Are they right to be alarmed? That is the question. If this decrease were to lead little by little to the complete disappearance of the species, there would be a cause for alarm, but this cannot be the case because procreation will always be safeguarded by a powerful factor, namely the love of children. At the present time, people are reluctant to have six children, but they are very keen to have one or sometimes two. Those individuals who find sufficient nourishment for their mental activity in their own minds or in the outside world are rare. A child satisfies a certain number of needs in an adult's heart: the need to love and be loved, the need to protect, the need to dominate. All of this is too great a part of life for us to need to fear that the present generation will succeed in deliberately suppressing future generations.

Thus it can be seen that the fears of the re-populationists are not based on a fear of the disappearance of the human species. Theirs is a narrower point of view; they think only of France and contemplate the numerical proportion of her forces in comparison with those of other nations. The supporters of population growth are for the most part men of reactionary opinions; they are in favour of authority, the subordination of the poor to the rich and they believe that the best means of maintaining a social hierarchy is to have a 'good war' from time to time ... . These conservatives wish to profit from patriotism but they refuse to accept its burdens. They believe themselves born to lead, believe that they have a right to a free and privileged life which is not compatible with a large family. A man of this class does not want to divide his fortune [among many children]; his wife feels the same, and what is more, she wants to keep a fresh face and a supple body in order not to become repulsive ... .

The number of births is diminishing in France rather more than elsewhere, it is true, but it is diminishing throughout Europe. Voluntary birth control and civilization go hand in hand ... . If France is less prolific than the nations which surround her, it is to her honour; she has taken a leading role on a path where others will follow or are already following.

In general, as long as there is no direct danger to a country, reasons of state cannot be justified. Above all the individual should be sacred, and provided that one does not do harm to others, the individual's liberty should be complete. One has the absolute right to live as one chooses, to reproduce or not to reproduce. Attempting to restrict individual liberties in the national interest always does more harm than good.

Doctor Pelletier

Editor's Note

Professor Lacasagne of Lyons has declared authoritatively in *Le Matin* (21 December 1910) that the crime of abortion has been committed 500,000 times. *La Liberté* raises the number to 700,000 but there is every reason to believe that it is higher. We are justified in inferring, therefore, that this crime is perpetrated at one time or another by a majority of French families and in general by the better off, with the complicity of the major newspapers (see advertisements in the big dailies) who represent, and are to a certain extent, the will of the state, so arbitrarily invoked here. There is no one article of the Criminal Code so regularly broken as Article 317. It has, therefore, been abolished in fact. Faced with these objections, every arrest for the alleged crime of abortion seems unjust and scandalous.

In any case, with reference to what right does the legislature think itself authorized to intervene in an act which there is no doubt is of a private and personal nature? If it is in reference to overseeing public order and to suppressing an act which disturbs public and private welfare, which is the only *raison d'être* of human law, it is in this case without any success. This law is the primary disrupter of public order and a threat to individual security. For in order to avenge 'a seed', the law sacrifices the future of living conscious beings who should be spared.

ON PROSTITUTION[13]

I may be blamed for speaking paradoxically when I say that prostitution has constituted a sign of progress. That, nevertheless in my view, is a fact. Primitive societies knew nothing of prostitution; men, stronger than women, simply took them and gave nothing in return. This state of affairs, one may add, was not limited to the early savages; it was also common among the peasantry. Women and girls avoid lonely places because they are afraid, afraid they will be raped. One has to call a spade a spade.

So it is a form of progress when it occurs to men, no longer to impose the sexual act on women, but to pay them. This is already a first step in liberation for women, who can no longer be raped at a whim, but demand money for the loan of their bodies. To be honest, often a woman does not sell herself; it is the man who directly or indirectly sells her to other men. A slave does not throw off slavery from one day to the next. In civilized countries and especially in the cities, prostitution constitutes a more or less tolerated trade. In general it is working-class girls who become prostitutes. They are often pressed into it by a lover who wants to live like a parasite at the woman's expense. Sometimes it is laziness or a weak intellect which leads women to sell their bodies. It is hard to get up every morning to go to the workshop or factory. It is also hard to work as a maid from morning to night, to be scolded by an irritable mistress. And when one has once experienced how easy it is to gain money on the street, one goes back to it and gets used to living in this way.

But in most cases it is poverty that pushes women on to the street. Society has not yet understood that women, like men, should be able to earn their living by working. The wages they are offered are inadequate. In order to live they must count on the help of family, of their husbands or lovers, and if they have neither the one nor the other, they have a choice between prostitution and death.

This is not an exaggeration. I had to look at the case of a girl who committed suicide thanks to her poverty. And her concierge said to me spontaneously these revolting words: 'She was well behaved, Madame, much too well behaved!' – 'Too well behaved!' What she meant was, that rather than kill herself, this girl, being young, should have profited from a career on the streets.

Prostitution does not take place entirely on the street and in brothels; there are also hotels and cars. What feeds it? Middle-class girls sometimes who have lost their fortunes, divorcees ruined by their divorce, lower-middle class housewives who go to the brothel to earn enough to close the gap in the family finances, and also working-class girls attracted by the idea of luxury. 'Why shouldn't I wear the beautiful dresses that I sew for rich women?', the seamstress of the Rue de la Paix says to herself.

This is a legitimate desire; after all, one must be ill-natured to blame them. Unfortunately for these poor girls, in prostitution many are called but few are chosen. They think they will be lodged in a palace and find themselves in a run-down hotel room. It is often argued nowadays that prostitution is a trade like any other and has nothing dishonourable about it. I agree. Honour is difficult to define. In reality in our world honour is confused with money; an honourable profession on the Champs-Elysées, prostitution is considered dishonourable on the Boulevard de Belleville [a working-class quarter].

What should one think about the regulation of prostitution? We must be clear that it is a barbarous law. In order to preserve themselves from venereal infection, men had the idea of treating one category of women like cattle. These women commit no offence since no one obliges men to consort with prostitutes. The prostitute is arrested, treated abominably and spends an unspecified length of time in prison. This is a shameful state of affairs in a civilized society. Notice that this arbitrary justice only attacks the poor, working-class prostitute. Those whom one sees at the Opera never go to prison.

Is prostitution useful? Yes, in the present state of our manners and morals. Women have fewer sexual needs than men and the few which they have are repressed by society. Women practise Freudian repression which can be the cause of nervous illness. Men are accustomed to satisfying their sexuality easily, provided that they have a bit of money. If prostitution were suppressed, there would be no other resource than rape (for men) and women, forced to live as recluses, would re-experience their former slavery.

In the society of the future, prostitution will be unnecessary. Firstly because women having entered the labour force will be able to live by their work, secondly because prejudices about feminine virtue, which consist of repressing sexuality if one does not have a husband, will have disappeared. The greatest evil arises from social repression. When sexuality is considered to be a natural function for both women and men, there will be no more prostitution.

Doctoresse Pelletier

LETTER FROM MADELEINE PELLETIER TO ARRIA LY

27 June 1908

Mademoiselle,

I will accept your article but I should warn you that it is solely to show you that I hold no prejudices against you, for the article will certainly harm my paper. At heart I share to some extent your ideas. One needs during a period of struggle a certain number of women motivated by this hatred of men; it is easy to make them into committed soldiers for the cause. But one must not say or above all write everything that one thinks, especially if one wishes to proselytize. What are the anti-feminists and even the lukewarm feminists (and there is no other kind, I tell you) going to think of this young woman who would commit suicide rather than consent to have sexual relations with her husband? They would say that we are abnormal and half-crazy and that we are supporting an unnatural and dangerous doctrine since it leads to nothing less than the end of reproduction.

I believe, and I tell you this in a friendly spirit, that your ideas are mistaken. This is the feminism of Renooz and Cleyre Yvelin carried to the furthest point, with greater passion and the zest of youth.[14] It has its source in spite: in spite in general, of course, for never having met them I cannot speak of any personal circumstances, which I would not make in any case. These women retreat into femininity. They declare it superior and overwhelm masculinity with their scorn. It is childish, you will agree.

Feminism should not be a feeling *but a rational idea*. We do not despise men, nor do we hate them; we simply demand our rights. If they do not wish to give them to us, we must protest by all possible means, if need be to do the greatest possible harm to our adversary, but only because he is the adversary, and not because of any hatred of the male sex.

I can assure you that I am capable of sometimes being a terrible adversary. That is why I am not liked and why I have had the honour to have been disciplined half a dozen times by the various political committees to which I belonged, but I have no sexual hatred of men.

Like you, I will not marry and it is probable that I will never take a lover, because under present conditions, sexual relations are a source of humiliation for a married woman and of scorn for an unmarried one. Since I am a woman and since I have not wished to educate my genital senses, my virginity is not a source of suffering and I am convinced that I have chosen the path in life that suits me the best, but such a life cannot, you understand, be advocated as the norm; it is only the consequence of the unjust situation in which women find themselves:

Cordially yours,

Dr Pelletier

NOTES

1. Edited versions of both 'The Feminist Education of Girls' and 'The Right to Abortion' have appeared in *Feminisms of the Belle Epoque*, eds, Jennifer Waelti-Walters and Steven C. Hause, London, University of Nebraska Press, 1994, pp. 253–69 and 101–16. Our selections tend to emphasize the political aspects of Pelletier's argument.
2. Arria Ly (1881–1934), pseudonym of Josephine Gondon, one of the few notable provincial French feminists, came from Toulouse. She and Pelletier corresponded over a 20-year period. Espousing a much more radical feminism than Pelletier, she advocated complete separation between the sexes. She committed suicide in Stockholm in 1934.
3. Jean Jacques Rousseau, *Emile ou De l'éducation*, The Hague, J. Néaulme, 1762.
4. See François de Salignace de La Mothe Fénelon, *De l'Education des filles*, Paris, P. Auborien, 1861, and Félix Dupanloup, *La Femme studieuse*, Paris, C. Douniol, 1869; also Claude Zaidman, 'Madeleine Pelletier et l'éducation des filles', and Felicia Gordon, 'Les Femmes et l'ambition', both in *Madeleine Pelletier (1874–1939), logique et infortunes d'un combat pour l'égalité*, ed., Christine Bard, Paris, Côté-femmes, 1992, pp. 127–40 and 27–34.
5. For an analysis of *Belle Epoque* costume see: Jean-Paul Aron (ed.), *Misérable et glorieuse: la femme au XIXe siècle*, Paris, Fayard, 1980.
6. Note: Translation of 'l'amour'. The word has a multiplicity of meanings in French, from sexual intercourse, sexuality and desire to platonic love. All these ideas emerge in Pelletier's text and I have tried to render the meaning according to context (Felicia Gordon). For general background on prostitution in France see: Alain Corbin, *Les Filles de noce: misère sexuelle et prostitution, 19e et 20e siècles*, Paris, Aubier Montaigne, 1978. A translation exists called *Women for Hire: Prostitution and Sexuality in France after 1850*, Cambridge, Massachusetts, Harvard University Press, 1990.

7. Madeleine Pelletier, Doctor in Medicine, Paris Vᵉ, M. Giard and E. Brière, Librairies – Editeurs 16, Rue Soufflot and 12, Rue Toullier, 1914.
8. Anatole France, *Le Crime de Sylvestre Bonnard*, Paris, C. Lévy, 1881.
9. Herbert Spencer, *Education Intellectual, Moral, Physical*, London, Williams and Northgate, 1861.
10. *Le Droit à l'avortement: pour abrogation de l'article 317*, by Madeleine Pelletier, Doctor in Medicine, Paris, Edition du Malthusien, 1913. Article 317 in the Criminal Code forbade abortion.
11. Jacques Bertillon, *La Dépopulation de la France*, Paris, Librairie Félix Alcan, 1911.
12. Emile Zola, *Fécondité*, Paris, Librairie Charpentier, 1899.
13. By Dr Madeleine Pelletier, Monthly Issue of *L'Anarchie*, November 1928.
14. Renooz, Céline, feminist and scientific popularizer in the *Belle Epoque* who published *The Vegetable Origin of Man* (*La Nouvelle doctrine de l'évolution*, Paris, Imprimerie de A.-M. Beaudelot, 1891) and wrote against doctrines of Darwinian and Lamarckian evolution, espousing the concept of the immutability of species. In discussing the comparative physiology of men and women, Renooz argued that women were superior. Cleyre Yvelin was the author of *Etude sur le féminisme dans l'antiquité* (*The Study of Feminism in Antiquity*), Paris, E. Buère, 1908, and a writer on contemporary feminist issues.

7.   Hélène Brion: syndicalist, pacifist and feminist

CONTEXTUAL INTRODUCTION

On 17 November 1917, after four months of preliminary interrogation and following several searches of her house, Hélène Brion was arrested and sent to Saint Lazare prison, best known as the prison for common prostitutes, where she remained until her trial of 25–31 March 1918. She was 36 years old. Her pre-trial arrest was prompted by Georges Clemenceau's accession, as Prime Minister, on 15 November 1917 and his determination to crush anti-war sentiment at a time when the war was literally mired in the trenches and demoralization among both civilians and the military was growing. Hélène Brion's prosecution for 'defeatism' throws light on a still relatively obscure moment in French political and military history.

'*L'Affaire Hélène Brion*' can be seen as drawing together a number of threads in the French military and political crises of 1917: army mutinies, trade union pacifism, feminist anti-war feeling and finally the determination of the French state to crush all manifestations of dissent at a time when the entire war effort appeared to be crumbling. Hélène Brion's trial was part of the government's ultimately successful strategy to revive flagging French patriotic morale by denouncing 'the enemy within' and thereby restoring faith in the military struggle. Pacifists, 'defeatists', left-wing socialists and trade unionists were targeted in this campaign, as were the genuine spies like Mata Hari, eventually to be executed. Anyone who advocated negotiation with the Germans as opposed to their unconditional surrender was suspect.

In the spring of 1917, the French army under its new Commander-in-Chief, General Nivelle, had attempted a disastrous push through the German lines. Nivelle (later termed 'The Butcher') claimed that with a massive build-up of troops, artillery and tank support, the German line could be breached and their forces defeated within 48 hours. The offensive, known as the *Chemin des Dames*, after an escarpment which the French attempted to take, proved to be a costly disaster with French troops massacred by the German artillery. Following this *débâcle*, Nivelle was forced to resign and was replaced by General Pétain. However, the effect of this defeat on the army, already de-moralized by poor food and clothing, inadequate medical services, harsh

189

discipline, lack of furloughs, no progress in military objectives, rumours of the Russian Revolution and the perception that civilians and generals outside the war zone were leading a luxurious life, was dramatic. Isolated mutinies began to break out in April 1917 and continued with increasing frequency into July. According to official figures, which almost certainly understate the extent of the disorders, the mutiny period saw 110 cases of 'grave collective indiscipline' and between May and October 1917 the *'conseils de guerre'*, which replaced the old court martial, found 23,385 men guilty of various crimes of whom 412 were executed, though only 23 mutineers are officially recorded as having been shot. According to informed estimates, at least 100,000 men were in active mutiny during those summer months. Meanwhile, on the civilian side, May and June saw a series of strikes in key war industries, and on the political front the *Union Sacrée*, the all-party government coalition formed to prosecute the war, appeared ready to fracture, as socialists became increasing disillusioned with the government.[1]

When Georges Clemenceau, long a campaigner for patriotic unity and a critic of what he considered to be governmental vacillation, was appointed Prime Minister in November 1917, the stage was set for a decisive period of repression against 'spies', 'defeatists' and mutineers. In all it is estimated that some 1 700 people of left-leaning sympathies, as well as a handful of genuine spies, were arrested. Hélène Brion found herself trawled up in the net that included far more subversive figures such as the Minister of the Interior, Malvy, the Editor of the anarchist paper, *Le Bonnet rouge*, Almereyda, and the adventurer, confidence man and spy, Bolo Pasha. A pervasive sense of public disquiet, of corruption in high places, swept the country. The patriotic press coined the epithet 'defeatist' as a substitute for 'pacifist' and all those not seen as whole-heartedly of the war party were branded as traitors. Clemenceau's speech to the Chamber of Deputies when he took office captures the flavour of the time.

> Alas there are also crimes, crimes against France which call for prompt punishment … . No more pacifist campaigns, no more German intrigues. Neither treason nor semi-treason: war. Nothing but war. Our armies will not be caught between two fires. Justice takes its course. The country will know it is defended.[2]

Hélène Brion's arrest and trial reflect both on the politics of wartime and on sexual politics. A British observer of the French scene, Lord Esher, Secretary of State for War, wrote from Paris in 1917 of the terrible discouragement and physical and moral fatigue of the civilian population. He noted too the growing reluctance of French soldiers to throw themselves into enemy fire and then commented on his perception of the national character, a perception which is revealing of the conjunction of pacifism and effeminacy. 'If the French should morally collapse, such is the curious working of the feminine strain that runs now, as ever, through the race, they would certainly blame Britain.'[3] The association of pacifism with femininity or the effeminate, though coming from a British source, gives symbolic resonance to the arrest of a feminist pacifist trade union militant.

What had Hélène Brion's wartime activities been? After the conversion of the FNSI to the Zimmerwaldian position, she had succeeded, along with the treasurer of her union, Loriot (another active peace campaigner), in holding the annual congress of the teachers' union in 1917, in defiance of a government ban. This must, at the very least, have irritated the authorities. They would have argued that exemplary punitive action against a leader of the FNSI would serve as an example to other trade union dissidents, but would not damage war industries. Though the Metal Workers Union boasted an equally problematic pacifist leader (from the government perspective), Alfred Merrheim, his prosecution would almost certainly have unleashed a strike in a key munitions industry, which the country could ill afford in wartime. Hélène Brion's prosecution, it was assumed, would provide a lesson to the pacifists without causing havoc in the crucial industrial sector.[4]

'*L'Affaire Hélène Brion*' is well documented, but has received surprisingly little analysis.[5] Initially her arrest sparked off a series of defamatory articles in the patriotic Parisian dailies, particularly by *Le Matin* which suggested that as well as having kept pacifist leaflets in her flat and distributed them to the public, she was also a spy. Though she was not in the end tried for espionage, the imputation risked being deeply damaging. Even the published account of the trial lists '*L'Affaire Hélène Brion*' under the general rubric: 'Trials for Treason'. The arrest and prosecution constituted, as her friend Madeleine Vernet put it in a pamphlet published in Brion's defence, '*Une sombre affaire*'.[6]

Hélène Brion was tried under Articles 1 and 2 of the Law of 5 August 1914, forbidding any actions harmful to the morale of the army or of the civilian population and of a nature to favour the enemy.[7] Soon after her initial interrogation by the civil magistrate in July her case was transferred to the military court, an alarming development. She was not the first teacher to have been prosecuted in this manner. In October 1917, Marie and François Mayoux received two-year prison sentences for having distributed their pamphlet '*Les Instituteurs syndicalistes et la Guerre*' ('Syndicalist Teachers and the War'). Louise Colliard, another active trade unionist and teacher, had been arraigned before a court martial but acquitted. Given the history of the political involvement of the army in cases of spying dating from the Dreyfus case, a court martial, or War Council as it was now called, was not a hopeful venue for Hélène Brion from the point of view of the defence.

It is clear that by 1917 Hélène Brion had become a particular focus of police and governmental concern. Police files of the period give an insight

into the evolution of official thinking. Whereas in 1915 it was noted that
she was a member of the *Fédération féministe universitaire*, but that there
were no suspicious circumstances attaching to her, by 1916–1917 she was
increasingly the subject of detailed police reports in her own right.[8] Thus on
17 May 1916 it was noted that Hélène Brion, along with Loriot and leaders
of the *Ecole émancipée*, was carrying out a vigorous pacifist campaign. On
26 June 1916 the following report was sent to the head of the *Sûreté*: '…
though these teachers are a minority, they are dangerous, given their authority over pupils and their relations with parents'. Urgent measures, the report
concluded, should be taken. At a meeting of 9 December 1916, Loriot was
quoted as proffering 'these impious words: "French or German, I don't give
a damn ['who wins', understood], provided that the war ends"'.[9] These
accounts were based on information from spies within the trade union
movement acting on behalf of the police. Finally a list of 'Notorious Individuals Carrying Out Pacifist Propaganda' (24 October 1916) includes Hélène
Brion, Secretary of the National Federation of the Trade Unions of Teachers. Without doubt, the police and the government had Hélène Brion in their
sights.

After her arrest, Hélène Brion's friends in the feminist movement, the CGT
and the Socialist Party set up a defence fund and held several meetings to
gather support. Resolutions of solidarity were passed by union branches all
over the country, as well as a resolution by the Central Committee of the
CGT (9 March 1918).[10] One item of the police report on the meeting which
agreed this resolution is of interest in suggesting a line of attack against
Hélène Brion, if the charges against her proved insufficient:

> Among friends, it was recognized that Hélène Brion is 'unbalanced' and 'exalted'
> and that at meetings of the Central Committee she was noticeable for her eccen-
> tricity and her lack of decorum.

This spiteful comment was based on the views of one unknown member of
the Committee who acted as a spy within the CGT's ranks. During her
imprisonment prior to the trial, Brion was subjected to a psychiatric examination which found entirely in her favour.[11] By attempting to classify Brion, a
woman political activist, as 'unbalanced', the authorities had hoped to undermine the cause as well as the individual. This tactic (which failed in the case
of Hélène Brion) was to prove successful with Madeleine Pelletier.

The largest meeting to be held in Hélène Brion's support took place at the
Grand Lodge on 6 January 1918, with over a thousand people in attendance.[12]
It had been jointly organized by socialists and by Séverine, the veteran
feminist/pacifist campaigner who also spoke eloquently at her trial. Paul
Meunier, Deputy for the Aube and a barrister, attacked what he saw as the

illegality of her trial. There was no case in law, he argued, for transferring Brion's case to a military court. From the point of view of civil liberties, this prosecution was an infringement of the laws of free speech.

What, then, was the charge that Hélène Brion faced? With her co-accused, Gaston Moufflard, a serving soldier and socialist with whom she had corresponded while he was at the front, she was accused of 'having distributed, or having made others distribute, brochures, tracts and leaflets of such a nature as to aid the enemy and to exercise a harmful influence on the army and civilian morale'.[13] As Paul Meunier and others had pointed out, the brochures that Hélène Brion held in her possession, the 'Zimmerwald Declaration', 'The Call to Teachers' and so on, were held by socialists all over the country, none of whom had been charged. The prosecution was obliged to focus firstly on letters received from Moufflard, which Brion, to her express regret at the trial, had kept; secondly, on the fact that as secretary of the FNSI she had sent pacifist material approved by the union to individual union members; and finally that she was alleged to have made pacifist or 'defeatist' comments to fellow teachers.

The trial was remarkable for the number of character witnesses called (between 57 and 80 in various versions). Among them were Séverine, Marguerite Durand (Editor of the feminist paper, *La Fronde*), Nelly Roussel, the birth control campaigner, Jean Longuet, grandson of Karl Marx and socialist Deputy, and a host of trade union, teaching and feminist colleagues. The court heard a series of eulogies on Hélène Brion's character, stressing her probity, sincerity, devotion to her principles, her disinterestedness, her energy, her commitment to helping the poor and her excellence as a teacher. Séverine compared her to Louise Michel and many witnesses stressed the connection between her feminism and her pacifism, the principal line of defence in Brion's own statement before the court.

Another noteworthy aspect of the trial was the extent to which Hélène Brion herself played a leading, indeed a dominant, role, cross-questioning witnesses and replying to the judge's questions with composure and force. Even the initially unsympathetic reporter for *Causes célèbres* acknowledged the effect she had on the judge and the prosecution witnesses. Dressed in a grey blouse with a large black bow, a dark skirt and without a hat (an explicitly feminist gesture at the period), she intervened authoritatively in a number of the debates and, though she had a lawyer, virtually conducted her own defence. She appears to have engaged the judge's sympathy although Lieutenant-Colonel Maritz with his pince-nez, handlebar moustache and array of medals must have presented a formidable figure. In the event, Maritz found himself on the defensive when it was suggested by Brion's lawyer,

Hélène Brion responds to the Commissioner

Oscar Bloch, that parallels could be drawn between Hélène Brion's trial and the Dreyfus case, a suggestion which he vehemently denied.

On the last day of the trial, Maritz made a speech defending the political independence of his court and denied that he would have withheld any important documents from the defence (as was alleged to have been the case in the contemporaneous Bolo spy trial).[14] Maritz said, to loud applause from the public gallery: '... the officers of the French Republic are incapable of condemning someone according to order ... .We are no longer in the period of those officers [associated with] the Dreyfus Affair.'[15] What is revealing about this incident is the extent to which Maritz felt himself and his brother officers on trial. A reading of the trial report demonstrates that his conduct in the Hélène Brion case was exemplary. Though Maritz decided on a guilty

The President (Judge) Lieutenant-Colonel Maritz

verdict, the suspended sentence, which the defendants received, suggests that Hélène Brion and Gaston Moufflard had stirred the conscience of the court.

It is clear that Hélène Brion saw her trial as an opportunity to gain maximum publicity to the cause dearest to her heart, namely feminism:

> ... it was an ideal chance for Hélène Brion, who had been obliged to do battle with her political and trades union comrades on the ground that they themselves had chosen ... to move the political debate for once on to the terrain of feminist demands. For her, the feminist path was a path to follow towards revolution.[16]

One of the greatest difficulties experienced by French feminist campaigners in pursuing their aims had been the problem of gaining public attention.[17] Their demonstrations were usually small and non-violent; the press coverage was correspondingly minimal. At her trial Hélène Brion had decided that feminism would star. Yet she was on trial not for her feminism but for her pacifist activity. Her line of defence in the 'Declaration', therefore, deserves some analysis.

In her 'Declaration' Hélène Brion challenged the court's right to bring her to trial on the grounds that she was being tried for political crimes but possessed no political rights. She was, she argued, effectively outside the law. 'I appear before you accused of a political crime; but I am stripped of all political rights.'[18] Brion's defence dramatized the absurdity of French laws in

M. Jean Longuet, Deputy, character witness

relation to women. Citizens when it came to paying taxes, they had no voice as to how those taxes might be spent. An illiterate man was considered by the law to be more 'responsible' than the most educated of women. Denying that she had ever tried to weaken public morale on the war Hélène Brion repeatedly emphasized that her feminism lay at the root of her opposition to the war, a view endorsed in later years by her socialist colleagues. She denied being a 'defeatist'. She was a feminist first and then a pacifist. Her feminism had been the prime motive of her life; pacifism was a concern linked to feminism and arising from the war.

A sceptic might suggest that Hélène Brion soft-pedalled her pacifism and emphasized her feminism in order to gain the sympathy of the court. This is not a convincing argument. All the evidence points to the fact that she was prepared

M. le Commandant de Meur: Commissioner of the Government (Prosecutor)

for a stiff prison sentence but was determined to gain maximum publicity for women and for feminism through her trial. Feminism, in any case, was not a cause to inspire official sympathy. Yet this she effectively did. 'I am the enemy of war because I am a feminist. War is the triumph of brute force. Feminists can only triumph by moral strength and intellectual power.'[19] Society, she argued, was based on a lie, the lie of the 'Rights of Man', which meant, with universal male suffrage, the rights of men only. Brion ridiculed the conception of masculine honour in war which required a seemingly endless massacre of men and the well-documented rapes of women to sustain it. She rested her case on the claim that it was women's exclusion from political life and their lack of power that made war more likely. She did not claim innate pacific qualities for women, but rather that war was entirely contrary to their interests.

Oscar Bloch, her defence lawyer, pleaded for her acquittal or at the very least a suspended sentence. She was given the latter, a three-year suspended sentence. In addition she was dismissed from the teaching service and not reinstated until 1925. Her letter protesting at her dismissal was not conciliatory.[20]

A final point to be made about Hélène Brion's trial concerns the reaction of mainstream feminist groups. Whereas prominent feminists had testified in her defence, there were others who objected to her claim to speak for feminism. *La Française*, a journal of moderate and now patriotic feminism, congratulated the court for not accepting Hélène Brion's arguments and acquitting her. Amélie Hammer, President of the patriotic '*Union fraternelle des femmes*', confessed herself shocked by Hélène Brion's pacifism and suggested she was the dupe of the Germans.[21] The French feminist movement for which Brion spoke so passionately at her trial was still bitterly divided.

Hélène Brion's other major published text, 'The Feminist Path', undated but probably written in 1917, should be read as addressing two debates: one on the future of feminism and the second on the future of socialist and syndicalist movements in the post-war period. Hélène Brion's pamphlet, written for socialists and syndicalists alike, was not an attack on those movements' theories or principles, but a critique of their practices. As we have seen, her credentials as a syndicalist and committed socialist were impeccable, a fact which sharpened the force of her criticism. Brion argued that these great parallel movements, the Socialist Party and the CGT, which committed themselves to ameliorating or transforming the lives of workers and the oppressed, had almost entirely ignored the position of women and the nature of female oppression, especially within the family. In not addressing the needs of women, reformers and revolutionaries had constituted themselves wittingly or unwittingly as oppressors in their turn. Further, by ignoring or neglecting the potential strength of the women's movement, both socialism and syndicalism had unnecessarily weakened themselves. This weakness, according to Brion, was nowhere better demonstrated than in the dramatic collapse of the Second International at the outbreak of the 1914–1918 war.

In 'The Feminist Path', Hélène Brion analysed the issue of separate spheres, or the conflict of public and private life as it affected women socialists and trade unionists. If proletarian women worked in factories, they also performed unpaid labour in the home. Neither socialism or syndicalism, she observed, recognized or quantified the nature of that work and thereby the reality of women's lives. Elsewhere when labour was performed by unpaid workers it was called serfdom or slavery; in the case of women's labour in the family, it was called their natural function. She argued that women suffered a double oppression of class and sex. Without an analysis of sexual oppression, that of class was largely meaningless. Finally women suffered not merely from poverty, but from being held in low esteem. In that sense, women, regardless of their class, formed a sexual proletariat.

Hélène Brion attacked the deep social conservatism of the syndicalist/trade union movement which purported to 'liberate' women from the drudgery of the factory in order to return them to unpaid housework. Trade unions had, moreover, led the way in enforcing restrictive practices against women, under the guise of protective legislation, thus condemning women workers to low wages and dependency on men. Her use of examples was telling: the woman forced into strike-breaking by her husband, as trade unionists stood by powerless to intervene because it was a 'private' matter: the woman bookbinder who disguised herself as a man in order to gain equal pay: the Couriau Affair of 1913 where a woman typesetter (and her husband) were forced from their jobs by the Lyons branch of their union because the husband refused to prevent his wife from working: cases of physical intimidation of women cab drivers by their male competitors, and so on. Here were clear-cut cases of oppression and injustice perpetrated not by the capitalist class, but by members of the very organizations which purported to end the evils of capitalism.[22]

'The Feminist Path' was an appeal to socialists and trade unionists to harness the power of women's energy and enthusiasm. It was also an appeal to women themselves. Feminism, for Hélène Brion, was not opposed to socialism or syndicalism but it could not be subsumed into those movements; it was a complementary strategy which, she believed, could immeasurably strengthen the power and the appeal of a revitalized post-war Left. Like her statement to the court martial, 'The Feminist Path' conveys an energetic critique couched in terms of often mordant irony, of institutionalized oppression of women.

TEXTS

'To All Feminists; To All Women'
Statement Read to the Court Martial, 29 March 1918 (Germinal Year 126)
Letter of Protest against the Psychiatric Examination
Letter to Mr Laferre, *Ministre de l'Instruction Publique*
'The Feminist Path'

TO ALL FEMINISTS; TO ALL WOMEN[23]

'In the tumultuous period which we are experiencing, the person who believes themself neutral is mad; the person who hides themself away is a criminal.' These words of André Léo to the women of the Commune, could be rewritten for us today. Let each person reflect while there is still time! The war has arrived. In a few days, perhaps, a terrible crisis will shake Europe to its foundations. The horrors you have read about in the Russo-Japanese War, the Balkan War, the terrible nightmare of 1870, we must relive all of that. What will you do, you who at this time by sheer intellectual torpor refuse to believe in the war? You will say: 'They will sort it out. It would be too stupid to get people killed for such silly reasons. At bottom no one wants to fight!'. Yes, that is the tragedy of it: no one wants to believe in it because it would be so horrible and thanks to this general indifference and to the sinister motives of our masters, this conflict that nobody wants could break out tomorrow.

Do you dare to imagine what this would be like? What kind of life would yours be, you women whose sons, brothers, husbands would join the ranks. Don't you think that a rebellion in broad daylight, while there is still time, would be preferable to the long hours of anguish and of heartbreak that you will live through afterwards, no longer daring to cry out or protest for fear of doing wrong to your loved ones; will you not be dumb slaves as you have always been? Aren't you tired of this suffering that these big crazy children, men, impose upon you? When they were little and their energy expended itself in fisticuffs, weren't you there to separate them, these warriors on the grass? You used to explain to them then how naughty it is to fight and that the strongest fists don't necessarily prove anything. Why, then, today don't you place yourselves between them?

And you, feminists, who are used to political action in groups, you who have struggled for so long and were on the point of seeing your dearest hopes realized, don't you understand the immense reaction that a world war would bring about in thought? Don't you understand that our efforts of years past will have been lost? Why do you not try to save our movement by rising up before the obstacle (of war) before it crushes us? There were 20,000 of us in the street for the Condorcet demonstration;[24] we were more than 500,000 to sign petitions for the right to vote. We must be thousands to cry out everywhere our hatred for war and by our firmness do everything in our power to prevent it.

Yes, I repeat, everything in our power. Beginning with words of common sense and persuasiveness, who would dare to blame us acting in such a way and who would punish us? Isn't it our role and the most sacred right that has ever been vouchsafed to us? Let us protest then, everywhere, always, in the street, at home, in the factory, at the office, at every moment of the day against the crime which is being prepared. We can; we must. It is the first and the most pressing of our duties. Let us fulfil it at once fully and to the bitter end.

Hélène Brion

STATEMENT READ TO THE COURT MARTIAL, 29 MARCH 1918 (GERMINAL YEAR 126)[25]

I appear before you accused of a political crime, yet I stand stripped of all political rights. Because I am a woman, the laws of my country have from the outset classified me as far inferior to all Frenchmen and all colonials. In spite of my intelligence which has recently been confirmed,[26] in spite of the certificates and the diplomas long since awarded to me, before the law I am not the equal of an illiterate Negro of Guadeloupe or the Ivory Coast. For they can participate by postal vote in running the affairs of our common country and I cannot. I am outside the law. The law should show itself logical and ignore my existence when it is a question of penalties to the same extent that it ignores me when it is a question of rights. I protest against the law's illogicality.

I protest against laws being applied to me which I have neither discussed nor voted for. These laws are not, as it says in the Declaration of the Rights of Man: 'the expression of the general will', for the largest fraction of the nation, women, have never been called upon to make them either directly or indirectly through their representatives. The law, which I am challenging, charges me with having propagated opinions likely to weaken the morale of the population. I protest even more strenuously and I refute it. My closely argued propaganda has constantly appealed to reason, to the power of intellect, to that common sense which is shared to some extent by every human being.

It is indeed dangerous to awaken a sleepwalker who dances on the rooftop in order to make him aware of the dangers of his situation. But I have never been able to liken my country to a sleepwalker. I love it too deeply not to recognize its absolute right to hear the truth. Truth is the manna of the strong. It alone is worthy of a great people.

I repeat, therefore, formally, that my propaganda never opposed our national defence and that I have never demanded peace at any price. I have always said, on the contrary, that there was only one duty, a single one seen under two aspects:

For those at the front, to hold firm.

For those at the rear, to think.

I have exercised this educational function above all in a feminist sense, for I am first and foremost a *feminist*, as all those who know me can testify. And it is through feminism that I am an enemy of war.

The prosecution claims that under the guise of feminism, I worked as a pacifist. This argument twists my campaigning to other ends. I maintain that the contrary is the case and I will easily prove it. I confirm that for years before the outbreak of war, I was an active feminist, that I have simply continued to be one since the war began and that I have never commented upon the evils of the present day without concluding that if women had a say in the matter of social policy, things would go differently. I hereby call upon the testimony of all those who have campaigned with me.

Under whatever angle I contemplated the present war, whether I believed in the possibility of a lightning victory over our enemies, or whether I only saw the possibility of a war of attrition, demanding yet more years of struggle, I have always looked at it from the feminist point of view and as a feminist. If someone had read all my articles since the war began, they would have been convinced, but no one took the trouble and they thought it better to prosecute me for opinions and pamphlets that were not my work. People are trying to see in me, not the convinced feminist that I am who, day by day, applied those lessons thrown up by the war for feminist ends, just as I used to apply commonplace current events to the same ends before the war, but a sort of shameful pacifist who under the vague pretence of being a feminist dupes innocent souls in order to poison them with pernicious doctrines. For those who know me, this is entirely absurd.

I never campaigned for pacifism before the war and never took part in any pacifist organizations, whereas for years I have campaigned in feminist organizations: *Suffrage des femmes, Union fraternelle des femmes, Fédération féministe universitaire, Ligue pour le droit des femmes, Union française pour le suffrage des femmes, Ligue nationale du vote* and so on. In 1908, 1910 and 1912 I supported the feminist election campaigns of Jeanne Laloë, Hubertine Auclert, Renée Mortier and Madeleine Pelletier.[27]

In 1914, I took part in demands for electoral registration in the 6th Arrondissement, took part in the Condorcet demonstration, myself pasted up some two hundred posters in Pantin and Le Pré-Saint Gervais for the *Union française pour le suffrage des femmes*, as much on my own behalf as on that of a colleague, who had undertaken to do so but did not dare to do it herself and could find no professional billsticker to do it during an election campaign. This woman is one of the two who now claims that my feminism is only a façade to conceal my pacifism.

1.   I concede nothing.

2.   My feminism is of twenty years' standing and my pacifism dates only from the beginning of the war, unlike many others whose pacifism died on 4 August 1914 or a few days before.[28] Before the war, the only pacifist propaganda that I am aware of having engaged in was to encourage as much as possible the reading of *Down with Weapons*, by Baroness Bertha von Stittner, who won the Nobel Peace Prize in 1905. And I encouraged this because it was by a woman.

Since the beginning of the war I have struggled continually, even and especially with my closest pacifist comrades, those who wrote the pamphlets for which you are prosecuting me, for their lack of feminism. There are proofs of this in *La Voie féministe* which is my own work, with my own turns of phrase, expressing my own thoughts which nevertheless has not been read by you or any other of my accusers, whereas, Sirs, you are preparing to judge me on my peace propaganda. I am an enemy of war because I am a feminist. War is the triumph of brutal force; feminists can only prevail by moral force and intellectual power. There is an unbridgeable gulf between the two.

I do not believe that in primitive society women's strength and value were inferior to men's but it is certain that in the present day, the possibility of war has established a scale of completely false values to the detriment of women. The inalienable and sacred right of every individual to protect themself when attacked has been withdrawn from women. Women have been defined as, and educated to be, weak, docile and insignificant creatures who need protection and supervision throughout their lives. Far from being able to protect their own children, as in the rest of nature, they are denied the right to defend themselves. In concrete terms, women are denied physical education, sport and practice in what is termed the noble profession of arms. Politically they are denied the right to vote, 'the keystone', Gambetta said, 'of all other rights', this right to vote, thanks to which they might intervene in their own destiny and have at least some of the resources necessary to try to stop the dreadful conflicts in which they find themselves and their children immersed like unconscious and powerless automata.[29]

'Women are distanced from public life', Michelet wrote: 'We forget too often, it is true, that they have a better right to be there than anyone else. They have a greater stake in the public sphere than any of us. A man only stakes his life, a woman stakes her child. She is far more concerned with informing herself about public events and looking ahead. In the solitary and sedentary life that most women lead, they follow the crises of their country and the manoeuvres of armies in their unquiet reveries. Do you imagine that they are staying at home? No – they are in Algeria and take part in the privations and the forced marches of our young soldiers in Africa. They suffer with them in combat.'[30]

Within the value system made inevitable by war, only men count. Men are the only mark of value; the future soldiers. A man may be a moral coward and physically weak but he is nevertheless given the title of 'defender' and 'protector', the born protector, the Master, and treated as such. His physical development is looked after whereas women's is neglected. He is inculcated with the idea of his own worth, of greatness, of his social role, and conversely a woman is made to feel a sense of humility and told to feel gratitude towards this protector who has been imposed upon her without her request and who, in civilian life, is often her greatest enemy.

The war which we currently see raging is the inevitable result of this oddly constructed masculinist society, a society in which an infinitesimal fraction of the world's people have attained a conception of the Rights of Man – the word Man being taken in the narrow sense of the male individual – a society where no nation has yet achieved this conception entirely – far less a proclamation of the Rights of Man in the wider sense of the word, the rights of human beings, man or woman, a society based on lies of which Jean Finot has written:

All public life founded and maintained by men is based on a lie. An armed peace, this supreme male fiction, is in reality nothing but a gigantic lie, which filters through all our consciousnesses. Putrid fumes of lies which corrupt the atmosphere we live in. Nothing escapes it, not even patriotism which has become part of an obscene traffic. Everyone trades in it, especially those who proclaim it the most claim a monopoly for themselves. And all this is the work of men, created by men for men's profit.[31]

This entire accumulation of social lies, of which women are by far the greatest victims, finally culminates in the supreme lie of war, in what Norman Angell has called: *The Great Illusion.*[32]

And to emphasize to what extent this lie is real and how it is to be found everywhere among all the world's history of such convulsions as you men bring about, listen to this:

We are not going to war against Germany whose independence we respect. We hope that the peoples who make up the great German nation will freely decide their destinies. As for us, we demand the establishment of a state of affairs which would guarantee our security now and in the future. We want to win a lasting peace, founded on the true interests of the people and to make an end to this precarious state where all nations eat up their resources by arming against one another.

These wise words, which could have been taken from a speech by Wilson, Lloyd George or Landsdowne are copied from the *Officiel* of July 1870. They are signed by Napoléon III, Emperor of the French, and extracted from a proclamation to French women to explain the necessity of war to them.

Alongside these male lies, listen to female common sense asserted in the words of George Sand:

This slogan 'an honourable peace' which is on everyone's lips, is, as is always the case when a slogan takes over from ideas, the one that makes the least sense. We cannot make a dishonourable peace after a war of extermination, which has been accepted so courageously for the past five months.[33]

I reiterate her words and with how much more force. I say to you: No we cannot make a dishonourable peace after the gigantic struggle waged so courageously for the past forty-four months. No – peace will not dishonour us. But what does dishonour us, what is an unspeakable shame for all male humanity is the profane continuation of this massacre, without our daring to whisper a word of reason to counsel its end.

A word? Yes: reasonable words have been uttered. President Wilson was able on several occasions to find words opening up a hope of peace. He was able, furthermore, to say words of admiration and sorrowful sympathy which only he could say because he has no censure to fear, words which thousands of people think privately, words for the unhappy Russian people and for those who have taken on themselves the great and difficult task of ruling them at this time. He gave the old world a fine lesson in intelligence and courage. And he gives me now the chance to emphasize, Sirs, that the only great country in the world where women have the right to vote, though not everywhere, is really the country which represents the head of civilization. I recall with pride that in 1912 the American suffragettes led by Miss Abby Wibbert then aged seventy-five strenuously campaigned for Woodrow Wilson, whose present stance is an honour to the world. And that alone can console me to see my country, which until now was the classic land of generous enthusiasms and actions so far distanced at the present time from the path of Goodness and Reason.

I am also obliged to emphasize to you that the only country in the world where statesmen have spoken publicly in the same manner as Wilson is England, where women play such an active part in political life and where eight million of them – in wartime – have just gained the right to vote.

Are the dignity of England and the fighting power of the United States weakened by this attitude on the part of their statesmen? Far from it! We can only regret that our government has not yet been moved to act on Victor Hugo's famous saying: 'In the twentieth century, France will declare peace to the world'. For us, feminists, this failure is explained by the poet's previously incorrect prediction. He said in 1853 at the funeral of Louise Julien: 'the eighteenth century proclaimed the Rights of Man; the nineteenth will proclaim the Rights of Woman'. But the nineteenth century failed to proclaim the Rights of Woman and France in the twentieth century has not risen to the historical task which confronted it.

You men, who alone govern the world, you aspire to do too much too well. You think that the better is the enemy of the best. You want to spare our children the horrors of a future war: a praiseworthy sentiment. I say that from the moment that the terrible battle going on not one hundred kilometres from here is finished, your aim will have been achieved and you can envisage peace.[34] In 1870 two European nations fought each other, for only two, and hardly for more than six months. The result was so dreadful that all of Europe, exhausted and terrified by the conflict, needed more than forty years before daring or being able to begin another conflict. If you reckon that at the moment we have been fighting not for six months but for forty-four full months and not only two countries but more than twenty, the so-called elite of the civilized world: that almost the whole white race is involved in the fray and that the yellow and black races have been dragged along in their train; say to yourselves, I beg you, that from *this moment* you have attained your aim. For the world's exhaustion is such that we will certainly be assured of one hundred years of peace from now on if the war were to finish tonight.

The future tranquillity of our children and grandchildren is assured. Think now about guaranteeing their present happiness and future health. Reflect on how you can give them unlimited bread and even a taste of sugar and chocolate. Think what effect their present deprivation could have on this happiness which you claim to guarantee by continuing to fight and by making them live in this atmosphere which is so unhealthy from every point of view.

You say that you want to restore freedom to enslaved peoples. You say that you wish to rally to freedom, in spite of themselves, people who do not seem ready to understand it as you understand it and you fail to notice that in this struggle each one of us has lost more and more of those scraps of liberty which we once possessed, from the physical freedom of eating what one pleases and travelling where one likes, to the intellectual freedoms of writing, speaking, meeting and indeed thinking: above all the possibility of thinking clearly. All this is disappearing little by little because all of this is incompatible with a state of war.

Take care! The world is going down a slippery slope which it will be difficult to clamber up again. Since the beginning of the war I have been saying: 'Unless you call for women to help you, the slope will not be surmounted again and the new world which you claim to be inaugurating will be as unjust and chaotic as the pre-war world'.

I will give you only one example. When the most understanding among you, those who appeal to the power of reason as well as cannons to win victory, tackle the question of Alsace-Lorraine, you accept the idea of a referendum for the population. But who among you imagine that women should have a voice in the matter come a referendum? No one. And yet, if conquered and scattered peoples like those of Alsace-Lorraine and Poland have kept their national identity in spite of a foreign yoke, is it not above all thanks to the energy of women, first of all mothers, those powerful teachers and relentless defenders of the home, inculcating from the cradle in the child the love of their native language, country and people?

What appals me about war, more than the dead and the ruins which it piles up, infinitely more than the material miseries it creates, is the intellectual and moral degradation that it brings, since everything that lowers the moral level of society contributes to women's subjection.

There is a particular rubric on morality that young conscripts are lectured on; I would like to speak about it here. I have learned from the newspapers of the arrival on French soil of men who have come from all over the world, representing all races and nationalities – come in order to defend me as a French woman. I am aware that great care is taken over their comfort and the cleanliness of their accommodation. And I cannot prevent myself from recalling that there are certain houses, you will know which ones, that one is almost certain to find in garrison towns, because, to be sure, their establishment is all part of the well-being and hygiene of soldiers.

Yes, I know it is very bad taste to speak of such things. Your morality, the morality created by you, for your profit, decrees that the evil or bad taste lies not in doing these things but in speaking of them, to let it be known, especially if one is a woman, that one knows that they exist and that one thinks of them. I know this, but I am first and foremost a woman and a feminist. I cannot help feeling more humiliated as a woman when I think of these things than I am proud as a French woman. I cannot help thinking that if the luck of battle had allowed us to invade some foreign country or other, the women of that country would have been treated by our allies exactly as the women of invaded countries have been treated by the German soldiery in this war, as Chinese women were treated by European soldiery of every country during the conquest of Peking.

I am reminded of Mr Clemenceau himself who has spoken so well against prostitution and wonder if he would not find it natural for women, having read his powerful words, to take them at their face value and to rise up against a war that incalculably reinforces this social evil.

Yes, war lowers our moral standards and unleashes the passions. It also corrupts the intellectual level. The mind no longer labours over subjects worthy of it. Intelligence and creative drive are only applied to works of murder and destruction: dumdum bullets, dreadnoughts, submarines, super submarines, asphyxiating gas, zeppelins, super zeppelins, tanks and so on.

I cannot believe that we human beings were given intelligence for this purpose, but I cannot pretend that this is not the course of events. The newspapers which control public opinion cover those scientists who dare to think of anything other than war with ridicule. Some time ago *L'Oeuvre* ('The Work') scoffed bitterly at those peaceful scientists of the French Academy who had listened with interest to a scholarly paper on the probability of the planet Mars being inhabited. The journalist behaved as though this was almost an act of treason, but it seems to me, simple woman that I am, that the old men discussing this issue showed more tact and dignity than those rowdy characters in the rearguard who, from the depths of their armchairs, energetically propel others forward to war, the dangers of which they themselves avoid.

As for the charge that I encouraged defeatism and national decline or that I ridiculed morality, let me give the Pope the last word:

Letter from the Pope to Mr Geoffroy de Grand'Maison.[35]

The evils resulting from the present war are not confined to the devastation of the countryside, to the destruction of flourishing cities, not even to violent death and wounds. There are two other evils of a different kind but of an equally serious nature. Amidst such misfortunes, mutual charity has disappeared from many souls; war has virtually erased the teaching brought by the Gospel which obliges us to love even our enemies. Some have even gone so far down this road that they have measured the love due to their country by the hatred they feel for those with whom they are at war. Those passions for conquest and domination which engendered the war, aggravated by its cruelty and long duration, have the result of removing all inhibitions to rancour, hatred and the desire for revenge. You can do nothing more useful for your age than to lead men together united heart and soul, through your teaching, persuasion and exhortation to understand the benefits of a peaceful future.

Gentlemen, I have done nothing different from the above. I followed the Pope's advice long before he thought to give it, for the good of my country, for the good of all humanity and for feminism. My propaganda was carefully reasoned and I made no appeals to violence. I call upon the testimony of all those who know me and have read my work. I call on the testimony not of her, who in her zeal to denounce me made a statement that she was herself partly obliged to retract, nor of her who was obliged to admit that I had only spoken directly to her once and who was reduced, in order to denounce me, to report conversations overheard while eavesdropping and to invent surmises about my actions: no. I call on those women and men who have known me for the past ten, fifteen or twenty years, and who since the beginning of the war have seen me campaign by their sides, who oversaw and followed my propaganda, whether they agreed or disagreed with it. From them I fear no rebuttals. They know that I have been a fierce opponent, that I am loyal and that if I have always defended my point of view until the bitter end – whether against or in favour of others – I will always continue to do so. At no stage did I ever dream of prevailing by blows or calumnies. Violence repels me and I have never used it or suggested its use. It is in order to end its dominion in this world that I have tried to arouse women to an awareness of Victor Considérant's words:

'When women are allowed to play a full part in social questions, revolutions will no longer take place by rifle fire'.

Hélène Brion

LETTER OF PROTEST AGAINST THE PSYCHIATRIC EXAMINATION

To *Monsieur le Capitaine Rapporteur*

I have heard from Mr Oscar Bloch, my defence attorney, that I am to become the object of a special medical examination by *three* legal doctors aimed at judging my degree of mental competence.

At the present moment, I still cannot believe in this absurd machination; nevertheless my great confidence in Mr Bloch's word leads me to behave as though I believed it, namely to ask you with the utmost seriousness to register my most energetic protest against this unspeakable measure.

I think, *Monsieur le Capitaine*, that you had some part to play in taking the above step. I do not think that I ever gave you the impression that my faculties were impaired in any degree whatever by imbecility when I replied to your interrogation. It even seemed to me that you found me possessed, on the contrary, of a clear and ready mind.

I therefore protest most energetically, not against you, but to you, because you are my judge and I have faith in your impartiality.

I protest in the name of my thirty-six years of robust health in the course of which I have not known a single illness. As a child I completed my six years of primary school without missing *a single day*; as a girl I completed my five and a half years of secondary school (Sophie Germaine) without missing *a single day*. I have always led, and especially since the beginning of the war, a super active life, if I may put it like that, both physically and mentally which would have been impossible without an iron constitution.

I protest in the name of the Education Service which has employed me for the past thirteen years; before entering the service I taught German, English and Russian students. Wherever I have been I have always been noted by my various superiors in the same way; 'an intelligent and energetic teacher'; as a pupil I was always marked as being an 'intelligent student'.

Finally I protest in the name of all the following groups and associations which have voted me to carry out various duties:

1.   The National Federation of Syndicalist Teachers, whose secretary I am.

2.   The Council for the Administration of Working-Class Orphans, *l'Avenir social* of Epône, of which I am the secretary.

3.   The Council for the Administration of the Teachers' Friendly Society, of which I am a member.

4.   The Confederal Committee of the CGT where I am the only woman delegate.

5.   The Action Committee of the Socialist Party of the CGT of the Federation of Co-operatives of which I am the only woman delegate.

6.   The Office of the Socialist Section of Pantin of which I am the archivist.

7.   The Editorial Committee of journals or newspapers: *l'Action féministe, la Paix organisée, les Semailles, l'Ecole émancipée.*

I protest as well in the name of all those women and all those feminists who for many years have seen me campaigning in feminist circles and here my protest is two-fold. Firstly against the very fact of a mental examination which it is proposed to make me undergo; secondly against the composition of the Commission charged with this examination, a Commission in which there is not a single woman although women doctors are plentiful in Paris and many have specialized in mental illnesses.

I end, *Monsieur le Capitaine Rapporteur*, by expressing the firm hope that you will spare the law and the medical profession the great ridicule to which both would be subject by suddenly discovering me to be 'irresponsible' or incompetent, for no one will believe it, except, perhaps 'them'.

And while officially I still retain my entire sanity, I wish to thank you for having been able to give me confidence in your impartiality and to assure you that if being found to be incompetent I do not lose all respect for the judiciary this will be entirely thanks to you. Saint Lazare Prison, March 1918.

LETTER TO MR LAFERRE, *MINISTRE DE L'INSTRUCTION PUBLIQUE*[36]

I have received my notification of dismissal dated 3 May from Mr Lefebre, Director of Primary Education of the Seine Department.

I have written to Mr Lefebre, acknowledging the receipt of his notification. I am addressing you now to make my most vehement protest against this action which you believe you are obliged to take and to ask for legal recourse which I have the right to do within 20 days following the notification.

My protest against dismissal is two-fold.

1.   Against the act itself. At the very moment when a public verdict, rendered with all the necessary formalities and preceded with enquiries, counter-enquiries, expert opinions and interrogations of every kind, came to the

logical conclusion and public proclamation of 1. my honesty, 2. my intelligence, 3. my intellectual development 'more developed than is usual in school teachers' (terms of the report), 4. my good conduct; at the moment where such a public recognition is given of my merits, it is a bit rich, believe me, to see myself barred from teaching and to be pompously declared to be unworthy to teach children of two to five years old, unworthy to blow their noses and to teach them to say 'thank you'. I know that intelligence is not obligatory in the exercise of our profession; illustrious examples prove it at every turn (there are more than three I could name!), still it might be more fitting, perhaps, not to set up special bonuses for stupidity and cowardice. I am afraid, Monsieur le Ministre, that the latter may not appear to arise all too clearly out of the fact of my dismissal for those who were able to see and follow the trial more closely than yourself.

2.   I protest against the fact that you have made this dismissal retroactive and I assure you that with all the intelligence which a special commission recognized that I possess, I have not been able to clarify the sense of this phrase in the notice of my dismissal:

'The judgement came into effect on 29 March 1918, backdated to 17 November 1917.'

Let me speak to you in the clear French of France. I was dismissed by the decree of 25 April 1918. Previously I had been administratively suspended with salary from 11 August 1917. No administrative action was taken again between 11 August 1917 and 25 April 1918. You owe me my entire salary between these two dates. Part of it has indeed been paid; that from 11 August to 16 November 1917. I await the other part: that of 16 November 1917 to 25 April 1918. I even expect something more, Monsieur le Ministre. I expect a gesture by which the Administration will rehabilitate itself and will make honourable amends towards the lay teaching profession which you betray at the moment, by restoring those good republicans to their posts, who have been dismissed at the moment: namely the Mayoux in the Charente, Lucie Colliard in Savoy and I myself in Paris.

Ministers of State come and go but the lay school system will remain. That is what we serve. Our devotion for it remains unshakeable. All our commiseration goes to the bosses who believe themselves obliged to betray it by striking down the teachers of the *avant-garde*.

Hélène Brion

THE FEMINIST PATH[37]

'Women dare to be', Félix Pécaut

Progressive political parties often say to us feminists when we are fighting the good fight in their ranks and we are driven by the logic of events to strengthen their demands with our own demands as women – these progressive parties, easily irritated and not understanding us often say: 'Come on, now, what is all this feminism, then? What are you asking for that we do not offer?'.[38] And here they divide into two equally convinced sects each singing the same refrain word for word. 'Socialism is the answer to everything. True feminism is to be a socialist. You do not need to be feminists. It should be enough for you to be socialists, fully and entirely – the whole social issue is subsumed in socialism.' And the other sect? 'Trade unionism is the solution to everything. A true feminist is a trade unionist. If you are really a trade unionist that should satisfy you, because integral trade unionism is the genuine solution to social issues and you do not even have to give sales talks on parliamentary action.' Quite a few feminist activists have begun to listen to these siren songs.

On behalf of all feminists I want to try to explain here why these views are false, why male activists themselves do not really believe in them and why they feel troubled and disturbed by this self-assertive feminist movement; they do not understand why women activists should more than ever continue to wear this political label representing the only theory which can bring a solution to the myriad social problems of whose existence socialism and trade unionism are entirely ignorant … .

Socialism and the Trade Union Movement both strive to better the lot of workers and of the poor. But women are more exploited by the male collectivity as women than they are by capitalism as workers. And without looking beyond the working-class world, it is easy for me to prove this, for the most flagrant injustice which hits the woman worker – be she in industry, or in white collar work – is inequality of pay for the same work, something everyone can see as a fact. Now this injustice is aimed not at the labourer but at the woman. It is the woman who is depreciated, *a priori*, as a worker by this stupid and odious action which custom has rendered sacred.

One example out of a thousand will suffice. Elizabeth Trundle, Gustave Téry tells us in *Le Journal*, was arrested in Brooklyn for wearing male clothing. 'What do you expect?', she said to the judges. 'I am a bookbinder by trade. If I work in a workshop dressed as a woman, I receive thirty francs a week. Dressed as a man, I earn seventy-five.' There is no need to comment further.

Having accepted the point that a woman is victimized as a woman more than she is as a worker, let us compare the workload that the female individual carries in the factory and in her family.

At the factory or workshop a woman has a fixed wage, however small it may be. She has settled hours of work, however numerous they may be and she has agreed time off. In the factory she feels herself to have the status of a producer. As a worker, she speaks proudly of 'my money' when talking of the wages that she draws, however little they may be. However awful her position, she will not be beaten by the boss or foreman without public opinion rallying to give her justice.

In the family, her working hours are not fixed. She has to devote herself at all times and all the time from morning to night to everyone: aged parents, husband, children, well or ill and she can never feel that her task is completed. For this crushing labour, for this perpetual slavery, she does not gain a farthing and she has no right to the fine title of 'worker'. And she produces nothing. One often hears a working-class or even a middle-class man say with pride: 'Oh, as for me, my wife doesn't do anything. I do not want her to work. She only does housework'. The man who speaks like this certainly believes that he is supporting his wife who does nothing. He will readily tell her so in order to make her feel that he is the master. And the law, an expression of the will and thinking of *men alone*, the law comes to the same conclusion and endorses this view – for example by the law on women workers' pensions which does not count housework as a trade unless it is carried out by a hireling.

This comparison of the two situations cannot admit of any doubt. It is in the family that women are the most oppressed; by coming to the factory they win a semblance of independence. Another powerful attraction is the much more varied life that women find there which is not a negligible factor in motivating more and more women to go out to work.

But it is precisely in the very place that they are the most oppressed, within the family, in their own hearth and home, that trade unionism can do nothing for them. Already nearly powerless to protect women workers doing piecework at home, trade unionism is completely powerless to defend women suffering from oppression and familial exploitation. The hell of the home, as it is presently constituted, weighs on a woman's whole life and prevents all independent or intellectual development. We feminists remember only too well a typical example at the Lebaudy strike some time before the war, an example which should give our male comrades food for thought if they took time to reflect on it.

It was in the midst of the strike. Women strikers and some male trade unionists were posted at the gate, guarding the entrance and stopping the entry of women workers too timid to strike if one did not give the impression of forcing them. So they 'forced' them. – To the few who came to take up work again, the guards at the door said a few words, indicated they were forbidden to enter and that was enough. The women turned away or stayed to watch. And what did all these men and women strikers then see, all of a sudden? A weeping woman, nearly dead with shame arrived, followed by a man, who with kicks and blows from a cudgel forced her to press on. She was a striker from the previous day and the day before that whom her tyrant had brought back to work because he was displeased that his wife was on strike. And the knights of the strike stood there, powerless in front of this man, who before their eyes, opened the gate and still raining down blows, pushed his wife back into penal servitude.

If it had been a question of a foreman beating a woman worker, all the trade unionists would have leapt forward: but this was a husband, a private affair, a domestic dispute. Trade unions are concerned only with work-related issues. We do not blame them, but they should not blame us either for concerning ourselves with those issues which concern us at least as much as labour conflicts.

Our comrades need to understand that for women, the centre of their lives is not the workplace, that to be a worker is just a moment of their lives as women. Family life absorbs them the most – even if this family is only represented by elderly parents for whom they must care. Women drag their domestic cares to work more often than they carry their work cares home. Their tasks at the factory or workshop are often only of a manual nature and make no demands on their intelligence, leaving their minds and hearts empty. Women do not have to expend their creative or inventive capacities in work. Their professional training, the openings available to them in manual trades, with the exception of dressmaking, are terribly circumscribed by convention. A man may be passionate about his trade and try to better himself in it or try to improve the machine and tools which he uses. Everything invites him to innovate, whereas everything drives women back to what at the present time is the only approved centre of her activity, the family.

Not only will trade unions be unable to bring about women's emancipation since they are only concerned with women as workers – and we feminists are incapable of confining our efforts to this – but we still fear that we may have to fight the unions one day if they do not soon clarify their views in relation to us. Many trade unionists in fact still maintain, as far as women are concerned, the old notion dear to Proudhon: housewife or harlot.[39] As harlot women have a clear function – as a housewife they have the same function and several others besides. They act as cook, dishwasher, washerwoman, laundry woman, mender, ironer, mother, nurse, child-minder, carer for invalids and so on. This frenetic life does not suit them any better than the first one mentioned. Women want the right to construct a third type of life, a free life whose elements they themselves wish to define.

These rights which feminists have always demanded, the right to work and freedom, have been refused us by many trade unionists. The notorious Couriau case, which occurred not long ago, proves my point.[40] Let me briefly recall the facts.

A woman typesetter, Mme Couriau, member of a trade union of many years' standing, as was her husband, and who had been paid wages at trade union rates, moved to Lyons and was taken on at a printing firm with her husband. But the trade union comrades of Lyons could not accept that a woman could work among them. They enjoined Mr Couriau to forbid his wife to work. Couriau would have none of it. He dared to suggest that his wife was a free being, as he was, and that they were harming no one since they were working at trade union rates.

Our good trade union comrades then went to the boss and threatened to unleash a general strike if Mme Couriau went on working. The boss was obliged to give in: Mme Couriau was dismissed, thrown out of the trade union to boot and her husband as well. All the feminist groups rose up in protest against this odious and arbitrary act, but not a single voice of the official trade union movement was raised to condemn it.[41]

Unfortunately this incident is not an isolated one. To mention only the well-known strike at Nancy, among intransigent typesetters also, a strike where women were blamed for having acted as blacklegs, many workers' movements have had as their objective the exclusion of women from certain trades, where the hard necessities of life, combined with their desire to work, drove them to earn their living.

I have heard Elizabeth Renaud say that she once attended a short strike against a joiner/furniture seller who had had the idea of hiring a woman who was literally dying of hunger.[42] The union did not allow the miserable creature to work for a single day. And without going back so far, did we not all hear at the outbreak of the war the blazing denunciations of the transport union which rose up against the employment of women as tram drivers, and urged the public in scarcely veiled terms to overturn the cars which were not driven by 'men'?

Recently in London, a huge strike of tram drivers had the same aim: to prevent women from earning their living as conductors. And do not tell me that our good trade union comrades act in this way to protect women's health and the public interest. As far as the public interest is concerned, experience proves that it is not in danger. Women tram drivers flourish just about everywhere; they travel the routes not only of Paris and its suburbs, but Bordeaux, Le Mans and so on. And military authorities, following the English example after a two-year delay, confide their convalescents, their wounded and even their heavy provision wagons to the weak and clumsy hands of these weak and clumsy women without any danger to anyone. Even better, at Fécamp there are already two women engine drivers – but let us not get carried away.

As for women's health, please forget it. Do not remind us of that famous law about night work, for example, proposed by men and voted by men, ending simply in making women typographers lose their jobs where before they earned six francs a night, without protecting, for all of that the newspaper folders who only earn, it is true, two or three francs. The weakness of women; the health of women. Do not dredge these up, when you know perfectly well that women have always worked at the hardest and most disgusting jobs, in mines, in agriculture, in weaving and in the sorting of cocoons [silk manufacture], in slaughterhouses, in the potteries, in the preparation of glue, wax and grease, in the tanneries as well as hospitals and in hospices where they care for horrible and fetid wounds. No! Do not come and talk to us about negotiating to improve women's health as workers while as women we remain subordinated to your absolute caprice as men. While you impose either multiple and exhausting pregnancies or abortions or sterility on us at *your* wish (which your laws condemn), which for women reduces the whole universe to your person. Do not talk about your concern for women's health or for the young as long as you accept the existence of brothels and the infamous regime of the morals police.[43]

No! What impels our trade union comrades to behave like this is simply the masculine instinct, accustomed for centuries to domesticate women, which is now terror-stricken at their possible liberation. It is the brutal domineering instinct of the Roman Caesars or of a slave owner who is infuriated by the idea that his cattle may escape. You can see him in all his glory in the following story which I copied from the newspaper *Lanterne* of March 1907.

Two cab drivers demonstrated in an ungallant fashion the pique they felt at the scarcely threatening competition caused by women cab drivers. First of all, one male cab driver made every effort to run into a cab driven by a woman. Having smashed in the back of the cab, he fled, well satisfied. Another was not so fortunate. Towards five o'clock in the afternoon, Mme Decourcelles, a cab woman working for the hire firm of Valentin, was driving two women home when at 144 Rue de Rivoli, a cab from the *Compagnie Urbaine*, driven by driver D__ suddenly cut across her path. In order to avoid a smash, the woman driver adroitly pulled her horse aside, but unfortunately her cab struck a car that was passing at that moment. The carriage springs were broken. Mme Decourcelles, who is not only a skilful cab driver but a strong-minded woman, jumped from her cab and set off in pursuit of D__ who whipping his horse was bolting at full speed. Courageously grabbing him by the collar, she dragged him back and called the police who interviewed witnesses. D__ has been booked by Mr Bureau, Police Commissioner for the Halles district, for hindering the freedom to work and for wilful violence.

You will find this same instinct at work at the other end of the social scale among young men of good family who at the end of the nineteenth century broke into a feminist congress singing obscene songs and throwing filth around the meeting room. You will find it among those students who one year pursued two of the first women doctors through the streets of Paris, shouting insults. It is the same which, not long ago, impelled chic young men to attack the models of the Rue de la Paix who were trying to launch the culotte skirt style. It is the same spirit which about 1851 raised a mob of Yankees in free America against the Bloomerists who had been daring enough to wear divided skirts.[44]

From woman doctors to woman cab drivers, from the Misses Garretts and Blackwells to Mmes Dufaut and Decourcelles, all those who have snatched or attempted to grab a few scraps of freedom have had to struggle against this spirit.[45] And this is not only in France and Europe but in Turkey, Persia, China and India, everywhere that the enslaved sex has at long last been moved by the sacred spirit of rebellion to try to react against a wretched condition.

Trade Unionism and Socialism concern themselves above all with the poor and with material welfare. But human beings in general, and women in particular and even wealthy women may suffer from mental depression as painful perhaps if not more so than poverty. I will not insult the great majority of our comrades by believing that they doubt my words.[46] If there is a small number of brutes who seem to believe and pretend to say that money is the answer to all evils, that one will have no cause for complaint when one has all one's needs catered for, I know that they are the exception and I repeat: the great majority have a truer idea of life's complexity and of the complexity of the human mind. The latter will understand us and all women will similarly understand us if we affirm that there are rich women, very distinguished women, who have suffered and suffer still from social barriers as much and perhaps more than do women factory workers. For the capacity for suffering depends on the cultural development of each individual. Some such 'great lady' who spends her life in charitable work to battle against poverty and vice has perhaps experienced more mental suffering from social injustice than some poor woman whom she has rescued who is too brutalized by her own poverty to reflect upon it.

Yes all those Josephine Butlers, those Paulines de Grandpré have suffered from social barriers, wearing out their lives in the struggle against prostitution. Miss Garrett and Miss Blackwell suffered from male injustice, spending their fortunes and their energy for years on end to plead against the Universities of London, Edinburgh and against fourteen American universities in order for women to have the right to study medicine. Elizabeth Cady Stanton also suffered. This passionate anti-slavery campaigner and feminist undertook a voyage of five thousand kilometres in order to attend an anti-slavery convention in England in 1840. She was refused entry to the convention, though she was a delegate, because she was a woman.[47]

And in the realm of feeling let us not enumerate the endless sufferings of women as mothers whatever their social rank, nationality or race. I simply want to evoke them. Every man and woman will see a crowd of martyrs surge forward, a product of the male organization of the world, from the Indian widows burned alive on the funeral pyres of their masters to the Chinese women with their bound feet ... .

Trades Union comrades: your ideal will not do! If we turn your own question back on you and if we ask you point blank: 'What is this trade unionism of yours?', it may be that there are not many of you who could immediately answer in one or two clear sentences. And if I asked a second question: ' What place does the trade union movement offer me as a woman?', then I am certain that there will be no answer whatever, a profound astonishment, a second's embarrassment, a vague unease on suddenly seeing the shadows of a thousand unsuspected problems rise up.

Then your usual self-sufficiency reasserting itself, we would see either a scornful shrugging of the shoulders or hear a series of commonplaces about women's role and her 'natural place' in the home, in the shadow and the wake of men. Banal and empty phrases, heartbreaking to hear for those who think deeply: phrases which are particularly shocking from the lips of fierce revolutionaries which we have so often heard and read in their banality and conventionality among the bourgeoisie and right-thinking people of every shade of opinion and every political party.

As for me, I cannot listen to them without being reminded of Chaumette's grotesque and bombastic speech on the 29th *Brumaire*, driving women republicans away from the Convention, women who had come yet once again to demand their rights.[48]

'The forum where the people's representatives debate,' cried out this fierce friend of his own liberty, 'must be forbidden to all those who *outrage nature*! ... . Since when is it permitted to renounce one's sex? Since when is it seemly to see women abandon the pious cares of their households to come into the public arena: into the debating chambers: to the bar of the Assembly? Imprudent women, do you want to become men?' ...

This speech leads us back to the issue of political rights and to the question of what that party which in political life represents the interests of the oppressed, has done for us women. Without going back to the Flood, without questioning Saint Simon, Fourier or even Proudhon on their ideas about our social role and the place which they reserve for us in any future society, let us just look at the Third Republic. And let us see what activity has been expended on us by that party [the socialists] which shamelessly forbids us to undertake any political action outside of its framework. Here in chronological order are some of the reforms which concern us:

1881–1886: Reintroduction of divorce, Loi Naquet.
1904: M. Vallé constitutes Commission for Reform of the Civil Code, reform *'pro femina'*.
1905: Charles Beauquier: Project to repeal married women's legal incapacity.
1906: M. Chéron: Forms parliamentary group 'Rights of Women'. Henri Coulon, extra-parliamentary commission on marriage reform.
1907: Goiran Law on married women's wages.
1907–1908: Women become eligible for the *Conseils de Prudhommes*.
1913: Paul Strauss: Maternity allocation of fifty centimes per day for women lying in.

The bill giving women the rights of guardianship which naturally languished in parliamentary files many years before finally emerging a few months ago, recalls the names of Castelnau, Marc-Réville and Maurice Violette.

As for proposals, they are legion: Dussaussory and Buisson's for women to vote on municipal councils: President Magnaud's proposal that women control their own property in common law marriages: a proposal of Martin and Maurice Violette asking for divorce by mutual consent: a proposal of E. Girard giving power of attorney to the wife of a husband interned in a psychiatric hospital: a proposal of Chautemps-Borel asking that cases of adultery and divorce be tried *in camera*: a proposal of Beauquier asking for the ending of married women's legal incapacity and proposing to make mental instability a ground for divorce and so on.

Among all these names, my socialist Comrades, not one of yours.[49] Among all these reforms or scraps of reforms dredged out by the constant labour and relentless effort of the feminist movement, there is not a single proposal coming from you. That famous law on the search for paternity which it took thirty years to pass owes nothing to socialist activity.

These fine gentlemen who drew up the bill achieved nothing effective in any case. And it was fatal. On such a sensitive issue and one which affects them so closely, only women could have found a satisfactory solution. The requirement to discover the father [of an illegitimate child] is a false concept which we radical feminists oppose because it tends to perpetuate the age-old error that the family is based on the man whereas its logical and natural basis is the woman and only the woman. Starting from a false premise, our good legislators, in spite of all their enthusiasm and legal knowledge, could only succeed in making a faulty law. And that is what they succeeded in doing. But we feminists cannot but be grateful to them for having given themselves so much trouble to try to remedy a flagrant evil whose underlying causes they failed to understand. And we are obliged to note once again that there were no socialists in their ranks.

Moreover it was not so long ago that our feminist delegations coming to Parliament with a feminist petition had to address themselves to Radicals or Radical Socialists whereas very often almost the entire delegation of feminists was made up of members of the Socialist Party. We are aware, to be sure, that you have included votes for women in your party manifesto. We even are aware that just before the war, at the last municipal and parliamentary elections, the party had made an effort to *support* (?) women and feminist candidates. Elisabeth Renaud in the Isère, Madeleine Pelletier and Caroline Kauffmann in Paris, stood as candidates – if I may put it like that – under the banner of the PSU [*Parti socialist unifié*], in unwinnable seats in any case and with no chance, simply as paper candidates.

We well remember the complex feelings which assailed us when taking a passionate part in this election campaign: a gleam of hope and happiness to be able to fight one's own battles, to serve the cause of justice for the highest but also for the most personal ends, and at the same time, shame, profound shame and painful, bitter humiliation. For we saw someone as intelligent as Madeleine Pelletier, for example, confronted with the popular stupidity of one of the most reactionary districts of Paris and felt that all this intellectual power and competence which could have been used by our party in Parliament was condemned to expend its efforts there, in this commonplace school hall before an uncomprehending audience, to see this while we knew that under more favourable circumstances, candidates of no greater worth and far less knowledge would be elected almost without opposition.

I accept that it was a great hour for the feminist movement when the Socialist Party endorsed female candidates. But it would have honoured itself far more and would have gained the right to our eternal gratitude if it had made it possible for a woman to be elected. Oh, I can hear the objections: you would have had to sacrifice a safe seat, upset certain arrangements, offend a few mediocre party hacks. What trepidation in the Republic of Comrades. But what a moral victory for the party and what enthusiasm this would have aroused in the feminist movement. A moral victory of incalculable effect on the eve of this tragic conflict in which the world is now engaged. A gesture of immense significance which would have hurled a new force of incalculable power into the political arena, with a limitless faith and enthusiasm, perhaps capable by itself of purifying, cleansing and renewing the Old World by sparing it the horrors and the crimes of the present day.

Therefore neither trade unionism nor socialism are adequate for the feminist movement. And we must, in the higher interest of justice and our own interests, continue to struggle as feminists on the margins of all other parties. We will not fail. We have set out our position clearly *vis-à-vis* our comrades of the far progressive left in the following note sent to them a year ago:

Feminist Message to the Committee for the Resumption of International Relations[50]

We who were unable to prevent war, since we possess no civil or political rights, are with you heart and soul to will its end. We are with you in our desire that after the war a more just and fairer social system be established in Europe which on the one hand would make wars less frequent, by some kind of federation of nations, and assure on the other, a better and less precarious life within each nation for the great mass of workers.

We women are among the mass of workers, because we are everywhere oppressed, much more so than any class of worker. Like you, we are workers, and suffer more than you from war which is why we want to try to prevent its recurrence. But before joining you in a more decisive phase of action, we want to clarify our motives and to comment on your attitudes as demonstrated by the facts. Workers, you have never been just to those women who have helped you in your struggles. In the dawn of 1789, at the moment when a new era seemed to be beginning for the world, women came to you full of confidence, because you promised them liberty and they thought they would gain their own. You rejected them.

Proud of your newly acquired rights as 'citizens', instead of reaching out a fraternal hand to all those women who for centuries had pulled the plough at your side and like you had eaten grass in the famine years, you scoffed, you scorned them. You, who wanted no more of despots, were horrified at the idea of the possible emancipation of your eternal slaves. You broke up the women's clubs, confiscated their newspapers, rescinded women's right to petition Parliament, forbade all thought and all action to women. You brutally drove women back into that ignorance from which they wanted to escape, back into the arms of the Church. More than half of those women who for fourteen years had sustained the revolt in the Vendée came to the Revolution of 1789 full of trust. But rejected, as the blacks from the colonies were at first, women, like the slaves, rebelled. And as Legouvé wrote at a later date: the Revolution failed because it was unable to enlist women.[51]

Note, nevertheless, that in spite of your harshness towards them, many still hoped and came to your aid. You have all heard of Mme Roland, Charlotte Corday, Théroigne de Méricourt, Rose Lacombe, Olympe de Gouges, Sophie Lapierre and the '*Babouvistes*' and so many others who sealed their revolutionary faith with their blood.[52]

Throughout the nineteenth century, at each moment of political crisis, women accompanied you or preceded you. In 1830, 1848, 1851, 1871 we find Flora Tristan, Jeanne Deroin, Pauline Roland, Eugénie Niboyet, Adèle Esquiros, Andrée Léo, Olympe Audreard, Louise Julien, Louise Michel, Hubertine Auclert, Eliska Vincent, Nathalie Lemel and so many others, whose names, scarcely known to you, are dear to feminists, as are the names of national heroes to oppressed peoples. At each one of these crises, women came to the aid of those men struggling for more liberty and well-being, for a more rational and a more humane life. The pioneers of feminism gave themselves to your cause without counting the cost, trying to link women's cause to yours and to make you understand the close connection between the two, not through selfishness or in order to derive personal profit, but for the love of justice, for the sake of all their sisters who suffer and for your sakes too, you workers who seem incapable of comprehending. You always accepted their help, sometimes somewhat shamefacedly, embarrassed at what you owed them, as happened at the time of the trial of Jeanne Deroin's women workers' associations.

But while accepting their efforts, you never dreamt, when the moment came, of sharing with them the slight concessions you had wrested from the authorities. You had not yet understood, or wished to understand, that your cause will not be genuinely just and holy until the day that you can no longer tolerate the existence of slaves among you. As long as it seems natural to you to maintain a privileged position in relation to more than half the nation, you will have no grounds for inveighing against privileges that others possess in relation to you. If you want justice for yourselves, try to practise it in relation to your female inferiors.

Workers, a social crisis more profound than all those in the nineteenth century, is currently in preparation. As always, women rally to you, ready to give selflessly of their devotion the day that you are ready to act. And feminists rally to you as well with the same devotion and the same goodwill. But, they say: 'If this time, yet again, you accept women's help – and you cannot not accept it – without planning to carry out social reforms: if you maintain women as serfs instead of making them your equals from an economic, civil and political point of view, your work will lie in ruins'. Women rally to your aid and remind you, or inform you that as early as 1843, a woman, Flora Tristan, first had the idea of a Workers' International, and they will quote this passage from her manifesto to you, a passage too often forgotten, with which it opened. 'We, the proletariat, accept that we have been genuinely enlightened and are convinced that the neglect of and scorn for women's rights are the sole causes of the world's evils, and we have resolved to inscribe their sacred and inalienable rights in a solemn declaration. We want women to be made aware of our declaration so that they no longer allow themselves to be oppressed and degraded by the injustices and tyrannies of men and we also wish all men to respect in women, their mothers, the liberty and equality which they, as men, enjoy.'

If you had taken heed of the provisions and of the spirit of this very first International, which you do not even count as part of your history, the Second International would not have undergone the lamentable collapse from which the world is now suffering. Workers, the women of the *avant-garde* await your response and leave you with these words of Considérant to ponder: 'The day that women participate in the public sphere, revolutions will cease to take place by rifle fire'.

No response has as yet been received to this message. And this tactic of not replying has the air of an answer, even a highly significant answer. I am not authorized here, for the moment, to draw broader conclusions, but one at least seems inescapable. It is not possible for feminists to merge their programme, at present at least, with that of trade unionists and socialists, while agreeing that these should remain linked. But conversely it is undeniable that the socialist and trade union movement is at the moment undergoing a crisis. By the crude light of facts, socialists and trade unionists have discovered how fragile their apparently sound organization is. They now realize that among their membership statistics there are as many noughts as positive numbers. This is why the disappearance of one man was enough to plunge the party into crisis.[53] They now recognize that they themselves grew drunk on empty words, when thinking that they had educated their fellow workers. May this be a useful lesson. May they reflect upon the causes of this fundamental weakness in a party which gave such an appearance of strength.

As for me, if I may hazard a personal opinion, perhaps an impression more than an opinion, I would venture the following: Among women's groups the contrary occurs. We have a seemingly much more defective organization and a far less centralized one. Our thirty-six little groups seem to be a scattered force, almost opposed to one another. Many of us do not belong to any group and carry out educative and propagandizing work without links with other women. But beneath this apparent disorder, there is a profound unity of thought, born of women's common suffering. There is an intense vitality, a profound faith among these little groups. There we examine ideas instead of manipulating words. There is more depth, more real experience of life and also more frankness as well as *naïveté*. We know more but do not dare to speak out or to assert ourselves.

And that is why I want to end these pages with the quotation with which I began; a profound and moving call from a great hearted person [Félix Pécaut], a call even more heartbreaking to hear at the present hour of madness:

Femme, ose être.
Woman, dare to be.

NOTES

1. For background on the French military mutinies and Clemenceau's repression see: Richard M. Watt, *Dare Call it Treason*, London, Chatto and Windus, 1963; David S. Newhall, *Clemenceau: A Life at War*, Lampeter, Edwin Mellen Press, 1991; John Terraine, 'The Aftermath of Nivelle', *History Today*, **27**, 1977, pp. 426–33; Gregor Dallas, *At the Heart of the Tiger: Clemenceau and his World 1841–1929*, London, Macmillan, 1988, and Guy Pedroncini, *Les mutineries de 1917*, Paris, Presses Universitaires de France, 1967, especially pp. 36–52, 'Le GQG et la propagande pacifiste'.
2. *Journal officiel*, Chambre de Députés, Débats parlementaires, Imprimerie Nationale, 1917, quoted in Newhall, *op. cit.*, p. 354.
3. Terraine, 'The Aftermath of Nivelle', *op. cit.*, p. 427.
4. Christine Bard, *Les Féminismes en France. Vers l'intégration des femmes dans la Cité*, Thèse de doctorat, Paris, Université de Paris VII, 1993, p. 189. D.R. Watson makes the point that Clemenceau was careful not to alienate the working class by attacking the large unions. He was conciliatory to Merrheim, Secretary of the Metal Workers Union and brought 'minor figures' to trial. D.R. Watson, *Georges Clemenceau, a Political Biography*, London, Eyre Methuen, 1974, pp. 285–7.
5. 'L'Affaire Hélène Brion, pacifisme et défaitisme', *Revue des causes célèbres*, Paris, 2 May 1918. For references to L'Affaire Brion see: Jean-Jacques Becker, 'Teachers and the War', pp. 150–60, *The Great War and the French People*, translated by Arnold Pomerans, Leamington Spa, Berg, 1985, and for a succinct and perceptive analysis, James F. McMillan, *Housewife or Harlot: the Place of Women in French Society, 1870–1940*, Brighton, Harvester Press, 1981, pp. 101–15. McMillan says of Brion: 'Her advanced political feminist views made her the object of vile abuse in the reactionary press, where she was accused of Malthusianism, defeatism, anti-militarism, anarchism and incompetence at her job, as well as a preference for masculine clothes', p. 114.
6. Madeleine Vernet, *Hélène Brion, une belle conscience et une sombre affaire*, Epône, L'Avenir social, November 1917.
7. See *Journal officiel de la République française*, 6 August 1914. The new law drawing on Article 23 of 29 July 1881, concerning the press, forbade the circulation of information other than that approved by the government relating to the movement of troops, wounded, defence installations and so on. It was also forbidden (Article 3) to circulate or sell magazines, newspapers and so forth printed abroad. Infractions could bring a term of imprisonment of between one and five years and a fine of 1 000 to 5 000 francs.
8. AN F/7/ 13266 'Vote des Femmes', Archives Nationales, Paris.
9. AN F/7 13575, Archives Nationales, Paris.
10. AN F/7/ 13343, Archives Nationales, Paris.
11. See pp. 209–10, 'Letter of Protest against a Psychiatric Examination'.
12. 'Les poursuites contre Hélène Brion', *L'Humanité*, 28 November 1917.
13. '*L'Affaire Hélène Brion, op. cit.*, p. 131. Gaston Moufflard was an electrician and socialist who had corresponded with Brion during the war. Conscripted into the army, he was twice wounded and twice demoted for 'insubordination'. At the time of his arrest, he was

working in a munitions factory, having been invalided out of the army. The court found him guilty and sentenced him to a six-month suspended sentence.

14. Bolo was executed in 1918, one of three to receive the death sentence for treason at this period.
15. '*L'Affaire Héléne Brion*, *op. cit.*, p. 166.
16. Huguette Bouchardeau, *Hélène Brion: la Voie féministe*, Paris, Syros, 1978, p. 40.
17. See Madeleine Pelletier, 'Memoirs of a Feminist', pp. 235–48.
18. Héléne Brion, 'Déclaration lue au premier conseil de guerre' (Statement read to the Court Martial), 29 March 1918, Epône, L'Avenir social, 1918, see p. 201. For a previous translation of this text see: Susan Groag Bell and Karen M. Offen (eds), *Women, the Family, and Freedom*, vol. 2, 1880–1950, Stanford, California, Stanford University Press, 1983, pp. 273–5.
19. *Ibid.*, see p. 203.
20. See Letter to Mr Laferre, *Ministre de L'Instruction Publique*, pp. 210–11.
21. Christine Bard, *Les féminismes*, *op. cit.*, p. 195.
22. For detailed accounts of the Couriau Affair see: Charles Sowerwine, 'Workers and Women in France before 1914: The Debate over the Couriau Affair', *Journal of Modern History*, **55**, September 1983, 411–41; Steven C. Hause with Anne R. Kenney, *Women's Suffrage and Social Politics in the French Third Republic*, Princeton, Princeton University Press, 1984, p. 279; and Patricia J. Hilden, 'Women and the Labour Movement in France, 1869–1914', *Historical Journal*, **29** (4), 1986, 809–32.
23. *La Bataille syndicaliste*, 30 July 1914.
24. The Condorcet demonstration of 5 July 1914 organized by Sévérine, was the largest and most successful gathering of French suffragists to date.
25. By giving a date from the Revolutionary Calendar of 1789, Brion signalled her loyalty to revolutionary principles and to the idea that the revolution was a continuous process, not yet achieved.
26. See 'Protest', pp. 209–10.
27. All four women cited in this paragraph stood as paper candidates in the 1908, 1910 and 1912 elections, in order to dramatize women's exclusion from political life. (See Chapter 7).
28. A reference to the majority of French feminists and many socialists who enthusiastically embraced the war effort. See Pelletier's strictures on Marguerite Durand and Gustave Hervé ('Memoirs of a Feminist', pp. 235–48).
29. Léon Gambetta (1838–1882). Republican Deputy and member of the National Defence government during the Franco-Prussian War. He was renowned for his patriotism.
30. Jules Michelet, *Histoire de la Révolution française*, Paris, Chamerot, 1847–53 (Hélène Brion).
31. Jean Finot, *Préjugés et problèmes des sexes*, 1913 (Hélène Brion).
32. Norman Angell, *La Grande Illusion*, Paris, Nelson Editeurs, 1913. A work of political economy which studied the military build-up to the Great War and the economic competition of the major European powers, arguing against the then current version of deterrence theory. Angell's title was employed for the great anti-war movie of the same name.
33. George Sand, *Letters, Correspondance 1812–1876*, Paris, C. Lévy, **6**, 1884 (Hélène Brion).
34. Probably a reference to the Great War slogan: 'A war to end all wars'.
35. 'La Croix', 11 March (*Vérité*, 1912).
36. Letter published in *L'Humanité*, 18 May 1918.
37. *La Voie féministe*, edited by La Société de la Librairie et d'Edition de l'Avenir Social à l'Epône, (not dated; –1917?).
38. By 'progressive political parties' Brion wished to indicate socialist parties grouped either in the SFIO or the CGT.
39. Proudhon argued that his definition of women's possibilities (housewife or whore) was not demeaning to women. The role of housewife as manager of the family economy was in no way inferior to a man's role ('Revolutionary Programme Addressed to the Voters of the Seine', 31 May 1848). Syndicalist movements embraced his views, partly from fear of

female competition on wages (Brion's point), partly from traditionalist views of gender roles and partly from nostalgia for a pre-industrial past.

40. Although the *Fédération nationale du livre* had championed women's rights in 1913, the national organization was not empowered to force its branches to accept women members. When in 1912 Emma Couriau and her husband were expelled from the Lyons branch of the union, the case became a focus for feminist protest. Madeleine Pelletier was one of many feminists writing articles to denounce '*hominisme*'.

41. *La Fronde*, Marguerite Durand's feminist daily, spearheaded the pro-Couriau campaign.

42. Elisabeth Renaud (1846–1932), teacher, feminist and socialist, stood as a socialist candidate in the 1910 parliamentary elections in the Vienne and gained an impressive 2 869 votes. She was a founder member (1896) of the Feminist Socialist Group. She ran a *pension de famille* where Madeleine Pelletier boarded during the 1914–1918 war. Renaud converted to the Seventh Day Adventist Church in 1925.

43. The campaign against legalized prostitution, the enforced medical inspection of prostitutes and their imprisonment to cure them of venereal disease was a central feminist concern of the period. See also Madeleine Pelletier, 'On Prostitution', pp. 184–6.

44. 'Bloomerists': Mrs Amelia Bloomer, an advocate of dress reform, proposed in 1851 that women who wanted to lead physically active lives should wear loose baggy trousers under their crinolines. The style evolved with the advent of the bicycle in the 1890s, when more and more women abandoned the over-skirt and wore some version of trousers. In France trousers for women had been banned under the Revolution of 1789 and were only legalized in 1909. One notes that Hélène Brion's cycling costume, knickerbocker trousers, was regarded by the right-wing newspaper, *Le Matin*, as evidence of her bad character at the time of her court martial. See 'Les Poursuites Contre Héléne Brion', *L'Humanité*, 28 November 1917, for a discussion on the press campaign in *Le Matin*.

45. Elisabeth Garrett (1836–1917), the first British woman to qualify as a medical doctor, obtained a medical degree in Paris in 1870, having been refused entry to study medicine at the University of London. Elizabeth Blackwell (1821–1910) was the first woman to qualify as a medical doctor in the United States and campaigned vigorously in Britain for women's right to enter the profession.

46. Brion here is arguing against a purely materialist and class-based Marxist analysis of oppression. She suggests that sexual oppression transcends class or material oppression.

47. Josephine Butler (1828–1906), from a secure middle-class background and married to a Unitarian minister, campaigned vigorously and successfully against the regulation of prostitution under the Contagious Diseases Acts. Pauline de Grandpré worked with the Saint Lazare prostitutes and campaigned against regulation. Elizabeth Cady Stanton (1818–1902) was one of the founders of the American feminist movement and a vigorous anti-slavery campaigner. Her exclusion from the anti-slavery conference in London had a radicalizing effect on her feminism.

48. Women's revolutionary clubs were closed by the Jacobins and by 1795 women had been excluded from all political assemblies.

49. Bouchardeau points out (*op. cit.*, p. 86) that Brion exaggerates somewhat in this section. Socialists and communists had submitted proposals for reforming the paternity laws and for liberalizing laws on contraception and abortion.

50. This refers to a minority in the French socialist movement who took part in the Zimmerwald and Kleinthal conferences of 1915 where the idea of a new International was launched by Lenin and Trotsky.

51. Ernest Legouvé (1807–1903), Professor at the *Collège de France*, early champion of women's rights, and author of *L'Histoire morale des femmes*, Paris, G. Sandré, 1849 was founder member in 1870 of *L'Association pour le droit des femmes*, with Maria Deraismes and Léon Richer.

52. The women listed here, though politically very diverse, had in common their prosecution of imprisonment during the Revolution. Rose (Claire) Lacombe was President of the women's club, *Républicaines révolutionnaires*. Théroigne de Méricourt, who argued that women should bear arms, was incarcerated in an asylum, Mme Roland, Charlotte Corday and Olympe de Gouges were guillotined.

53. Jean Jaurès (1859–1914), one of the founders of the modern French Socialist Party, headed the *Parti socialiste unifié* and was assassinated by right-wing extremists at the outbreak of the Great War.

8. Madeleine Pelletier: autobiographical writing

We are fortunate in possessing a wealth of autobiographical writing by Madeleine Pelletier. Her two published novels, *Une Vie nouvelle* (1932) and *La Femme vierge* (1933), were based on her own life. She also left three unpublished autobiographical texts, translated and published here for the first time: her 'War Diary, 1914–1918'; her Memoir, 'Anne, dite Madeleine Pelletier', a fragment dictated at Perray Vaucluse in 1939; and her 'Memoirs of a Feminist' (*c.* 1933).[1] The Memoir, taken down by Hélène Brion at the asylum of Perray Vaucluse where Pelletier was incarcerated when she was found too ill to plead on an abortion charge in 1939, is overshadowed by the dark and tragic circumstances in which she died. Yet it is also illuminated by the vivid glimpses of Pelletier's childhood in a two-room slum house where she lived with her parents in the heart of the Les Halles market district. Pelletier understood her past as formed from her working-class milieu, from the world which had constructed her political, social and gender consciousness. 'Memoirs of a Feminist', on the other hand, is a considered public account of Pelletier's career, often betraying disappointment and disillusion, but breathing a spirit of defiance and a belief in social justice. Finally, Pelletier's 'War Diary' records valuable glimpses of her experiences in the 1914–1918 period, when she, like Hélène Brion, was under police surveillance, though she avoided arrest and prosecution.

'Anne, dite Madeleine Pelletier', which details many sordid aspects of her family's poverty, more importantly illuminates the basic political/gender tensions of Pelletier's childhood in the 1870s and 1880s. Madeleine Pelletier's mother, Anne Passavy Pelletier, was a devout Catholic. She had married a cab driver, who was an invalid for most of their daughter's childhood. The father shared the anti-clerical views of his class and gender. The Pelletier marriage in its religious divisions reflected the preponderantly Catholic education of girls and the lay education of boys in France.[2] Madeleine Pelletier's mother, according to her daughter, was a religious fanatic and a royalist. Living as she did in a republican working-class quarter, and cherishing a dream of noble origins, Mme Pelletier was far from popular. In opposition to this maternal atmosphere of the *ancien régime*, her father's religious scepticism ('when we are dead, we are dead') and his admiration for the modern achievements of the Republic, as well as the republican sympathies of other people in the neighbourhood from whom young Madeleine learned revolutionary songs, the child developed a precocious and radical political awareness. The Church for this daughter of poverty seems to have represented warmth, beauty, music, zealotry, sexual hypocrisy and the fear of hell fire. The Republic stood for modernity and social cohesion. Though this 'Memoir' is only a fragment, it reveals a powerful sense of the psychological and social origins of Madeleine Pelletier's remarkable political energy.

Pelletier wrote 'Doctoresse Pelletier: Memoirs of a Feminist' in the early 1930s, presumably intending it for publication. In it Pelletier developed two main themes: firstly, her involvement in mainstream and therefore 'male' politics (including anarchism, Freemasonry and especially socialism), and secondly her feminist commitments in their varied forms. Sub-themes were education, professional life and the birth control or neo-Malthusian movement.[3] Only a few lines were devoted to her childhood, but these are telling by raising the theme of thwarted ambition, central to her understanding of her own career. The great general she had wished to become, modelled on her childish idea of Napoléon, epitomized Pelletier's burning desire to figure on the stage of history and her belief that she had the intellectual and moral qualities to do so.

In Pelletier's account of her life, the two poles of analysis are class and gender. As someone who had escaped from a poverty-stricken and repressive milieu and who hated its dirt and squalor, she nevertheless remained loyal to her working-class roots and displayed an ambivalent attitude towards the bourgeoisie whom as a medical doctor she had in class terms theoretically joined, but from whom she dissociated herself politically. She spoke of herself as an 'integral', that is a total and militant feminist. One of the central tenets of her political analysis was that the interests of different oppressed groups did not always coincide; the working class, as Hélène Brion also discovered, did not necessarily understand the notion of the oppression of women.

In the male political sphere, Pelletier moved from her early contacts with anarchists (where she met the legendary Louise Michel) to the centre left faction of the Socialist Party led by Jules Guesde, to the revolutionary Left led by Gustave Hervé.[4] She recounted the difficulties faced by a woman in the overwhelmingly male atmosphere of French socialist gatherings. Pelletier was not alone in her perception of the 'masculinism' of such meetings. Marie Guillot (1883–1934), a teacher who wrote for the journal the *Ecole émancipée* and who was an active syndicalist and socialist, commented on the allegation that women were always quiet at meetings: 'I think that women form a silent element because they are not accustomed to attending public meetings; they lack the self-assurance which the habit of participation brings'.[5] When we recall that Pelletier was a tough and aggressive individual, her difficulties give us some inkling why the French Socialist Party was so unsuccessful in attracting female recruits. Her successes, notably the inclusion of women's suffrage on the socialist platform and her election to the CAP in 1912 were negated in her mind by in-fighting, jealousies and pervasive anti-feminism. She was attracted to socialism by its promise of social justice but we also note her dismissal of both Bebel and Marx as either conventional on gender issues or pretentiously long-winded.[6]

If Pelletier was uncomfortable in socialist circles as a woman, she was equally ill at ease in bourgeois feminist circles (Solidarity). As a self-made woman of working-class origins, she felt herself patronized by bourgeois feminists. These tensions emerged in her acerbic comments about those feminists whom she called the '*demi-émancipées*' or '*demi-féministes*', especially flirtatious women in low-cut dresses, the fashion of the *Belle Epoque*. Pelletier's strictures about the glamorous Editor of the feminist daily paper, Marguerite Durand, a former actress turned journalist, reflected her unease at the class divide within feminism as well as a critique of gender politics in dress.

Pelletier's feminism expressed itself first in her successful battle to enter the competitive examination to become an intern in the psychiatric services, then in her leadership of '*Solidarité des Femmes*' (Solidarity of Women), in her editorship of her journal, *La Suffragiste*, and in her lengthy, though unsuccessful, struggles to gain the vote for French women, her campaigns of militant action (one of the few French suffragists beside Hubertine Auclert to attempt it), and finally in her dress code. Pelletier's bourgeois 'ladies' in Solidarity were alarmed by the enthusiasm and single-mindedness with which she pursued her feminist programme. Yet even in her teens, when involved with Astié de Valsayre's feminist group which advocated teaching women to fence, Pelletier had been sensitive to the double standard infecting feminist thinking. Why were women so reluctant to throw off what she called servile attitudes? The issue of dress reform and the right to undertake traditionally masculine pursuits formed part of Pelletier's overall strategy to conquer the masculine sphere, not by flirtation, as she accused some fellow feminists of doing, but in open competition.

Madeleine Pelletier's 'War Diary', which she kept between 24 August 1914 and 27 September 1918 is a document of absorbing psychological and historical interest. Drawing on her work in psychiatry, Pelletier analysed the war fever and spy mania which overwhelmed public opinion, turning normally harmless individuals into bellicose chauvinists. Pelletier focused on the psychological transformation which events forced on individuals, a transformation which threatened to destroy individuality and civil liberties. Her extreme depression on Bastille Day 1914 resulted from the loss of faith in socialist and scientific ideas of progress.

Ever striving to compare her capacities to men's, Pelletier recorded how she conducted a psychological experiment on herself to test her courage by visiting the battlefields of the Marne, shortly after the battle. Since women were alleged to be incapable of physical bravery, Pelletier came as close as she could to facing enemy fire. Her account conveyed a mixture of bravado, cynicism and pathos. Finally, she was concerned to document the effect of war on ordinary people, especially on the poor. Her description of the march-past of soldiers on the Boulevard St Michel remains especially haunting. One may also speculate that Pelletier's own close escape from arrest and the fact that she was under police surveillance may help to explain why she did not testify at Hélène Brion's trial for 'defeatism' in 1918. Pelletier's political links with revolutionary socialists and anarchists and her uncompromising feminism, as well as her anti-war sympathies, continued to make her an object of suspicion to the authorities. For both Pelletier and Brion, the Great War marked a watershed in their political activism. Thereafter the threat or the reality of repression were always to hang over them.

TEXTS

Memoir: dictated on 23 November 1939 in the *Asile de Perray Vaucluse*, by '*Anne, dite Madeleine Pelletier*'
'Doctoresse Pelletier: Memoirs of a Feminist', April 1933
'Doctoresse Pelletier: War Diary', 24 August 1914–27 September 1918

MEMOIR: DICTATED ON 23 NOVEMBER 1939 IN THE *ASILE DE PERRAY VAUCLUSE*, BY '*ANNE, DITE MADELEINE PELLETIER*'

I was born in Paris on the 18th of March 1874 in a fruit and vegetable shop on the Rue de Petits Carreaux, number 38. The house was very old and was demolished a few years ago.

My mother was extremely intelligent but was completely uneducated. Her customers called her Mme de Sévigné.[7] My father was far less brilliant but he had a great fund of good sense. Whereas my mother, a fervent Catholic, was a veritable fanatic, my father was a sceptic. He would say to me: 'The priests know no more than we do; when we are dead, we are well and truly dead; it lasts a long time; we are in the kingdom of the moles'. I was about four years old when my father had a paralytic stroke which confined him almost completely to the house.

As I have said, my mother was a religious fanatic. She wore a figure of Christ on her breast, not just a simple crucifix, and if a customer complained about the rain she would say: 'The Good Lord makes the weather; you have only to submit to it'. Her profound faith, this attachment to religion, did not help her business. Customers who came to buy a kilo of potatoes had no desire to hear a sermon. They preferred to shop across the street at a grocer with less pronounced opinions.

My earliest memory is of a walk in the botanical gardens. I was about four years old. For the occasion I had been bought a grey woollen dress and a straw hat from Italy decorated with blue ribbons. My little sister who was two had a similar hat.[8] We hired a cab for this excursion – a magnificent gesture, for my mother was very miserly. I also remember an enclosure occupied by Negroes. One of them held out his big hand to me saying: 'Good day, Mademoiselle'. That evening we went to a restaurant and then to a concert. All this seemed splendid to me, especially the singer dressed in pink, but I went to sleep in the middle of the performance.

Another memory is the winter of 1879–1880. The snow accumulated in untidy heaps in the gutters or on the pavements. It was fun for the neighbourhood children, for the traffic stopped and the kids monopolized the street for snowball fights. Our family huddled in the back room which was heated by a cast-iron stove.

Another event in my childhood was the 14th of July celebrations.[9] In those days they had an extraordinary glamour. Houses disappeared under the tricolour flags; all the windows as well as the lamp posts bore flags. Firecrackers and Roman candles exploded. I thought this was wonderful but my mother did not agree. She did not put out the tricolour flag and on the contrary displayed the *fleur de lys* [symbol of the monarchy] as a gesture of protest for she was *Henriquinquiste* [an avowed monarchist]. She called the Republic the *'Ruine publique'*. Her extreme right-wing views made her an object of hatred in the neighbourhood. Once I was chatting with Pavillet, a cobbler, who was making a big lantern. I asked him what he wanted to use it for. He replied: 'It's for locking up Jesuits'.

The *crêpe* seller was also very republican. She would say that my mother belonged to the 'Black Commune', an expression which was evidently meant to be very abusive. The café owner across the street was, so it was said, a Freemason and my mother told me dreadful tales about this association. She claimed that before she died, her greatest joy would be to strangle a Freemason.

I remember another occasion when my mother woke me at eight in the evening which I found unusual. 'Come,' she said, 'we are going to see the Good Lord'. I was seven years old and could be treated as an adult. The church seemed splendid to me. Behind the altar there was a bright blue hanging, the colour of the Holy Virgin, and blue flowers everywhere. An innovation, 'Drumont's Lights', lit up the chapel brightly and for the first time I heard the well known hymn:

It is the month of Mary
It is the loveliest month.

After this there was the sermon. I struggled with all my might to keep awake; I wanted to be like the big girls, to listen to the sermon and to understand it, but at nine o'clock we had to go home. My mother was afraid that my father might have a second attack.

On our return home, she repeated the preacher's sermon for my father. She had a great deal of natural eloquence and was pitiless in her sermons. The damned, in spite of their supplications, wheeled about from abyss to abyss, until they came to a vast cavern filled with fire. I dreamt about it all night.

Eventually it became necessary to send me to school. I was seven years old. I should have gone at least a year previously, but my mother always hesitated. To send a child to school assumed that the child was clean, washed, combed and so on, all of which were profoundly contrary to her habits.

My father had taught me to read from an alphabet book which cost all of fifty centimes. I recall the following sentence: 'When an animal has one hump on his back, we call it a dromedary; when it has two we call it a camel'. At school, because I had an excellent memory, I shone at recitation time. I was much less skilful at writing. My fingers, covered with chilblains and numb with cold, were utterly clumsy and I envied the well-kept little girls whose agile fingers turned out fair copies and conjugations. My vertical lines were awkward and bulbous; I had great difficulty in forming my letters, especially the capital letters the lines of which terrified me. The school was run by nuns – lay schools were not yet the rule. One day, it was a Saturday, I had the good fortune to win the prize for English, having shown myself capable of counting up to twenty in that language.

At about this period my father began to walk again and took me to see the new horseless trams, on the Boulevard Sebastopol, which were a mechanical novelty. On another occasion, he took me to see the construction of the new Post Office building. My young mind mulled all this over. My mother always said that the Republic was worthless, but I thought these things were very fine and of great value. For the rest, old Father Bessard thwarted my mother's influence. He had taught me '*le Chant du Départ*' which I was careful never to sing within earshot of my mother.[10] He used to say to me: 'Ah, your mother is full of prejudices'.

I greatly admired the B__ family whose two grown daughters went to boarding school wearing coats with fur collars. Their house was spotlessly clean, ours repulsive with dirt. I admired their shining red tile floors; my mother's were horrible. We did not dare open our front door wide for fear the neighbours would see this filth.

My mother's shop was the meeting place of a group of devout women, called *'Notre Dame de Bonne Nouvelle'*. They were all old women dressed in black. I remember especially one with a big black cape and the most zealous one, with buckled shoes imitating a priest's shoes. There was a woman who sold newspapers in the neighbourhood, but these women said that she sold 'red' papers and she was regarded with suspicion. A young 'child of Mary' was discovered to be six months pregnant, apparently thanks to a priest. This amazed me. 'But, Papa, is it possible for a priest to have a child?' 'Naturally, priests are men like any others.' 'But isn't it very wicked?' 'To be sure. But it is not as though people only do what is right.'

It was my father who first informed me about sexual matters; I was twelve years old and was entering into a woman's life. 'But, Papa, Mama also?' 'Yes, your mother as well – she is a woman.' I had never loved my mother, but I had felt a certain respect for her. I lost it at this moment when I imagined her to be like me. I retained this distaste for a long time.[11]

In class I was not liked. I was dirty; I was badly dressed. Horrors! I had lice. They teemed in my hair and fell upon the table. What a difference to compare me with the confectioner Labbé's daughter, always perfectly turned out with her big white lace collars. In spite of all this I gave brilliant replies in class which were taken note of and a nun told my mother that I should be encouraged to do my Brevet [school certificate]. My mother was not opposed to this, but when I was twelve years old I decided to leave the hostile and repressive milieu of my school and gave up my studies.

I should mention here a trip to the Auvergne. My mother, who was an illegitimate child, had the letter 'P' branded on her skin. 'Passavie' was my mother's maiden name and like all illegitimate children, she imagined that she came from some illustrious but secret origin. A fortune teller had predicted that she would find her family if she went back to her region of origin. I cried a great deal at the thought that my mother was going away and she agreed to take me. After eleven pregnancies, she had only two surviving children, a big brother, whom we never saw, and me. Seeing my despair, she was afraid of losing another child.

This trip was far from entertaining for me. Immersed in her researches, my mother left me in the hotel throughout the long days, where I was terribly bored. Nonetheless I remember a hill where my mother had gone to visit her foster father. He urged her to settle down there, but she preferred her business in Paris. A flock of sheep which I saw on this journey marked my first moment of disillusionment. I had imagined them being white, clean and with ribbons tied round their necks. These sheep were dirty, muddy as one could wish and wore no ribbons.

'Are those sheep?'

'Of course,' said my mother. 'What do you think they are?'

In order to take my first communion, I went to catechism classes. I achieved only relative excellence because I never got the gold star which was the highest mark of achievement. This went to the little girls with well-brushed hair who came to the classes by carriage. No one knows better than the Church how to maintain social distinctions. Among us children there were clearly four classes: 1, Privately educated children who had governesses and specialist teachers; 2, Paying boarders; 3, Pupils from religious schools; 4, Pupils from state schools.

This first communion was a great festival. A neighbour, who had not yet quarrelled with my mother, came to offer me a ticket for the theatre. My mother refused with indignation. 'In three months, she will be taking her first communion.' Finally the long heralded day arrived.

My loved one is not come.
Dark night, will you last forever?

DOCTORESSE PELLETIER: MEMOIRS OF A FEMINIST, APRIL 1933

I can affirm that I have always been a feminist, at least from the age that I was old enough to understand things. Even as a child, the remarks I overheard concerning the inferiority of women, which were repeated every day in conversation, shocked me profoundly. When in my childish ambition, my head stuffed full with stories from French history, I announced that I wanted to be a great general, my mother rebuffed me curtly saying: 'Women are not soldiers; they are nothing at all; they marry, they cook and they bring up their children'.

I was a precocious child and had an independent dispositon. Any order for which I was not given the reason threw me into a state of rebellion. When I was thirteen years old, I began going out in the evening, leaving my parents' house to attend political meetings. That is how I came to join a feminist group, who met at the Rue de Turenne in a ground floor flat. Among the members were Astié de Valsayre,[12] an engraver, Champly, who had been a parliamentary candidate, a few women about whom I remember nothing and a tall schoolboy who intrigued me because of his voice. This person was in fact a woman writer, Hertyal d'Estève. So one could dress up as a man! I discovered here a brightly lit road towards liberation. But I realized that this particular road was not open to me; one needed to be entirely free and to have money.

Among other subjects, these feminists would talk about sport, and especially fencing. Astié de Valsayre had fought a duel with another woman. I thought this was noble. Nevertheless, the arguments which they used to uphold women's right to fight duels did not appeal to me at all. They argued that there was nothing like fencing for developing the breasts. Reduced in this way to a better means of breast-feeding, fencing lost all its nobility in my eyes.

There is more to be said on this issue. Fencing, the final goal of which is destruction, is a less noble activity than breast-feeding which gives life. Nonetheless, I had a confused notion that in order to liberate women, it would be necessary to change their habits. Furthermore, the right to fight duels was a right that should be demanded like any other, because it was a right and not under the hypocritical shield of developing a femininity which had only resulted in women's slavery.

My association with Astié de Valsayre's group caused me to have a number of arguments with the anarchists. I tried in vain to explain to them that political suffrage, in spite of its possibly illusory character, was a stage women must pass through in order to liberate themselves. They believed that women were inferior beings. They accepted them only as helpmeets, to propagate their doctrines, if need be, as Louise Michel had done.

I met Michel fairly often at meetings. She was tall and extremely thin. Her distinguishing feature was the nobility of her expression which blotted out her ugliness. She was always very poorly dressed, the result of her indifference to fashion much more than her lack of money, since she earned a good deal from lectures which were always well attended. But she took absolutely no care of her person, forgetting to comb her hair or to wash. In addition, when she had a bit of money, there was always someone to take it from her. And she did not know how to turn people down. She felt obliged to uphold the character created for her. It was understood that 'la Bonne Louise' was incapable of refusing anything and might take the shirt off her back to give it to a beggar woman.

Her eloquence was entirely emotional. She spoke of the misery of the poor, of freezing hovels, of children without bread. The revolution would avenge all that, and after a few days of disorder, everyone would be happy. This revolution was, in her mind, something mystical. It was a force of nature. In the images which decorated her speeches, Louise Michel compared the revolution to a torrent, to an avalanche, to an earthquake, to a tide that submerges everything. Fundamentally, although Louise Michel called herself an atheist, for her the revolution was a form of divine justice.

In my heart of hearts, I reproached her for not being a feminist, for consecrating her gifts, the power which her fame gave her, to the service of men. I went to see her once in London where she was voluntarily exiled for fear of Constant, Minister of the Interior, who had threatened her with incarceration in an insane asylum. I told her of my reservations. She told me that she was a feminist, but that the women's movement was too narrow. She had gone along with men because action in masculine political parties was greater and more interesting.

During this period I had read widely and had come to the conclusion that I knew nothing. I decided to prepare the Baccalaureate on my own. In the distant future, I anticipated studying medicine but only as a vague possibility. My mother, who was my only surviving relative, being very poor, could never give me the money I needed. Henceforth academic study fascinated me, or rather the ardent desire to succeed did, for in themselves the course books for the *bachot* were not amusing. I gave up my political meetings without regret. The anarchists did not care for me because I wanted to liberate women but also because I refused to take a 'companion'. They called me the 'unique Madeleine', a sexless Joan of Arc. They were happy to have one 'Red Virgin' [the nickname for Louise Michel], but they did not want two.

The fate of the women companions did not appeal to me; taken up and then abandoned, they were passed from one man to another. They dragged babies after them, because the means of avoiding pregnancies were not well known. This was not the future that I sought. I wanted to succeed, to leave my family background where I was placed by birth, and I believed that I could succeed by intellectual endeavour.

The feminists did not like me either. My tailored suits and my mannish starched collars seemed an unheard of audacity to them. According to some of them, this was going against nature and harmed feminism. Yet I still wore my hair long. What would they have said if I had dared to cut my hair? In any case, at their meetings, these feminists only spoke about women in the noble role of wife and mother. Fencing developed the breasts; intellectual endeavour made one a better cook. A woman's kitchen is a veritable chemical laboratory; as for her knowledge of physiology and hygiene, she would use it obviously to look after her husband and children and to cure their illnesses.

All this hypocrisy shocked me. I thought it was humiliating to look for utilitarian rationalizations for activities which are in fact rights and for feminists to accept their servitude as natural and inevitable. In any case at meetings my contributions were not very great. I was timid, as a result of my education, which had left me with a huge inferiority complex. Moreover I was short, badly dressed and very young. The feminists called me 'little Madeleine' and I did not interpret this as a sign of benevolence from my elders ... .

It was at about the same period that a feminist congress was held at the *Société des savants*, presided over very energetically by Maria Pognon.[13]

There was opposition to her leadership. Some feminists said aloud in the congress hall itself that she ran a bawdy house and that she followed a profession that sullied her honour and that she was not capable of chairing a congress. The accusation of running a bordello turned out to be based on her having an hotel. In those days women were very proper. The congress was stormy. Male students came to heckle as was their custom. They shouted: 'And the kitchen! Back to your sock mending', not to mention the cartload of obscenities borrowed from their medical studies.

A few years later, *La Fronde* began publication.[14] This *was* an event. Huge posters depicting a crowd of poverty-stricken women served to break the news of the paper's publication all over Paris. It was my ambition to write for it and I took along an article I had written to the editorial offices. A woman in a very low-cut dress greeted me haughtily. She took the article saying that if it appeared I would see it and must buy the paper every day. I did not look well off, obviously, with my ready-made dress which had cost less than twenty francs, and that was much more important than anything my article might contain.

I easily consoled myself for this disappointment for at that time I was, above all, a disciple of the School of Anthropology.[15] The professors recognized that I was someone out of the ordinary, but I had the misfortune to be a woman and on top of that I had no money. One of the professors advised me to commit suicide because without powerful contacts and without money, it was clear that I would never succeed at anything. I said to myself that human progress in goodness had not developed much since the *itechanthropus erectus*, the skull of which had just been discovered. In addition, I was advised to go in for flirtation as the only means for a woman to succeed. 'Become the mistress of a politician. When he is tired of you, he will find you a good job.' In the first place, I did not know any politicians, and secondly I could not imagine myself in the role of a ridiculous and imploring mistress. I found all this shameful, and still find it so today.

But I was approaching the end of my medical studies [1902]. I wanted to put myself down for the *concours* [a competitive examination] for an internship in the Psychiatric Service. I was very interested in psychology and hoped to discover the laws of natural selection which cause madness. In addition there was a small salary with the post which would be of help to a poor student. The salary would tide me over while I waited for my private patients who were slow in coming to me as a newly qualified woman doctor. However, for the examination there was a rule requiring that candidates possess political rights, a rule which had been instituted in order to exclude women.

I began a campaign in the press. It is hard to imagine what this simple phrase means in terms of rebuffs, endless waiting in newspaper anterooms and finally not being seen, and promises, easy to make to a poor girl without connections. However I finally succeeded. I became an intern and on top of that I was famous. My photograph appeared in the newspaper! But all this did not earn me a penny.

I found a flat for 420 francs a year on the first floor of a new building, a little lodging of two rooms: a kitchen and an entrance hall. I furnished it as well as I could, rather badly in fact, with second-hand furniture which I repaired myself. Brightly coloured lined curtains – everything was clean – it smelled of paint. I was enchanted. Downstairs I put up an enamelled plate: 'Woman Doctor – Tuesday, Thursday, Saturday 2–4'. I had moved in. But the patients were slow in coming. Though I stayed at home regularly during my office hours, noone came. In three months I only looked after a baby on the fifth floor and my concierge who was in labour. The concierge gave me twenty francs, and the fifth floor family nothing at all.

One winter evening when it was raining hard, I suddenly heard the ring of the bell. I trembled with joy on going to open the door. I recall that my entire capital consisted of three sous; even before the war, that was not a lot. Who knows, perhaps someone wanted me at a lying in – fifty francs for the bill. But at the door was an old woman with white hair. She was dressed in an unbelievable old coat which was soaked through. I made her come into my office which was simultaneously my bedroom, though one could not tell. 'I am not a patient. I am Caroline Kauffmann and I lead a feminist group, "*La Solidarité des femmes*".[16] I am getting old. Furthermore I have business interests in Alsace that I must look after. I need someone to take over Solidarity. I had thought of asking Elizabeth Renaud, but she is more of a socialist than a feminist and that would never do. So I thought of you. I read interviews with you in the newspaper; you have opened the door to women to pursue careers in mental hospitals – that was a fine thing. Would you agree to be my successor?'

I knew this group, about thirty women all speaking at once … . Still, it was a lucky break for me; by that I mean a psychological break. I suffered more from boredom than from poverty. At the asylum the male interns harassed me constantly, so I only went there to do my morning rounds; I had given up thinking I could do research in psychology there. The nurses and care assistants ran everything; they watched flabbergasted this strange animal, a woman medical intern who was just like a man. As for the director, he spent all his time signing letters. I had quickly become discouraged … .

The day of my inauguration at Solidarity arrived. There were at least fifty people present at the Saint Sulpice town hall. Caroline Kauffmann introduced me, saying: 'We need younger women to re-invigorate feminism'. I gave my speech which I had memorized. In it I said that in my view feminism ought to shake off vague notions about the social value of housewives and mothers and to abandon comparisons between feminine virtue and male vices. We were not men's enemies; what we wanted was equality, nothing more. One question must dominate all others, namely the right to vote – this was what feminist action ought to aim for.

A young woman lawyer exclaimed: 'Lead us to victory!'. I felt my heart pounding; for a minute, I give you my word, I thought victory was in our grasp. But it was not as easy as that. I soon realized that I was not going to lead the members of Solidarity to anything at all. Victory? First of all they would have had to have genuinely sought it, but what they wanted above all was to amuse themselves. Most of them were past their first youth, widows or divorcees; they had small private incomes and wanted something to do in the afternoons. If they did not come to our group, they went to public lectures at the Sorbonne or the Medical Faculty.

In spite of what Caroline Kauffmann had said, I turned out to be not at all suitable. My followers and I were poles apart. Thanks to my work, I had climbed several rungs of the social ladder; I was down to earth; I knew what I wanted and I got it. They had always lived in the shadow of their families and had received that ladylike education given to middle-class girls at that time. Sometimes the leaders of other feminist groups came to our meetings. They put on a condescending manner with me, putting their hands on my shoulder; they would say in a protective tone: 'You are a very praiseworthy person'. I felt like hitting them.

Many of the group hated men, as women do who have suffered under men all their lives. One had had her dowry eaten away by her husband's financial speculations, by gambling or by debauchery; another saw herself abandoned when she was in her forties: her husband divorced her in order to marry a younger woman. Having lost her husband, such a woman also lost her social position. She had had a fine apartment and servants; she received friends in her salon. Now she only had a little flat and a charlady – what poverty! Her old friends no longer visited her. Another member of the group, who had been the mistress of a government minister, was cast off and to add to her misfortunes, locked up in an insane asylum so that she would not cause a scandal. 'Ah, if only men would do their duty,' these women would lament. 'That is all we ask – we do not want to be men.' On the contrary – in my view, we must be men, socially speaking. Men will never do their duty. They will support you for a time, you become dependent on them and when they are tired of you, they will drive you away.

The real evil is that even in marriage, women are prostitutes. What we need to achieve is political and social equality. The day that women can earn their living in all the jobs and professions that men currently occupy, divorce will no longer be a catastrophe. A woman would no longer lose her rank in losing her husband. Women should not exist through men, but through their own efforts.

I soon realized that I was speaking in a vacuum. What I was asking was to change the world and my Solidarity members were not keen to do so. They wanted a few protective laws for women, so that they could live better lives without changing their condition as women ... .

However, the parliamentary elections were approaching. We feminists needed to gain some publicity for ourselves. If I took my fifty women out on the street to demonstrate, only about half of whom would come: it would look ridiculous. But if we hired carriages, that would be entirely different. Taxis had not yet been invented. We only had open hackney carriages, pulled by miserable nags. For two francs, one could be hauled about for an hour. For twenty francs we could have ten carriages which would make a fine procession.

The demonstrators wore multicoloured sashes on which we had inscribed our demands. I chose snappy slogans. Hubertine Auclert had adopted: 'Women's Suffrage'.[17] I carried 'Women Must Vote'. That, the least cultivated of men in the street would understand, whereas 'suffrage', a more abstract word, would mean nothing to them.

So I had my banners printed: 'Women Must Vote', 'They are subject to the law and pay taxes', 'We want universal suffrage not uni-sexual suffrage'. An elderly seamstress with fine taste mounted the slogans on streamers. We marched through Paris. I had arranged for everyone to meet at my flat and the Rue Gergovie, normally very quiet, was flabbergasted. In my heart of hearts, I knew that such schemes were not the sort of thing to improve my clientele. What would people think of this woman doctor who, instead of being satisfied with bleeding her patients, organized subversive demonstrations? But too bad – let the chips fall where they might. That is what I thought then and I still think the same today, even though time has brought me many disappointments. Our ideals may be illusions, but without these illusions, our lives are not worth living.

The passers-by looked at us oddly. They thought we were advertising something. Then when they had read our banners, on the whole, they became indignant, unless they broke out into insulting laughs: 'Women must vote! I like that. I'd as soon allow my dog to vote!'. After that we had the classic dismissive send-off to the kitchen and to mending socks. Oh, those socks, symbol of women's servitude! Could one not replace them with something else?

We also organized public meetings, either at the '*Sociétés savantes*' or less ambitiously at the Free College of Social Science. To save money we pasted up our own posters, also to gain publicity by attracting public attention. Nevertheless, each time we received insults. People would not acknowledge that women were capable of pasting up posters, especially if it involved a demand for this outrageous thing, the right to vote. One lout emptied my pot of paste over my head, and an elderly member of our group had her arm pierced by a hat pin by a woman who doubtless was deeply attached to her slavery and did not want to be liberated from it.

All these arguments ended at the police station where the officers would lead us, followed by a hostile crowd. There we would be treated ironically but paternally. They did not lock us up. In any case we had not committed an offence. Once freed we would go to the newspapers to make our adventures known. On the whole, we were not well received. The issue of women's suffrage lacked interest. If it had been an actress who had lost her necklace, that would have been splendid. Nevertheless, a few minor papers were willing to take down details and sometimes these details sprang into life as articles. There were a few favourable ones. 'Still,' a young editor said to us one day, 'your posters that you paste up everywhere are hopeless. If you want press coverage, let off a bomb.' Obviously bombs give one publicity, but all the same ... .

At the time of the next elections [1908], I had the idea of taking Solidarity along to break windows at a polling station. I made my fell plan known to the group and of course they did not approve. They thought that going out into the street was vulgar; that was all right for working-class women; a decent woman should stay at home. Public meetings were a last resort, but a demonstration in the street could only harm the cause, especially with this violent character. One of my members objected that stones thrown into windows might injure someone inside. She suggested replacing stones with potatoes. 'Potatoes!' People would think that we wanted to feed the voters. I would take stones – let whoever loves me follow me. I knew perfectly well that even with stones, we would not do much harm. At the first stone we would be arrested. I was not keen that there should be much damage. For publicity purposes, the gesture alone was enough.

We were about a dozen at our rendez-vous, Rue de l'Arbalète. I threw my stone at a window shouting: 'Women must vote!'. The window broke, without hurting anyone and there we were, another member of the group and I, led off to the police station, Rue Dante. A constable telephoned for orders to the *Prefecture*. No doubt they asked him if it was a major disturbance; the constable replied: 'Well, no – hardly anything – two women – they are here. I must admit, I'm a bit ashamed – obviously not – nothing happened – it's not my fault'. They let us go, but I was told to appear before the magistrate's court.

All of Solidarity was there the day of the magistrate's hearing and even some of Hubertine Auclert's group and Madame Oddo's.[18] I was congratulated. It was the first time that feminism had appeared in court. They gave me every encouragement. Courage was not necessary. I knew perfectly well that the authorities did not wish to make a martyr of me and that in the affair noone had been hurt. But we had to wait a long time before the Pelletier case was called into court. There were a whole lot of thefts, frauds and fleecings, that came up before my case and I was able to see how hard justice is on ordinary people. A miserable woman furrier, guilty of having solicited, was given three years in prison – and such a lack of decorum from the judges. The chief magistrate made witticisms at the expense of the unhappy accused. I was revolted.

Finally my turn came. The chief magistrate's face lit up. Feminism was, one could tell, a bit of a change from stealing potatoes and the petty pilfering that had bored him stiff earlier. He asked me to explain the reasons for my detestable action. I did so. Sixteen francs fine with suspended sentence. That was not expensive. At that price, one might re-offend from time to time.

However, the leaders of the other feminist groups saw this childishness as some kind of outrage. They made me sound like a terrible revolutionary whose extremism and violence could only do harm. There was a bit of jealousy in all this, but this characterization made me better known. I was talked of more than those feminists who were satisfied with meeting with their little groups on set dates. Though in theory I am a revolutionary, in practice I only kill the fleas which from time to time my patients make me a present of – and I let the spiders live, which makes my cleaning woman think that I have a screw loose [French pun: that I have a spider in the head].

I had joined the Socialist Party [1906] in the Fourteenth Section sometime previously. Louise Michel was right: feminism was too narrow and further-more this atmosphere of tittle-tattle disgusted me. Was I a socialist? I had not yet really thought about it properly. I had never studied political economy, finding all that sort of thing tedious. It was too abstract. Wealth, a wealthy country, what does that mean? I often heard it said that France is wealthy; that does not prevent me from being penniless. I had occasionally been to big socialist rallies. There it was claimed that capital holds within it the seeds of its own destruction, that little businesses were disappearing, absorbed by big business. The workers applauded wildly – doubtless they understood. As for me, I did not understand very well, even though Letourneau had made me read *Das Kapital* by Karl Marx, which had been a great strain. Not that the subject was difficult. I had read much drier works of philosophy, but I thought that Marx strove to complicate things which are simple. The fact that workers are exploited is something we have always known; there is no need for hundreds of boring pages to prove it.

What I do know is that I am in favour of social justice and that I lean rather towards Robespierre's teaching, a radicalism pushed to the limits, abolition of inheritance, free education at every level, generous state benefits for chil-dren, the old and the sick, no more class distinctions, no more worship of money. Intelligence and hard work should be the only means to success.

However, the Radical Party had long since forgotten Robespierre's programme and anyway, if I had taken it into my head to knock on his door, he would have had none of me. Robespierre did not like women.

At the Fourteenth Section I was given the cold shoulder. Noone would sit next to me and they did not even say 'hello'. I was very ill at ease and was reduced to fiddling with my gloves and my pen knife and my watch to put myself at ease. I was a woman, that was the problem. If, in theory, women were admitted, in practice they were only welcomed if they accompanied a man: husband, father, brother, lover. 'A woman doctor, who came all alone, what devil or what devious motive sent her? Fournière recommended her; no doubt he has plans for the Fourteenth Section. Fournière is on the right of the party. He has probably sent this woman to set things up for the leader of the Jauresian right.' ... .

Eventually I made the acquaintance of K., a man of about fifty. He invited me to his house for dinner the following Sunday. K. lived in a ground floor flat in the Rue Daneau in a poor artisan's dwelling with his wife and two children. He was an unshakeable Guesdiste and he explained to me how the section worked. Obviously he wanted to draw me towards the Guesdistes. I was not opposed to this. The Guesdistes seemed to me more genuinely socialist; the Jauresians were scarcely more than advanced liberal republicans. And if I could not accept everything in Marxism, I did understand the necessity for the socialization of the means of production in order to abolish the class structure. K. explained to me that as far as the Socialist Party was concerned, my 'votes for women' had no interest for them. Socialism liberates women, but prior to achieving socialism one must not undertake a sex war. However, if I really wanted to draw up a motion on 'votes for women' he would arrange for me to present it to the National Congress which would be held Limoges six months hence.

I was delighted. Women's suffrage accepted at the Congress of a major political party, this would be marvellous! And nevertheless, the party was anything but feminist; I could see that easily in the Fourteenth Section. The few women who appeared at the meetings only accompanied a man. Most of them understood nothing from all those speeches.

In order to give me an idea about socialist views on women, I was advised to read *Women and Socialism* by Bebel. I had read it long before. It is an anti-feminist work. Bebel describes the life of working-class women realistically, the work which crushes them both in the factory and at home. But there is no protest against their sexual slavery, which is considered to be natural and unchangeable. According to Guesde, the bourgeoisie, by taking women away from the home and putting them in factories, have committed the crime of crimes. I do not think there was a particular crime in this. Certainly women are exploited in the workplace and in the home, more exploited than men.

There is sexual prejudice that operates here as elsewhere. The employers take advantage of the low esteem in which women are held by paying them less. But nevertheless, the possibility of earning a little money directly by selling their labour partially relieves them from the necessity of selling themselves sexually. Socialist parties all over the world have adopted Bebel's thesis, and by a really bizarre form of hypocrisy, some women have been elected as deputies; a few are today ministers or under-secretaries of state, all for having maintained for their entire lives the idea that the natural place for women is the kitchen and that the bosses have committed the worst of crimes by dragging them out of the kitchen.

Naturally socialist women were careful not to appear sexually emancipated. Rosa Luxembourg wore long skirts, long hair and a veil and flowers on her hat. Clara Zetkin did the same. In those days women wore great pins which held their hats on to their chignons and when Clara Zetkin spoke at the rostrum, the breadth of her gestures made her hat wobble from side to side with comic effect. Laura Lafargue, Karl Marx's daughter, was occasionally nominated to chair the congress. She appeared with her face covered by a heavy veil. From afar, she gave the impression of a bundle of fabric. She was no longer young – but are men afraid of showing their wrinkles and white hair? It was thought that a woman should only allow herself to be seen as long as her face could please the stronger sex.

I would never adopt such a tactic which in my eyes was and is a moral degradation. Am I not a human being? Do I need to evoke the bedroom by my exterior appearance while expounding my political ideas? I stood up for feminism as a matter of justice, a question of a woman's right to be treated as an equal. I was blamed for not being a socialist. The Fourteenth Section constantly tried to run me down for my connections with Solidarity where, they claimed, I was guilty of class collaboration. It was not as though the party did not indulge in class collaboration in parliament and elsewhere. Further, my feminist demonstrations by carriage, my banners which proclaimed 'Women Must Vote', indicated an eccentricity of which the party took a dim view.

Nonetheless, I was able to attend the Congress.[19] I was even nominated secretary of the meeting. These are harmless honours which the party confers willingly on persons of the 'weaker sex', but this is only a meaningless kind of chivalry. The question of women's suffrage came right at the end. I even thought it would not be discussed, so little importance was attached to it. When I was given leave to speak, three-quarters of the audience left the hall in order to show the contempt in which they held both the subject under discussion and my puny person. My motion was unanimously adopted, minus a few abstentions, but behind me, a Congress member, doubtless to please me, spoke up: 'You know, we have voted for your motion because votes for women has no chance of success. If it did, you would have seen some real opposition'.

At this time I was able to carry out an old dream of mine. I went to a meeting of the CAP (*Conseil adminstratif permanent*) of which I was a member, dressed as a man. There was a general outcry. A ... comrade made a drawing of me which showed me in Berlin as a homosexual prostitute. A dilettante wearing a Prussian helmet followed me tantalized by my rear-end sex appeal. The caption read: 'And this is why Madeleine...'. This brute obviously only thought of his own sex and believed that if Madeleine dressed as a man this could only be with lustful designs. Once at a meeting I was not recognized and was taken for a police spy. But all the same there was one chap who understood. 'This at least,' he said to me, 'is equality.'

I was not able to adopt masculine dress permanently; my profession was incompatible with this kind of freedom, especially as I had few patients through personal contacts. Most of my patients came accidentally, and it was difficult when they arrived, preoccupied with their own health worries, to make them a speech on the enfranchisement of women. In any case, masculine dress did not entirely suit me. I am little and plump; I had to dissemble and fake my voice. In the street I was obliged to walk quickly so as not to be noticed. But in male attire I was freed from being followed. Normally, in the street after nightfall, a woman who is still young is likely to be accosted at every step.

I had by this time joined the Hervéiste faction, which was on the extreme left of the party. I found the other factions too moderate and too preoccupied with electoral success. Hervéism had few followers. This is why I rose in the hierarchy to the summit of the party within eighteen months of joining, thanks to proportional representation: the theoretical summit. In actual fact, the CAP did not direct anything and the problems submitted to it were purely administrative. The party leadership was held by *l'Humanité* and the parliamentary group ... .

I had a little newspaper, *La Suffragiste*. It cost me fifty francs for one thousand copies. I had about five hundred subscribers, or rather, five hundred persons who had paid once for a subscription of from one to six months ... . One day I wrote an article in *La Suffragiste* entitled: 'Women Soldiers'. One of the most commonly deployed arguments opposing women's suffrage was that women do not do military service [and therefore have not 'earned' the vote]. There was some logic in this, for if women were not forced to do military service, it was because they do not count in society. Between them and society, there are men, their direct masters. In spite of my paper's title, my article was commented upon in the press world-wide ... .

My article on military service for women caused quite a stir. Hervé was very angry. How could I, an editor of *La Guerre sociale* and a pacifist, how could I suggest that women should be allowed to do military service? I tried to explain. Obviously I was in favour of the abolition of armies. But at the present time, armies exist, and the fact of being excluded from military service puts women in a state of inferiority. This is so true that the opponents of women's suffrage constantly put forward this objection of the absence of military service. Women lag behind; it is necessary to put them on the same footing as men. But Hervé was not convinced. If women were in barracks, he said, men would make the soup and look after the kids. Obviously he was not a feminist. He had never given serious thought to the question.

He wanted me to make a retraction in *La Guerre sociale* and to declare that I had written '*La Femme soldat*' as an error. He did not know me. Even if he had thrown me out of his faction and off his newspaper, I would never retract on a question that I considered to be important. He had already tackled me about my short hair and my tailored suits. He maintained that Louise Michel had succeeded because she dressed like other women. It seemed to me that it was not worth succeeding if one could not use the position one had attained to defend one's ideas. I was perfectly willing to accept party discipline, but feminism was my own business ... .

When the war came, most of the feminist groups were transformed into sewing circles. In my opinion sewing is a servile occupation. I had not carried on feminist propaganda for eleven years in order to come to the point of knitting socks. I preferred to stop calling meetings of Solidarity. I broke off with Caroline Kauffmann because of her spiritualism. It seems that she had the privilege of seeing 'astral pictures'. But I saw nothing at all; there was no further agreement possible. In any case, the old campaigner, crippled with rheumatism, scarcely went out any more.

But I remain a feminist. I will remain one until my death. Even though I do not like women as they are, any more than I like the working class as it is. Slave mentalities revolt me.

I wrote an article in the *Intransigéant* in which I argued that women should replace men who had gone to war, in the heavy labour industries. The article had a great deal of success and some of the ideas I had put forward were put into practice. But the article got me into trouble with the comrades who said I had become a 'patriot'. I was nothing of the kind. I find love of one's country outdated and as a woman I cannot love the country which shackles me and constrains me to a tedious life. But the war had become a paradise for working-class women. They had never been so happy, at least from a material point of view. Never before had they earned so much money. They became metal workers and chemists and earned forty francs a day, before the cost of living had risen. What silk stockings, rabbit fur coats, eau de Cologne! Bourgeois women blamed them with pained expressions for being prodigal. They [the working-class women] should save their money. As though one could save when one did not know what was going to happen tomorrow. Women drove trams. I listened to jealous recriminations from old pointsmen.

Come the peace, the men returned and the women retired to their kitchens, satisfied to grumble. Women's emancipation will not come about tomorrow, alas. I tried to revive *La Suffragiste*. Two or three editions came out, but prices had risen astronomically. Instead of fifty francs, my printer demanded five hundred and it was impossible to go on.

Of course I still retain my ideals. I publicize them in pamphlets which I bring out from time to time and in articles which appear in smaller papers or in lectures. Nowadays women vote nearly everywhere. It is only France, in spite of its pretensions to human rights, which appears in reality to be a very backward country.

DOCTORESSE PELLETIER: WAR DIARY, 24 AUGUST 1914–27 SEPTEMBER 1918

24 August, 1914:

The war has stirred up patriotic feelings. Everyone is excited by events; they talk of nothing else. Even women are aware of the situation and talk about current events just like the men. In general, evil feelings are stirred up far more than good ones. Mlle Ollier, an old feminist, an inoffensive person and *deaf* to boot, has been enjoined by the mayor of the village of Yens where she has a small property, *to abstain from all demonstrations because there is a war on*. Because she spent several years in America and has a vaguely British air, this was enough to turn her into a German and to cause her to be harassed.

At Nancy, my masculine appearance was sufficient to draw a crowd of more than two thousand people around me. An old woman grabbed me violently by my jacket. I only saved myself by climbing into an officer's car. The following day it was enough that I spoke to some adults on a tram for me to be arrested by a policeman who suspected me of spying. Though my papers which I showed him were in order, this only partly convinced him.

'But, nonetheless, you have short hair,' he said. 'Why?'

Oh, Individual Liberty, where are you now? I had to offer to go with him to see his superior officer in order to convince him.

A very elegant, slender woman in my train compartment said to her husband that German prisoners ought to be killed. In the X prefect's office a well-dressed and gloved visitor, to whom someone had recounted the story of an officer killed on his horse, said that it was better for the man to be killed than the horse, no doubt because horses are more difficult to replace than men. Human life no longer counts.

My colleague in the middle ranks of the army explained his feelings to me. 'My wife is very ill, but I do not think about her; it's all the same to me. I am cut off from home; I no longer exist; I am only a number with whom one can do what one likes.' The few officers whom I have seen giving orders are quite paternal. It is true that we are not in combat and they use conditionals rather than imperatives. The soldiers do not seem to lack supplies.

Mme Durand has republished *La Fronde*. She is as unfeminist as it is possible to be. She makes vests for children of the poor. The poor are helped but unemployment is the real curse. I have received four hundred letters asking for work and not a single offer.

The Red Cross: a clerical organization where dedication is fanned by ostentation. I was welcomed there more or less as someone turning up who is not at all wanted because I do not have a car and a *valet de chambre*. Volunteers are offering themselves in far too great numbers. All the rich middle-class women want to be nurses. There are also a large number of men that they do not know what to do with. The charities make workers labour at a very low wage, twenty sous a day, sometimes no money, only the mid-day meal.

25 August, 1914

I was sadly drinking a cup of coffee at a café in front of the Gare du Nord. A tyre exploded like the sound of artillery fire. This reminded me of the fire-crackers I had bought the previous 14th of July. Mme Renaud and the other tenants thought I was ridiculous to buy firecrackers. But of course it is they who are silly. I wanted to seize again those feelings of my childhood. I am so unhappy that I look for the fleeting joys of the past. On those early Bastille Days, people let off masses of firecrackers and when they exploded they shouted, '*Vive la République*'. The Republic then appeared to me as something very fine and strong which burst like an explosion. With my firecrackers in my hand, I thought how futile it is to run after phantoms. The Republic will never again 'explode'. It is embodied by sensible, down-to-earth gentlemen who only think about how to earn the greatest possible amount of money for their dinners, their cars and their stupid mistresses.

But if the Republic seems to be exploding loudly, it is only the cannon down at Charleroi like the one I heard at Nancy. The feelings of my childhood will not reawaken. '*Vive la République*,' bang, bang. This is not grand; it is only sad, terribly sad. It means one may be killed and afterwards cease to exist! – Terror – To give my blood, my life's blood, to suffer, that is fine, no big deal. But to cease to exist. Though it is true that one day, obviously, I will be no more. No, the war is definitely not a higher form of life. It is true that I am living through it in a Paris lodging house, where I await events that probably will not happen. For this to be a finer existence, one would have to be one of the major actors and this can never be. I am poor and, alas, a woman.

27 August

I saw Dr Buillar and he stunned me with his extreme chauvinism. As I was saying to him, in accordance with normally accepted ideas, that I would care for German and French patients without distinction, he said to me that I had no patriotic feeling, that I was a bad French woman, that I deserved death and made a gesture with his hand as if to shoot me. 'I would feel obliged,' he said, 'to kill off the enemy wounded, to blow out their brains', and then seeing that after all he was going a bit far, he told me that there are cunning means of avoiding giving succour, and that one should reserve medical care for the French. Furthermore, B. has become politically reactionary. He declared himself an anti-Semite, an anti-Dreyfusard, and an anti-fichard.[20] I do not know how he stood on these issues before but at least he was an active Freemason. He told me, without it is true seeming entirely convinced, that since God has given us a combative instinct, we must not curb it but exercise it fully. I do not know whether Buillar is sincere in his chauvinism. Before the war, I had never spoken to him on the subject, but all the same he is moving oddly to the right, showing a reactionary tendency that was doubtless already under way. Nevertheless, the war is a great experiment in human psychology.

Another letter from S. about the spy mania of the people of Nancy. I said that they were capable of shooting people first and asking questions afterwards. 'It is better,' he said, 'to kill ten innocent persons than to let one guilty one escape'. This, it is true, is a reason of State. But if we agreed that it is permissible to kill on suspicion, half of the population would kill the other half.

Long files of Belgians who are fleeing the invader. They are lodged all over the place, in public buildings. They drag along children, parcels tied up in string. There are women weeping.

Braemer is happy with Guesde's appointment to the Cabinet.[21] He reckons up the possible scenarios. Socialism, in effect, is a joke. If people held firm convictions, their ideals would not go up in smoke like this. He too says that Germany must be crushed. He bears a grudge against the German socialists and he is right. With four million voters, they should have been able to do something. It is also true, as I saw in Stuttgart, that German socialists despise the French.[22]

28 August

Now spy mania has conquered Paris. This morning, because I have short hair and ride a bicycle, a policeman asked me for my papers. I showed them to him; he turned them over and over; in the meantime a crowd gathered. Already a man was commenting that I did not look like a nice person. The policeman took me to the station which was at sixes and sevens. Meanwhile there had been an undertaker in the crowd, more or less of a socialist, who said he knew me. All this left me feeling depressed. Women's emancipation will obviously never come. Formerly my emancipated appearance only provoked cries of 'cazzi' [cock, shit, fool] from hooligans; now I am arrested because I do not look like a slave, unlike all other women. Evidently I was born several centuries too early.

4 September

I have had no luck with my naive desire to devote myself to my country. It was in vain that I tried to move heaven and earth, that I petitioned everyone that I knew even slightly in positions of influence in order to be sent to the army. Complete failure. Even though Dumas has made it to the top and he is on my side, or so he says. Surely those thousands of wounded lack care. Administrative stupidity is the same everywhere.

The invasion of Paris is feared. The government has gone off to Bordeaux.[23] In my ministry it is a general exodus. There is a baby in the treasurer's office. A great crowd of civil servants rush in to be paid and run about like the clappers saying that Paris is in flames. Extravagant fears haunt the minds of even educated people. 'The metro is to be blown up.' Socialists say that they will be shot as being held responsible for the defeat. The railway stations are under siege. People fight each other to get on the trains. The common people, however, are not afraid. The old have seen 1870 and they reassure the young. 'A siege isn't so bad. If they drop bombs we'll go into the cellars, that's all.'

In the evening, a crowd on the Boulevard St Michel was awaiting a troop march-past: a working-class crowd. Most of the women were bare-headed: people sat on the edge of the pavements or even on the ground alongside the buildings. It was a carnival-like atmosphere with, nevertheless, an unaccus-

tomed casualness. It was a tragic moment and people felt this. Luminous
bands of searchlights seeking out zeppelins, swept the sky. A man in rags cut
through the crowd. 'Ah, well,' he said in a sepulchral voice, 'since we must
croak, we might as well croak straight away.' I had the feeling that something
terrible and inevitable was imminent. The boulevard was scarcely lit, the
quays of the Seine not at all. The silhouette of Notre Dame stood out tragi-
cally in the moonlight. The white edges of the parapets shone with phospho-
rescent light on the black backdrop of the river bank. The arches of the
bridges reflected in the water gave the illusion of great round tubes. The
towers of the Conciergerie, the massive bulk of the Louvre surged up blackly.
A real St Bartholemew's Eve. I heard the clock strike on St Germain
l'Auxerrois.

I saw some Algerian infantrymen. Their eyes were shining; they were
going off to war as if to make love. They were taking a lad of twelve or
thirteen years old with them. 'Where are you going?' someone said. 'I am
going to war,' he answered in a tone which conveyed all his joy at being
included with the soldiers in spite of his tender years. They anchor their lives
to a trinket. A little flag worth two sous, a pencil, a mirror, a notebook given
to them, these it seems will bring them luck. I would gladly be in their
knapsacks but not in their skins, by golly. How dreadful if my life only
depended on these little knick-knacks.

In passing by, the soldiers routinely insult the women spectators. Ah, war
is anti-feminist. 'Does grandmother have tits then?' and so on. They kissed
everyone in the front row so I prudently placed myself in the second. The
women, of course, did not take offence. They answered the '*cazzis*' with
expressions of pity. 'Poor things, what a sad day all the same.' A young
woman in front of me allowed herself to be kissed by at least one hundred
men. She was a tart, that was obvious, but all the same there was nothing
lecherous in her kisses. She believed she was performing a good deed, by
giving men courage who were going out to risk their lives. That night twenty
to twenty-five thousand men marched by with all kinds of weapons, with
75mm guns, trucks, even cattle which will serve to re-supply the troops with
food.

I was to see three of these infantrymen on a tram after the battle. They
were much less cocky. 'Ah,' they said to me, 'this isn't anything like Mo-
rocco. The Moroccans surrendered straight away. But this here war is dreadful. We were in a trench, fighting almost one against two. The captain had an
order passed along our ranks on a bit of paper, and we read that we had to
fight to the death. You can imagine how pissed off we were.' Evidently most
men, however courageous they may be, only brave a danger in the hope of
escaping it.

8 September

Trains full of the wounded or trains of English troops. The inhabitants of Montgeron bring them all sorts of things: milk, fruit, bread, meat. A nun brings two carafes of clear water, with an ostentatious air. For the time being, the passage of the trains was the chief entertainment for Montgeron. The whole population came to the station, society girls in elegant bright coloured dresses, women and children of the common people. When night fell everyone was sent away. A train full of soldiers arrived. They came from the north and will guard Paris. There were two who knew me; one was a socialist, the other, a cab driver, had once driven me to the Gare de l'Est. 'Ah, all my ideas are overthrown,' the socialist said to me. 'Now one sees things differently.' How fragile socialism is. These soldiers do not know anything, even where they are going. They think there is a revolution in Paris only seventeen kilometres away.

They told me that in the north the peasants refused to feed them, even when offered money. They had been fasting for twenty-four hours. That was bad luck for the peasant woman who arrived with two heavy baskets of peaches on her arm. As she generously tried to offer a few to the soldiers, everyone rushed to crowd round her baskets and it was a proper pillage.

11 September

I have been of some help in the course of my walks. Wounded men who needed attention saw my Red Cross arm band and I helped them as best I could. Today I will carry a few bandages. The summer weather has been glorious. I decided to go to Meaux.[24] En route I met an infantry regiment of Algerians going to the front. I endured salvoes of insults directed at my pronounced physique. This chilled my desire to be useful down to zero degrees. Evidently for their sort, I represented approximately the equivalent value of a dog and in society in general I do not count for much either. Since that is the way it is, I would be stupid to take part in this public misfortune.

Ah, what a terrible calamity it is to be a woman. Yes a calamity, for I do not love my disdained and oppressed sex. On balance, women get what they deserve. The most liberated women are only partly free.

All the same, there were a few cries of '*Vive la Croix-Rouge*' addressed to my armband. I carried on. At Chelles I was stopped because I did not have a safe conduct pass.

12 September

Undoubtedly war does not reinforce solidarity; it reinforces egotism. The Paris population are kind to the soldiers; people in cars give them lifts, whereas ordinarily they drive past arrogantly. But it is merely fear that makes them behave like this. Soldiers are their defenders against the gunfire of triumphant Prussians, therefore they look after them. Shopkeepers, normally polite by profession, are of an unheard of rudeness. They almost refuse to sell. Obviously they feel their profits are unstable and they guard them even more jealously. Most of the smaller shops are shut and the impression in the streets is of a half-holiday.

16 September

Set off for Meaux. Bridges at Lagny blown up. The iron bridge is cut in an S shape as if by a knife. One has to cross by pontoon bridge. At Meaux almost noone about. Found a room in a little hotel. Very pleased. Lice. The inhabitants are still terrified, their voices shaking. A courageous inn-servant, who calmly recounts how a shell exploded next to her. The courage of simple people is partly a function of their incomprehension of danger.

Varredes: I crossed a wood laid waste by the battle; tree trunks cut in two by high explosive shells, branches strewn on the ground. Further along, the dead buried along the road. It was getting dark. I took a walk on the battlefield looking for a piece of howitzer shell. I stepped over graves; all at once something stirred next to me. For a moment I felt ridiculously afraid. But common sense returned. If something is stirring this means it is not dead. I must try to dig up the person buried alive. I waited, but there was nothing more; no doubt an animal after its quarry.

The following day, after a dozen kilometres, Barcy; a vast plain, grey sky, it has just been raining. In the distance a troop of black capes was silhouetted against the sky. Men carrying something on the ends of poles. I approached them. These 'things' were shovels and the men dismal gravediggers.

Every five metres, the body of a French soldier with his wine-red trousers. Here and there a few Germans in grey. Not at all terrifying this battlefield; the bodies resembled dolls dressed as soldiers. I consciously had to force myself to feel frightened. If after all, I were one of those: nothing more, nothingness. What a folly it had been for this 'doll' to mix himself up in all this. Life is the only reality. Everything else is just words. All right, then, is this 'doll' losing out on a great deal? I too will die, but not in battle. One day I will be like him. What then?

Fundamentally these people have got what they deserved. Humanity is stupid. Have I not sung to the workers in every key that they must start a revolution in order to free themselves? I only succeeded in frightening them. Now they are dying all the same, and not for liberation but for the opposite purpose. Oh, everything is futile. Progress does not exist; what is the use of living? It would be better for me to be in this dead man's place. But, no, the self is the sole reality, and if social struggle is only a false glimmer, the blue sky is still lovely to look at; let us enjoy it in the time that remains to us.

The village of Barcy was half destroyed. The inhabitants tell me their view of things. 'Barcy, you understand,' one peasant said to me, 'was the bull's eye.' One would think that he was proud of it.

20 September

Senlis: A whole street burnt to the ground, the houses reduced to four walls, sometimes a heap of stones. There are still bodies about. A publican, to whose establishment I went to quench my thirst, tells me amid tears of the pillage of her house. The French, she said, were as bad as the Germans. They left their filth in corners. She showed me a room turned upside down; a mattress on the floor. When people left the café they shook her hand in leaving, in single file as at a funeral.

From Senlis to Crepy-en-Valois by bicycle. Traces of the Germans passing through. Boxes which must have held shirts, bits of great coats, bandages, boxes of jam, bottles. I was alone on the open plain. All at once above me, 'vroom, vroom'. I looked up and saw a German plane. I was scared stiff. What the devil was I doing in this place? True, if I had stayed at home I would have seen nothing. All the same, if he chucks a bomb at me, my life ends here. Too bad, hard luck. There is nothing for it, no houses to hide in. There is indeed a tree, but that will not help me. But after all he ignored me; a mouse like me is not worth a bomb. He disdained me and went off. I breathed again.

A soldier on the train ... possibly an anarchist. He said he had been wounded and was now better. They want to send him back to the front, but he will not go. There were fifty of them in his position. There was no justice. Some men never went to the front, why? He spoke of the officers, who, he said, were no better than us. 'They work with their heads, people say. Well then, they are like artichokes.' He said that if he went to war it was only to keep the Prussians out of France, but afterwards, if they did not improve the workers' conditions, they would go to war; he meant the revolution.

This man expressed some of my ideas but he disgusted me. He looked like a scoundrel who dresses himself up with theories to hide his baser instincts.

Everyone in the railway carriage, of course, was quiet. It was a second-class carriage full of small shopkeepers. They were shocked by this soldier's tepid patriotism.

24 September

An example of the ascendancy of the collective over the individual. I went into a cinema wearing my Red Cross arm band. A working-class woman said loudly to her neighbour: 'Look, the Red Cross. She shouldn't be here; she should be on the battlefield.' The feelings behind her words were complex. The Red Cross is no longer popular because it recruits exclusively from the bourgeoisie and many of its functions have little use. But women are hard on other women like myself whose apparent rise in rank makes them jealous. There was a British officer in front of me who also entered the cinema. They made no comment about him, and nevertheless in their eyes, he too should have been at the front.

26 September

Arrest of spies or suspected spies on the Boulevard des Italiens at 1 p.m. A motorcycle with sidecar pulls up. A minute later two other cars arrive. On the first, officers with a young man with round shaped head and pale blond hair. He was dressed in some sort of military uniform and wore a military medal. The crowd, a well-dressed crowd, shouted: 'There he is! Oh, the scum, and he's wearing a medal! Put him to death!' He halted for a few seconds in front of me. The officer made a gesture as if to say, 'Leave us alone. This business has nothing to do with a rotten mob like you'. The man himself stood upright, his hair blowing in the wind, his eyes bright, a smile on his lips; a magnificent statue of courage. People shouted: 'You've had your chips; you will be shot; four bullets in your carcass'. He did not flinch.

I notice yet again that it takes a little while for a crowd to move from words to deeds, because during the short time when the car was stationary, the crowd had time to leap on the man and drag him off. They did not do it however and satisfied themselves with insults: 'He's a Frenchman. Traitor, swine' and so on. This sight moved me profoundly. The thought of this exuberant life which was perhaps going to be suddenly annihilated, overwhelmed me. Energy is really a beautiful thing. This man must be a German, for I did not recognize my idea of traitor in this superman. He must be working for his own country. I may be wrong. I would like to think that he is a German. All this power then, this willing sacrifice of a life for Kaiser

Wilhelm. Wilhelm who will know nothing about it, lost as this man will be in a crowd. Oh what futility. It is true that everything is pointless. The liberation of the proletariat is as futile as *'Deutschland über alles'*. In the second car, some civilian or other in a bowler hat, properly dressed, ordinary face. 'Kill him, kill him! Oh, they should have given him to us', said a woman worker or shop assistant wearing a hat. People said that the two cars had pursued the motorcycle from the Italian border and had finally succeeded in cornering it. There only remains their new car draped with a British flag. On the seat a sheepskin and an aviator's helmet.

29 September:

A few years ago, Sobillard, a sex maniac who killed a little girl after having raped her, would have been guillotined. The idea of murder was not even hateful; it did not belong to the present but to history and to fiction. Today death is common currency; there is nothing but stories of killings, stabbings with bayonets, decapitations, and people are not shocked. They laugh. De Ribeaucourt told me how on the Boulevard Port Royal he saw on a train some Algerian riflemen who had slit the throats of German prisoners. 'There was a professor there who burst out laughing, but I laughed too. You have to go along with things in order not to seem to be a wet blanket.' De Ribeaucourt ended with a story about cannibalism: 'You know,' the rifleman was supposed to have said, 'on the battlefield there was nothing to eat. We were hungry so we cut up some Prussian and cooked it. It was *very* good. You would have thought it was mutton'.

20 December 1915

At the present time the war is no more than a part of life which has scarcely any more importance than political events do in peacetime. Paris is still here but one still fears death from possible zeppelins which have not been seen for nine months. By contrast, night life has slowed down considerably. People seldom go to the theatre and most people go to their local cinema. They are accustomed to this state of affairs and think no more about it. When soldiers finish their period of leave they go back to the trenches in the same way as before the war they would have gone back to work, mechanically with neither courage nor weariness, as though to a necessity that did not need explanation. Municipal councillors are paying themselves salaries of 15,000 francs while at the same time whittling down, by some pretext or other, the allowances paid to soldiers' wives. But the public is used to these sorts of iniquities; this does not even seem shocking any more.

The curses to Kaiser Wilhelm on everyone's lips that one heard at the beginning of the war are forgotten. Noone speaks any longer either of the Kaiser or of the Huns [*les Boches*]. A normal life of work and material cares has reclaimed its usual place in people's minds. No more caricatures ridiculing the enemy; the saucy stories of the pre-war period are regaining, little by little, their place on the front pages of the illustrated papers. The only difference is that from time to time they are given a military flavour. The war shirker or the badly wounded soldier have become stock figures. At the cinema they have reverted to police dramas; war issues no longer stir the emotions. They are relegated to the newsreels, the serious part of the evening.

The cost of living has risen by a third.
Methylated spirits: 1 franc 80 per litre
Anthracite: 7 francs 50 for 50 kilos
Balm 'ordenon': 5 francs per pound

An attempt has been made to freeze prices, an initiative taken by the Prefecture of Police. But supplies stopped getting to Paris and the plan was dropped. On the trams people tell stories of relatives killed or wounded in the war, but do so without emotion, as though retelling ordinary events. No one bothers to read the communiqués from the front, which in vague terms always recount the same thing, these never ceasing artillery bombardments.

27 September 1918

Frequent and dangerous air-raids. A concierge, 5 Avenue Thénard, neglects going to the catacombs during the alerts. She stays in her bed and puts the photograph of her son killed in the war under her pillow. She thinks that because her son has been killed, she will be saved.

NOTES

1. The Perray Vaucluse Memoir is entitled, '*Anne, dite Madeleine Pelletier*', Dossier Madeleine Pelletier, Bibliothèque Marguerite Durand; '*Doctoresse Pelletier: Mémoires d'une féministe*', Fonds Marie-Louise Bouglé, Bibliothèque Historique de la Ville de Paris; '*Journal de Guerre*', Dossier Pelletier, Bibliothèque Marguerite Durand.
2. For a moving account of a similar case of marital division based on the gender–clerical/anti-clerical divide see Suzanne Voilquin's autobiographical fragment in Claire Goldberg Moses and Lesley Wahl Rabine, *Feminism, Socialism and French Romanticism*, Bloomington, Indiana University Press, 1993, pp. 147–77.

3. See: 'The Right to Abortion', pp. 177–84.
4. Louise Michel was a legendary revolutionary and anarchist who fought in the Commune. Jules Guesde was leader of the moderate socialist faction. Gustave Hervé was founder and Editor of *La Guerre sociale*, and led the revolutionary socialist faction until the outbreak of the war, whereupon he had a political conversion to the patriotic Right.
5. *l'Ecole émancipée*, no. 19, 4 February 1911.
6. Auguste Bebel (1840–1913) was the author of a seminal socialist feminist text, *Die Frau und de Socializmus* (Berlin, Internazionale Bibl. 9, 1879), translated as *Women in the Past, Present and Future*, London, 1885.
7. Madame de Sévigné (1626–1696), Marquise de Sévigné, author of a remarkable series of letters to her daughter. The reference here is as a member of the aristocracy and a representative of the *ancien régime*.
8. Pelletier makes no other mention of the little sister who may have died in infancy. There are references to an older brother, but in general Pelletier writes as though she were an only child.
9. The republican 14th of July celebrations, 'Bastille Day', were still politically charged events in Pelletier's childhood. The first national holiday after the 1871 Commune was not permitted until 1878 and the tricolour was a living symbol of radical republican hopes for the working class, expressed in the celebrations taking place in Pelletier's own quarter (see Felicia Gordon, *The Integral Feminist: Madeleine Pelletier 1874–1939*, Cambridge, Polity Press, 1990, pp. 1–2).
10. 'Le Chant du Départ' (1794) by Marie-Joseph Chénier, the second national anthem of republican France.
11. This episode is recounted at greater length in Madeleine Pelletier, *La Femme vierge*, Paris, Bresle, 1933 where the heroine, when she begins to menstruate, can obtain no information about her 'illness' from the nuns at school or her mother. It is her father who explains that she is now a woman. Pelletier clearly saw the menarche as a formative moment of shock and her rejection of women's biological destiny.
12. Astié de Valsayre, at the period when Pelletier knew her, described herself as a socialist feminist, though later she espoused ultra-nationalist opinions.
13. Maria Pognon (1844–1925), President of the *Ligue française pour le droit des femmes*.
14. *La Fronde*, feminist daily newspaper, founded by Marguerite Durand and published between 1897 and 1914.
15. The School of Anthropology, founded in 1875 from its parent organization, the Anthropological Society of Paris, was dominated for many years by Paul Broca. Charles Letourneau (d. 1902) was a socialist and proponent of social evolution (see *The Evolution of Marriage*, London, 1891 and *Property: Its Origin and Development*, London, 1892).
16. Caroline Kauffmann (1840–1926), Secretary of Solidarity before Pelletier was known for her campaigns in the physical culture movement. A republican with socialist leanings, she was less radical than Pelletier. She participated in a number of feminist demonstrations. During and after the First World War she became interested in spiritualism.
17. Hubertine Auclert (1848–1914), an indefatigable for women's suffrage, led a group called '*Le Suffrage des femmes*'.
18. Mme Oddo – Jeanne Oddo-Deflou – feminist and journalist who covered Pelletier's electoral campaign of 1910 for *La Fronde*.
19. The SFIO Congress of 1906 at Limoges.
20. Affaire des fiches: A scandal provoked by a corrupt system of promotion established in the French army from 1901–1904 by General André, Minister of War, and based on notes relating to officers' religious and political opinions.
21. Max Braemer (b. 1860), militant socialist, sculptor by trade, active in socialist politics from 1883 onwards. In 1914 he was an adherent of the policy of national defence and was a member of the committee of aid to refugees. He served in Jules Guesde's ministry. (See Jean Maitron (ed.), *Dictionnaire biographique du mouvement ouvrier français*, vol. 11, Paris, Les Editions ouvrières, tome 11 p. 41.)
22. Pelletier here refers to a meeting of the Socialist International which met in Stuttgart in 1907 and which also hosted the International Socialist Women's Conference, organized by

Clara Zetkin and dominated by the German SPD (Social Democratic Party). The Conference opposed women's suffrage and co-operation with bourgeois feminists. Though Pelletier attended the conference she was unhappy both with its tone and its outcome.

23. On the 31 August 1914, Poincaré's government fled Paris for Bordeaux, fearing that the Germans would take the capital.

24. Pelletier was anxious to visit a battlefield and made her epic journey to Meaux and the battlefields of the Marne shortly after the battle.

9. Conclusion

In this Reader we have grouped together five women political activists campaigning from the 1830s to the 1930s under the broad rubrics of socialism and feminism. We have sought to emphasize both continuities in their aspirations and experiences, and contrasts in their personal circumstances, professional lives and political philosophies. Yet when reading letters, diaries, memoirs or published works from the past in an academic context, it is easy to overlook a central reality present to or threatening all these feminists' ambitions, namely the blight of poverty. Even to find the time or a place to write must be counted as an achievement. Financial hardship did not only form the basis for their political analysis, it took a toll on their personal lives. For example, Pauline Roland's attempts at independence crumbled when thanks to her poverty as a prisoner in Algeria, she had to beg former partners for child support. Flora Tristan, treated as a pariah by her aristocratic family, suffered from a sense of social displacement as well as from poverty. Pauline Roland and Jeanne Deroin became journalists and lived precariously in part by their writing. Hélène Brion, though her father was an officer, had no means of support other than her teaching. She lost her livelihood thanks to her pacifist involvement which also had its effect on her subsequent political activism. Madeleine Pelletier achieved minimal financial security, eking out a living as a medical doctor in a working-class district. For all five women included in this Reader, the effect of poverty in undermining successful political and feminist organization needs emphasizing. The clubs or journals they founded were poorly funded and consequently ephemeral. The dream of class and gender solidarity eluded them.

The second major factor curtailing the revolutionary and reformist programmes to which Tristan, Deroin, Roland, Pelletier and Brion committed themselves was that of repression. This operated powerfully, both on the level of social opprobrium, even within parties of the Left with which these women were ideologically aligned, and through the state. Brought to trial, Pauline Roland and Jeanne Deroin were punished particularly severely for their desire for independence. The character assassination in the press which Hélène Brion faced at the time of her arrest was directed as much against her alleged 'unladylike' activities, for example wearing trousers when delivering coal in her war relief work, as against her pacifism. Madeleine Pelletier's forays into cross-dressing made her the butt of socialist comrades' obscenities. State repression was also entirely real for all five women. They risked their liveli-hoods and in some cases their lives by espousing two sets of subversive causes: the liberation of the working class and of women. It may be difficult today to appreciate the extent to which feminism was viewed by the authori-ties as potentially undermining the state. If we only consider the small number of women who belonged to feminist groups or who attended demonstrations in France in the 19th and early 20th centuries, we may underestimate the seriousness with which the authorities took such movements, a seriousness underscored by the lengthy reports on feminist activity in the police archives. Feminists were subversive because they opposed war, because they were in favour of equal pay, of paid work for women, of the abolition of the double standard, of family limitation and women's suffrage. These were all aims which, it was claimed, would undermine French society, founded on the twin ideals of the patriarchal family and the mother-educator. In retrospect, the contempt and ridicule with which feminists were treated in the popular press have tended to trivialize their activities even today. Ridicule functions as a powerful weapon of oppression, more powerful perhaps than the threat or reality of imprisonment, but it is also paradoxically a recognition of the seriousness with which the feminist movement has been perceived.

The question which arises with each of our five writers in relation to their activism is: what kind of socialist: what kind of feminist? What was the common ground between Flora Tristan, nourishing her aristocratic identity, and Pauline Roland, a petty bourgeoise, Jeanne Deroin and Madeleine Pelletier, daughters of the people? To answer such questions requires an assessment of varieties of socialism and feminism. With regard to the former, the impact of utopian socialism, particularly of Saint-Simonianism, was, as we have seen, crucial to the generation of the 1830s and 1840s as was its relationship to, and reaction against, organized religion. For Flora Tristan, for example, the messianic impact of utopian socialism left a particular imprint. Yet while seeking to create a genuinely working-class movement, Tristan, like Pelletier after her, took an elitist position in relation to the working class. For Roland and Deroin, on the other hand, Saint-Simonianism offered an opportunity for education, self-valorization and political and journalistic activity. There were also negative psychological effects, as Pauline Roland's debilitating worship of Enfantin demonstrated. Hélène Brion and Madeleine Pelletier, a genera-tion later, cut their political teeth on varieties of Marxist socialism, but honoured their predecessors as feminists and socialists. Curiously, in their own historical analyses there is an almost complete silence about the Saint-Simonian movement.[1] The Saint-Simonian appeal to a feminine identity, the reinstitution of separate spheres ideology and the emphasis on religious feel-ing and hierarchical religious observance would have been distasteful to both

Pelletier and Brion. The latter's interest in spiritualism from the 1920s onwards, however, could be compared to Saint-Simonian and early republican varieties of religious fervour.

Saint-Simonianism, like Catholicism, like even the anti-clerical Republic, gave a privileged place to women. It was a place, however, separate from the male sphere, and which functioned either as a refuge or a prison, depending on one's point of view. The ambivalence that so many feminists betrayed on this issue is hardly surprising. Contesting that place and space in education, the professions and in political life constituted the essence of the feminist project from Deroin to Pelletier. These early feminist socialists sought to mould new political structures and to create space for women in the public sphere.

For Deroin Saint-Simonianism's greatest contribution was to promise women a release from the prison in which the Napoleonic Code incarcerated them:

> One day I opened the book of the law [the Civil Code] and read these words: 'The husband must protect his wife; his wife must obey her husband'. I felt a profound indignation. Never, I told myself, would I buy happiness at the price of slavery.[2]

Divorce for Flora Tristan was both an important personal and a public political issue. Domestic misery and social crime, she believed, could be laid at the immovable door of the indissoluble institution of marriage. Jeanne Deroin, though content in her personal relationships, was similarly motivated by indignation at the Civil Code to try to change the marriage laws. Pauline Roland, eschewing marriage, also created a political statement out of her personal circumstances, claiming the right to single parenthood. Flora Tristan compared her own unhappy marriage with that of women everywhere, placing her personal situation in an international context. In her petition 'On Women Travellers' she similarly extolled internationalism, the breakdown of national barriers through education, dissemination of information and travel. This theme presages her creation of an international workers' association, which pre-dated Marx's First International. Tristan also dwelt, although to a lesser extent, on the nature of women's exclusion from political institutions.

Deroin, though believing that Saint-Simonianism under Enfantin heralded the regeneration of society through economic reform and that it would put an end to women's subjugation, nevertheless admitted its faults and declared a preference for the Republic for which she and Roland passionately fought during the short Second Republic.

Saint-Simonianism fell into disrepute with the republican Left which in turn was superseded by scientific socialism in its analysis of capitalism, dialectical materialism and class conflict. This and the fact that in practice the Saint-Simonians' emotional relations were often exploitative[3] may account for Pelletier's and Brion's silence about the movement. Yet Pelletier's call to sweep away the double sexual standard in order to achieve genuine equality was not dissimilar to Jeanne Deroin's. The attraction of Saint-Simonian socialism was that it saw gender relations at the heart of social relations and that the latter were not reducible to material questions alone. However, Enfantin's insistence on the re-institution of masculine/feminine natures in his philosophy re-inscribed a system of separate spheres at the heart of this supposedly gender liberating movement.

Turning to socialisms of the *Belle Epoque*, one finds that the aim of integrating an economic analysis for class liberation with sexual liberation was relegated to sexual libertarians like Paul Robin or the anarchist movement. Mainstream socialists espoused Marx's materialist analysis which regarded women's oppression as another symptom of class exploitation.[4] While such an analysis did serve to demystify marriage and prostitution by showing their historical and economic bases, it failed to account for women's subjection beyond the working class. Middle-class feminists tended to be dismissed by socialists as class enemies. Within the context of socialist women's politics, Hélène Brion and Madeleine Pelletier represented an attempt by feminists of the Left to remain simultaneously, feminists, socialists and trade unionists. Pelletier and Brion may have lost faith in socialist parties but not in their ideology nor in their belief that feminism could revitalize socialism.[5] Though the texts included in this Reader often function as critiques of socialist institutions, there is no doubt of Tristan, Deroin, Roland, Pelletier and Brion's passionate identification with a broad movement of social transformation while differing on the means of achieving it, whether through association, education, syndicalism, reform, party politics or revolution. In spite of the difficulties they experienced, it remains the case that socialist parties offered a difficult but nonetheless possible mode of access into the male political sphere where other democratic parties did not.

The writings of these five ideologically linked women demonstrate the richness and diversity of their feminist analyses and aims. From a late 20th-century perspective, Flora Tristan may not appear to have made feminism (as opposed to workers' associations) her central concern, but in 'The Need to Provide Hospitality for Women Travellers' and in her 'Petitions on Divorce', she focused on the realities confronting independent women while demonstrating an understanding of wider issues: 'A whole class, making up half of the human race, is among these unhappy creatures which our civilization is condemning to live in distress'.[6] For Pauline Roland, adequate and universal educational provision was the overriding need. Education was for these feminists the key to women's advancement. They were all to some extent autodidacts, conscious of their struggles to gain a purchase on ideas and language and convinced that the ability to write and express themselves gave them an identity in the public world. Roland, like Pelletier, argued powerfully for the abolition of the double standard and for the right of women to affirm their sexuality without the trappings of shame and modesty enjoined by tradition.

The suffrage issue became a major focus for Deroin, Pelletier and Brion who struggled for full civic recognition for women. France since the revolution of 1789 had put the idea of citizenship at the core of its moral and political identity. The exclusion of women from the polity reduced them not only to an inferior social and legal status but condemned them to an inferior ethical status. Much of the anger and frustration that we hear in the voices from this anthology stemmed from the writers' perception of the injustice and immorality of a state in which women were forced to live out their lives in a form of internal exile. They saw both action (in the form of political involvement, demonstrations and marches) and words (writing and speeches) as necessary to overturn this denial of personhood by the male-authored state. In the modern state it was self-evident that to be a full person one must be a citizen. 'When women gain entry to public life through having the vote, they will become individuals worthy of the name.'[7]

All five women demonstrated the psychological cost of their struggles against poverty, conformity, state repression and sexual subordination. They died young or went into exile, were assaulted or suffered political imprisonment, were incarcerated as mad or threatened with psychiatric incarceration. They were liable to physical and mental suffering, to exploitation, mistrust, *naïveté*, enthusiasm and disappointment. Their talents were not allowed to develop fully. Flora Tristan, Jeanne Deroin, Pauline Roland, Madeleine Pelletier and Hélène Brion were women for whom the political world in its broadest sense was a passion. They sought to place themselves not only in the politics of the present but within a historical tradition: to give women a place in the history of revolutionary radicalism, a history which within their own lifetimes had not completed its liberating, egalitarian and socially healing mission.

NOTES

1. An exception to this silence is Brion's comment in 'The Feminist Path': 'Without going back to the Flood, without questioning Saint Simon, Fourier or even Proudhon on their ideas about our social role and the place which they reserve for us in any future society, let us just look at the Third Republic' (p. 219) Brion's linkage of Saint Simon and Fourier (supposedly champions of women's emancipation) with Proudhon (a known anti-feminist) suggests that in her view all three held traditional attitudes towards women's roles.
2. Jeanne Deroin, '*Profession de foi*', Fonds Enfantin, Bibliothèque de l'Arsenal, Paris.
3. See 'Letters', in Claire Goldberg Moses and Lesley Wahl Rabine, *Feminism, Socialism,*

and French Romanticism, Bloomington and Indianapolis, Indiana University Press, 1993, pp. 218–81.

4. See: Frederich Engels, 'The Origin of the Family, Private Property and the State', 1884.
5. Hélène Brion, 'A Feminist Message', pp. 221–4.
6. Flora Tristan, 'On the Need to Provide Hospitality for Women Travellers', p. 28.
7. Madeleine Pelletier, 'Feminism and its Militants', p. 147.

Bibliography

Archival sources in the following libraries:

Archives nationales, Paris (AN)
Bibliothèque historique de la Ville de Paris (BHVP)
Bibliothèque nationale, Paris (BN)
Bibliothèque Marguerite Durand, Paris (BMD)
Bibliothèque de documentation internationale contemporaine, Nanterre (BDIC)
Fonds Enfantin, bibliothèque de l'Arsenal, Paris (BA)
Fonds Puech, Castres (FP)
Institut français de l'histoire sociale, Paris (IFHS)
Institute of International Social History, Amsterdam (IISH)

PRIMARY SOURCES

Deroin, Jeanne

(no date), *Profession de Foi*, Fonds Enfantin, BA.
(no date), *Aux électeurs du département de la Seine*, Paris, Imprimerie Lacour, rue saint-Hyacinthe-St-Michel, 33, et rue Souflot, 11, BN.
(1849), *Campagne électorale de la citoyenne Jeanne Deroin, pétition des femmes au peuple*, Dépôt central de la propagande socialiste, rue Coquillière, Paris 13, BN.
(1849), *Association fraternelle des Démocrates Socialistes des deux sexes, pour l'affranchissement politique et social des femmes*, Paris, Lacour Printers, BN.
(1852, 1853, 1854), *Almanach des femmes*, London and Jersey, BMD.

Roland, Pauline

(1833–1852), *Correspondance*, Fonds Enfantin, BA, BN, BMD, IISH.
(1842), 'Du travail des femmes et des enfants dans les mines de houille' in *La Revue indépendante*, tome IV, juillet, 184–95, BN.
(1849), *Aux instituteurs: l'Association des instituteurs institutrices et*

professeurs socialistes, Paris, par la société typographique de Paris, Imprimerie Schneider, rue d'Erforth, 4, BN.

(1849), *Programme d'enseignement de l'Association fraternelle des instituteurs institutrices et professeurs socialistes*, Paris, par la société typographique de Paris, Imprimerie Schneider, rue d'Erforth, 4, BN.

(1851), 'La femme a-t-elle droit à la liberté?', *La Feuille du peuple*, 25 avril, BN.

(1981), *Bagnes d'Afrique Trois transportés en Algérie après le coup d'Etat du 2 décembre 1851* (textes de Pauline Roland, Arthur Ranc, Gaspard Rouffet), Introduction et notes de Fernand Rude, Collection Actes et Mémoires du Peuple, Paris: Maspéro.

Tristan, Flora

(1835), *Necessité de faire un bon acceuil aux femmes étrangères*, Paris: chez Delaunay, BN.

(1835), Correspondance, quoted in Jules Puech (1925), *La vie et l'oeuvre de Flora Tristan*, Paris: Marcel Rivière.

(1838), *Méphis*, roman, 2 tomes, Paris: Ladvocat, BN.

(1838), *Pétition pour l'abolition de la peine de mort à la Chambre des Députés*, Paris: Imprimerie de Mme Huzard, AN.

(1838), *Pétition pour le rétablissement du divorce à Messieurs les Députés le 20 decembre 1837*, Paris, Imprimerie de Mme Huzard, AN.

(1838), *Pérégrinations d'une paria*, Paris: Arthur Bertrand, BN.

(1843–44), Correspondance, FP.

Re-editions

(1978), *Promenades dans Londres* (première édition 1840), édition établie et commentée par François Bédarida, Paris: Maspéro.

(1979), *Les pérégrinations d'une paria 1833–34*, Paris: Maspéro.

(1980), *Flora Tristan's London Journal 1840* (*Promenades dans Londres*), translated by Dennis Palmer and Giselle Pincetl, London: George Prior Publishers.

(1980), *Le tour de France. Etat actuel de la classe ouvrière sous l'aspect moral, intellectuel et matériel*, journal inédit de Flora Tristan, texte et notes établis par Jules Puech, réédité par Michel Collinet, introduction nouvelle de Stéphane Michaud, 2 tomes, Paris: Maspéro.

(1983), *The Workers' Union* (*Union Ouvrière*, troisième édition, 1844), translated and introduced by Beverly Livingston, Urbana, Illinois: University of Illinois Press.

(1986), *Flora Tristan's London Journal* (*Promenades dans Londres*, 1842 edition), translated, edited and introduced by Jean Hawkes, London: Virago.

(1986), *Union Ouvrière* (troisième édition 1844), une édition de Daniel Armogathe et Jacques Grandjonc, Paris: Des Femmes.

(1986), *Perigrinations of a Pariah* (translated, edited and introduced by Jean Hawkes), London: Virago.

(1988), *Necessité de faire un bon acceuil aux femmes étrangères*, édition présentée et commentée par Denys Cuche, Paris: L'Harmattan.

(1993), *Utopian Feminist: Her Travel Diaries and Personal Crusade*, selected, translated and with an Introduction by Doris and Paul Beik, Bloomington and Indianapolis: Indiana University Press.

Brion, Hélène

(no date), 'L'Encyclopédie féministe', BMD and IFHS.

(1918), 'Déclaration lue au premier conseil de guerre', Epône: L'Avenir Social.

(no date: 1917?), 'La Voie féministe, les partis d'avant-garde et le féminisme', Epône: La Société de la Librairie et d'Édition de l'Avenir Social.

(1919), 'Flora Tristan, la vraie fondatrice de l'internationale', *La Voie féministe*, Epône: L'Avenir Social.

Pelletier, Madeleine

(1908), 'La Question du vote des femmes', *La Revue socialiste*, septembre–octobre.

(1909), 'Le Féminisme et ses militantes', *Les Documents du progrès*, juillet, 19–26.

(1911), *Le Droit à l'avortement*, Paris, 2nd edition (1913), *Pour l'abrogation de l'article 317*, Paris: Editions de 'Malthusien'.

(1914), *L'Education féministe des filles,* reprinted with other works and with preface and notes by Claude Maignien (1978), Paris: Syros.

(1914–1918), 'Journal de Guerre', dossier Pelletier, BMD.

(1928), 'De la Prostitution', *L'Anarchie*, 20 novembre.

(1931), 'Le Droit au travail pour la femme', *La Brochure mensuelle*, Nminiov.

(1933), 'Doctoresse Pelletier: Mémoires d'une féministe', dossier Madeleine Pelletier, Fonds Marie-Louise Bouglé, BHVP.

Correspondance Arria Ly–Pelletier, dossier Madeleine Pelletier, Fonds Marie-Louise Bouglé, BHVP.

(1939), 'Anne, dite Madeleine Pelletier', MS in the hand of Hélène Brion, dossier Pelletier, BMD.

SECONDARY SOURCES

Actes du Colloque d'Albi des 19 et 20 mars 1992 (1993), *Femmes Pouvoirs* (sous la responsabilité de Michèle Riot-Sarcey), Paris: Editions Kimé.

Actes du Colloque Blanqui (1986), *Blanqui et les blanquistes*, Société d'histoire de la Révolution de 1848 et des révolutions du XIXe siècle, Paris: SEDES.

Actes du Colloque International 12–14 avril 1989 (1990, 1991), *Les Femmes et la Révolution française* (3 vols), (sous la direction de Marie-France Brive), Toulouse: Presses Universitaires de Mirail.

Adler, Laure (1979), *A l'aube du féminisme: les premières journalistes 1830–1850*, Paris: Payot.

'L'Affaire Hélène Brion: pacifisme et défaitisme: Compte rendu des débats judiciaires d'après la sténographie, avec croquis pris à l'audience' (1918), *Revue des causes célèbres*, **5**, 2 mai.

Agulhon, Maurice (1983), *The Republican Experiment 1848–1852*, translated by Janet Lloyd, Cambridge: Cambridge University Press.

Albistur, Maïté and Daniel Armogathe (1977), *Histoire du féminisme français*, 2 vols, Paris: Des Femmes.

Ambrière, Francis (1993), 'Qui était Flora Tristan' in *1848 Révolutions et mutations au XIXe siècle*, **9**, 21–35.

Angell, Norman (1913), *La Grande Illusion*, Paris: Nelson.

Arnaud, Angélique et Caroline Simon (1990), *Une correspondance saint-simonienne Angélique Arnaud et Caroline Simon 1833–1838*, Textes recueillis et présentés par Bernadette Louis, Paris: Côté-femmes.

Aron, Jean-Paul (ed.) (1980), *Misérable et glorieuse: la femme du XIXe siècle*, Paris: Fayard.

Baelen, Jean (1972), *La vie de Flora Tristan: socialisme et féminisme au XIXe siècle*, Paris: Seuil.

Bard, Christine (ed.) (1992), *Madeleine Pelletier (1874–1939), logique et infortunes d'un combat pour l'égalité*, Paris: Côté-femmes.

Bard, Christine (1993), *Les féministes en France. Vers l'intégration des femmes dans la Cité. 1914–1940*, Thèse de doctorat, Paris: Université de Paris VII.

Bard, Christine (1995), *Les filles de Marianne: Histoire des féminismes 1914–1940*, Paris: Fayard.

Becker, Jean-Jacques (1985), *The Great War and the French People*, translated by Arnold Pomerans, Leamington Spa: Berg.

Bell, Susan Groag and Karen M. Offen (eds) (1983), *Women, the Family and Freedom: The Debate in Documents*, Volume 1, 1750–1880, Volume 2, 1880–1950, Stanford, California: Stanford University Press.

Bellet, Roger (ed.) (1978), *La femme au XIXe siècle*, Lyons: Presses Universitaires de Lyon.

Bidelman, Patrick (1982), *Pariahs Stand Up! The Founding of the Liberal Feminist Movement in France, 1858–1889*, Westport, Connecticut: Greenwood.

Blunden, Katherine (1982), *Le Travail et la vertu. Femmes au foyer: une mystification de la révolution industrielle*, Paris: Payot.

Bouchardeau, Huguette (1978), *Hélène Brion, la Voie féministe*, Paris: Syros.

Bouët, Louis (no date), *Les pionners du syndicalisme universitaire*, Paris: Edition de l'École émancipée.

Bryson, Valerie (1992), *Feminist Political Theory: An Introduction*, Basingstoke and London: Macmillan.

Bulciolu, Maria Teresa (1980), *L'école saint-simonienne et la femme*, Pisa: Goliardica.

Carlisle, Robert B. (1987), *The Proferred Crown: Saint-Simonianism and the Doctrine of Hope*, Baltimore and London: Johns Hopkins University Press.

Clévenot, Michel (1992), *Les hommes de la fraternité. Un siècle cherche sa foi: le XIXᵉ siècle*, Paris: Editions Retz.

Cohen, Yolande (ed.) (1987), *Femmes et contre pouvoirs,* Alberta: Boreal.

Collini, Stefan (ed.) (1989), *On Liberty with the Subjection of Women*, Cambridge: Cambridge University Press.

Corbin, Alain (1978) (1990), *Women for Hire: Prostitution and Sexuality in France after 1850*, Cambridge, Massachusetts: Harvard University Press.

Correspondance (1992), *De la liberté des femmes. Lettres de dames au Globe (1831–1832)*, Textes recueillis et présentés par Michèle Riot-Sarcey, Paris: Côté-femmes.

Cross, Máire (ed.) (1995), Special Issue, *Modern and Contemporary France*, NS3 (2), 127–58.

Cross, Máire and Tim Gray (1992), *The Feminism of Flora Tristan*, Oxford: Berg.

Dallas, Gregor (1988), *At the Heart of the Tiger: Clemenceau and his World, 1841–1929*, London: Macmillan.

David, Marcel (1992), *Le printemps de la fraternité: genèse et vicissitudes (1830–1851)*, Paris: Aubier.

De Beauvoir, Simone (1983), *The Second Sex*, (first published 1949), translated by H.M. Parshley, Harmondsworth: Penguin.

Derré, J.R. (ed.) (1986), *Regard sur le saint-simonisme et les Saint-Simoniens*, Lyons: Presses Universitaires de Lyon.

Desanti, Dominique (1972 and 1980), *Flora Tristan: La femme révoltée*, Paris: Hachette.

Dijkstra, Sandra (1976), *Tristan and the Aesthetics of Social Change*, unpublished PhD thesis, San Diego: University of California.

Dijkstra, Sandra (1992), *Flora Tristan: Feminism in the Age of George Sand*, London: Pluto Press.

Duby, Georges and Michelle Perrot (1991), *Histoire des femmes, le XIX*ᵉ *siècle*, Paris: Plon.

Duby, Georges and Michelle Perrot (1992), *Histoire des femmes, le XX*ᵉ *siècle*, Paris: Plon.

Durand, Pierre (1987), *Louise Michel, la passion*, Paris: Messidor.

Engels, Frederick (1884), *The Origin of the Family, Private Property and the State in the Light of the Researches of Lewis H. Morgan*, translated by Alick West, from the 4th German edition, 1891, London: Marxist-Leninist Library, 1943.

Evans, Richard J. (1977), *The Feminist*, London: Croom Helm.

Evans, Richard J. (1987), *Comrades and Sisters*, Brighton: Wheatsheaf.

Fauré, Christine (1991), *Democracy Without Women: Feminism and the Rise of Individual Liberalism in France*, translated by Claudia Gorbman and John Berks, Bloomington and Indianapolis: Indiana University Press.

Fichet, Françoise (1992), *Saint-Simonisme, libéralisme et socialisme: la doctrine de la production*, Paris: Ecole de hautes études en sciences sociales.

Flammant, Thierry (1982), *L'école émancipée*, Paris: Les Monédières.

Fortescue, William (1993), 'Divorce Debated and Deferred: The French Debate on Divorce and the Failure of the Crémieux Divorce Bill in 1848', *French History*, **7** (2), 137–62.

Frader, Laura Levine (1991), *Peasants and Protest*, Berkeley and Los Angeles: University of California Press.

Fraisse, Geneviève (1994), *Reason's Muse, Sexual Difference and the Birth of Democracy*, translated by J.M Todd, Chicago: University of Chicago Press.

Garny, R. and H. Dubief (1963), 'Le legs Hélène Brion', *L'Histoire sociale*, **44**, 93–100.

Gemie, Sharif (1994), 'Docility, Zeal and Rebellion: Culture and Sub-cultures in Women's Teacher Training Colleges c.1860–c.1910' in *European History Quarterly*, **24**, 213–44.

Gemie, Sharif (1995), *Women and Schooling in France, 1815–1914*, Keele: Keele University Press.

Girard, Louis (1986), *Napoléon III*, Paris: Pluriel, Fayard.

Goldstein, Leslie (1982), 'Early Feminist Themes in French Utopian Socialism', *Journal of History of Ideas*, **XVIII** (1), 91–108.

Gordon, Felicia (1990), *The Integral Feminist: Madeleine Pelletier 1874–1939*, Cambridge: Polity Press.

Gouges, Olympe de (1986), *Oeuvres*, présentées par Benoîte Groult, Paris: Mercure de France.

Grogan, Susan K. (1992), *French Socialism and Sexual Difference: Women and the New Society, 1803–44*, Basingstoke and London: Macmillan.

Groult, Benoîte (1991), *Pauline Roland ou comment la liberté vint aux femmes*, Paris: Robert Laffont.

Guilbert, Madeleine (1966), *Les femmes et l'organisation syndicale avant 1914*, Paris: CNRS.

Hause, Stephen C. (1978), 'Women who Rallied to the Tricolour: The Effects of World War 1 on the French Women's Suffrage Movement', *Proceedings of the Annual Meeting of the Western Society for French History*, **6**, 371–81.

Hause, Steven C. with Anne R. Kenney (1984), *Women's Suffrage and Social Politics in the French Third Republic*, Princeton: Princeton University Press.

Hilden, Patricia (1986), 'Women and the Labour Movement in France, 1869–1914', *Historical Journal*, **29**(4), 809–32.

Huard, Raymond (1991), *Le suffrage universel en France 1848–1946*, Paris: Aubier.

Hyams, Edward (1979), *Pierre-Joseph Proudhon, His Revolutionary Life, Mind and Works*, London: John Murray.

Klejman, Laurence and Florence Rochefort (1989), *L'Egalité en marche: le féminisme sous la Troisième République*, Paris: Des Femmes.

Krakovitch, Odile (1990), *Les femmes bagnardes*, Paris: Olivier Orban.

Krop, Pascal (1983), *Les socialistes et l'armée*, Paris: Politique d'aujourd'hui.

Kruse, Darryn and Charles Sowerwine (1986), 'Feminism and Pacifism: "Women's Sphere" in Peace and War', in Norma Grieve and Alisa Burns (eds), *Australian Women: New Feminist Perspectives*, Melbourne: Oxford University Press.

La Fournière, Xavier de (1986), *Louise Michel Matricule 2182*, Paris: Librairie Académique Perrin.

Landes, Joan B. (1988), *Women and the Public Sphere in the Age of the French Revolution*, Ithaca and London: Cornell University Press.

Landes, Joan B. (1994), 'Women and the French Revolution', *Gender and History*, **6** (2), 281–91.

Le Bras-Chopard, Armelle (1986), *De l'égalité dans la différence le socialisme de Pierre Leroux*, Paris: Presses de la fondation nationale des sciences politiques.

Lefrançais, Gustave (1972), *Souvenirs d'un révolutionnaire*, texte établi et préparé par Jan Cerny, Bordeaux: Edition de la Tête de Feuilles.

Lejeune, Paule (1978), *Louis Michel, l'indomptable*, Paris: Des Femmes.

Lejeune-Resnick, Evelyne (1991), *Femmes et associations (1830–1880)*, Paris: Publisud.

Letourneau, Charles (1891), *The Evolution of Marriage and the Family*, London: Walter Scott.

Letourneau, Charles (1892), *Property: Its Origin and Development*, London: Walter Scott.

Louis, Marie-Victoire (1994), *Le droit de cuissage France 1860–1930*, Paris: Les Editions de l'atelier.

Magraw, Roger (1992), *A History of the French Working Class*, Volume 1 'The Age of Artisan Revolution 1815–1871', Volume 2 'Workers and the Bourgeois Republic 1871–1939', Oxford: Blackwell.

Maignien, Claude (1978), *Madeleine Pelletier: L'éducation féministe des filles*, Paris: Syros.

Maignien, Claude and Charles Sowerwine (1992), *Madeleine Pelletier, une féministe dans l'arène politique*, Paris: Éditions ouvrières.

Maitron, Jean (ed.) (1964), *Dictionnaire biographique du mouvement ouvrier français*, première partie 1789–1864; seconde partie 1864–1871; troisième partie 1871–1914; Paris: Les Éditions ouvrières, 15 vols.

Mayeur, Françoise (1979), *L'éducation des filles en France au XIXe siècle*, Paris: Hachette.

Mayeur, Jean-Marie and Madeleine Reberioux (1983), *The Third Republic from its Origin to the Great War*, translated by J.R. Foster, Cambridge: Cambridge University Press.

Mayoux, Marie and François Mayoux (1917), 'Les instituteurs syndicalistes et la guerre', *Fédération nationale des syndicats d'institutrices et d'instituteurs publics*, Section de la Charente.

Mayoux, Marie and François Mayoux (1918), 'Notre affaire: la propagande pacifiste pendant la guerre', *L'Avenir social*, Epône.

Mayoux, Marie and François Mayoux (1992), *Instituteurs pacifistes et syndicalistes*, Chamalières: Éditions Canope.

McDougall, Mary Lynn Stewart (1984), *The Artisan Republic: Revolution, Reaction and Resistance in Lyon 1848–1851*, Kingston and Montreal: McGill Queen's University Press.

McMillan, James (1981), *Housewife or Harlot: the Place of Women in French Society 1870–1940*, Brighton: Harvester.

McMillan, James (1991), 'Religion and Gender in Modern France: Some Reflections', in Frank Tallet and Nicholas Atkin (eds), *Religion, Politics and Society in France since 1789*, London: The Hambledon Press, 55–66.

McPhee, Peter (1992), *A Social History of France 1780–1880*, London: Routledge.

Melzer, Sara E. and Leslie W. Rabine (eds) (1992), *Rebel Daughters: Women and the French Revolution*, Oxford and New York: Oxford University Press.

Merriman, John (1978), *The Agony of the Republic: The Repression of the Left in Revolutionary France 1848–1851*, New Haven and London: Yale University Press.

Michaud, Stéphane (ed.) (1985), *Un fabuleux destin: Flora Tristan*, Dijon: Editions Universitaires de Dijon.

Michaud, Stéphane (ed.) (1994), *Flora Tristan, George Sand, Pauline Roland: Les femmes et l'invention d'une nouvelle morale 1830–1848*, Paris: Créaphis.

Mill, John Stuart (1869), *The Subjection of Women*, London: J.M. Dent.

Moses, Claire Goldberg (1984), *French Feminism in the Nineteenth Century*, Albany: State University of New York Press.

Moses, Claire Goldberg and Leslie Wahl Rabine (1993), *Feminism, Socialism, and French Romanticism*, Bloomington and Indianapolis: Indiana University Press.

Newhall, David S. (1991), *Clemenceau: A Life at War*, Lampeter: Edwin Mellen Press.

Noak, Paul (1992), *Olympe de Gouges: courtisane et militante des droits de la femme 1748–1793*, Paris: Editions de Fallois.

Offen, Karen (1984), 'Depopulation, Nationalism and Feminism in Fin-de-siècle France', *American Historical Review*, **89** (3), June.

Offen, Karen (1988), 'Defining Feminism: a Comparative Historical Approach', *Signs*, **14**, 119–57.

Offen, Karen (1991), 'Exploring the secual politics of republican nationalism', in Robert Tombs (ed.), *Nationhood and Nationalism in France: From Boulangism to the Great War 1889–1918*, London: Harper Collins Academic.

Pedroncini, Guy (1967), *Les mutineries de 1917*, Paris: Presses Universitaires de France.

Peignot, Jérôme (1988), *Pierre Leroux inventeur du socialisme*, Paris: Editions Klincksieck.

Phillips, Roderick (1988), *Putting Asunder: A History of Divorce in Western Society*, Cambridge: Cambridge University Press.

Plamenatz, John (1952), *The Revolutionary Movement in France 1815–1871*, London: Longman.

Price, Roger (1972), *The French Second Republic: A Social History*, London: B.T. Batsford.

Price, Roger (ed.) (1975), *1848 in France* (Documents of revolution, with 48 illustrations), London: Thames and Hudson.

Price, Roger (ed.) (1975), *Revolution and Reaction: 1848 and the Second French Republic*, London: Croom Helm.

Puech, Jules (1925), *La Vie et l'oeuvre de Flora Tristan 1803–1844*, Paris: Marcel Rivière.

Rabaut, Jean (1978), *Histoire des féminismes français*, Paris: Stock.

Rancière, Jacques (1981), *La nuit des prolétaires*, Paris: Fayard.

Rendall, Jane (1985), *The Origins of Modern Feminism: Women in Britain,*

France and the United States, 1780–1860, Basingstoke and London: Macmillan.

Reynolds, Siân (ed.) (1986), *Women, State and Revolution: Essays on Power and Gender in Europe since 1789*, Brighton: Harvester.

Reynolds, Siân (1994), 'Le sacre de la citoyenne? Réflexions sur le retard français', unpublished paper, *Colloque féminismes et cultures politiques nationales*, Lyon: 30 novembre–2 décembre, published in shortened form as 'Le sacre de la citoyenne: Pierre Rosanvallon and the Significant Other' in *Modern and Contemporary France* (1995), NS3(2), April, 208–12.

Reynolds, Siân (1994), 'Women and the Popular Front in France: The Case of the Three Women Ministers', *French History*, **8** (2), 196–224.

Riot-Sarcey, Michèle (1993), 'De l'utopie de Jeanne Deroin', *1848 Révolutions et mutations au XIXᵉ siècle*, **9**, 29–36.

Riot-Sarcey Michèle (1994), *La démocratie à l'épreuve des femmes. Trois figures critiques du pouvoir 1830–1848: Désirée Véret, Eugénie Niboyet, Jeanne Deroin*, Paris: Albin Michel.

Riot-Sarcey, Michèle (1994), 'La démocratie représentative en l'absence des femmes', *French Politics and Society*, **12** (4), 53–63.

Ronsin, Francis (1980), *La grève des ventres: propagande néo-malthusienne et baisse de la natalité en France, XIX–XXᵉ siècles*, Paris: Aubier.

Ronsin, Francis (1992), *Les Divorciaires: Affrontements politiques et conceptions du mariage dans la France du XIXᵉ siècle*, Paris: Aubier.

Rosanvallon, Pierre (1992), *Le sacre du citoyen: Histoire du suffrage universel en France*, Paris: Editions Gallimard.

Rosmer, Alfred (1935), 'The Fight Against War in France During the War', in Julian Bell (ed.), *We Did Not Fight*, London: Cobden-Sanderson.

Rosmer, Alfred (1936), *Le mouvement ouvrier pendant la guerre*, Paris: Librairie du travail.

Roudinesco, Elizabeth (1991), *Théroigne de Méricourt: A Melancholic Woman during the French Revolution*, translated by Martin Thom, London and New York: Verso.

Rowbotham, Sheila (1992), *Women in Movement*, London: Routledge.

Saint-Simon, Henri de (1969), *Le nouveau christianisme et les écrits sur la religion*, Textes choisis et présentés par H. Desroche, Paris: Seuil.

Sanchez, Luis Alberto (1987), *Flora Tristan: Una mujer sola contra el mundo*, Lima: Mosca Azul Editores.

Sauret, Henriette (no date), 'Hélène Brion, héroïne de la paix', unpublished MS, BMD.

Serret, Bernard, Louis Bouët et Maurice Dommanget (1938), *Le syndicalisme dans l'enseignement*, Grenoble: Institut d'Études Politiques de Grenoble.

Sewell, William H. Jr. (1980), *Work and Revolution in France: The Language of Labour from the Old Regime to 1848*, Cambridge, London and New York: Cambridge University Press.

Simon, Jules (1977), *L'ouvrière* (facsimile of 1861 edition), Saint-Pierre de Lalerne, Brionne: Gérard Monfort.

Slater, Catherine (1981), *Defeatists and their Enemies: Political Invective in France 1914–18*, Oxford: Oxford University Press.

Sohn, Anne-Marie (1979), 'Féminisme et syndicalisme: les institutrices de la fédération unitaire de l'enseignement de 1919 à 1935', doctoral thesis, 3ᵉ cycle, Paris: Université de Paris X.

Sowerwine, Charles (1976), 'The Organisation of French Socialist Women 1880–1914: A European Perspective for Women's Movements', *Historical Reflections/Réflections Historiques*, 3 (2), 3–24.

Sowerwine, Charles (1982), *Sisters or Citizens? Women and Socialism in France since 1876*, Cambridge: Cambridge University Press.

Sowerwine, Charles (1983), 'Workers and Women in France before 1914: The Debate over the Coriau Affair', *Journal of Modern History*, 55, 411–44.

Spenser, Samia I. (ed.) (1984), *French Women and the Age of the Enlightenment*, Bloomington and Indianapolis: Indiana University Press.

Strumingher, Laura S. (1988), *The Odyssey of Flora Tristan* (University of Cincinnati Studies in Historical and Contemporary Europe, 2), New York: Peter Lang.

Strumingher, Laura S. (1989), 'Women of 1848 and the Revolutionary Heritage of 1789', in Harriet B. Applewhite and Darline S. Levy (eds), *Women and Politics in the Age of the Democratic Revolution*, Ann Arbor: The University of Michigan Press.

Sullerot, Evelyne (1966), 'Journaux féminins et lutte ouvrière (1848–1849)', in *Société d'histoire de la Révolution de 1848*, Paris: CNRS, 88–122.

Terraine, John (1977), 'The Aftermath of Nivelle', *History Today*, 27, 426–33.

Thébaud, Françoise (1986), *La Femme au temps de la guerre de 1914*, Paris: Stock.

Thomas, Edith (1956), *Pauline Roland: Socialisme et féminisme au XIXᵉ siècle*, Paris: Marcel Rivière.

Thomas, Edith (1963), *Les Pétroleuses*, Paris: Gallimard.

Thomas, Edith (1980), *Louise Michel*, translated by Penelope Williams, Montréal: Black Rose Books.

Thomson, David (1969), *Democracy in France since 1870*, Oxford: Oxford University Press.

Tilly, Louise and Joan Scott (1987), *Women, Work and the Family*, (first published 1978), New York and London: Routledge.

Timms, Margeret and Gertrude Bussey (1980), *Pioneers for Peace 1915– 1965*, London: Allen and Unwin.

Traugott, Mark (1993), *The French Worker: Autobiographies from an Industrial Era*, Berkeley and Los Angeles: University of California Press.

Vernet, Madeleine (1917), 'Hélène Brion, une belle conscience et une sombre affaire', Epône: Société d'Édition et de Librairie de l'Avenir Social.

Voilquin, Suzanne (1978), *Souvenirs d'une fille du peuple*, Introduction de Lydia Elhadad, Paris: Maspéro.

Waelti-Walters, Jennifer and Steven C. Hause (eds) (1994), *Feminisms of the Belle Epoque*, Lincoln and London: University of Nebraska Press.

Watson, D.R. (1974), *Georges Clemenceau, A Political Biography*, London: Eyre Methuen.

Watt, Richard M. (1963), *Dare Call it Treason*, London: Chatto and Windus.

Wiltshire, Anne (1985), *Most Dangerous Women: Feminist Peace Campaigners of the Great War*, London: Pandora.

Yarrow, P.J. (ed.) (1975), *Victor Hugo: Les Châtiments*, London: Athlone Press.

Zylberberg-Hocquard, Marie-Hélène (1978), *Féminisme et syndicalisme en France*, Paris: Editions Anthropos.

Zylberberg-Hocquard, Marie-Hélène (1981), *Femmes et féminisme dans le mouvement ouvrier français*, Paris: Les Éditions ouvrières.

Index